REFLECTIONS OF A SUCCESSFUL DROPOUT

Sort of a "How To" Story

by **Val Barry**

Illustrations by Michael LeMay

Reflections of a Successful Dropout
Sort of a "How-to" story

Edited by: Dee Dees
Ronda Downey

Published by
J.W. Publishing
10165 E. Caron Street
Scottsdale, AZ 85258
(480) 625-4684

For more information regarding this book, please contact
J.W. Publishing.

I dedicate this book to my wife, Julie.

Absent her encouragement and belief

in me it wouldn't have been written.

Acknowledgments

It is clear the blessings permeating my life were produced by a power far superior to my abilities. That awesome authority weaved a tapestry of personalities in which each touched me in their own fashion and created a success recipe for which I'm ever grateful. I thank those who extended a helping hand as well as those who made life hard because they strengthened my resolve to do the things needed to be accomplished. I want the angels who encouraged me during the dark days—and you know who you are—to realize I'm aware of my massive debt to you. I thank God for my family who fills my heart with joy and for Julie who understands me better than I understand myself.

TABLE OF CONTENTS

PREFACE

I'm so very grateful that I'm living what I would describe as the *good life*. A basic reason for my joy is that I share my world with Julie, who I love and cherish, and I know she feels the same about me. Biblical proverb 31:10: *"A truly good wife is the most precious treasure a man can find"* makes me think of Julie. We support our common goals and each other's individual goals without reservation. Our mornings begin with a lively discussion of our plans for the day. During this relaxing period, Julie reads a few pages to me from an enlightening variety of books that have captured our interest. It's a great way to start our daily adventure.

Of course, financial independence plays a huge part in the blessed sense of well-being that fills my universe. Is monetary freedom a requirement of a happy life? Some will posit it is not entirely essential, but I believe it is. I've been broke and I've been rich and which side of that equation worked best for me wasn't hard to figure out.

Looking back over the decades, I realize how easily I acquired wealth once I made a concerted effort to figure out how to make it happen. Severe economic deprivation—which I certainly knew— helps one develop what I refer to as a *Deep Desire* to overcome the humiliating misery of poverty. When I truly learned to respect the power of money, I began to think of myself as an entrepreneur. I set a goal and created a plan to reach my target. Once I had my success formula firmly fixed in my consciousness, nothing could deter me from my objective. By the time I reached the age of

1

thirty-seven, if I wanted I could have retired. Even though the choice was mine, not working didn't present an acceptable option.

The proverbial "silver spoon experience" had no part of my introduction into life. No, I sure didn't live the *Father Knows Best* type of childhood. My existence as a child included all the negativity that came with a severely alcoholic father. Dropping out of school to get married at age eighteen with no marketable job skills, and the father of three kids by the age of twenty-two, placed me and my family firmly in the poverty category. Nevertheless, at least I learned at an early age what sort of life I didn't want my family and myself to endure.

I worked through a succession of dead-end, yet informative jobs until, at the age of twenty-five, I began a career as a licensed residential real estate salesman. It seemed as if I had been born to sell real estate and perform the many ancillary tasks connected to that profession. Though hard, I loved the work. In a few short years it seemed we had it all; we had arrived . . . finally! At that time I thought with our financial difficulties behind us, a wonderful, trouble free future dawned on our immediate horizon. My wife didn't see things quite the same way and overnight our eighteen-year marriage came to an end.

Decades have passed since that heart-rending experience, but all has worked out well. My time is spent doing whatever I wish, totally free of the restrictions of a lack of money. The life I live is fashioned in a manner in which I'm able to afford most anything that strikes my fancy. I'm grateful I have the ability to help smooth off the rough edges of those close to my heart, and I exercise that ability. As I mentioned earlier, it wasn't always this way. Now and then I examine old scars that remind me of who I used to be. I hope my story might interest you or even be of some practical use to you. It is my wish that this book demonstrate that my life meant more than merely filling in the gap between the last generation and the next one.

PART ONE

THE FIRST EIGHTEEN YEARS

"family life in a war zone"

CHAPTER ONE

As far back as I'm able to remember, sometime in 1938, when I was three, Dad drank to excess. His boozing surely contributed to my mom's continual angry frustration. Both my parents were blessed, or maybe cursed, with extraordinary good looks. Dad resembled Henry Fonda as he appeared in the movie, *Grapes of Wrath*. Mom could double for Jean Tierney, a Hollywood beauty of that era. As a young child, I didn't mind that Dad drank so much and Mom yelled at me a lot. At that age, I thought living in a war zone was perfectly normal. It occurs to me now that events that happened long, long ago are as fresh in my memory as if I experienced them just today.

Dad—born on February 3, 1913, had four siblings; two older sisters, Marlas and Joanne; an older brother, Randolph and a younger brother, Hobert. Dad grew up on a dairy farm in Christian County in the gorgeous verdant landscape of the Missouri Ozark Mountains. He often told me of the joy he experienced being raised on the farm. As a youngster—long before the booze took control—he delighted in fishing, hunting and horseback riding and doing all the things that most men wish they could have experienced during any period of their lives. Years later, separated from the serenity of his youth, Dad longed to return to those halcyon days. He promised us that someday he, Mom, my little sister and I would live on a cattle ranch in the Ozarks, and I believed him.

My paternal grandparents, Carl and Betty Barry, doted on their five children, especially their boys. During their early twenties, the girls, Marlas and Joanne, were school teachers. They both married decent, hardworking ambitious men and lived happy productive lives. My dad and his brothers, spoiled by my grandparents, all became alcoholics; a condition that hastened the deaths of two of them and diminished the quality of the lives of all three brothers.

Grandpa Barry, along with many small-farm owners in Southwest Missouri, worked for the Frisco Railroad Company in Springfield, about thirty-five miles from the home place. Farm income was usually not enough to provide for the family. Dad worked for Frisco as well, until 1938, when Mom, Dad and I moved to the small lumber town of Pe Ell, Washington.

Pe Ell, a town of around six hundred residents located in the central western part of the state, had become home for many Missouri immigrants who relocated there to work in the thriving lumber industry. Many of those people were friends and acquaintances of my parents, and Dad decided to join them, ostensibly to take advantage of the opportunity for work, but maybe for other reasons too, because he actually held a secure position with the Frisco Railroad in Springfield.

By 1938, his drinking had led to a rather dissolute lifestyle. In all likelihood, the true reason for leaving Missouri had less to do with work opportunities and more to do with escaping the scrutiny of his parents. He wouldn't stop drinking, but he couldn't do it in sight of my grandparents.

In January of 1938, Mom and Dad and I arrived by train at Chehalis, Washington, where we were met and driven to Pe Ell by friends my parents had known in Missouri. Dad hoped to get a job there as a lumberjack. We stayed with their friends for a few days until we moved to a rustic, tiny three-room apartment above a two-pump gas station. Within a few rainy days, Dad found work as a logger. Each weekday before sun up, I watched him from our living room window as he climbed aboard the back of a canvas-covered truck that took the lumberjack crew to the woods. After sundown, I watched for the truck to drop him back off in front of the gas station. He started drinking as soon as he got home. Dad drank too much and raised a lot of hell, and I adored him.

Soon after we arrived in Pe Ell, I had a very frightening incident. Access to our second story flat could only be gained by way of exterior stairs that ascended to a small landing at the entrance of our apartment. As a rambunctious three-year old, I didn't always use my head. One day, while playing alone, I hung by my hands from the edge of the twelve-foot high stairway landing. After a few minutes, I realized I hadn't the strength to pull myself back onto the landing. I dangled there, terrified, yelling for help, but nobody came to my rescue. I remained there for an eternity, until my aching arms forced me to let go. As I fell, even at that young age, I knew that could be bad. Surprisingly, I didn't get hurt. I picked myself up, walked away, and minutes later involved myself in some other fun-filled, less dangerous activity. Thank goodness for young, pliable bones.

CHAPTER TWO

We didn't live above the gas station very long. In our next home, sometime before midnight, September 17, 1938, Mom gave birth to my sister, Sherie. While Mom labored to deliver what I hoped to be my new baby brother, Dad made me stay next door with the widow, Mrs. Criswell. I ran in the dark from Mrs. Criswell's home to our back door several times, hoping to meet the new arrival, only to be hustled back to Mrs. Criswell by Dad.

I didn't get to meet my sister until the next morning because by the time Sherie arrived, Mrs. Criswell had finally gotten me to sleep. Well, Sherie wasn't the brother I expected, but I loved her anyway. She sure had our parents' good looks, but that didn't make me jealous. Well, maybe just a little. I've never figured out the reason, but after the birth of my sister, I began receiving some pretty severe beatings from Dad, not spankings—beatings. He scared the daylights out of me, but I still loved him.

A few months later, we moved into a comfortable two-bedroom, dark brown, shingled home situated on a pleasant residential street, not far from the business district of Pe Ell. One day, the landlord arrived to make a plumbing repair. The friendly elderly widower remarked to Mom that he felt as if he would soon be taking that long journey to rejoin his wife who awaited him in heaven. Overhearing the conversation, I stood before the gentleman and with hands on my hips stated, "Mr. Meyers, before you go on that trip, I sure hope you get our toilet fixed." Mr. Meyers smiled and said to Mom, "I wish I could be around to see that kid when he grows up."

In 1940, I was five, and we still lived in Pe Ell. The commercial district ran along Main Street for about four blocks. On the west side of the street, situated near the center of the stores and other commercial outlets, there stood a small single-story freestanding brick structure with bars on the windows: our town jail. On Saturday nights, the rough and tumble lumberjacks spent the evening drinking in the Main Street saloons. Occasionally an unruly drunk started trouble and found himself arrested and placed behind bars until he sobered up.

Sometimes an arrestee made the egregious error of physically challenging Pe Ell's sole peace officer, Fats Smith. Fats, whose appearance clearly indicated why he had been given his nickname, sometimes maintained order by utilizing a high pressure fire engine type water hose attached to an exterior wall of the jail house. Whenever Fats felt it necessary, he turned the hose on the more combative offenders. The painful and humiliating drenching occurred outdoors, in front of the jail, in full view of the public. The experience always produced a calming effect and hastened sobering. Watching Fats—a huge intimidating force, especially to a five year old boy—in action, scared me. It didn't help that both Mom and Dad warned me that Fats wanted to talk to young boys who misbehaved.

We lived near a large, empty farm-type house situated on a wooded site overgrown with weeds and dry grass. Neighborhood kids often romped and played there. One morning while playing in front of the old house with stick matches swiped from Mom's kitchen, I caused a serious problem. I had a great time repeatedly striking a match and tossing it into the dry grass and weeds. They ignited immediately. Before the flames could spread more than a few inches, I extinguished the small fire by stomping on it. What fun! I continued the exciting game until I reacted a little too slowly. The fire quickly expanded into an out-of-control full-fledged conflagration. Terrified, I raced home. By the time I scrambled up our back porch, I heard the fire engine siren.

I never returned to the scene to determine the extent of the damage, nor until now, some seventy years later, did I reveal my guilt. Back then, I worried that Fats Smith would figure out who started that fire and subject the blameworthy party to the water punishment. When Dad and I walked along Main Street, I think he must have wondered why I always insisted on walking on the side of the street opposite the jail.

Often, Mom sent me to various stores with a note requesting items which were charged to our account. One day I decided to do some shopping on my own. I scribbled what to me looked like writing on one of Mom's marketing lists. I selected a red, white and blue toy whistle and took it to the counter and handed the note to Mr. Milicoski, the proprietor of Milicoski's Variety Store. He took the note, smiled and placed the toy whistle in a paper bag and handed it to me.

About three years after we moved from our apartment above the gas station, I returned to the station frequently. World War II had begun, resulting in extreme shortages of materials needed to support the war. The station owners bought used rubber and resold it to the government. I continually scrounged around the countryside for old tires and other items made of the scarce material, which I sold to the gas station operators for a penny a pound. A penny doesn't sound like much money, but in those days a consistent multi-penny income kept a little kid well supplied in candy and inexpensive toys.

CHAPTER THREE

Toward the end of 1940, we moved to the Chehalis River Place. That truly beautiful five acre farmette backed up to a gorgeous river, which flowed through a five hundred foot deep, verdant, fern-covered, wooded canyon. The property fronted on a graveled county road which ran parallel to the river. The quarter-mile depth of the little farm equaled the distance from the county road to the river. A narrow dirt road bordered the west boundary of the farm from the county road and led to the river's deep embankment, which served as an unofficial regional dump site.

For years people dumped their trash over the edge of the embankment. In my late forties, on a vacation drive up from California, I paid a visit to that long abandoned dump. I found the site to be even more isolated than when I lived in the adjacent little farm as a small child. Though it was covered with blackberry bushes and dense foliage, I managed with difficulty to salvage a few antique collectables. Sometimes I daydream about returning with a large truck and spending a few days harvesting hidden treasures.

A large contingent of the area's population worked in the logging industry. Many had come from Missouri, as we did. It seemed that when they arrived in Pe Ell their inhibitions disappeared. They drank to excess and played too hard for their own good. Dad enjoyed cutting hair. He turned his barbering ability into a social event. Often, on Saturday mornings some of his Missouri pals stopped by our home for a haircut. The unspoken customary charge for Dad's service required that each recipient bring along a bottle to share with Dad and the others. Even though everyone had a good time on those Saturday mornings, I think the quality of the trims diminished as the day wore on, but nobody cared.

In addition to a trout stream that flowed through Chehalis River Place, the property's other amenities included a two-seater outhouse which Dad and I sometimes shared. There were two 300-foot long chicken houses which Mom put to good use. Shortly before the outbreak of the second World War, the United States Army began conducting battle games in the vicinity of our little farm. Mom took advantage of the situation and stocked the processing buildings with very young chickens. She fattened them up and sold them at a handsome profit to the Army for consumption by the soldiers on maneuvers. Mom prospered in her thriving poultry business. After all, she grew up on a farm. It made her proud to be making money and helping her country at the same time.

Dad still boarded the truck to the woods before dawn and didn't arrive back home until dark. After he got home he had regular farm chores to do. While we resided at the Chehalis River Place, Dad rarely beat me, possibly only because he didn't see me that much. No matter though, Mom filled in efficiently for Dad when she figured I needed discipline. Dad didn't have to be worried about me getting spoiled—not with Mom on the job.

Mom's method of torture differed from Dad's. She applied punishment in a more refined manner; more painful, yet perhaps with less risk of causing permanent physical damage. Dad's assaults consisted of uncontrolled violence and ended when his temperamental outburst subsided. Instead of using a thick belt or stick of firewood as Dad did, Mom preferred to use a narrow flexible whip she cut from the willow tree in the front yard. Getting whipped with a switch really stings. When it first strikes the buttocks and back of a little guy's legs, there is a moment of numbness followed by intense pain. When Mom laid into me, I tried not to cry, to show her she couldn't hurt me. But before she finished, she had me screaming. Even though only five, I knew that a parent shouldn't do that to their kid. I suppose the emotional damage resulting from Mom's abuse compared to Dad's beatings was about equal. Did I deserve punishment for misbehaving? Sure, but maybe not quite so intense. Nevertheless, I had tons of fun. I loved to romp over the farm, slapping my right thigh, pretending to be both horse and cowboy. I dreaded the thought of growing up. Somehow I knew it wouldn't be acceptable behavior for grownups to play horse and cowboy.

Paradoxically, small kids adore their parents even when they are mistreated by them. The stories my Dad told me about growing up on a farm in Missouri fascinated me. Regardless of the angry beatings, I just loved him, and I knew he loved me too.

When people think of the climate in Washington, cool and wet usually comes to mind. Actually it is sticky hot there in summer. Sometimes, to help recover from the ill effects of too much booze, and to beat the oppressive heat, Dad napped stark naked on the smooth rock shores of the river. I relished accompanying Dad on those treks to the bottom of the ravine where the clear refreshing waters of the Chehalis River flowed. The steep trail down that beautiful naturally landscaped ravine bordered the dumpsite where Dad and I sometimes dallied to search for abandoned treasure. Those special memories will stay with me all my life.

In 1941, I turned six, and we moved from the Chehalis River Place to as beautiful a site as we had ever seen. Our new home, a forty-acre farm about five miles from Pe Ell, went by the name of the Jennings Ranch. In my opinion, due to its size, the designation of farm rather than ranch more accurately described the place. I suppose someone by the name of Jennings either owned or had once owned that pastoral piece of heaven. Improvements included a spacious modern house, a barn and a detached garage plus agriculturally related outbuildings. Every building and even the mailbox had been roofed and sided with matching light green colored shingles, all of which served to further enhance the beauty of Jennings Ranch.

The house, the barn and other buildings were near the county graveled road at the front entrance of the farm. The ranch was contained within a gently sloped narrow valley around seven hundred feet by nearly a half mile in length. A strikingly beautiful serpentine, fast moving creek bisected the luxuriant green valley and traveled the entire length of the center of the property. Most of the landscape on the south side of the creek consisted of a splendid apple orchard, while a mature cedar forest graced the northern slope.

Often, I'd tie a safety pin to one end of a length of string attached to a slender branch or stick. I then impaled an earth worm on the pin and proceeded to toss the lure into the creek. Occasionally, a Brook or Rainbow trout took the worm and got hooked, or more accurately, pinned. I then tried to yank the fish onto the shore. Most of the time, the unbarbed pin allowed my catch to escape, but not every time.

Dad, impressed that his six-year-old could enjoy any degree of angling success in that fashion, presented me with a new metal

12

fishing rod. Excited and proud of my new gift, I planned to put it to use the very next day. Before daylight, the following morning, while still in bed, I took my pole in hand and pretended to be fishing.

Unfortunately, I stuck the end of the rod into an electrical wall outlet, causing the metal tip to melt. I knew that amounted to an offense worthy of a painful switching or beating depending upon which of my parents elected to administer my punishment. I hid the useless pole under my bed until I could select a more secure hiding place. Perhaps the only good result of the situation lay in the fact that the Jennings Ranch trout population avoided decimation.

Ma, our dear angelic, lovable, maternal grandmother, traveled from her home in Springfield, mainly to visit Sherie and me. Mom drove to Chehalis to pick up Ma at the train depot. When they arrived back home, Dad wasn't on hand to welcome Ma. Sherie and I insisted on giving our grandmother a tour of our captivating home site. When we entered the barn, we found Dad, asleep on a stack of straw, passed out drunk. Solitary drinking had become a regular part of his life.

Ma looked at Dad in his impaired condition, smiled and said, "Let's not wake him, he will be fine when he sleeps it off." Ma wasn't angry or upset. She knew about Dad's drinking problem and loved him anyway, just as Sherie and I did.

A couple of weeks later, just before Ma returned to Missouri, Mom and Dad hosted a large picnic in our magnificent park-like apple orchard. Most of the guests consisted of families who formerly lived in Missouri. There were a lot of hard drinkers in the group. Dad and a few of his inebriated pals had a good time tossing an unopened bottle of beer up in the air and catching it before it fell toward the ground. After each catch they tossed the bottle a little higher. As usual, Dad had too much to drink and the falling bottle struck his face with enough force to knock him down. Over the following week his black eye remained swollen closed. He acknowledged that it hurt, but he just laughed it off.

During the four and a half years we resided in Pe Ell, we lived in five different homes. Years later I wondered why we moved so often, until it dawned on me that when the head of the family is a confirmed alcoholic, you can be sure there will be money problems. A lack of adequate income throughout my early life greatly affected my future attitude regarding money. I experienced some very difficult times, paradoxically for which I became sincerely grateful.

Shortly before 1941, my folks sent me back to Missouri to live with my Grandma and Grandpa Barry temporarily. I started first grade there in a one-room school house where each row separated grades one through eight. My cousins, Annie and Rachel, who also lived with my grandparents, attended the school as well. I'll never forget those happy periods of my life. No drinking, no fighting, just delicious food, and lots of fun and lots of love. The times I lived with my wonderful Grandparents helped mitigate the psychological damage inflicted on me by Dad and Mom. If there is a heaven, and I'm pretty sure there is, that's where Grandpa and Grandma Barry must surely reside.

In 1942, at my parent's insistence, I returned to Washington, heartbroken. To fight World War II the U.S. Navy desperately needed warships. I heard the adults talk, and I feared that the Japanese military, commonly referred to as the "Japs," might successfully invade the United States mainland. Workers of all skill levels found high paying jobs in the burgeoning ship-building industry. Our family moved from Pe Ell to Tacoma, and Mom and Dad went to work in the Tacoma shipyards. The war ended the Great Depression, and it seemed as if our financial hard times had ended, at least temporarily. Dad even bought a brand new Nash automobile.

We rented a flat in an old two-unit Victorian style building on Olympia Boulevard directly across from Puget Sound. My parents worked the night shift and my little sister stayed with a sitter. I spent many nights alone in our gloomy apartment. Long before television, I relied on radio drama for my evening entertainment. I thrilled to *The Shadow* from its opening question, "Who knows what evil dwells in the hearts of men?" I waited for the narrator to answer, "The Shadow knows." I hung on every word of *Inner Sanctum,* cringing at the frightening sound of that squeaking door. Those wonderful programs both thrilled and terrified me while I listened in my bed from under the covers.

I enrolled in the second grade at Central Elementary School, about a half mile from our flat. Until arriving in Tacoma, I couldn't remember ever having met or seen a black person. Vaguely aware of the race, I'd only ever heard of them referred to as niggers. I honestly had no idea of the pejorative connotation of that word. One morning during recess, I observed an older boy with light skin and kinky hair. Without a smidgeon of bigotry, I politely asked if he was a "nigger." In an instant, I found myself sprawled on my back on the ground. When I became more enlightened, I realized I got off easy.

During our family's stay in Tacoma, Mom placed first in a beauty contest at the shipyards. The experience thrilled her and made Dad, Sherie and me very proud of her. To the best of my memory, I don't believe I received any severe beatings while we lived in Tacoma. Maybe my parents were too fatigued from their long work schedules to administer corporal punishment or maybe my conduct had improved.

Dad came home late one afternoon, sporting a swollen black eye. Clearly battered, he joked that I should have seen the other guy. Willy Nelson and Waylon Jennings could have been describing my dad in their song about "A Good Timing Man." Dad fought, gambled, chased and clearly did not hold up as a good role model. No matter though, Sherie and I loved him dearly. Obviously, our notion of the values that constitute a competent, well-rounded parent was skewed.

CHAPTER FOUR

During the summer of 1943, the family moved to Salashan, a government developed housing project located near Tacoma. The subdivision, built primarily for families of shipyard workers, consisted of about 2000 units divided into single family homes, duplexes, triplexes and six-plexes. The modern suburban ambiance of the community better served families with children than the congested environment of Tacoma.

Lots of kids lived in Salashan, and those kids really knew how to have fun. In addition to engaging in the usual sports of baseball, football and basketball; impromptu, no-special-theme parades formed in which hundreds of gleeful children of all ages marched through the streets. Occasionally they set up their version of a carnival, with gypsy-costumed fortune tellers, and dart throwing competitions in which contestants could win prizes. Awards included toys, marbles, comic books, makeup for teenage girls and just about any inexpensive item that appealed to youngsters. Many carnival prizes were donated by local stores and some parents. Others had been purchased with borrowed money and repaid from the event's earnings.

The kids, with the help of some fathers, constructed a contraption which they called "The Salashan Carousal." It consisted of two eight-foot long, four-by-four inch crossbeams mounted in the center on a vertical support about five feet tall. Two husky teenage boys ran while pushing the crossbeams, spinning it at a dizzying speed. The carousel accommodated four riders per each two-minute spin with one kid seated at each of the four ends of the two crossbeams. It cost two cents to ride the carousel, and a consistently long line of kids waited to climb on board. Some kids kept riding until they ran out of pennies.

World War II raged and dominated the thinking of children and adults alike. Americans stayed unified in their knowledge of what had to be accomplished. Political correctness didn't exist and would be considered ludicrous in those times. The only successful conclusion of the war required total defeat of the axis powers. The kids loved playing war. The varied topography and forests with a creek bordering Salashan served as perfect battlegrounds to conduct simulated battles. Two opposing armies formed and sophisticated military combat strategies developed. The competing troops started with an equal number of participants. Each combatant wore a blue or red armband identifying to which force he or she belonged. Yes … the Salashan kids were ahead of the times—girls fought alongside the boys.

Whichever side won had to be considered to be Americans, and the losing side became the axis powers because they could never be allowed to leave the field of battle victorious. Monitors who acted as referees determined when a soldier had been killed by a pretend bullet from a homemade rifle. The first side reaching a predetermined percentage of casualties surrendered and peace reigned until we did it all over again.

When Dad drank he sometimes forgot his fatherly responsibilities. One winter Saturday morning, Dad took Sherie and me for a ride in his new car. We were thrilled—we loved spending time with him. He told us he just wanted to be with his two kids. About ten in the morning, he stopped by his friend's home for just a quick hello. He instructed Sherie and I to wait in the car and promised to return in a few minutes. Undoubtedly, those friends were heavy drinkers because all of Dad's pals were alcoholics. He returned very drunk just as the sun had begun to set.

In 1943, lacking diversions such as television, video games and all of the electronic entertainment devices that came much later, we made our own fun. On warm summer evenings, kids in sizable groups played games like "kick the can" and "hide and seek." We continued playing after dark and right up until bedtime. Yet, we never heard of child kidnappings or molestations occurring. Years later parents became fearful of permitting their children to walk to school in broad daylight.

One family living in a single family home on our street attracted the neighborhood kids like an irresistible magnet. The mom, dad and six children all told terrific stories. Often, after the sun went down, many of the kids in the neighborhood gathered in their backyard around a campfire and thrilled to funny and exciting tales. The delightful recollections of heroic harrowing exploits and adventures involving various members of the family were represented as having occurred before they arrived in Salashan. Of course, we heard exaggerations and even outright lies, but we didn't care because those after-dark yarns so thoroughly entertained us.

The Thomas family; Mr. and Mrs. Thomas and their two sons, Duane and Clayton, lived in the duplex unit adjacent to ours. Duane was a year older than I, and Clayton a year younger. Mr. and Mrs. Thomas always acted pleasantly. They didn't drink, and I loved hanging out with the Thomas family. The boys became my closet pals.

As in Tacoma, I spent a lot of nights alone. Sometimes on Friday nights the Thomas's invited me to join them in their living room to listen to our favorite radio programs. While we listened, we enjoyed freshly prepared popcorn and hot chocolate topped with delicious marshmallows. One cold, rainy night, I was alone and Mrs. Thomas came to our gloomy apartment to check on me.

Aware I had a bad cold, she massaged my chest with Vicks ointment. That really felt good. I envied Duane and Clayton.

My parents' quarrels seemed to become more violent. One night Dad progressed well beyond the beginning of a binge; he discovered Mom had hidden his pint of bourbon—an act of cruelty which made the situation worse. She often did that, and Dad always reacted in the same manner. Desperate for a drink, he pleaded with her to give his bottle back. Clearly enjoying her advantage and Dad's agony, Mom smugly pretended to ignore him. He turned dangerously furious and physically attacked her in our kitchen. She fought back, but I saw the fear in her eyes. Terrified, and—thinking Dad might kill her—I squeezed between my parents and did my best to separate them. Their hostility immediately turned on me. My efforts to intervene at least resulted in an uneasy truce between them. Mom returned the liquor to Dad and he continued with his binge.

Christmas morning, 1943, Dad sat on the couch. He wore only his underwear and stared through a boozy fog at his precious half empty bottle. Mom and Sherie got out of the apartment before I awoke. The previous evening, I heard my parents' angry exchange after Dad stumbled through the front door on Christmas Eve. This time I didn't intervene. I learned my lesson the last time I tried to play referee. The presents under the decorated Christmas tree remained unwrapped; there could be no Christmas for me without my mom and sister.

Mom's endless, loud, harsh, beyond reason, non-constructive criticism of Sherie and me left us with lifelong psychological damage. Paradoxically, concurrent with the ego-shattering disparagement we received, she could behave toward us in a manner that defined her as a responsible parent in other ways. We always received highly nutritional and delicious meals. No one could cook like Mom. Nothing short of our punctual classroom attendance would be tolerated by our mother.

While living in Salashan, Mom purchased the beautiful *Child Life* encyclopedia set for Sherie and me. The series consisted of several volumes designed to instill a broad range of fascinating educational material including poetry, mythology, history, science, astronomy, math, etc. Into my twenties, I continued to absorb information from the superb publication. Mom's true feelings toward her children continued throughout our lives to be highly confusing.

Soon after I turned nine and shortly before we left Salashan, Mom and Dad gave Sherie and me a Cocker Spaniel puppy. For obvious reasons, we named him "Chocolate." He was a thoroughbred and quite beautiful, but Chocolate turned out to be an ill-tempered cur. My sister and I despised him. Even so, we took good care of the vicious little beast and never let our parents know how we felt about him. When we were about to move to California, Mom informed us that taking Chocolate would simply be too much trouble. With difficulty, we concealed our joy.

CHAPTER FIVE

Mom's father, Sam Benson, and Myrna, his new wife, had migrated from Missouri to Richmond, California. Sam, a large man, standing over six feet tall with gigantic hands seemed very intimidating, at least in my eyes. Violence had been integrated into his persona.

My grandmother, "Ma," at age eighteen married Sam, age twenty, in 1913. Ma became pregnant with my mother right away. Sam, true to his ill nature, denied being the father of the unborn child. As they rode in a horse-drawn carriage one day, he attempted to abort my mother by abruptly driving off the country road, hoping Ma would be thrown out. Although the carriage, the passengers and horse all tumbled down the embankment, Sam failed in his vicious maneuver to kill his unborn child.

Sam's parents, Grandma and Grandpa Benson—prosperous and decent farmers—in order to protect their granddaughter from Sam's jealous rages, took on the responsibility of raising Mom. Ma and Sam went on to have five more children. On Sundays, Ma brought the other kids to Grandma and Grandpa Benson's farm to visit Mom. Although Mom always acknowledged the loving treatment she received from her maternal grandparents, she admitted that it hurt that she couldn't live with her immediate family. When a Sunday visit ended, she watched her family drive away … and cried. Eventually, Ma escaped Sam's drinking, gambling, and abuse when she divorced him.

As years passed, Sam seemed to realize his cruel mistake. He could not deny Mom's beautiful blue eyes—a perfect match to his. She and her father eventually developed a relationship; not warm and loving, but one that acknowledged their biological connection. Mom never displayed any outward condemnation of her father; nevertheless, perhaps some things can never really be put right.

Mom also told me that her dad had once enjoyed considerable wealth, after he had won title to a profitable farm in a poker game. But when a lover's husband learned of his wife's adulterous affair with Sam, things went bad. The cuckolded man confronted Sam in his barn at gunpoint, and gave him the choice of being shot dead on the spot or agreeing to pay him five thousand dollars within the week. In 1930, that represented a tremendous sum of money, but Sam paid up to save his life. In Missouri in those days, the man could have killed Sam and likely walked free with a verdict of justifiable homicide.

Sometime in 1940, Sam and Myrna moved from Missouri to Richmond, California. He wrote to Mom and Dad and explained that there were plenty of jobs available in the shipyards in Richmond. Mom's sister and brother-in-law, Pauline and Gene Frazier, had also recently moved from Missouri and settled in nearby Oakland, and worked in the shipyards there.

At the beginning of 1941, around twenty thousand people lived in Richmond. In 1942, over one hundred thousand workers were needed in Richmond shipyards to build ships for the war effort. Tens of thousands of victims of the Great Depression rushed there to take advantage of the high paying employment opportunities while performing their patriotic duty of our country, but mostly, they came for the high paying jobs. After all, the depression had dominated the country's economy for the past ten years. They swarmed to Richmond from Oklahoma, Arkansas, Texas, Missouri, and all over the United States. By 1944, the massive influx of migrants combined with the abrupt and dramatic economic changes resulted in a boomtown environment.

The letter from Sam tempted Dad and Mom who just weren't happy together. Both had strayed beyond the boundaries of their marriage vows. Dad continued drinking and they quarreled incessantly. Their lives seemed to reflect the constant cold and wet gloomy Washington weather. In hopes that more than just the climate might be better in California, my parents decided to relocate to Richmond.

We arrived in Richmond near my ninth birthday in early 1944. The memory is fuzzy, but I think my parents had separated when they left Washington and planned to get together in Richmond. Dad arrived first to get a job and find a place for us to live. It took a few weeks to wrap things up in Washington and prepare for the move.

During that period, while in California I had to stay with Sam and Myrna until my parents and sister and I could be together again. In the process of moving, Mom and Sherie and I drove back and forth between the evergreen state and the golden state three times. On one trip to California, Mom stopped to pick up a young soldier hitchhiking to a California destination. The soldier and Mom shared driving for the remainder of the trip. During this period, people often picked up military hitchhikers—times have changed!

For about two months, I lived with Sam and Myrna in their first floor, one bedroom apartment in a six-plex in the projects. As in Salashan, the federal government developed the projects in Richmond to provide housing for workers employed in industries related to the war effort.

Sam, not a typical grandfather, preferred that Sherie and I address him by his first name. At that time, he made his living gambling at the legal card rooms in the nearby City of San Pablo and regularly played against some pretty disreputable characters. For protection he always carried brass knuckles and a revolver, which I'm sure he wouldn't have hesitated to use if he felt the need to do so.

Sam and Myrna, clearly alcoholics, shared a love of ale in long neck green bottles. Even at nine years of age. I knew they weren't the same type of alcoholics as my dad. They never appeared drunk, whereas Dad's demeanor always gave a clear indication of whether or not he had been drinking. They didn't live in a trailer, but in every other manner Sam and Myrna aptly fit the description of "trailer trash."

They spent much of their lives in cheap taverns, and their dissipated appearance testified to those wasted years. I could see that Myrna had once been pretty, but too many men and too much booze had taken their toll, despite her excessive use of cosmetics. Sam and Myrna fit together well, and neither of them could do better.

While I lived with them, I saw them quarrel a lot. On two occasions, Myrna launched vicious verbal attacks, and Sam retaliated by punching her to the floor. Both times, within minutes after she picked herself up, they calmly chatted and sipped their beloved ale. If not for Myrna's bleeding nose and swollen black eye, no one would know the assaults had occurred.

While with them I developed a skin disorder, later diagnosed as shingles, likely resulting from the stress of my situation. The malady resulted in deep and painful sores on my lower back and stomach area, and the intense pain made sleep nearly impossible. Sam allowed my condition to remain untreated. I suppose he just didn't give a damn. In time the sores subsided but scars and numbness remain to this day.

Early in 1944, after my ninth birthday, I reunited with my family in a two bedroom, second story project apartment within a few blocks of Sam and Myrna's unit. By now, Sam's long time arthritic condition had grown much worse. He gratefully accepted assistance cheerfully given him by Dad and Mom. He began to depend on them to pick him up and gently help him in and out of their car for his frequent doctor visits. During this time, Sam and Dad seemed to develop a genuine fondness toward each other. I wonder if Sam ever considered the irony of the situation—the girl he had tried to kill and rejected as a child became the daughter who provided him comfort and care.

The irony didn't stop there. Mom and Dad first met at a church sponsored picnic on the banks of the beautiful Finley River in Stone County, Missouri. Most of the Benson family, including Sam, belonged to the same church, although he rarely attended. Dad's presence at the church likely had something to do with his interest in meeting girls, rather than religious motivation. Each Sunday Mom and Dad met secretly after services and carried on a courtship.

One Sunday morning Sam showed up and saw Mom and Dad together. He challenged Dad to a fistfight. Dad knew how Sam had treated Mom and he accepted the angry challenge without hesitation. He welcomed the opportunity to beat his future father-in-law to a pulp, and proceeded to do so. Bloodied and enraged, Sam left to retrieve his gun. When he returned with the weapon, he found himself under arrest. Strange but true—years later Dad and Sam became close friends.

CHAPTER SIX

Mom and Dad secured employment in the Richmond Shipyards, performing the same type of work they had been doing in Tacoma, and we settled into our apartment on Canal Street. We lived less than a half mile from what I believed to be the first market of the future gigantic Lucky grocery chain. Although tiny compared to the stores that later evolved, it probably was the largest grocery store in Richmond. Practically everyone in the projects bought their groceries at the Lucky market.

In the 1940s, most people traveled by foot within the city. There wasn't much in the way of bus service. In addition to many commodities, the war brought about shortages of gasoline, oil and tires. Rationing had become a way of life. Those without the means to drive depended on walking or bicycling.

Enterprising boys in the community constructed carts made from packing cases and wheels from discarded old tricycles, baby carriages or whatever they could find. The young entrepreneurs, ages about nine to mid-teens, gathered with their carts in front of the Lucky market, where they negotiated with the shoppers to haul their groceries home. For each delivery the boys charged around ten to fifteen cents; good pay for a kid back then.

Shortly before the shopper's weekly payday, delivery opportunities dropped significantly, and competition between the cart owners became fierce. The older boys pushed in front of the smaller kids, and the intimidated younger boys often went home empty-handed.

Some of the Lucky market customers lived in Richmond Terrace, located nearly two miles from the store. Reaching it required a long, uphill trek and most of the boys wanted nothing to do with Richmond Terrace deliveries. One slow shopping day, I had been hanging around for a couple of hours with nothing to show for my time. A chubby lady, who reminded me of Grandma Barry, asked if one of us would take her groceries to Richmond Terrace. No one wanted the job. Because she reminded me of my grandma and I had made no other deliveries that day, I agreed to haul her groceries for twenty cents.

My new customer and I walked together and became acquainted. I enjoyed talking with her and she seemed to like me. Instinctively, I already knew it served my interest to be friendly. Sometimes shoppers remembered me and specifically chose me to serve them. When we reached the apartment of Grandma Barry's look-alike, she insisted on paying me a whole dollar. She explained that prior to that day, getting her groceries home had been a real problem. I agreed to meet her at the same time each week, thanked her for the dollar, and told her I would only charge her seventy-five cents thereafter.

From that day on, I held up a small placard that read, "Will deliver to Richmond Terrace." I charged seventy-five cents; around five times what the boys were paid for regular deliveries. Sometimes I received tips, which never happened on short distance deliveries. Best of all, I had no more slow days. As with my first Richmond Terrace patron, I pre-arranged convenient delivery scheduling. My grocery delivery niche provided an income that handsomely met the financial needs of a fourth-grade boy. I had no way of knowing then that the Richmond Terrace inspiration would serve me well in the future.

CHAPTER SEVEN

While living on Canal Street, I enrolled in the fourth grade at Washington Elementary School in Point Richmond. I didn't know it but my future wife, Julie, lived just a few blocks away from Canal Street on Oil Street (damn, those street names were ugly.) At four years old, she didn't go to school yet, but her eight-year-old sister, Charlene, attended Washington the same time I did. Decades later I'd meet Julie for the first time in another city and eventually marry her. The peculiar story of how we came together will be told later.

I spent many delightful hours at the Richmond Plunge, a large indoor swimming pool, across the street from the Washington School playgrounds. Although incomparable to the water-oriented theme parks in vogue these days, Richmond Plunge meant the world to a nine year old boy in 1944. I was thrilled the moment I discovered myself actually swimming, when seconds earlier I wondered if I'd ever catch on.

Sixty-eight years have passed since that memorable day. Recently, while taking a nostalgic drive in the area, I discovered that the venerable Richmond Plunge is still intact, though not in use. I noticed a sign asking for support to "Save the Plunge," which stirred in me the hope that maybe someday another nine-year old boy might duplicate my wonderful experience at the delightful old pool.

Sometimes I could be incredibly stupid. My parents rented the Canal Street apartment furnished. One day I carefully examined the top opening of one of the lampshades, and saw a brass ring from which three spokes extended to the inner perimeter of the shade. I used wire cutters to snip off the spokes from the brass ring, creating a nice looking piece of jewelry—a gold colored ring for my finger, but I'd ruined the lampshade.

Dad discovered my handiwork and when I saw the look in his eyes, I knew my punishment would far exceed the extent of the offense. He beat me mercilessly with his folded thick leather belt. Dad had beaten me severely in the past, but this ranked as the worst I had ever received. The onslaught ended when Dad became too winded to continue. His being a chain smoker helped me. I considered later that had I been a soldier captured and tortured by the enemy, and if the hurt caused by the enemy had been commensurate with Dad's infliction of pain, I would have given up every military secret I knew.

I began to smarten up. I wouldn't be beaten by my Dad ever again. Normally we couldn't have asked for a more devoted father, and most of the time I loved being in his company. Both Sherie and I adored him. He would give us his undivided attention, and he treated us as if we were intelligent and deserving of his respect and admiration. He told us fascinating true stories, read to us, and took us to movies in downtown Richmond. During the six mile round trip walk, we discussed the movies we had watched and he genuinely wanted to know our opinion of them. But at some point in his mood swings, his disposition darkened, and he became quiet, nervous and withdrawn. In that condition anything might throw him into a rage. After the lampshade incident, I stayed out of sight until the threat of his potentially violent behavior receded; and I knew it would … after his next binge.

Not long before I turned ten, I began to understand more about the devil with which Dad had to deal. He belonged in the binge drinker category. Between binges he didn't drink at all. I noticed that he became distant and irritable a week or so before he inevitably succumbed to the irresistible craving for alcohol. During that period, I really needed to stay out of his sight. Once he began drinking I easily avoided him, because he'd come home from the shipyards and go directly to bed with a bottle. Even during a binge he never missed work.

During the weekends of his drinking bouts, Dad stayed in bed. After a week or so he had drank himself into such a state of severe dissipation that he couldn't ingest more booze. Then the sobering process began, and it took Dad about a week to get back to normal. During the first days of recovery I still kept my distance. He soon regained his health, and I guess in an effort to make up for the misery and insecurity he had inflicted, he lavished us with love and affection. For the next few weeks, a palpable happiness filled our home.

CHAPTER EIGHT

In 1945, my family moved from Canal Street to a first floor six-plex apartment located at 925 South Ninth Street, also in the projects. Sherie and I enrolled in Nystrom Elementary School on South Tenth Street, a block from our new apartment. I attended the fifth grade and Sherie, the second. We had moved too far from the Lucky market for me to continue my grocery delivery service. However, Sam at that time operated an "ice house" from which he sold twenty-five-pound blocks of ice for the ice boxes in the projects. Due to the war-related shortages, very few people in the projects owned electric refrigerators.

I began using my grocery cart to transport blocks of ice to Sam's customers' apartments. Generally, the boys who delivered the ice received ten cents per trip. The short distances allowed for several daily deliveries, and I soon replaced my income from my discontinued Lucky Stores operation.

Between deliveries, I hung around the ice house with the other boys. Sam's mean streak showed up there as well. One afternoon, he told a boy named Jack, who lived across the street from the ice house, that his grandson could kick his ass. Jack, two years older than me and considerably larger, immediately issued a challenge. I didn't want to fight, but I couldn't back down in front of my pals. Any boy in the projects who wouldn't fight lost the respect of his peers and could look forward to being bullied. I had to fight Jack.

We deliberately squared off. Jack towered over me at what seemed to be at least a foot. He threw the first punch which landed hard over my right eye, which quickly swelled nearly closed, impairing my vision. I fought back, throwing a barrage of punches, missing with most, but landing a couple of solid smacks. I'd been doing some boxing at the Boy's Club on Cutting Boulevard and tried to apply the little I'd learned there. I could see that Jack's confidence had waned. The battle lasted only a few minutes but it seemed like hours to me.

A surrounding crowd urged us on. Because of my size and obvious age disadvantages, the onlookers, mostly adults, seemed to make me their favorite. Shamefully, grownups urging kids to fight just for the pleasure of watching the conflict represented the mentality of many of the project's residents. Soon Jack and I reached a point of total exhaustion. We called a truce and later became friends. When I observed my black eye in the mirror, I reckoned Jack had won, but I knew he wouldn't like to repeat the experience.

Another time, Sam posited to the ice house delivery boys that he wanted to sponsor a "long dick" competition. He proposed to measure the penis of each kid. The best endowed would receive an award of twenty-five cents. The contest never happened. We all refused to participate. Sam's abysmal behavior didn't make him a pedophile, just morally reprehensible.

Several fellows competed for the icehouse delivery assignments. Sam made sure I got all the hauling jobs I could handle. His condition from rheumatoid arthritis became so severe that he eventually had to give up the icehouse operation. With Sam no longer in charge, I had to compete on an equal basis with the other boys for deliveries, which reduced my income considerably. I spent the same amount of time there, but earned half the income I had made before Sam's departure.

I quit delivering ice to sell newspapers; a job I liked much better. Each day fifty papers printed by the Richmond Independent News Company were delivered to me at the corner of South Ninth Street and Cutting Boulevard, right where I sold them. I paid two cents for each paper which I then sold for five cents. I could sell them all in forty minutes. During school I usually sold all my papers during my lunch period. Each day I traded three papers with local merchants for my lunch; a sandwich, a banana and a maple bar.

No traditional newspaper routes existed in the projects in 1945. I marketed my papers by standing on the corner and yelling, "Hey, get your Richmond Independent Newspaper," followed with teasers related to the current headlines. With no television and few radios, newspapers kept the public informed on current events. We were at war, the end of which might have thrown the country back into a depression. People were hungry for the latest news and at ten years old I helped satisfy that hunger at Cutting and South Ninth.

As a kid selling newspapers, I cannot ever forget April 12, 1945, the day President Franklin Roosevelt died. Most Americans credited him with leading our nation out of the misery of the Great Depression. We looked to him to guide our country to a victorious conclusion of the war. His sudden demise shocked the populous. His passing affected us at a level equal to the shock of the tragic death of President Kennedy, almost two decades later.

The public hungered to learn everything about the death of President Roosevelt, and the best source of that coveted information existed on the corner where I hawked the Richmond Independent. I sold a mountain of newspapers on that fateful day. Only fifty papers were delivered at a time, but the deliveries came frequently. I suppose my boss believed I might lose control if I had more than fifty papers on site at one time. He might have been right, but I think not. I sold out within minutes of each delivery all through the day. That day's earnings were probably more than all the other days that I'd sold the paper, combined.

CHAPTER NINE

Late one night, our family experienced a truly terrifying event at the South Ninth Street apartment. Sherie and I slept in separate beds in the same bedroom. Her bed, adjacent to the only window in the room, looked out onto a vacant parcel. I awoke to the hysterical screams of my seven-year-old sister. Street lights sent a pale glow into the room, and I saw a man lying on top of my sister in her bed.

He wore khaki colored work clothes, similar to those our dad wore, and I mistook him for Dad. I asked "Dad, what's wrong?" My father, followed by Mom, rushed into the room. The stranger quickly jumped to the floor, wielding a large hunting knife. I never, ever heard screaming as loud as my sister screamed that night. In an instant, Dad—thankfully my sober Dad —grabbed the intruder's wrist and yanked him hard down off his feet, sending the knife clattering across the floor in Dad's direction. He snatched the knife and held it to the throat of the stranger, who offered no further resistance. My parents strong-armed him into the living room and pushed him down onto the couch.

Dad stood over the obviously intoxicated belligerent trespasser. I recognized the wild expression in Dad's eyes that said any show of resistance would be met with unbridled violence. No private telephones existed in the projects. Mom frantically fumbled through her pocket-book for a nickel so she could call the police from the pay phone on the corner. When she couldn't find one, she asked Dad for a nickel. Smugly, the guy on the couch reached into his pocket and extracted a handful of change which he extended toward Mom. What a mistake. She responded to his arrogance by launching a furious physical attack. It took all of Dad's strength to pull her off the target of her rage.

Mom made the call and the police arrived to arrest the potential molester. As the officers placed their prisoner into the back seat of their cruiser, they purposely slammed his head into the top of the car door opening. Each family member testified at the trial, held very soon after the arrest. The court agreed with the prosecutor's contention that Sherie's ripped pajamas left little doubt as to the defendant's intentions.

The man received a seven year prison sentence. He came from Alaska which hadn't yet achieved statehood. Not being a citizen, after serving his sentence, he faced deportation with no chance to ever return legally to the United States.

Other than her initial terror, Sherie seemed to have sustained no physical or emotional damage as a result of the experience. But she and I got a lot of mileage out of telling the "Alaskan Molester Story" in the coming years.

As a young boy, I had lots of fun fishing and exploring around the wharfs in the Richmond bay, located less than a mile from the Ninth Street apartment. Occasionally, I got lucky and hooked a fish, which Mom cooked for me. One afternoon I caught a strange looking fish like none I'd seen before. It turned out to be a Rock Cod, and I soon learned that the ugly creature's barbed fins are poisonous, and they should be handled with great care, which I failed to do. The severe pain in my hand from the sting necessitated a visit to the emergency room of the small Kaiser Permanente medical facility on Cutting Boulevard.

The war resulted in a severe shortage of sugar. While fishing off the docks one day, I watched a ship being unloaded. Longshoremen transferred what looked to be sacks of some kind of material from the vessel onto trucks. One of the bags accidentally dropped from the gangplank to the pier. When all the sacks had been loaded onto a truck, I noticed no one tried to retrieve the one that fell. After the workmen left, I discovered that the impact of the fall broke a sack of sugar. I felt as if I'd found abandoned treasure. I happily carted my prize home and my delighted parents treated me like a hero for the next few days.

CHAPTER TEN

Dad continued drinking but it appeared the effects of the alcohol on his body had begun to change. It took longer to recover from the binges and he needed a drink just to keep his hands from shaking. Drinking no longer gave him the pleasure that it used to do. I overheard him tell Mom, he now considered liquor the medicine he needed in order to function.

Dad's attempt to overcome his addiction led him to join Alcoholics Anonymous, and he responded to their wonderful program by remaining sober for around six months. During that period the dark moodiness disappeared, and Mom, Sherie and I couldn't have been happier. Our family did what normal families did. We loved to visit the San Francisco Zoo and frequently enjoyed other Bay Area points of interest. Those excursions often included a picnic lunch featuring Mom's delectable fried chicken and potato salad.

Sadly, our lives changed. One rainy Saturday afternoon, Dad came in the front door and walked right by us, with no acknowledgement. He went into the bedroom and shut the door— an old familiar scene. I asked, "Mom, is Dad drinking?" As stunned as I, she nodded yes, with tears spilling down her cheeks. The blissful respite had ended, and we would never again enjoy the level of happiness with Dad we had treasured during his six months of sobriety.

My eleventh birthday arrived. The quality of our family life had sunk to its lowest ebb. Dad drank more than ever. The other war, the one outside our apartment, had ended along with the well paying shipyard jobs. It wouldn't take a high degree of psychic ability to foresee how that promised to go. Our family needed a timeout. Our parents sent Sherie and me to Missouri to spend the summer with our grandparents.

Before going to Missouri in 1946, I had managed to scrounge an impressive collection of war-related memorabilia. The dozens of items I acquired included two Japanese rifles with bayonets, several disarmed Japanese and American hand grenades, a large Japanese flag, a Japanese officer's uniform, and both American and Japanese military merit decorations and medals. I used a portion of the money earned delivering groceries and blocks of ice and selling newspapers to buy the collectables from military people, shipyard workers and other collectors. I worked hard to accumulate my prizes and put together a fine aggregation of souvenirs. When I left for Missouri, I asked my parents to take care of my treasures.

Sherie stayed with Ma in Springfield in her quiet and comfortable rooming house. We loved her home. I lived with Dad's parents on a pastoral dairy farm about thirty miles from Springfield. Sherie and I were elated. We had been with our grandparents occasionally over the years and had bonded with them. In addition, our many uncles, aunts and cousins seemed to genuinely welcome us. For the first time since Dad's six-month involvement with Alcoholics Anonymous, we felt secure.

Also sharing my grandparent's home was my uncle Randolph and his two daughters, Rachel and Annie. My two cousins were six and eight years older than me, respectively. Rachel married soon after my arrival and she and her husband moved to their new farm. Like my dad, Randolph couldn't stay away from the liquor. When he and his wife divorced, the court awarded custody of their girls to Grandma and Grandpa. Soon after Rachel and Annie arrived at our grandparents' farm, Randolph moved in as well. Unlike Dad, Randolph couldn't hold a regular job during that period because of his drinking, but he managed to share the farm-related chores.

About mid-summer I learned from my uncle Hobert that Mom and Dad had divorced. I suppose that the inevitability of that process led to Sherie and I being sent to Missouri. Dad took a construction job in Okinawa and Mom worked as a waitress in Richmond. My dad and grandparents had decided if I wished to live with my grandparents in Missouri, I could if Mom agreed.

CHAPTER ELEVEN

Near the end of that greatest summer of my life and Sherie's, Mom wrote that she would soon be coming to Missouri to take us back to California. The thought of leaving my loving Missouri family broke my heart. I begged Grandma Barry to intercede on my behalf and try to persuade my mother to allow me to live in Missouri permanently. Grandma promised to do everything she could.

I went into the smelly outhouse and got down on my knees and prayed for more than an hour. I'm not sure of exactly how it came about but I think that my grandparents enlisted the help of Dad's brother, Hobert and his sister, Marlas, to plead my cause to my mother. In any event, a letter soon arrived saying that I could indeed live with my grandparents permanently. I truly appreciated all that my Missouri family did for me, but I knew beyond any doubt that I owed my good fortune to God. I've gone through some difficult times in life, but I've never lost the faith I developed when God answered my outhouse prayer.

Randolph's presence on the farm taxed the patience of his parents and his alcoholism brought shame to his family. It would have been better if he had removed his debauchery from their sight, as Dad did back in 1938. Even though Dad would not or could not change, unlike Randolph, he still held the respect, love and admiration of his parents and siblings because they weren't forced to witness his seamy lifestyle. Grandpa Barry commuted five days each week from the farm to Springfield to his job with the Frisco Railroad Company. Randolph's work on the farm earned him just enough to keep him intoxicated.

Randolph drank gin—lots of gin. No matter where I roamed over the rolling pastures and wooded areas surrounding the little farm house nestled in the peaceful ambiance of the Missouri Ozarks, I would find a hidden half-filled pint of gin. Any outbuilding, log, tree fork and boulder might harbor a partially filled bottle of Randolph's addiction.

The Barry family enjoyed a high degree of respect in the community. Randolph's weakness presented a constant source of embarrassment to them. In cases of severe alcoholism, well-connected family members occasionally had their wayward loved ones committed to a state mental asylum.

Whether my grandparents actually initiated the legal process to have Randolph committed or simply pretended to do so, the result was the same. One Saturday morning, while most of the family went into Springfield to shop, someone came to the farm and told Randolph that on the next Monday morning he was to be taken into custody and delivered to a state mental institution.

Terrified of the prospects of being locked up for an indefinite period, Randolph fled the farm. He caught a Greyhound bus to Peoria, Illinois, where he soon found work at Caterpillar Tractor as a machinist, the same type of work he did at the Frisco Railroad company before alcohol took him over.

The prospect of losing his freedom had sufficient impact to cause Randolph to stop drinking. In Peoria, his life transformed. He fell in love, married and continued working at Caterpillar Tractor until he retired after many prosperous happy years.

Later, Randolph with his wife returned to Missouri and bought a home in the small agricultural town of Nixa, about twenty miles west of Springfield. His two sisters, Marlas and Joanne, and his widowed mother also resided in Nixa. There, he lived out his life contented and respected until he passed away at age eighty-seven. Things didn't go that well for his brothers.

CHAPTER TWELVE

When I first began living on the farm, much of the time I acted like a little shit. I often tried the patience of everyone in the house. I didn't know how to act. I argued over things I knew nothing about, probably just for attention. The hostile insecure environment I endured for most of the first eleven years of my life had undoubtedly shaped my unpleasant pattern of behavior, and I just didn't know any better. It embarrasses me to this day to remember how stupidly I conducted myself back then.

During my time on the farm I began to experience terrible headaches at the rate of about one a month. Although I suffered in agony, I rarely complained and just endured the severe discomfort during their four to five hour duration. One day, I told Grandma that my head hurt so badly that I had to lie down. As I lay on the couch, Annie thought I was asleep and I heard her ask, "Do you think Val really has a headache?" Grandma answered, "Maybe he does, I sure do."

It disappointed me that Annie didn't believe me. While in Missouri, I never mentioned my headaches again, but the condition plagued me for decades.

Annie adopted the role of my older sister and tended to be bossy. I resented my cousin giving me orders and responded rudely to her well-intentioned efforts to help me adjust to my new life. Ironically, notwithstanding my treatment of Annie, I secretly adored her. I've met few people in my life possessing the degree of charm and magnetic appeal that equaled Annie's irresistible personality.

We attended the same school—grades one through twelve—in the small town of Billings about twenty miles from the farm. Each weekday we rode to and from our school in a school bus. One day I left my notebook on the bus, and I really needed it that day regarding a special study assignment. I knew Annie had an extra notebook. I received permission to go to her class to borrow it. The binder she lent me had been partially used.

When I opened the borrowed notepad, I came upon the beginning of a letter from Annie to her best friend, Sharon Mangel. Sharon's family owned the Mangel Mortuary in Billings and actually lived in the same building that held the expired subjects of their enterprise and ostensibly thought nothing of it.

I read my cousin's preparatory draft to her friend and learned that Annie indicated she would accept the Mangel family's invitation to spend the summer with them at the mortuary. She explained that because of my hostility she looked forward to passing the summer away from me. As I thought about what Annie had written, regret filled my heart. It hurt to know that I had treated her so shabbily that she preferred to sleep in a house with dead people than be near me.

Had Annie openly confronted me regarding my lousy attitude, I likely would have angrily defended myself. However, the non-confrontational manner in which I learned how she felt simply made me ashamed. I clearly understood that I had repaid badly needed love and kindness with callous disrespect. I promised myself to do everything I could to make things right.

I made every effort to keep my promise. I let her know I truly appreciated her guidance. Of course, conditioned by my previous rudeness she would not quickly be convinced. Whenever the opportunity arose in which I could assist Annie with her farm chores, I did so. Such occasions occurred rarely because she could easily double my output.

She gradually began to respond to my unwavering efforts to win her affection and a bond of love, deep respect and friendship evolved between us. I had finally been able to make things right. The fact that Annie didn't spend the summer of 1947 sharing accommodations with corpses underscored the success of my project. Decades passed until I began to wonder if Annie's message to Sharon Mangel had truly reached me by chance.

Basketball almost religiously dominated school sports in our section of Missouri. Within the region, basketball teams represented each class from the sixth through the twelfth grades. Teams throughout the school system regularly competed with each other.

My competitive nature and the fact that my cousins, boys and girls, were members of their schools' teams made me ashamed of my lack of skill. I explained my dilemma to Grandpa Barry. The next Saturday morning we went shopping in Springfield. Annie drove us there in the family's 1935 black Chevrolet sedan. Rachel had married and moved away, and Randolph was gone, leaving Annie as the only person remaining on the farm who could drive.

Our purchases included a new basketball and hoop. When we arrived home, Grandpa installed the hoop on the back wall of Grandma's chicken house. The very next morning I began what became a daily ritual of dribbling and shooting hoops. Occasionally, a couple of boys from nearby farms stopped by to practice with me. The more I played, the better I became. During school recess and lunch period all the boys in our class played our favorite sport. The official class team honed its skills competing against us non-team players. We were usually easily defeated, until the ability I developed behind the chicken coop began to balance the previously lopsided competition.

Surprised, the official team members discovered we non-team players were getting hard to beat, and believe me, that felt real good. Even though the official team still won most of the time, they could no longer prevail without putting forth their best effort. My diligence to achieve some degree of proficiency at playing basketball reached fruition. Unflagging determination had earned the acceptance, admiration and respect of the sixth grade team.

At the beginning of that summer, my Missouri family had occasion to attend the funeral of a neighboring farmer. At the service I ran into James Mathew Merrit, the captain of our sixth grade basketball team. James told me that I had been selected to be an official member of the seventh grade team. Although circumstances arose that prevented me from experiencing that honor, my sense of satisfaction lasted a long time.

At twelve years of age, in 1947, I occasionally joined my grandfather and Uncle Hobert and a few of their companions on a fox hunt. Fox hunting, conducted in the Missouri Ozarks seemed to be completely understood only by those actively engaged in the sport. On selected moonlit nights, owners set their hounds free to roam the countryside in pursuit of the crafty little prey. The basic stages of the hunt included the hounds searching for the scent of a trail, locating the trail, and jumping and chasing their quarry until the fox went underground which concluded the event. The hunt generally began near eight in the evening and ended around six in the morning.

Over fields and through the forests the men ambled after the pack at a distance near enough to enjoy what they referred to as the "music" of the constantly howling hounds. The pitch each dog emitted enabled the human segment of the pursuers to determine the progress of the hunt as well as determine which hound had taken charge. The nocturnal canine symphony constituted the essence of the sport. Discussion of every nuance of the hunt went on for days after the event, just as other sporting events are discussed in great detail after a big game.

Fox hunting in that region intended no harm to that sleek little creature. I believe the pleasure derived by the hounds and men ranked second to their elusive quarry's love of the chase. The fox's participation in the contest happened to be entirely voluntary, and it could generally end the chase at will.

The clever animal seemed to derive great satisfaction in matching wits with its pursuers. Full of fun, the cunning trickster delighted in teasing the dogs. A favorite ruse involved leading the clamoring hounds on a long circular route, come up behind the pack, and perhaps momentarily pretend to be the pursuer. I think foxes have a sense of humor.

Sadly, though it didn't happen often, a fox would be overtaken before it could escape underground. Such an occurrence always proved fatal to the hapless animal. Equally unfortunate, as the result of a particularly taxing chase, a truly dedicated hound would occasionally expire from exhaustion.

Being invited to join Grandpa Barry and the others in their revered sport pleased me immensely. Notwithstanding the fact that fox hunting has endured for centuries, it meant much more to others than me. I didn't mention that to them.

One bright full moon night, while sitting on a grassy countryside knoll listening to the singing pack doing what they were born and bred to do, I looked skyward at a passing airliner. I saw lights shining through the plane's windows and imagined the passengers were having a good time. For the first time since I'd come to live with my grandparents, I felt lonely. I realized at this moment, life on the farm for me had come to an end. I missed my mother.

Summer had nearly passed when I received a letter from Mom. She let me know that she would soon be in Missouri to take Sherie back to California and that she planned to visit me the next week. She drove out to the farm in a rental car the next Sunday afternoon. We walked over the acres talking until the sun began to set.

Mom was truly beautiful. She rarely turned on the charm but when she did, she glowed. When we returned to the farmhouse, I told my grandparents and Annie that I would be going back to Springfield to visit with Mom and my sister before they left for California. In truth, I'd already decided to return to California, but I needed time to figure how best to inform them.

My grandparents had no telephone. The next day I called Aunt Marlas in Jamestown—colloquially referred to as "Dogtown,"— where she and Uncle Armon owned a grocery store. I asked her to tell them what I'd decided. Aunt Marlas drove from her home to the farm to tell Annie and Grandma and Grandpa that I wouldn't be returning to them.

A few days later, they came to Springfield to say goodbye. It was a difficult meeting, as it hurt them to see me and Sherie go, but they were resigned and understanding. I loved them and knew I would miss them. I often wonder where my life might have gone had I stayed in Missouri. The next time I saw my Missouri family would be on a very sad occasion.

CHAPTER THIRTEEN

Mom, Sherie and I arrived by train in Oakland, California, a few days later. We shared a three bedroom duplex apartment with Mom's youngest brother, Jeremy, and his wife, Sandy, and their baby, Phillip. Jeremy had recently been discharged from the army in California. He decided to stay in the Golden State with his little family for a while. The duplex was part of a government project originally developed for people in war-related jobs, similar to those units we had occupied in Salashan and Richmond. By 1948, the war had been over for three years, and the projects would soon be razed.

We were crowded in the small apartment, but we all got along well. Early one Saturday morning, Uncle Jeremy and a neighbor and I went on a Pacific Coast deep sea chartered fishing venture out of Half Moon Bay, about fifty miles down the coast. I caught a nice Ling Cod and had a terrific time until I became seasick. One with severe seasickness doesn't care whether they live or die; at least that's how I felt. I may have been sicker at some point in my life, but I couldn't be sure.

The following day, still feeling weak and nauseous, I lay on my bed with my head resting on the window sill under the raised window, just in case. Sherie felt sorry for me and lay down beside me, and we lazily stared out the open window Tall dry grass just below us grew against the building. Soon, we noticed a thin spiral of smoke rising out of the grass and weeds.

We ignored the smoke and continued quietly conversing. Then flames appeared. Incredibly, we kept talking, paying no attention until the fire engaged the entire height of the structure, and we were driven from our resting place. A fire engine with siren screaming arrived and the firefighters quickly extinguished the flames. Fortunately, not much damage had occurred. Sherie and I said nothing about watching a tiny stream of smoke develop into a full blown conflagration, while doing nothing to prevent it. We had no idea why we behaved as we did, but we still laugh when we recall the incident.

I thought about the fine array of World War II memorabilia that I left in my parents' care when I went to Missouri, and I asked Mom about it. She changed the subject, and I assumed she had given away my collection. I was disappointed, but Mom and I were getting along well so I didn't make an issue of it.

Within a few weeks of our return to California, Uncle Jeremy and his family moved back to Springfield. Mom, Sherie and I relocated to 1355 95th Avenue in the Elmhurst district of Oakland. Sherie and I shared the bedroom and Mom slept on the couch in our circa 1930s auto court apartment.

Mom and I had remained on good terms. She bought me a new bicycle and a baseball mitt and bat. She worked as a waitress and didn't earn a lot. She insisted that I get a job delivering papers which would keep me busy and provide me with spending money. By that time, I'd turned thirteen and attended the seventh grade at Elmhurst Junior High on 98th Avenue. The obligation of maintaining a daily paper route prevented me from hanging out with classroom pals after school let out.

Even though the paper route interfered with my social life, I gained some sound business principals from the experience. To avoid complaints and encourage tipping, I delivered the paper in a timely manner and made sure to deposit it on the porch rather than on the lawn or in the shrubbery. I strove to establish a friendly rapport with my customers.

I learned the importance of being a diligent bill collector while conducting my paper delivery business. Newspaper boys received their pay from the monthly funds they collected from their customers. Lazy fellows or shy collectors often received no payment at all from some of their deadbeat clientele.

I discovered a small percentage of customers met their financial obligations only in response to aggressive collection methods. Indeed, I had to practically haunt those who avoided paying until I wore them down. *Damn … who wants to work for nothing?* In most cases when reluctant payers realized the uselessness of trying to avoid me, they began to pay up in a reliable fashion. Such lessons are only learned in the real world, not in academia. My experience as a thirteen-year-old newspaper delivery boy helped prepare me to successfully manage collections in the coming years.

CHAPTER FOURTEEN

Elmhurst Junior High School had seven homerooms. The students were assigned to homerooms according to their perceived intelligence levels. Political correctness hadn't come into vogue yet. The faculty homeroom assignment committee placed who they thought to be the most intelligent students in homeroom number one, and placement descended accordingly down to homeroom number seven. But for the fact that they were so big and tough, I think homeroom seven students would have been teased by all the other seventh graders. I drew homeroom number two, Mrs. Firenzi's class.

The school counselor, Mr. Bowles, interviewed each intellectually above-average seventh grade student. He was a likable little man, who, after interviewing a student, gave them a bag of corn nuts, which he produced after school hours in a small plant he owned. Some say he invented corn nuts—I don't know. Mr. Bowles informed me my I.Q. happened to be considerably above average, and he encouraged me to select college preparation courses whenever possible. Foolishly I didn't follow his advice.

During the summer before entering Elmhurst, I read Dale Carnegie's classic, *How to Win Friends and Influence People*. Utilizing the techniques advocated by Mr. Carnegie, I became an instant social success at Elmhurst. In the seventh grade, I did indeed win friends and influence people. The homeroom seven classes competed in intramural sports competitions, and my classmates selected me to be captain of the baseball, basketball and football teams.

My teachers and fellow students liked me and I excelled academically. However, in the eighth grade I began to change and my short-lived success declined rapidly. I got attention by becoming one of the class clowns and my interest in academic and athletic achievement dwindled. Mom worked long, hard hours as a waitress to support us and just didn't have the time or energy to notice.

My behavior continued to slide downhill. When I enrolled in high school, I began drinking on weekends along with other wayward friends. I earned barely passing grades throughout high school and invested just enough effort to avoid failing. If not for Mom's non-negotiable insistence that I graduate, I would have dropped out as several of my loser friends had already done. I spent more evenings and weekends with the dropouts instead of school chums.

Although I never placed the blame for my stupid lifestyle on anyone other than myself, maybe family problems exacerbated my poor attitude. Shortly before I entered the eighth grade, Mom remarried. I still adored Dad and rebelled against the authority of my step-father, John Beltran.

John never had children of his own and tried to make a happy family—I didn't give him a chance. Probably because of me, Mom and John began to quarrel a lot. It took time and changing circumstances, but the time came when John and I developed a close father/son relationship.

CHAPTER FIFTEEN

At the beginning of the summer of my fifteenth year, I landed what I considered my first real job. My best pal, Don Dennis' father held the position of superintendent of the Longview Fiber Box Company located at 85th Avenue and San Leandro Boulevard in Oakland. Mr. Dennis arranged for Don and me to work at the corrugated cardboard box company through our summer vacation. I worked eight hours each weekday and received a dollar and forty seven cents per hour. I felt a strong sense of pride.

Although grateful for the job, I noted the value of influential connections. Don, the son of the superintendent got assigned to a job in a pleasant office environment while I labored at bottom of the plant's caste system as a "tailslitter." An operator fed flat rectangles of corrugated cardboard into a machine known as the slitter which cut the slots necessary for each sheet of cardboard to be transformed into boxes.

The slotted pieces emerged on a conveyer belt from the machine and formed a stack six to eight inches high. Working quickly, I placed the heavy cardboard sheets onto a wooden pallet. When the stack reached a height of around three feet, I quickly replaced the full pallet with an empty one. I continued the hard labor until the ten minute morning break, the thirty minute lunch and another ten minute afternoon break. Believe me; those breaks were like palm-shaded fresh cool lagoons in the blazing desert.

My summer stint at Longview made me feel grown up, even though I didn't even shave yet. I kept up with the older guys and earned their respect. More often than I should have I joined my box plant pals after work at a nearby tavern and enjoyed two or three beers while listening to forlorn Hank Williams type ballads. I preferred rhythm and blues, but after a couple of Pabsts it really didn't matter.

CHAPTER SIXTEEN

After the war, Dad worked in construction overseas. Between jobs he lived in inexpensive but clean hotels in San Francisco. Sherie and I visited him a lot during those brief periods. Often I took off school and stayed with him a few days at a time. During one of his San Francisco stopovers in 1949, I helped him through a particularly severe drinking binge. I still loved Dad, and he could still break my heart. I remember with tears in my eyes, telling him, "Dad, I think you are going to die very soon."

His answer came in the form of a simple question, "Val, do you really think so?"

Dad would be leaving for Portland, Oregon in a few days to meet with his construction crew before flying to Iran where he would help develop oil field infrastructure. Before he left, I misbehaved in school, earning a three day suspension. I walked slowly home, dreading the wrath I'd face from my mother. Along the way, I ran into two of my friends, Larry Groves and Chuck Mitchell, who recently dropped out of school. Chuck and Larry were out joy riding in a car that Chuck had swiped from his uncle that morning, and they invited me to join them. They knew there would soon be a reckoning resulting from the theft of the car, and they agreed to my suggestion that the three of us run away.

We bought a twelve-can case of Burgermiester beer financed with dimes that filled a fruit jar that Chuck found in the trunk of his uncle's car. We took off for Orland, a small agricultural town, 150 miles northeast of Oakland. We hoped to locate our pal, Jack Fenton, a former classmate who had been sent to live with his grandfather on his olive ranch. I suppose Jack's parents relocated him to separate him from kids like Larry, Chuck and me.

By the time we reached Vallejo, about forty miles north of where our adventure began, we'd consumed the beer. Chuck rear-ended another car, rendering his uncle's vehicle inoperable. Thankfully, neither we, nor the passengers in the other car suffered any injuries. Before the police arrived, we started out on foot to find the Greyhound Bus Depot. We financed our bus trip with the remaining dimes from the fruit jar and continued our journey to Orland.

Around two in the morning, the bus spilled us— hungry, broke and hung-over—out onto the bitter cold January streets of Orland. Wearing a short-sleeve golf type shirt and no jacket, I suggested we might be better off to turn ourselves over to the police. At least, we could sleep off our hangovers in a warm cell. In a few minutes we spotted a police station. We were extremely disappointed to find it closed. Sacks of grain stacked outside at the front of a feed store served as our beds until dawn.

Starved and shivering, we wandered around until Orland began to wake up. Chuck, as always, anxious to gain approval, provided a delicious breakfast of shoplifted sliced cheese. Hunger sated, we started back to the police station, when we ran into Jack. What a stroke of good luck! The adventure continued.

Jack explained that on Saturdays, he and his grandfather and his uncle came into town to shop for things needed at the ranch. Jack drove separately in his own pickup so he could visit his town friends. He introduced us to his grandfather and uncle and let them know he would be home late that evening. Although Grandpa agreed to let us stay at the ranch that night, I knew by the way he looked us over that his thoughts were centered on how to get rid of us. Looking back, I can't blame him.

That afternoon, Jack, always popular wherever he lived, introduced us to his Orland buddies. We had a great time partying with Jack's friends past midnight. Flowing beer, friendly girls; I loved Orland. Early Sunday morning, we arrived at the ranch.

Larry, Chuck and I slept—or passed out may have been more accurate—on Jack's bedroom floor. At dawn, Jack and his grandfather and uncle left to work the olive orchards. Jack told us we were welcome to prepare ham and eggs for breakfast. We couldn't find any food at first. I clearly understood Grandpa's message. Even so, we were hungry. A quick search turned up a suitcase full of eggs and a ham hidden under the uncle's bed.

After a delicious breakfast, we cleaned up and planned to hitchhike back to Orland, hoping to meet up with our new pals. We walked out of the farmhouse right into the custody of Glenn County Deputy Sheriffs who were accompanied by Larry's dad and uncle. Jack's grandpa had outfoxed us. Larry's uncle seemed impressed as we described our adventure. We enjoyed a pleasant ride back to Oakland.

The relief of our safe return exceeded Larry's and my parents' need to discipline us. Larry let me know Chuck didn't get off so easily. I never saw Chuck again. I felt sorry for Chuck. He seemed to be continuously doing stupid things in a futile effort to gain approval of his friends. A few years later, I learned he had been fatally shot by a San Leandro Police Officer while fleeing a botched bank robbery.

Home from Orland, I needed to be reinstated into school. For that to happen one of my parents had to meet with the vice principal, Mr. MacMasters (Mac), an intimidating appearing man a little over six-feet-three inches tall, with a deep authoritative voice. My step-father, a merchant seaman was at sea. Dad hadn't yet left for his new job. Mom insisted that he get me back into school which he agreed to do.

The meeting went surprisingly well. Dad, still a handsome man with a pleasing personality, dressed in a suit, white shirt and tie got on well with Mac. Dad made me feel proud. Mac explained that I lacked respect for authority. I think Dad empathized with me. Lack of respect for authority was a subject he knew something about.

Mac credited me with above average intelligence. He said he knew I could successfully do my assignments, but I refused to apply myself. Indeed, Mac stated the case accurately. I had the ability to do well in school, but I simply wasn't interested. For example, while getting "C"s and barely passing grades in most of my classes, I received an "A" in physiology, a difficult subject. I suppose something about dissecting frogs held my attention. In addition, I typed well and earned an "A" in that subject. Otherwise, I goofed off and received the grades I deserved.

Later, Dad said very little to me about my poor classroom performance. He told me if I didn't wise up there would be a price to pay. However, he believed we needed to have a serious father-son discussion regarding my drinking. I ran with a fast crowd and most of my weekends involved alcohol. He assured me, as an old sot, he could give me some helpful guidance relative to drinking. Dad, only thirty-eight, qualified as a sot perhaps, but not an old sot.

Dad surprised me. He never mentioned whether I should or should not drink. However, he said, "If a fellow is going to drink, it helps to do it right. To get the most out of a drinking spree, a guy should start with two or three belts in quick succession which produces a pleasant 'glow'." He let me know that even though I would experience a nice high, I wouldn't be intoxicated. He went on to tell me that about an hour after that initial double or triple, a savvy drinker would have another single shot to maintain the feeling of euphoria. That process should be repeated hourly. He persuaded me if I followed his advice I'd always be in control, never get sick and generally have a good time.

I reasoned, though he didn't say so, my drinking disappointed Dad. He clearly understood that I used alcohol as a social crutch and he knew it could ruin my life, just as it ruined his. Even so, I believe he instinctively understood if he launched into a lecture about the evils of booze, I wouldn't listen. What Dad told me likely had to be among the most helpful lectures I ever received. I loved him and until I decided to quit drinking, which I knew would happen, I planned to follow his advice.

CHAPTER SEVENTEEN

Dad gave me a beautiful Seamaster Omega wristwatch, which he won in a poker game on the flight home after he completed his job in Guam. I treasured that watch. Just before he left for Portland, he asked me if he could borrow the watch for a short period. He figured an Omega; a high-ticket item might help create a good impression with the people he would meet in Portland. He assured me I'd have my watch back soon. He didn't know the accuracy of his statement.

A few days later, while alone at home on a Sunday afternoon, I received a telephone call from Western Union. The telegram from Portland came from "Flanagan," a friend of Dad's who would be working with him in Iran. The telegram, addressed to me, simply stated: "YOUR FATHER HAS DIED."

Confused—at first I thought the telegram informed Dad that his father had died. Sure, that made sense. After all, Grandpa Barry had recently suffered a stroke. We had expected Grandpa's demise to occur soon. However, within the hour the message became clear. Shocked and devastated, I finally understood that Flanagan had notified me that *my* father had died.

I called the Geneva Hotel at 218 Southwest Salmon Street in Portland where Dad had registered. I spoke with Edith P. Hughs, the hotel owner. She said a hotel maid discovered Dad's body in his bed Sunday morning and that the City Of Portland's morgue had Dad's remains. I telephoned the office of the Portland Coroner. Someone there told me an autopsy had been performed and my father had died of natural causes, and his family could claim the body. I called Missouri. My Uncle Hobert, who idolized Dad, agreed to meet me at the Geneva Hotel on Tuesday morning.

Mom arrived home and heard my news and by the look on her face—I knew her pain equaled mine. Our mutual loss brought us very close. Mom borrowed money from Aunt Pauline and Uncle Gene to pay my expenses and airfare to Portland. The next morning, I boarded a plane to claim my father's body in Portland. I took a taxi from the airport to the YMCA in downtown Portland. My room at the "Y" for the night cost a dollar and thirty-five cents. I headed for the Geneva Hotel to get more information and pick up Dad's personal effects.

A block or so before I reached the Geneva Hotel I observed a large, stocky, red-haired man staring at me. He walked up to me and asked, "Excuse me son, is your name Val Barry?"

I answered, "Yes."

He smiled and said, "I knew it, you look just like Don." Flanagan walked with me to the hotel, where I picked up Dad's Samsonite suitcase containing his personal belongings. I spotted the Omega watch Dad gave me that I had lent back to him.

Flanagan explained he and Dad were friends and had worked together in Okinawa and Guam. In his awkward manner, he told me Dad began drinking as soon as he arrived in Portland. He had been playing poker late Saturday night and when a fight erupted during the game, Dad came out second best. He went to his room and was found dead Sunday morning. As Flanagan described his dear friend's final hours, I remembered when I told Dad in San Francisco that I thought he would die soon. Maybe I had been preparing for it. Flanagan showed me a short newspaper article memorializing Dad's demise with the caption, "Drinking bout ends in death."

I thought about something Dad said in response to the remark about me believing he would die soon. He mentioned that prior to leaving the country on work assignments, crews generally spent a few days in staging hotels such as the Geneva, where considerable heavy drinking occurred. Hotel doctors routinely injected the alcohol debilitated men with morphine to help them feel better and appear well enough to report for work

The injections cost a lot, and likely a portion of the revenue from the illegal and dangerous practice went to corrupt officials so they would look the other way. Since Dad usually went on a binge while at a staging hotel, it normally took him a few days to recover. One visit from the hotel doctor and he felt terrific. Dad admitted that after receiving a "sobering up" injection of morphine in an Omaha hotel he had experienced a severe negative reaction. The doctor said that in Dad's condition, the mixture of morphine and alcohol in his system could prove fatal, and he advised him never to repeat the procedure. The binge in Portland so debilitated him that he probably felt he could not report to work without an injection. He gambled and lost. I thought about Dad's lecture to me and wished he had followed his own advice.

My dad was gone, and I missed him terribly. Some may think, *What's the big deal? After all, he even described himself as "an old sot."* Dad often told me, "Someday, Val, we're going to own a large cattle ranch. It will have a lake filled with bass and trout, so whenever we're hungry for fresh fish we can take them out of our own lake. It'll be a big spread with alfalfa pastures for the cattle and timber forests full of deer and other game."

Naturally, in that dream we owned saddle horses and deer rifles which we used on our occasional hunting outings on our own property. Of course, he and Mom had reconciled and our family was intact again. In my dream, Dad's craving for booze no longer existed.

It wasn't total fantasy. During his time between jobs, which sometimes lasted several weeks, Dad traveled to Grandma and Grandpa's farm. He stocked the farm with cattle he bought at auctions. My cousin Annie cared for the cattle in his absence. Dad sincerely believed we would someday own that dream ranch. That dream ended on a cold, rainy morning, February 15, 1952, in a lonely room at the Geneva Hotel in Portland, Oregon.

Flanagan introduced me to Taylor Abercrombie. Taylor explained that he and Dad worked together on overseas jobs and had been close friends. Taylor was well built and a congenial man. He appeared to be in his early forties and came off as a man of authority. He would have been Dad's superintendent on the Iran job. He told me that Dad often spoke with him of Sherie and me.

Taylor explained that the night before Dad died they played poker in Taylor's room in the company of two women picked up in the hotel bar, and Dad, heavily intoxicated, became belligerent. A fistfight erupted between Taylor and Dad. The dispute ended quickly, followed by mutual apologies. Dad retired to his room with a bloody nose.

Taylor appeared shaken. With tears in his eyes, he told me he felt miserable about what had happened. He expressed his wish to stay in touch with me. He said, "Val, I will miss Don. If ever I can be of help to you, just ask." Taylor's sincerity seemed palpable. The time came when I responded to his offer.

I met my Uncle Hobert at the hotel later that day, and we arranged to have Dad's body shipped back to Missouri. We accomplished the transfer through a mortuary in Portland. The coroner's office asked that a member of the family view the body at the morgue to confirm identity. Thank God, Uncle Hobert performed that gruesome task. Visibly shaken, Hobert explained the autopsy left Dad's body open like a butchered steer.

After the Portland mortuary prepared Dad's remains for burial, I viewed the body. He looked good in his nice brown suit—the one he had worn to get me reinstated in school. I placed Dad's gold Eversharp pen in his breast pocket. When he arrived in Missouri, the pen had disappeared. Uncle Hobert, Dad and I traveled to Missouri on the same train, although not in the same coaches. I sometimes imagine that in a parallel universe or another dimension that Dad had indeed found his ranch and lives there sober and happy with his loved ones.

A few days later, I attended Dad's funeral in the small country chapel at the Delaware Cemetery, not many miles from the tiny farming village of Boaz. Lots of people came to show respect for Dad and his family. Despite his careless lifestyle, people remembered his charm and congenial wit. His demise saddened the close-knit rural community. We laid his body to rest in a grave among several headstones inscribed with the name of Barry within our family plot. I said "Goodbye" to my father and returned to Oakland.

CHAPTER EIGHTEEN

I spent the next year feeling sorry for myself and continued drinking on the weekends. I recalled Dad's lecture on that subject, and at least I no longer suffered hangovers. Just before turning seventeen, a friend introduced me to Sheila Drake, a fifteen year old who lived in Alameda. Sheila, a very attractive girl, seemed to like me a lot and we began dating.

She attended Saint Agnes High School, a Catholic school for girls. Even though Saint Agnes was located a half block from her home, she actually lived at the school on a room and board basis. That confused me and she didn't explain. The time came though when I discovered why she lived in a boarding school, a minute from her home.

Life becomes complicated for teenagers when they start behaving as if they are adults. We pretended we loved each other to justify what we did together, but it was a sporadic relationship. Sheila puzzled me. On more than one occasion, she knocked on my bedroom window after midnight on a school night. She wanted to take me riding in cars she said she had swiped.

Sheila explained that in the wee morning hours while the cars' owners slept, she "borrowed" their cars. According to Sheila, her hairpin lock-picking skills permitted her to enter a locked car and start the engine. Even though she had no driver's license, Sheila loved to drive. After a few hours of joy-riding, she returned the cars while the owners still slept. I'm not sure I believed her, but what did I know?

Since the eighth grade, I'd had a secret crush on one of my classmates, Bonnie Midland. She definitely belonged on what people referred to as the "A" list. Bonnie was popular and throughout her junior and high school years she always held an elective student government office. Although we never developed an intimate relationship, or even really dated, we became close friends. Each Friday night, our high school hosted a dance in the gymnasium. Bonnie and I danced together. I sure looked forward to those school dances.

In our senior year, she flattered me by inviting me to escort her to her sorority's formal dance at the exclusive Sequoia Country Club in the Oakland hills. Of course I accepted. Most of the popular girls in our school belonged to that sorority. Their escorts naturally included their popular male counterparts; the jocks, class officers and others on the "A" list. I got along okay with that group, but I wasn't one of them.

When I say I acted like a jerk, I mean it, my behavior qualified me as a first class rat-creep. I JUST DIDN'T SHOW UP. When I think of the humiliation she suffered—waiting at her home with her parents in her formal gown, I still cringe with shame. She didn't speak to me ever again. Her friends never spoke to me again. My social standing among the school's "A" list fell slightly less than that of a child predator. In the following years, I never attended any class reunions.

I knew how badly I had behaved and knew just as well that an apology wouldn't help. My offense had been so egregious I just didn't know how to make it right. The part that bothered me most lay in the fact that I couldn't even understand the reason for my miserable misbehavior.

Around the time I turned seventeen, a subtle change began to occur at home. My step-father and I began to get along well together. Actually, John had become the father Sherie and I never really had. He showed interest in the things we wished to accomplish, and we appreciated his encouragement. I suspect our relationship had improved so dramatically because he no longer had to compete with Dad. With Dad alive, John just didn't have a chance. John was a man of high integrity, and I regretted that it took me so long to recognize that fact.

A good example of his standard of conduct is reflected in the following incident: When the war ended and ships returned from the Pacific theatre of war, John worked as a security guard for the U.S. Navy. The ships emptied troops as soon as they arrived into the bay, adjacent to the Richmond shipyards, where they were chaotically stored temporarily. John's guard duties required him to travel from ship to ship in a small outboard motor-powered boat and board and inspect each ship.

One evening as he checked out a vessel's purser's office, he heard a loud clanging noise in rhythm with the movement of the rise and fall of the choppy bay waters. He discovered what he heard was the banging of the steel door of an open safe. Inside the safe he found $75,000 in cash, a fortune in those days. Without a moment's hesitation, John delivered and turned over the money to his superiors. In recognition of his honesty, he received a letter of commendation from the Department of the Navy. When John recalled that story in my presence, Mom made some remark like, "damn fool." John responded with, "At least I know I can't be bought for $75,000."

Mom didn't get along with any of us and yelled at the three of us constantly. Her verbal abuse left emotional scars on her children. The continual criticism diminished our self-confidence. In the years that followed, Sherie and I worked hard on ourselves to mitigate the damage. I believe Mom's anger and hostility hurt my sister more than me. When Mom was at home, I stayed away as much as I could. As a boy, I found it easy to avoid her. Sherie, being a girl, found it difficult to stay out of Mom's way.

Even though our mother made life hard for us, I knew she loved us. Mom faced daunting challenges. She got up every morning at four and went to her job as a waitress/manager in a donut shop. As always, she made sure that my sister and I ate well and attended school.

In spite of my lack of academic interest, I possessed artistic skill. I constantly drew pictures of either serious or cartoon depictions of people or animals or whatever subject interested me. I believed I had a future as a political cartoonist. After graduating from high school, I hoped to enroll in the Golden Gate Academy of Art, located on Broadway in Oakland.

By the time I became eighteen, my life had improved considerably. Although, the "A" list kids continued to ignore me, I became good friends with other quality classmates. I planned to graduate in June and had accepted a few invitations to pregraduation parties. I'd stopped drinking and generally had a great time. Although I still socialized occasionally with a rough bunch, they were now only at the perimeter of my life.

Until the end of April, 1953 turned out to be an especially good period of my life. I dated a couple of neat girls and kept excited about finishing with high school and making arrangements to enroll in the art school. I looked forward to a career as a cartoonist. I didn't know exactly how to finance my plan, but I knew would figure it out.

I had still been seeing Sheila off and on during all this time, but in March of 1953 we decided to go our separate ways. There were no recriminations—we hoped to remain friends, but we both wanted to move on.

One of her close school friends had recently moved to Oxnard, and Sheila planned to run away and visit her. Even as we split up, we said goodbye in our usual intimate fashion. She left and I believed we wouldn't meet again.

Near the end of April, I received a call from her. She told me she had returned from Oxnard and needed to see me right away— she had something important to tell me. In the meantime, her mother called Mom and scheduled a meeting at our home which included Sheila, her mother, my parents and me.

At that meeting, I learned that I was to be a father. Sheila's mother contended we had to get married. I sat there, stunned … I'd just turned eighteen and planned to enroll in art school in September. We weren't even going together. "Can't this be handled some other way?" I asked. Mom didn't speak.

My step-father looked at me and said, "Let's you and I step out back and talk this over, Val."

I had the utmost respect for John. He viewed me as an honorable man and knew I would do the right thing. He said, "You know Val, a child born to an unmarried mother is known as a bastard."

I couldn't argue—I knew what I must do. I took John's advice and agreed to marry. Someday I would again heed his counsel regarding Sheila.

We decided to get married in Reno. At that time I had no money and my parents were really financially strapped. My future mother-in-law felt she couldn't tell her husband what was going on, and she was broke as well. We didn't have the funds to finance our Reno wedding. I called Taylor Abercrombie at his home in Woodard, Oklahoma and explained the situation. Taylor said, "Son, I think you are making a mistake, but a check is on its way."

Two days later, the check and a letter arrived. Taylor wished me the best and repeated that in his opinion, I was making a mistake and admonished me, "Val, a poor man must do things in a poor way." His words would resonate over the years that followed.

Early morning, May 1, 1953, John drove Sheila and me to the train depot on Sixteenth Street in Oakland. We arrived in Reno, got a marriage license and became husband and wife via the services of a justice of peace. During the ceremony, something made us laugh. We just didn't understand the import of what we were doing. We had dinner, spent a few more dollars at the crap tables and rented a room at the Golden Hotel before heading home the next morning.

PART TWO

"a poor man has to do things in a poor way"

CHAPTER NINETEEN

John picked us up the next day at the Oakland depot. My mother-in-law had generously rented an apartment for us on Chestnut Street in Alameda and paid our first month rent of forty-two dollars and fifty cents. Now a married man, I suddenly had new responsibilities. I had rent to pay, and I had a pregnant wife to support. The fun-filled life I had envisioned just days before, of a young bachelor pursuing an exciting, lucrative career as a political cartoonist, no longer existed.

As an unskilled high school dropout, my employment opportunities were sparse. I landed a job at American Can Company on High Street in Oakland. I worked a revolving shift schedule. I hated the eleven p.m. to seven a.m. graveyard shift. There must have been more boring jobs, but I couldn't be certain of that. I worked in the lithograph department where an operator fed three-by-three foot sheets of tin—which would eventually become tin cans—into an oven, 200 feet in length. While being conveyed through the oven, the sheets were lithographed with a printed design for the future cans.

When the sheets reached the end of the oven, the printing had dried, I sprang into action. About four times during my eight-hour shift I transferred several hundred sheets at a time in two-foot high stacks from the oven onto a pallet. It took a couple of hours for enough sheets to accumulate to be removed from the oven. During that waiting period, I couldn't sit or read and I had no one to talk with. On the graveyard shift, the only people in the lithograph building were myself and the operator at the other end of the oven. I ate lunch at three o'clock in the morning alone in my car.

One day I felt particularly depressed. On that beautiful sunny California afternoon, I had to be at work by three o'clock. I thought about my single days before I became an expectant teenage father. I might have been having a great time at the beach with my pals and the beauty I dated before I had to get married. Just then, my in-laws, Ray and Pat drove up in their new Chevy Bel Air convertible. They wanted to show it off so they offered to drop me at American Can. Sheila agreed to pick me up when I finished my shift. They left me off at my job, and I watched Sheila and her parents drive away with the wind blowing in their hair, having a great time. I began to suspect why Pat seemed so cheerful those days.

Anticipating the arrival of our new baby, Sheila and I wanted to make the best of our situation. We got along pretty well, and although maybe only pretending to be in love, we had determined to make a good life. Suddenly, to our surprise, we discovered Sheila wasn't pregnant after all. No matter—she missed her next period—she was pregnant for real this time.

Shortly after our hastily conducted Reno marriage necessitated by Sheila's nonexistent pregnancy, her mother decided that a Roman Catholic Church wedding would erase the shame of our misconduct. Sheila approved her mother's wishes. Of course, in order for their aspirations to happen, I had to become a Catholic. I didn't object; after all, I wanted to make Sheila and her mom happy. So I converted and we married in the church. As I stated earlier, from childhood I held a strong faith in an altruistic creator. Nothing about becoming a Catholic affected my belief in God.

As a matter of fact, I found the elaborate rituals to be boring and superficial. I thought the massive wealth controlled by the Vatican to be somewhat at odds with the teachings of Christ. Nonetheless, I went with the program and kept my reservations to myself. For years, Sheila and I complied with the rhythm method of birth control, the only birth control procedure other than abstinence permitted by the Church. I didn't find the process to be very effective.

I came to think that maybe Sheila's strong attraction to the church had something to do with the fact that no matter how egregious one's behavior might be, a short visit to the confessional booth followed by an ingestion of a communal wafer made everything alright.

CHAPTER TWENTY

I learned something important. Working in a factory, doing the jobs available to a person with my limited education and skills, didn't appeal to me. I wanted to work in a clean, pleasant environment in which I could interact with people. I applied for and obtained a job as a trainee sales clerk at Burt's Shoe Store at Fourteenth and Washington Streets in downtown Oakland. I loved working at Burt's, but there wasn't enough business to keep me on full time. While at Burt's I learned that I could sell.

I visited the employment office on Webster Street in Oakland to see if they had any retail store job opportunities on file. They sent me over to Cannon Family Shoe Store at Eleventh and Washington. The manager, Bob McQueen, interviewed me. Bob came across as a no-nonsense, outspoken, chain-smoking manager of the largest store of a two-hundred-eight chain of shoe stores. The retail shoe business formed the core of Mr. McQueen's life. I liked him and he seemed to like me. He asked when I could report for work.

I loved working at Cannon. While there I acquired a valuable lifetime skill that simply, to the best of my knowledge, wasn't taught in any college. I started with Cannon in 1954; not that many years from the Great Depression. Due to their experience during that depression, Cannon emphasized teaching their full time salesmen (no salesladies worked at the store) the art of selling. They understood that most any clerk could sell a pair of shoes to a customer that came into the store to buy a pair of shoes.

However, at Cannon I learned that to sell that same customer the shoes they entered the store to buy, plus another pair, plus slippers, socks and polish, took a talented salesman. In addition, a real salesman often convinced the initial customer's companions who didn't intend to buy that day to also purchase something.

For me, working at Cannon seemed comparable to being in a classroom learning a skill I loved. The salesmen worked on commission. We were paid six percent of the gross sum of our sales. It happened now and then that a particular shoe style just wouldn't sell. Maybe it looked ugly or uncomfortable or both. After a year in stock, the company placed such poor performing footwear into the PM category (I have no idea what the letters PM stood for). In addition to the regular six percent commission, the salesmen received a fifty cent bonus for each PM they sold. Most of the sales personnel didn't try to sell them—they thought it a waste of time.

In the beginning, each day at Cannon excited me. I interacted with every type of personality imaginable. To insure my chance of success, I learned I had to quickly make my customers like me. How did I accomplish that? Bob explained that even the grumpiest customer couldn't resist a friendly, sincere smile. Greeting people with a warm smile not only caused people to like me but it let them know I genuinely liked them as well. What a wonderful, valuable, yet simple lesson.

Most of my customers clearly showed a positive response to my sincere friendliness, but not always; some people were just naturally cross, even though they may have still made a purchase. But when those hard cases returned to the store at a future date and insisted that they be served by me, I knew I had done my job well. I continually experimented, using different sales techniques. I discarded what didn't seem to work and improved on those approaches that produced good results.

After a few months, I became the store's top salesman. At only nineteen, with limited experience, I out-sold men much older and far more experienced than me. My skills rapidly continued to improve. I didn't recall ever feeling that good about myself before. Bob McQueen never stopped telling me how much my sales performance pleased him.

I learned that "clerks" sold shoes. Real salesmen sold happy dreams. For instance after a young woman had selected the shoes she actually came into the store to buy, I showed her a pair of PMs and explained how well suited those shoes would be to stroll the beach at Waikiki, Honolulu at sunset with her boyfriend or fiancé. Corny? Yes . . . but it worked more often than you might guess.

Cannon had shoes for every member of the family. Sometimes a family came in to buy shoes for only Mom or Dad. The military was highly popular to young boys in those days. They all seemed to want to emulate soldiers and sailors. We carried a boys' shoe that resembled shoes worn by soldiers. While Mom or Dad walked around the store testing the footwear I had tried on them, I surreptitiously pointed to a pair of shoes on display and asked the boys, "What do you think of these army shoes?"

Often, I heard, "Mommy, Daddy, I want a pair of army shoes."

My ploy worked with most families and always with black families. I'm not sure why, but I'd observed that black parents never denied their childrens' requests, at least in that Cannon store. A similar strategy worked with young girls. I showed them a pair of our popular patent leather "Mary Janes" and asked, "Aren't these pretty dancing shoes?" Cannon did not teach me that method of selling shoes to children. I developed it on my own.

We catered to men who wished to try on and buy women's footwear and to women who wished to try on and buy men's shoes. The store had a special, amply-mirrored fitting room for such customers. That took a little getting used to. An older, grizzled fellow dressed in construction worker clothing quietly informed me he wanted to try on a pair of the women's high heels with open toes and straps displayed in our window. The shoes he liked were PMs and I gladly obliged him. I removed his left high top, steel toe work shoe to measure his foot. It surprised me to find he wore nylon stockings through which I observed bright red toenails. As he left the store with his new shoes, I felt a little sorry for him. His life must have been complicated.

Each week, Cannon mailed out a sheet to each of the company's stores, listing the top ten producers in the chain. A few months after starting at Cannon, it thrilled me to see my name on that list. What an honor to be recognized as one of ten best salesmen out of at least a thousand other salesmen. In a few weeks I rose to the number one position and continued to be the company's most productive salesman for the next six months.

A high executive official at Cannon, Mr. Kalmeyer, flew out from the east coast to meet me and personally congratulate me. He wanted me to explain some of my selling techniques that might be of use in training procedures. When I explained how I managed to sell such a large amount of army shoes and dancing shoes, he laughed, saying he didn't think the company would print that in a training manual. He mentioned something that I wouldn't forget. He told me that the highest paid people in our country were sales people. He said, "Val, right now you're selling shoes, but there is no reason you couldn't sell airplanes or trains someday."

Each store had a manager and an assistant manager. The manager received a salary and a generous bonus depending on the volume of business the store did. The assistant manager earned an adequate salary plus commissions, as the assistant manager still sold in addition to his other duties. The manager did no selling whatsoever. Generally, when a salesman was promoted to assistant manager, his commissions decreased because of the time he spent performing the duties required by his new position. The salary purported to compensate for the reduced commissions, but it didn't always happen that way. Clearly, Frank Campos, the assistant manager, worked harder than anyone else in the store, yet I earned as much or more than Frank.

Bob invited me to have lunch at Sam's, a Greek café a half block down Eleventh Street from the store. All the tables were occupied so we ate at the counter. I ordered the "merchant's lunch" which consisted of thin slices of roast beef, mashed potatoes, gravy, peas, small green salad and Jello-O dessert. I really enjoyed eating at Sam's. I didn't get to eat in restaurants much. Bob informed me that Frank Campos was leaving our store. Beginning next Monday, Frank would be managing a store in Kansas City, Missouri. Bob wanted me to accept the position of assistant manager of our store. He told me what I already knew. My responsibilities would increase significantly. He convinced me to accept when he explained that the store managers were highly paid and the job of assistant manager is the doorway through which one passed to become a manager.

The job kept me challenged. My new duties included, but were not limited to, decorating display windows one Sunday each month, which made a seven-day work week, and taking inventory through the week which reduced my selling time significantly. I had to supervise the salesmen. They were very competitive, and I had to settle disputes which always left somebody mad at me.

Competitive salesmen? You bet. This is how it worked. We operated on a commission basis. The more we sold, the more money we made. Each salesman strove to serve customers likely to buy the most merchandise in the shortest amount of time. Generally, the most sought after customers were men who came into the store alone. Usually, men didn't like to shop for shoes.

They wanted to get in and out of the store quickly. A man by himself generally picked out a style and if it fit, he bought. A good salesman could complete a sale to a man within fifteen minutes. If he brought his wife or girl friend along, she generally insisted that he try on several styles before making a final decision, slowing the process.

Men's footwear cost more than our other merchandise. The dollar amount of the sale of one pair of men's shoes in fifteen minutes could be double that gained from a woman who it might take twice as long to serve. A woman could tie up a salesman for forty-five minutes and then decide she didn't feel like buying that day—it never happened that way with men.

With the store packed with customers, I recall waiting on an elderly woman one very busy afternoon. Commonly, at busy times we waited on more than one shopper at a time. But the lady had me so busy bringing different styles for her to try on; I had no opportunity to help anyone else. With my stomach in knots, I watched the other salesmen wrap up two or three sales while I remained trapped. An hour passed and my fake smile hid my extreme distress when she told me she wouldn't be buying shoes that day and explained she really just dropped in to get out of the rain.

Cannon had a strict rule that the sales staff make every reasonable effort to complete a sale to every customer that came into the store. Now and then, a salesman and customer just didn't click. When that happened, the salesman waiting on such a customer picked out one of his associates and said, "Mr. Jones I need a thirty-three." In a minute or so, the selected salesman came over and said, "Mr. Barry (or whoever), you have an important telephone call. "May I take over here for you?"

The "thirty-three" policy resulted in many saved sales (I have no idea as to why we used the number thirty-three to identify the procedure). However, sometimes salesmen abused the practice. For instance, while waiting on the previously described rainy day time-waster, I might have "thirty three'd" the old gal to Mr. Jones and grabbed a man entering the store. I didn't do that, but sometimes it happened. If I had done that to Mr. Jones, I think he may have wanted to "discuss" the matter with me in the store basement later.

As assistant manager, I left the store last each night. On Monday nights we didn't close until nine and it fell to me to see that the premises were cleaned and the shelves properly stocked and ready for business the following day.

Sheila gave birth to Danny early in 1954. In my assistant manager position I couldn't spend much time with them which created stress. We got along well before Danny came along. Sheila at seventeen and I at nineteen made us children raising a child. We began to compare our lives to others our age. Our friends did things like water skiing, dating, becoming educated in preparation for learning skills to help them lead an easier life than we had. We envied our single friends.

Sheila stayed at home and took care of Danny. As assistant manager at Cannon, I worked long hours. My average work week consisted of around sixty hours. Even though I had a difficult job, I did get to meet and interact with interesting people. I wished that I had more time to spend with Sheila and Danny, but I didn't.

In 1955, the company promoted Bob McQueen to the position of district manager. His area of responsibility covered the Midwest, so Bob, his wife and two children moved to Ohio. Bob had taught me a lot, and I missed him. Under his guidance I had developed a marketable skill. He assured me in his new position he would help me advance in the company.

Joe Goodyear replaced Bob as manager of the Oakland store. Joe's wife, Marylynn, also worked in the store as the cashier, as had Mrs. McQueen. Joe looked to be around fifty, and I think he had worked for Cannon most of his life. Joe's method of managing stood in stark contrast to Bob's style. Bob loved his career and constantly struggled to improve the operation of the store, while Joe—fat and tired—did as little as possible. When the store closed he and Marylynn spent hours totaling the day's receipts while drinking bourbon and Coca Cola. Clearly, the Goodyears were alcoholics. Totaling the day's receipts took the McQueens no more than thirty minutes. The Goodyears took hours and expected me to stay with them until they finished. If I left before they did, they sulked.

Marylynn acted like my boss, and Joe let her get away with it. She liked to flirt with the salesmen and picked out favorites, which made Joe jealous and complicated my relationship with the sales staff. My workload under Joe grew burdensome; a lot of the paperwork that Bob had done, Joe insisted that I do.

I spent less and less time with my family which made Sheila angry at me more and more. She nagged a lot, and I knew she had good reason to do so. It seemed we fought all the time. The job used to be exciting and fun—not anymore.

Ray, my father-in-law, had an important civilian job with the U.S. Air Force. His job placed him in charge of setting up quality control criteria with aircraft overhaul companies that contracted with the U.S. Air Force. The Air Force entered into a contract with Cal Eastern Airways under which the company would overhaul several dozen C-46 aircraft. Ray worked closely with Cal Eastern management to coordinate inspection requirements.

My father-in-law knew about my working conditions at Cannon. He mentioned that he could use his influence with Cal Eastern to secure a job for me as an aircraft mechanic trainee. Ray told me he'd try to get me into a department that paid well with good chances of advancement.

I informed him I appreciated what he wanted to do for our family. I let him know I'd get back to him in a few days. A good paying job, a forty-hour week with Saturdays and Sundays off, sure sounded good. I hoped Sheila and I would get along better if I had a job with regular working hours.

We didn't have a telephone. Our neighbors in the flat above ours let us give their phone number to our relatives and my employer for emergency purposes. One evening, Anita, our upstairs neighbor told me I had a call. It pleased me to hear Bob McQueen calling from Toledo, Ohio. Bob said, "I know Joe Goodyear and I know that Cannon will lose you if we can't get you away from Joe and his wife." He told me of an opening for a manager at the store in Chickasha, Oklahoma.

"Val, it's a highly productive store in which a manager can earn generous quarterly bonuses. We need you in the store within two weeks. The position is yours if you want it." I let Bob know I'd talk over the offer with Sheila and give him my answer within twenty-four hours.

Bob had given me a terrific opportunity and a conundrum as well. If I accepted the offer, I would be the youngest manager in the chain. Sheila had lived in Alameda all her life. She didn't know about moving to Oklahoma. I probably made a mistake by not accepting the offer, but living in Oklahoma didn't appeal to me either. Danny's grandmothers definitely wouldn't like their first grandchild living 1500 miles from them.

I called Bob McQueen and thanked him for his efforts on my behalf. It disappointed him when I told him I had to turn down the Oklahoma position and resign from Cannon immediately. I expressed gratitude to Bob for all I'd learned from him and regretted letting him down. I hoped we would remain friends, but I couldn't be sure of that. The essence of Bob's life centered on his career. He had just turned thirty-three when I last spoke with him. In the years to come, it saddened me to learn that at age forty-seven he died of a sudden massive heart attack.

The next day I gave Joe a letter of resignation. He became furious. Both Joe and his wife tried to convince me to change my mind. I had a great reputation with Cannon and Joe thought the company might blame him for losing me. My job at Cal Eastern wouldn't be ready for a few months, and I knew Joe needed me to stay on until he had trained my replacement. I told him I could continue at Cannon until he had someone to take my place. I knew Joe hadn't the ability or energy to do his job and mine. I felt sure he would gladly accept my offer. No way; the Goodyears angrily wanted me gone.

Sheila was pregnant again and our second baby would soon be arriving. I needed a steady income until I would begin working at Cal Eastern. I realized the mistake of giving my notice of resignation so far in advance of starting my new job. I thought I should do the right thing. Live and learn.

CHAPTER TWENTY-ONE

I decided to go into debt to buy a new Ford Thunderbird. Sheila argued that we would have two children soon, and she insisted we needed the stability of owning our own home. She had looked at a two-story Victorian that originally had been a single family home. It had been divided into three apartments during the World War II housing shortage; a common occurrence in Alameda. Sheila reasoned we could squeeze into one apartment and the income from the other two apartments would take care of our monthly house payments.

Sheila made a convincing argument. Shaw and Lunt, a long established Alameda Realty firm, had the property listed for $11,000. We asked the listing agent to prepare an offer to purchase for $10,000. The agent explained that the owner, Mrs. Thompson, a recent widow, no longer wanted the responsibility of owning rental property. She didn't need cash and wished to finance a substantial portion of the purchase price.

Mrs. Thompson accepted our offer and agreed to carry back nine thousand dollars at six percent interest per annum, payable at sixty per month, including principal and interest. We raised the down payment of $1000 by borrowing $500 from Sheila's maternal grandmother, Angelina Netti and $500 from my mom. We paid the closing costs from our meager savings. The purchase of our property located at 1222 Park Avenue proved to be a wise decision for which I give Sheila full credit.

Our second son, Steven, arrived in the fall of 1955. Wow! At the age of twenty—the father of two sons and the owner of a three-unit apartment building—my life sure seemed to be moving fast. Lack of money continued to be a growing problem. Our living expenses fought to exceed our income. We gave a thirty-day notice to vacate to the young navy couple who rented our least expensive apartment, the one we intended to occupy.

In anticipation of moving into our apartment in thirty days or so, we gave a month's notice that we would be vacating the apartment in which we resided. Our landlord immediately found a tenant for our unit. We had to vacate our apartment exactly according to the terms of our notice. Unfortunately, we learned that the young navy couple couldn't give up possession until two weeks after we had to move.

Upon learning of our problem, Sheila's parents offered to let us move in with them at their home on San Antonio Avenue in Alameda until we could move into our Park Avenue apartment. My father-in-law had spent all his spare time over the previous few years remodeling their three-story Victorian, built in the 1800s. Since he currently concentrated on working on the kitchen, we took our meals in one of the basement rooms.

Even with the renovation project, Sheila's parents' house gave us all plenty of space. Ray knew his stuff. In remodeling the San

Antonio Avenue house, he'd taken on a daunting, complicated project. He did it all: plumbing, electrical, plastering, concrete work and everything necessary to reach his goal and he did high quality work. I didn't know it then, but in the future, his fix-up talent would benefit me immensely.

CHAPTER TWENTY-TWO

I answered an ad for a linoleum installer helper placed by Alameda Linoleum on Park Street. Flunky, rather than helper, more accurately described the position for which I applied. The owner, Frank Anderson, hired me and explained that if I worked out okay, I maybe could work into a linoleum layer apprenticeship and eventually become a journeyman. I liked what he said. I didn't mention anything to Ray but that might even be better than Cal Eastern. My duties included loading and unloading tools and linoleum goods, sanding floors, and moving refrigerators and furniture from rooms in preparation for the installation of new linoleum.

Occasionally, when Frank or Garth, Frank's journeyman linoleum layer, had time, they taught me the fundamentals of the trade. Frank, in his late sixties, experienced poor health and constant irritability, which made it difficult to work with him. I didn't take his bad moods personally. I concentrated on the big picture. My responsibilities loomed heavy, and the job could be my way out. Early one morning after I loaded up the truck, Frank pulled into a service station on the way to the job site. Frank told me to check the oil. Embarrassed, I had to explain I couldn't find the dip stick. On Frank's truck, the dip stick wasn't where they usually were located.

No big deal—if he had told me the location of the damn thing, I would have retained the information for all time. He didn't feel well that morning; he acted especially grouchy and took his bad temper out on me. He asked, "What the hell am I doing with you?"

I didn't answer; I could recognize a rhetorical question. I smiled patiently and said nothing, even though I wanted to smack him.

Later at the job site we awkwardly struggled to move a heavy, old motor-on-top refrigerator through a kitchen doorway, and Frank's hand got smashed between the door jamb and the appliance. Of course, it had to be my fault. The day didn't shape up well. When we returned to the store after work, Frank handed me my final check and said, "You ought to go back to selling shoes because you will never be a linoleum layer."

Frank didn't intend to, but he did me a favor. I proved him wrong. In the years to come, I skillfully installed dozens of linoleum floor coverings.

While Sheila bought gasoline at the Regal Service Station on Park Street in Alameda, she told the manager of the station that her husband needed work. He let her know that if I didn't mind pumping gas, he had a job for me. Pumping gas, checking oil and tires, giving out Blue Chip stamps, and enjoying lighthearted chatter with the customers seemed like being on vacation compared to the heavy responsibilities at Cannon. My gas station job didn't last long because I soon began my job at Cal Eastern.

CHAPTER TWENTY-THREE

In 1956, I was 21 and employed as a mechanic by California Eastern Airlines at the Oakland International Airport. The company had contracted with the U.S. Air force to overhaul a few dozen C-46 airplanes. I worked in almost all mechanical phases required to complete the overhaul of each aircraft. What a wonderful job. The broad variety of my assigned tasks totally held my interest. I made pretty good money, and I enjoyed the camaraderie shared with my fellow workers.

I started out in a small shop around a quarter of a mile from Cal Eastern's two large hangers at the Oakland Airport. I worked with the shop foreman, Carl Anderson, and three other trainees. One of the trainees was a fellow by the name of Milt Armstrong. I met Milt before coming to work at Cal Eastern and it pleased me that we'd be working together. Milt, six years older than me, had been close friends with Ray's two half-brothers, Bert and Doug Maples, for years. Just as he had done for me, Ray used his influence to secure the Cal Eastern job for Milt.

My regular duties included installing what were referred to as boots onto the leading edges of the wings of the aircraft. The boots were thick black rubber bladders. They were mechanically inflated with air, in flight, to prevent ice from forming on the wings' leading edges. The build-up of ice on the wings compromised an aircraft's aerodynamic integrity. Attachment of the boots to the leading edge of the wings was accomplished by inserting holding pins through metal grommeted holes in the top and bottom edges of the boots into corresponding threaded holes in the top and bottom of the wings' leading edges. The attachment holes were spaced about six inches apart along most of the leading edges of the wings. Once the boots were held in place by the holding pins, the pins were removed, one at a time, and replaced with screws, which secured the boots to the wings.

Normally, a mechanic working from a stable scaffold in a warm hanger in which the boots would be relatively soft and pliable accomplished the installation. One bitterly cold early January morning, I received instructions to install boots on an aircraft that would be flight-tested as soon as I finished the job. Production had fallen behind schedule and it became vital that the airplane be completed as soon as possible. The hangers were full and I had to work outside. Additionally, I would have to work on a ladder, as all the scaffolding was in use.

I began by draping the unattached boots over the leading edges of the wings while balancing on a shaky ladder about ten feet above ground level. The holding pins were inserted into the attachment holes in the cold stiff rubber boots. A 15-inch long steel rod with a handle at one end, like a screwdriver handle, was used to manipulate the holding pins to attach the boots to the wings. The rod end opposite the handle end had a half inch deep hole into which a holding pin was inserted. About one inch of the one-and-a-half-inch long pin protruded from the end of the rod. The pin inserted in the end of the rod was pushed through a metal grommeted hole in the boot. The circumference of the rod was larger than the circumference of the hole in the grommet, which enabled me to leverage the rod to bring the holding pin in the boot to the corresponding hole in the wing. The cold rubber resisted stretching. It took all my strength to force each pin into place. As I awkwardly struggled to leverage a holding pin into place, I got my body into a configuration in which the pin inserted into the end of the leveraging rod was being pushed hard directly toward my face. Suddenly, the pin dropped out of the end of the rod resulting in the end of the rod smashing into my right eyeball.

When I consider this unfortunate incident, I am still puzzled and even a little amused by my initial reaction. I recall no pain; just the sensation of cold steel penetrating about a half inch into my eye. As I withdrew the tool, I became aware of blood streaming down my face. Descending the ladder, I observed with relief that no one had witnessed the mishap. It would have been embarrassing if any of my fellow workers had observed my carelessness. I wondered if carpenters with missing digits are embarrassed in the presence of other carpenters. As I calmly walked toward the nurse's office, I assumed that the vision in my injured eye was permanently lost. With little emotion, I contemplated how best to adjust my life to accommodate being rendered blind in one eye. Was this a normal reaction? I still don't know. Fortunately, perhaps miraculously, I'm forever grateful that the accident actually did not result in the permanent loss of sight in my injured eye.

Each airplane to be overhauled consisted of thousands of parts. Our shop dismantled and cleaned various parts, which were sent out to be magnafluxed, wherein the units went through a process similar to X-raying for the purpose of identifying cracks. The parts with no cracks came back to us. We reassembled them and painted them with aluminum colored paint. The reconstructed parts then got reinstalled onto the airplanes being overhauled.

The work fascinated me, and I especially enjoyed my co-workers. We all got on well with Carl, who seemed to enjoy teaching us. We enjoyed the relaxed, friendly environment. During our breaks we played a fast-moving card game called Crazy Eights. The breaks were supposed to last fifteen minutes, but if we had our work caught up, Carl didn't mind if they went a little longer. During lunch, while enjoying our brown bag fare, we played horseshoes.

I didn't stay in one place very long. I transferred frequently. Ray saw to it that I spent enough time in one area to learn the department's operation. I really gained a lot of knowledge and loved doing so. A few of my new skills included rigging flight controls, installing oxygen systems, sheet metal fabrication, riveting and overhauling hydraulic systems. I thought about Frank Anderson telling me I needed to go back selling shoes. My experience at Cal Eastern confirmed what I already knew about Frank—he was full of it.

CHAPTER TWENTY-FOUR

It looked as if we'd be moving from Sheila's parent's house into our Park Avenue mini-apartment in about a week. On our way home from work one afternoon, Milt and I stopped at the Driftwood bar on Park Street to celebrate my recent twenty-first birthday. Sometime into our third round, Milt told me he needed to pass on some information he thought I should know. He told me that Ray's two half-brothers, who were considerably older than Sheila, always hung around Ray and Pat's home as Sheila grew up. Milt told me the reason Pat didn't want them around her daughter and arranged for her to live at Saint Agnes.

When I arrived back at the San Antonio Avenue house, I told Sheila that we needed to talk. Everyone else was upstairs in bed. We sat on the couch in the dark living room. Very deliberately and quietly, I told her what Milt Armstrong had said to me less than an hour before. She listened and began to cry. She confirmed the truth of what Milt had said. She explained the abuse began shortly after her fifth birthday. I knew then positively why she lived at Saint Agnes. Even so, I couldn't understand why her parents failed to protect her more aggressively. She expressed relief that she no longer needed to hide the truth from me. I let her know we could deal with this. I hoped that with the information "on the table" we might get along better.

In a move to bring everything into the open, what Sheila said next stunned me. She told me that she had cheated on me. She said that while I worked at Cannon she had a romantic encounter with someone else. With heartbreaking emotion, I told her, "Hon, I'm so confused; I've just got to get away from you for a while." What happened before our marriage didn't really matter, but what happened while I worked my ass off at Cannon fell into a different category.

I went to my parent's home. Sheila told Ray and Pat what Milt Armstrong had said. She didn't let them know about her adulterous behavior. A couple of days passed and I got a call from Ray asking me to meet with him in Alameda. We discussed the situation while parked in his driveway. He understood the difficulty I had experienced in getting along with Sheila. He said that before we married, she often initiated what he described as "hate campaigns" directed against him. I suggested that perhaps her anger had something to do with her dysfunctional childhood. He said, "Maybe you're right. I should have been a better father." A few days later, Milt told me Ray stopped by his job and "gave him hell" for revealing a family secret. I wouldn't hold a grudge, but my relationship with Ray and Pat had changed.

In time, I realized I'd handled the situation wrong. It took a lot of trust and courage for Sheila to level with me. I became a judge instead of a loving mate, which I believe diminished Sheila's will to communicate effectively with me thereafter. We agreed to put the past behind us and moved into our Park Avenue property. We had been regularly attending mass at St. Joseph's Catholic Church on Union Street in Alameda. We took advantage of a free marriage counseling program offered by the diocese. We met one evening a week with a priest psychologist at his office in Berkeley, where we discussed all aspects of our relationship. I felt comfortable with the priest and receptive to what he told us. We wanted to make our marriage work.

CHAPTER TWENTY-FIVE

Sheila had called it right—by squeezing our family into an apartment consisting of one room, plus a tiny kitchen and a shared bathroom (with a pull chain toilet), the income from the other two units covered our loan payments. We rented out three of our four attached earthen-floor single-car garages for five dollars each per month. Being young, we could put up with the inconvenience for the promise of future rewards.

The Park Avenue units needed a lot of work, which accounted for the reason we had succeeded at negotiating such favorable purchase conditions. We had no money, so I'd have to handle most of the necessary repairs. Great! My knowledge regarding property improvement didn't reach beyond lawn mowing. I knew I had a lot to learn. Ray attempted to enlighten me. I thought with practice I might become handy at remodeling, but certainly not on par with Ray.

We had no sooner moved into the tiny apartment when Sheila announced she was pregnant again. Apparently, the rhythm method of birth control recommended by our marriage counselor lacked effectiveness. We struggled; we had very little money and barely got by. In addition to often working overtime at Cal Eastern, I took residential painting jobs to earn extra money. Sheila stretched our food dollars by buying twenty-five cent per pound hamburger—consisting of mostly fat—from which she made spaghetti sauce. Our family ate lots of spaghetti back then.

I had a friend from Malaysia who worked as a mechanic with me at Cal Eastern. I didn't know his real name, but at work we called him "Zook Zook." He didn't seem to mind his strange appellation. Zook Zook lived alone in a basement apartment a few doors away from us. To save expenses we traded off driving to work. Sheila prepared a sack lunch five days a week for Zook Zook for which he paid her one dollar for each lunch. Boy, were we busted.

We had no hot water in our tiny kitchen. For some reason unknown to me, seven feet of water pipe between the water heater in the basement and our kitchen had been removed. Until I could get a few dollars ahead to restore the missing plumbing, we heated water on the stove. I began to fully grasp the meaning of Taylor Abercrombie's cautionary words to me.

Sheila loved watching a television show out of Los Angeles called *Queen for a Day*, hosted by Jack Bailey. Ladies in the television studio audience submitted cards on which they described why they might be entitled to qualify as *Queen for a Day*. Mr. Bailey read the cards and selected three ladies with the most heart-rending stories. Each of the three then told their story on television and by way of the studio audience applause, a queen emerged.

Sheila and her friend, Carol Benz, made reservations to be part of the show's studio audience. The girls drove to Los Angeles, stayed overnight in an inexpensive hotel and arrived at the television broadcasting studio the next morning. Sheila's card presented a touching story about an expectant teenager with two young children living in a one-room shared bathroom apartment, whose husband couldn't afford to see that his family had running hot water in the kitchen. I took a sick day off so I could watch my wife humiliate me on national television.

Had Sheila been chosen queen, she would have been awarded a seemingly endless array of prizes, including a new speedboat and a remodeled kitchen. But she didn't get selected. The studio audience thought the lady whose husband perished in a fire deserved to win. Sheila, as second runner up, won a year's supply of cheese and aluminum foil.

Within a few months, we moved down the hall into an apartment that had a bedroom. Although still cramped, our living conditions improved considerably. Our two toddlers shared a spacious bedroom, and Sheila and I slept in our living room on a hide-a-bed.

We couldn't afford babysitters, but we sure enjoyed a social life. We developed a circle of young married friends and some single ones too. On Saturday nights, we'd get together and play poker or canasta for very small stakes, of course. Sometimes we had drinks, but not many and not always. We really liked entertaining our friends and they enjoyed reciprocating. On Sunday evenings, the Alameda drive-in theatre charged only a dollar a car, no matter the number of people in the car. So, when we could afford the gas on the Sunday nights, we packed up the kids and headed for the drive-in movies.

Even though I didn't earn enough money to support my family properly, I made some progress. I'd worked in a sufficient number of departments at Cal Eastern to qualify for the tests required for a promotion. I passed the tests and earned promotion to Journeyman Aircraft Mechanic.

As a Journeyman, I earned more money, of course, but that didn't really do a lot to ease our oppressing financial burden. Supporting a family with two small children on basically one income proved difficult. Any extra money got soaked up repairing and making sorely needed improvements to our property.

Occasionally, Sheila helped out financially and at the same time got a break socially by selling merchandise at house parties at friends' homes for companies such as Santa's Helpers and Tupperware. She did that work in the evenings while I watched our children. Often, I told the kids bedtime stories about three little boys named Herman, Sherman and Merman. I improvised the Herman, Sherman and Merman adventures. I totally made them up as I told them.

Although I never repeated a story, they all shared a commonality; in each telling I included a morality lesson. Generally, Herman, Sherman and Merman broke one of their mother's rules, which sent them off on an exciting but dangerous adventure, from which they were eventually rescued. The stories always ended with the boys tearfully promising their mom they would never disobey her again, but they always did, which led to the next bedtime story.

I'm convinced my children loved to hear about Herman, Sherman and Merman because over the years they frequently clamored for more. Telling extemporaneous tales and keeping them interesting is a very taxing mental exercise. I like to think that the activity helped keep my brain agile. Over many years, I have engaged in the telling the Herman, Sherman and Merman stories not only to my children but also to nieces and nephews and grandchildren.

Sometimes I succumbed to the temptation to compare our situation with that of some of my co-workers and friends, some single, or maybe married, with both spouses working. They involved themselves in activities such as water skiing, restoring antique cars, like my best pal Jim Kerr, or engaging in a myriad of activities that brought them pleasure they could easily afford. As I saw it, they had fun while we survived. Damn—jealousy is ugly. I thought about what a dope I had been. But I didn't feel sorry for myself very long. In spite of the financial hardships Sheila and I endured, and the heavy responsibilities we faced, we deeply loved our two little guys. We gave them abundant love and did our best to be good parents. It didn't cost much to have a picnic and let them play at a park, which we often did.

Sometimes when the boys misbehaved, they received a spanking. We administered mild spankings—not beatings. We mistakenly thought that to be a proper way to discipline our children and we just didn't know better. As we matured, our parenting skills improved.

Louie and Norma Alexander rented our first floor and by far the nicest and largest apartment. They were in their forties, and excellent tenants. Norma had recently given birth to their only child, a girl. The baby "accident" seriously disrupted their finely tuned life and they decided to divorce. Each of them moved back in with their elderly parents, and Norma took the child, which suited Louie.

We liked the Alexanders and felt sorry for them, yet thrilled that they gave up the apartment. At last, our family would enjoy adequate quarters. While living in our other units, we accomplished substantial improvements to those apartments. Constantly, we had lived in a remodeling mess. We faced no financial loss by moving into our best unit because of the income from our two second-floor apartments.

It pleased us to take possession of our downstairs apartment, approximately the same size as the other two units combined. My carpentry skills progressed to the point I successfully converted a portion of our large covered back porch into a small bedroom for Sheila and me. We still had no money left after we met our basic survival expenses. Notwithstanding our continuing financial oppression, we felt happier in our new accommodations. I'd become aware that property values in Alameda had increased. Until then, I'd never really thought of our property as a financial investment, just as a place to live.

Sheila gave birth to Valarie midyear, 1957. I adored my beautiful blond, blue-eyed baby daughter. As the twenty-two-year-old father of three kids, I didn't feel poor, but I sure felt broke. I can't repeat it too often—being poor is a state of mind, while being broke simply means you have no money. There is a big difference between the two conditions.

Our parents dropped by often. They enjoyed visiting their delightful grandchildren, but they were not about to babysit them. They were not getting caught in that trap. Sheila and I understood, but quietly wished they might offer us an occasional break.

It had been at least six months since Sheila and I had been out together; just the two of us. Oh sure, we often had friends over on Saturday nights, which we enjoyed and could afford, but with friends and family we weren't really together. We did what we had to do to get by, but I couldn't be sure we really knew each other, or even if we ever had. We bickered incessantly. I thought if just the two of us had an occasional relaxing evening out, we might get along better. I felt sorry for Sheila—a pretty twenty-year-old girl caring for three pre-school children. I knew I hadn't given her the life she once envisioned for herself.

I picked up a few extra dollars by doing odd jobs. We splurged, hired a babysitter and took in the movie *Peyton Place* at the beautiful Paramount Theatre on Broadway in downtown Oakland. Even though we had a great time, I realized another six months would probably go by before we could do something like that again. During that period, Sheila relieved her tedium by joining a group that played the card game "Whisk" one evening each week. She loved playing cards, and I didn't mind babysitting.

There wasn't a lot of time left on the Cal Eastern C-46 contract and not many planes left to overhaul. The company began initiating layoffs. If another contract didn't come through—and Ray Drake knew of nothing in the works with the Air Force—I knew I wouldn't be employed there much longer. I'd learned that the aircraft overhaul and maintenance industry was prone to frequent layoffs.

Paradoxically, the more people that got laid off, the better my chances were of keeping my job longer. Thanks to Ray's guidance and influence, I had concentrated on learning as many phases of the overhaul process as possible. When work in a department slacked off, the employees whose knowledge was limited to the work accomplished in that particular department were being let go, whereas the company could utilize my skills in any other department as needed.

By mid-1957, the Cal Eastern work force had reduced in number to around half of what it had been when I was hired. An interesting situation developed, which allowed me to stay on at Cal Eastern until the completion of the overhaul of the last plane. Earlier, I spoke of my pal Zook Zook. A citizen of Malaysia, he began working on C-46 aircraft for the U.S. Air Force in Guam during World War II. The hectic conditions under which Zook Zook worked in Guam required drastic time-saving efforts. We discussed a part known as the yoke, to which the rudder attached and is manipulated from the cockpit, to determine in which direction the plane travels.

The yoke functioned under severe stress and could develop cracks invisible to the human eye. If the yoke broke in flight, the consequences were devastating. The part had to be removed from the aircraft and sent to a shop where magnafluxing determined if hidden cracks had occurred.

To detach the yoke from the aircraft the rudder had to be removed. That time consuming job required the use of a cherry-picker, a small crane with a platform on which a man could could be raised to the necessary level to access the bolts attaching the rudder to the plane. Zook Zook explained to me that in Guam he learned to squeeze his upper body through an inspection opening into a tight interior space beneath the area where the yoke attached to the rudder.

From that awkward position, he manipulated a mirror and an extended hinged socket wrench, and removed the yoke from the aircraft within twenty minutes. He then installed an inspected yoke in the same amount of time. Zook Zook demonstrated he could accomplish a job in forty minutes that normally took two men two days to complete.

Additionally, the removal of yokes often had to be delayed until one of the limited numbers of cherry pickers became available. Zook Zook worked in sheet metal, and before his demonstration to me, he had never performed his yoke removal act at Cal Eastern. Almost immediately after teaching me, he left Cal Eastern to get married in Malaysia. Thanks to Zook Zook, I remained among the last mechanics to leave Cal Eastern when the company filed for bankruptcy about six months later.

I loved working at Cal Eastern. I found that I was mechanically inclined, which served me well over the years to come. Sloppy workmanship is unacceptable in the aircraft industry where lives are at stake. My training there helped me form the habit of doing the job right. Whatever project or task I take on, I do my best to do it correctly. I made many friends at Cal Eastern; most of whom I'd never see again. I missed them and wouldn't soon forget them. A few, though, remain part of my life to this day.

CHAPTER TWENTY-SIX

After Cal Eastern, at twenty-three I found myself unemployed and as usual, broke. I needed a job, and soon. It didn't appear that I had much chance of being employed in the aircraft industry. The fellows let go before me at Cal Eastern had filled all the mechanic

92

positions around the Oakland Airport. I located work at Bethlehem Steel Company, situated at the west end of Alameda.

The primary operation in progress during my time at Bethlehem Steel involved the fabrication of steel girders used in the construction of freeway overpasses. The constant noise from the grinding, welding, hammering and clanging movement of tons of steel came close to intolerable, and it made conversation at work stations nearly impossible. I could only talk comfortably with co-workers in the lunchroom or washroom.

At least I had a job—admittedly an awful job, but I had to earn. I worked in an immense, dirty, ugly, old brick, glass and steel building. The depressing, open 500 x 150 foot work area made me think of what "Hell" must look like. It was about 175 feet from the dirty concrete floor to the roof with no separating floors to break up the space. The one-story office area, lunch room and washrooms were attached to the exterior of the main structure.

My primary task consisted of grinding down the rough edges left on steel parts by the cutting torches. I used a heavy portable electrical grinder to smooth the parts. The grinding operation produced a shower of glowing sparks, which when cooled, covered me with a coat of black ash. After finishing my shift, I spent at least forty-five minutes trying to get clean. I knew my stint there would be short, thank God. But I also knew that many people were destined to spend their entire working lives at Bethlehem. I fantasized that when I got rich, I'd buy a new pickup truck for every one of those guys.

CHAPTER TWENTY-SEVEN

While employed at my version of "Hell," I continually applied for positions at other companies. I knew each job I'd held contributed to my acquisition of an informal, yet valuable education. I answered an ad for a job in the Quality Control Department of Standard Register Printing Company in Oakland, which presented me with an interesting situation.

If I accepted the position, I would be the only person in my department without a college education. In keeping with my quest to achieve a well rounded, even though informal education, working at Standard Register might serve me well. The salary started at only $275 per month. I couldn't support a wife and three kids on that amount. Yet I figured such an opportunity might not show up again. Things were going to be even more financially difficult, but I took the job. I felt sure my decision would pay handsome dividends in time. With the rental income and me doing more odd jobs when available, we got by, barely.

Working at Standard gave me even more than I had hoped. I learned several new skills there. Red Penny, my supervisor, taught me to measure the weight of carbon on carbon paper. If too little carbon had been applied, the copies would be too light and illegible. Too much carbon resulted in smudged and messy copies. In future years, I may not be weighing carbon samples, but certainly I would utilize my newly acquired knowledge of advanced math.

It amazed me that so many things could go wrong in the production of multi-page business forms. When a customer received defective forms they had to be reprinted and redelivered.

Reprints resulted in financial loss, which included the cost related to reproducing the forms, as well as compensating customers for ancillary damages.

The production of multi-page business forms required the participation of several departments. When a customer rejected sub-standard forms, we had to determine at which stage along the manufacturing chain the mistake occurred. Often we experienced difficulty pinpointing the exact origin of the fault.

For example, sometimes registration between the pages of the forms didn't align properly. In such a case, perhaps the problem originated in the collation operation where the binding of the pages of the form occurred. If we informed the collation supervisor that the pages were misaligned in his unit, he often claimed the paper was of uneven thickness. If his claim held true, then the problem wasn't the fault of his department.

Of course, the collation supervisor was attempting to divert the responsibility for the misaligned forms to either the Press Department or Quality Control, or both. As rolls of printing form paper arrived at the plant, a member of Quality Control tested random samples to determine if the paper thickness remained consistent.

When confronted with allegations of errors within their units, most supervisors vigorously tried to avoid responsibility. The cost to reprint an order accrued against the culpable department's budget and negatively affected the unit boss's annual bonus.

My department conducted a thorough investigation in an attempt to determine which department had caused a defect. Once we determined where the fault originated, it became the job of a member of Quality Control to convince the appropriate supervisor to sign a form personally accepting responsibility. Nobody wanted that job. Even when we were not demanding they take responsibility for errors, the Production Department heads generally held Quality Control in low esteem. The nature of our job annoyed them and they considered us a "pain in the ass."

Initially, the head of the Quality Control Department, Bob Wilkins, considered the task of negotiating a reprint situation with a recalcitrant supervisor to be beyond my job description. However, so that I might get a feel for the process, I accompanied Red Penny during several such meetings and silently observed that very nice and mild man do his best to get overbearing, even bullying department heads to accept responsibility.

Sometimes, Red's efforts to resolve such matters simply failed. In such cases, Mr. Wilber, the plant superintendent, settled the dispute, which made our department look bad. We were expected to do such a complete investigation that the culpable department head could not deny responsibility. Wilber believed if we did our job properly, he wouldn't have to waste his time doing our work.

Wilber might have been right about us not doing a good job. However, the fault didn't lie in our failing to conduct thorough investigations. Recalling my valuable experience with Cannon Shoe Company, it became clear to me that Red, though a very smart man, knew nothing about selling, and convincing those supervisors to do the right thing required selling.

A customer complaint involving a large order came to our attention. A valued upset customer threatened to pull his future business with Standard Register. The reprint promised to cost plenty. The customer claimed the printing ranged intermittently from almost illegibly faint to excessively heavy. Our department concluded the Press Department to be at fault. We wished that any other department would have been culpable. The head of the press unit rarely cooperated with our department under normal circumstances and that situation exceeded normal. The expense of reprinting such an order might substantially reduce the responsible party's annual bonus. Additionally, a career minded person wouldn't want a mistake of that magnitude to appear on his record.

Red had to handle the matter with Phil Shaw, the supervisor of the Press Department. Red, a person I truly respected and admired and a fellow I considered a friend, confided that the thought of meeting with Phil Shaw nauseated him. I asked, "Red, how about letting me handle this one?" Reluctantly, he consented to let me try, but I knew he had little confidence in my success.

That settled, I went back to my cubbyhole office in the Carbon Department and spent the morning preparing for my encounter with Mr. Shaw. Later that afternoon I dropped by Phil's office. I had a perfect right to be there, but he treated me as an intruder. He let me know he had no time to meet with me right then.

I told him, "I understand, just let me know when it will be convenient for us to talk." I acted friendly and relaxed but not overly so. He agreed to see me in his office at nine the next morning. I answered "That's fine, Mr. Shaw; I'll leave my file with you now. If you get a chance to review it before we meet, it might help us get through a little faster. I know how busy you are."

I definitely wanted him to go through the file before we met because it showed the results of an exhaustive investigation. Many of the arguments he might normally make, I'd addressed in the file. I showed up at his office at nine sharp. He stayed on the phone for nearly ten minutes and then had a discussion with a press operator for another ten minutes. During that time, he never asked me to have a chair, and he didn't even acknowledge my presence. I could have rightfully been angry at his rudeness, but I didn't let him get to me. I recognized his strategy. He tried to intimidate me, but it didn't work, because I knew I stood on the right side of that equation.

When he finally decided to acknowledge my presence, I smiled and sincerely thanked him for taking time from his busy schedule for me. He poured himself a cup of coffee and although I saw clean cups, I wasn't offered one. Even so, I sensed him to be a decent fellow. Photographs of family on his desk told me he had a son around my age. I instinctively knew that if I remained relaxed and congenial his attitude would soften. He, not I, opened the discussion about our reason for meeting. He began to tell me that paper with uneven thickness often caused varied shades of printing. I explained that I'd only worked for Standard Register for a short period and asked him if he would mind explaining more completely how such problems developed. I did not intend to argue with Phil. If I tried to debate with him, I would lose, as everybody expected I would anyway.

He finally offered me a chair and began to explain various defects that initially appear to emanate from errors in the Press Department. Many times, Phil explained, such imperfections actually started in other departments in the plant. I asked him if he minded if I took a few notes because what he said might help me do a better job. About ten minutes later he asked, "By the way, what is your name again?" I answered and he said, "Please pour yourself a cup of coffee, Val."

Phil led me out into the pressroom. He knew those presses better than anyone, and I genuinely appreciated the information he gave me. We returned to his office, and I felt comfortable enough to inquire about the photos on his desk. He seemed glad I asked. Among other things he told me that he and his son were avid fishermen; that they often took their cabin cruiser out in the bay to fish for striped bass. We had something in common. I enjoyed fishing in the bay and was actually in the process of building a small boat. I hadn't spent five minutes talking about the reprint situation. Phil smiled and said, "I really don't know whose fault this is, but I do know we should have caught it here. Where do I sign Val?" He then said, "How about stopping by for a cup of coffee now and then?"

For a few days, my department elevated me to hero status. Red assigned me to permanently handle reprint situations. Three weeks passed and I was called into Wilber's office. He told me he wanted to meet the Quality Control operator whom the supervisors had been talking about. A raise of my pay grade from level four to level six pleased me immensely.

CHAPTER TWENTY-EIGHT

Despite my limited handyman ability, our Park Avenue property looked good. During the two years that had passed since we acquired ownership in 1956, we had continually made improvements. Some upgrades turned out better than others, but there were two skills at which I had become quite proficient—retexturing over old cracked plaster walls and installing new linoleum; the latter, thanks to my former employer at Alameda Linoleum. Sheila worked just as hard as I did at fixing up our property, and our efforts generated lots of compliments.

Park Avenue, so named because, for a distance of two long blocks, the two one-way lanes were bisected with a pleasant, quiet park with beautiful mature trees. On a bright Saturday afternoon, I sat under a large shady Oak tree with my friend, Jim Kerr, from Cal Eastern watching my plump, brown-eyed two-year old, Stevie, play. I cautioned my boy not to stray too close to the street. I continued visiting with my pal, a fascinating conversationalist. Relaxing with him while babysitting my toddler was a swell way to spend a couple of hours. Then I noticed Stevie had wandered a little too close to the curb. I feared he might start across the narrow street toward our home.

I called to my little guy to come back toward me. As I started in his direction, he laughed and wanted me to chase him. He darted into the middle of Park Avenue, turned and faced me. A half block away a car slowly approached. I stayed perfectly still; afraid if I moved Stevie might start running again. I thought surely the driver would stop. Although plenty of distance existed between my boy and the car, it didn't slow down because the driver just didn't see Stevie. I watched, horrified, as the car smashed into Stevie, throwing him to the ground.

I didn't wait for an ambulance. I bundled my son into the car, and Jim and I rushed him to the Alameda Emergency Clinic. Amazingly, even though the major force of the impact was to Stevie's head, his injuries were not serious. Sheila blamed me for the accident. Neither Jim Kerr nor I could have convinced her otherwise. A part of me thought she may have been right.

Mom and my step-father lived in the pleasant East Bay town of San Leandro. We visited them now and then and liked the small town's ambiance. Alameda had a much larger percentage of renters than San Leandro. Additionally, San Leandro had better schools and lower property taxes, all of which caused me to think that it might be a good place for us to settle. We decided to put 1222 Park Avenue on the market. Shortly after listing the property for sale, we received and accepted an offer for $13,000.

While waiting for our escrow to close, we shopped for a home in San Leandro. We set our upper price limit at $15,000. Most of the homes that offered the amenities we needed were priced beyond our budget. Twice, through Realtors, we made offers of $15,000 for homes listed at much higher prices. Both sellers responded with rejections. We looked at a 1930 vintage bungalow located at 854 Juana Avenue, in upper San Leandro, an excellent family-oriented location.

We liked the Juana property. It had a spacious park-like rear yard, containing a variety of fruit trees. I enjoyed barbecuing, and the large inviting patio, shaded under grape-vine covered lattice work, particularly appealed to me.

We recognized the huge detached garage might serve as a combination work shop and recreation room. The house had only two bedrooms and, of course, with three kids another bedroom would have been preferred. The thought occurred to us if we bought the home, we might eventually add a third bedroom when our financial condition improved.

The advantages far outweighed the drawbacks—we instructed our Realtor, Bert Kirkpatrick with Bay Homes Realty to submit our offer to purchase the Juana Street property for $14,250. We requested that the seller help with the financing by carrying back a second loan for $2,500. Our down payment of $1,425 and the seller's $2,500 loan left a balance owing of $10,325, which we hoped to secure from a savings and loan association.

We proposed to secure the seller's loan with a promissory note, secured with a second deed of trust to encumber the property. The terms of the promissory note provided that the seller's loan bear seven percent interest per annum, payable at $25.00 per month, including principal and interest. If the seller accepted our offer, the remaining balance owing on the promissory note would be due in full in seven years in the form of a balloon payment.

I had two reasons for requesting the seller to help with the financing. The first was that my potential financial success with the Park Avenue property had inspired me to continue investing in real estate. If I had funds left from the sale of Park Avenue, after making the down payment on Juana, I might have tried to make a down payment on a house we could rent out.

Of course, we had just begun but it excited me to be traveling along a path that could possibly lead to financial independence. I came across a book written by William Nickerson, entitled, *How I Turned $1,000.00 into a Million* which fired my enthusiasm for real estate investments as a way of escaping financial deprivation. The author, a telephone company employee, explained in detail how he reached total financial freedom, beginning with the purchase and renovation of a single residential property.

Mr. Nickerson's wonderful composition provided a complete guide that covered every aspect of residential real estate investment. The book spoke to the potential investor who knew little or nothing about the subject. Everything a person might encounter on the path to success in real estate investment—including how to deal with people, financing, renovation, appraisal, buying and selling—had been clearly addressed.

I was convinced that by enthusiastically directing my energy toward the principals described by Mr. Nickerson and by incorporating my own innovations, my dream of financial independence would come true. I expected to have a great adventure during the process. Though purchasing the hard-bound book strained my austere budget, I couldn't afford not to have access to the information it held.

My second reason for asking the Juana seller to carry part of the financing: I figured in time the seller might be willing to discount his loan for an early cash payoff. Eventually, I thought I might accumulate enough capital to make the Juana seller a discount offer. The quest to becoming financially free required lots of thought and planning and the process promised to be fun.

The Park Avenue escrow closed and the Juana seller accepted our offer. Our family loved our new home. We set up a ping-pong table in the garage and invited our friends over to play. I fancied myself a "barbecue gourmet." Chuck roast is a very inexpensive cut of beef, but the way I prepared it on the Weber made it taste like the finest prime rib. We still spent most Saturday nights with other couples playing pinochle, canasta or varieties of poker for very small stakes. That period seemed to be the best of our hard times.

CHAPTER TWENTY-NINE

In 1959, my five-year-old son Danny began to feel ill. We assumed he had caught some sort of a bug while attending kindergarten. We viewed it as common and were not too concerned. He seemed to have an insatiable thirst. We had productive orange trees in our eclectic backyard orchard which resulted in abundant quantities of fresh juice in our refrigerator.

One evening, Danny violently threw up after drinking several glasses of orange juice. I scolded him, accusing him of making a pig of himself. He continued feeling poorly over the next week or so. Soon after, our family went shopping at Montgomery Wards and we spent a considerable amount of time in the store. Every few minutes, Danny requested that I take him to the water fountain, where he drank copiously. Right after the water fountain we headed for the restroom. Once again, I acted stupidly. To my everlasting shame, I again admonished him for acting like a little pig.

A few days later, our doctor gave us the devastating news that our son had sugar diabetes. We learned that his blood sugar level was dangerously elevated. The need for abundant quantities of fluid required to flush the raw sugar from Danny's kidneys accounted for his insatiable thirst. He spent the next two weeks in Children's Hospital in Oakland for the purpose of regulating his body chemistry. At first, the hospital's medical staff couldn't lower his blood sugar level. His food intake included no sugar and he received daily insulin injections, yet his blood sugar content remained dangerously high.

An astute young nurse solved the mystery. She noticed Danny swallowing his sugar-laden tooth paste as he brushed his teeth. Once he stopped ingesting toothpaste, his body chemistry responded properly and we brought him home. We learned no cure existed for Juvenile Diabetes. Danny's fragile health responded directly to the level of care he received. Inadequate monitoring of a person with his condition could result in devastating consequences, including death.   Glucose testing, administering insulin injections, meeting strict dietary requirements and a myriad of additional duties necessary to care for our son became part of the daily routine.

Sheila responded to Danny's needs beautifully. She took extraordinary steps to help compensate for his handicap. She strove to minimize the perception that his condition made him different from other kids. She involved herself with organizations that sponsored holiday celebrations and other events in which every child in attendance was a diabetic.

For a few years following his diagnosis, Sheila arranged for Danny to spend his school vacations at a special summer camp. The family delivered Danny to Bearskin Meadow, a camp for diabetic children, located in Kings Canyon National Park. It is truly a wonderful place situated in the Sierra Mountain Range east of Fresno, California.

The camp facilities included several attractive one-story rustic structures, encompassing bunkhouses, hobby and crafts buildings, and the mess hall where diabetic-friendly meals were prepared and served. The children were divided by gender and age groups and assigned to bunkhouses. Each accommodated about a dozen children and counselors in their late teens.

My first impression of Bearskin Meadow left me with a profound sense of gratitude that such a place existed. It seemed that the organizers had thought of everything. These kids could participate in a seemingly endless variety of fun-filled activities, including—but not limited to—horseback riding, fishing, swimming, boating, roasting marshmallows and listening to stories around an evening campfire.

A particularly humiliating aspect of child diabetes is the fact that the kids frequently wet the bed. It isn't their fault. These kids pee a lot and regularly experience bedtime accidents. At Bearskin Meadows, each morning the kids hung their urine soaked sheets and blankets on outdoor clothes lines. They soaped and hosed them down, and in the afternoon when the bedclothes were dry, they took them down and made their beds. No big deal if a kid needed to repeat the process daily; nobody took notice.

Danny was six the first time we took him to Bearskin Meadow. The family spent the entire day with him. As the sun began to set, we had to leave. Danny had never before been separated from us. He stood in the middle of the gravel road and watched us drive away. His eyes were filled with tears—as were mine. I suppose most people love their children equally but in different ways. I never really worried about my other children. I believed that they could take care of themselves. Danny was very smart—totally self-assured and independent. Why then, when he was out of sight, did I feel uneasy?

CHAPTER THIRTY

Even with the many challenges at home regarding Danny's health, I had to earn a living. My duties at Standard Register brought me into contact with Herb Otto. Herb came across as a pleasant, mild mannered, slight fellow in his mid-forties. We enjoyed each other's company and often visited during our lunch period. Herb held the position of supervisor of the shipping department. He'd been with the company for over ten years and earned relatively good money and his job seemed quite secure.

Herb took me into his confidence; he surprised me when he informed me he planned to leave Standard Register in the near future. I learned he had been working part time as a real estate salesman for the past couple of years, and he planned to soon go into the real estate business on a full time basis. Herb had a wife and three children. The following year his daughter, his oldest child, would be entering college. He had committed to finance her education as well as helping his two sons when they became ready to enter college not far in the future. I opined that Herb's financial obligations were substantial.

I asked, "Herb, are you joking—what would possess you to consider resigning a secure, well-paying job with future retirement potential to go into a business in which your income is dependent upon commissions?"

Herb smiled at my concern and explained his reasoning, "Val, last year, selling real estate part time, I earned over twice as much as I made working full time here."

As he saw it, working full time as a real estate agent, the person who decided the amount of his income would be Herb. "Sure, I make pretty good money here, and I'll receive a small retirement if I last another ten years. But, it's clear I'll never get rich at Standard Register, and I might just make it big in real estate." He explained, "guys like us who settle for mere security while working for other people can never really become truly financially independent. Selling real estate successfully is hard work, but I'm good at it, and I love it. I am constantly meeting interesting people who I have the opportunity to help, and I am well paid for doing so."

Talking with Herb really made me start thinking. My experience in dealing with the Park Avenue and Juana Avenue properties and reading William Nickerson's book led me to believe Herb had the right idea. Reflection on my success as a shoe salesman and what I had accomplished settling reprint disputes at Standard Register caused me to toy with the idea that I might make a good real estate salesman.

I asked Herb everything I could think of about working as a real estate agent. He seemed so positive that I became convinced I should explore the subject further. A license is required to operate as a real estate salesperson. Passing a state administered examination is necessary to obtain a license. Herb told me he found the test to be difficult, and I would need to study aggressively in order to pass. My interest had been stimulated sufficiently; I decided to try to obtain a license. There were several real estate schools available that prepared individuals for the test.

My Standard Register salary had increased, and we still had some of the proceeds from the sale of Park Avenue. Even so, in view of ever-increasing expenses and our years of financial deprivation, I hesitated to fork out tuition money to attend real estate license school. Although I found the idea enticing, I hadn't yet been entirely convinced that a real estate career loomed in my future. I ran my thinking by Herb.

He pointed out that even though he attended Anthony Real Estate School to prepare for his examination, he mentioned a book entitled *Westcox Primer*, which contained all the material covered in the test. Tuition to attend school ran around $300. I could buy the primer for around seven dollars. Actually, I wouldn't even have to buy it. Although Herb attended school to prepare for his test, he happened to own a copy of the primer, which he would be pleased to give to me. I accepted his offer and began preparation.

An opportunity arose which could enhance the quality of our life and leave me more time to study for my real estate examination. Phil Shaw, the Press Department supervisor with whom I had become friends made an interesting suggestion to me. We discussed the fact that most of the workers in the plant belonged to the Printers Union, but the Quality Control Department workers were not in a union. Phil extolled a few of the advantages the Printers Union members enjoyed that were not available to the Quality Control staff.

One union benefit particularly appealed to me. The Quality Control staff worked a forty-hour week, while the union members worked only thirty-five hours per week. Phil informed me that if our department became unionized I would receive the same pay for working thirty-five hours as presently received for forty hours. I spoke with the union officials who encouraged and assured me I could expect their assistance. They instructed me on how to proceed toward unionizing our department.

They warned me that management would aggressively discourage any move that might lead to a vote to become union members. According to the union organizers, someone within the department, namely me, needed to surreptitiously convince more than half of the department's work force to vote in favor of joining the union in the event of an election.

The union officials had to believe that more than fifty percent of the staff favored joining the union to justify scheduling an election. Timing was crucial—if the issue came to a vote and failed to pass, another chance might not ever come along. The union officials warned that if my superiors discovered my efforts to sell my co-workers on joining the union, they definitely would concoct an excuse to fire me. As I planned my strategy, I realized how much I wanted and needed that union opportunity. I thought, *I'm a good salesman, and I can make this happen.*

There were a dozen staff members in our department. I determined that four of those were staunch management types. Those four—in my opinion—would never vote in favor of unionizing. Another five would be fearful of incurring the wrath of our employers and would worry about losing their jobs if they openly favored joining the union.

However, if handled very carefully, the substantial benefits of being in the union might override their fear of management. The remaining three department members, Dick Partido, my close pal, Bill Foley and I would readily strive to convince our co-workers it served our best interest to belong to the union. Bill, Dick and I quietly and gently began explaining to each of the five potential supporters how much better off we would be under the protection of the union. At first, they were reticent, which I had expected.

Softly, I continued pointing out the many benefits available to us by unionizing. Not only would we receive the same amount of pay for a shorter work week, but we'd be more likely to receive considerably higher pay raises in the future. I didn't have to convince anyone that union members in general enjoyed greater job security than non-members. I posited that if three-quarters of our department stood together, management—out of fear of litigation—wouldn't dare fire any of us over our desire to belong to the union.

I let the union officials know that eight workers in our department were committed to voting in favor of belonging to the union. They scheduled an election date, we voted, and happily became card-carrying Printers Union members. A week or so after the election, Bob Wilkens called me into his office and said, "Val, I just want you to know you aren't fooling me. I damn well know it's because of you and you alone that my department is unionized. No one else around here, except you, could have pulled this off."

I don't think Bob meant to compliment me; just the same, he couldn't have given me a better compliment.

CHAPTER THIRTY-ONE

Benefits accruing to the Quality Control staff had the effect of dramatically raising our moral. We were happier, working harder, and management appreciated our improved attitude. Actually, we got more done in seven hours than we did previously in eight hours. Bob Wilkins became quite friendly with me. I knew it wouldn't happen, but I believe he wanted to thank me.

Late in 1959, I began to study in preparation for the real estate salesman license test. The material I had to learn fascinated me and I absorbed it like a sponge. Wherever I went, the *Westcox Primer* accompanied me. I believed I stood on the threshold of a very positive breakthrough in my life . . . and I felt happy.

Money continued to be in short supply and making ends meet didn't happen easily. Two new income sources became available. Sheila's elderly maternal grandfather, Lorenzo, had lived with Sheila's mother and step-father for many years. They both worked and felt that Lorenzo had reached a state of infirmity that required someone to watch out for him full time. His children asked if Lorenzo might live with us, for which we would be paid $100 each month.

The choice came down to, either; Lorenzo lived with us or in a home for the aged. His children decided he would fare better living with us. We would be less expensive than a home for the aged and maybe he would be happier with family. We welcomed Lorenzo into our home. We all liked that pleasant little man who spoke very broken English, having immigrated from Italy around 1914 to work as a laborer for Southern Pacific Railroad. Having few skills and little formal education, he hadn't been employed in decades. I'm not sure how we managed it, but Lorenzo got a bedroom and the kids were quartered in what had been a storeroom that we turned into a bedroom. Crowded? Sure, but we were young and used to being crowded.

We were delighted to have Lorenzo with us. He fixed his own meals and cleaned up after himself. I'm not sure how to describe Lorenzo's cuisine. Its Italian origin survived with adjustments resulting from decades of living the nomadic life of a railroad laborer. The fragrance of garlic and tomato sauce pervaded our home.

Lorenzo was excellent at yard maintenance, which he enjoyed immensely. He filled his days trimming, mowing, raking and keeping our heavily landscaped property looking gorgeous. I suppose drinking wine represented his first love . . . he consumed four gallons each month. He sang to himself all through the day and sometimes in the evening, always a little tipsy.

The second income source came from my sister, Sherie, who was in the process of getting a divorce. She had moved to an apartment in Berkeley to be near her job, and her husband wasn't capable of helping care for the children, ages four and two. Sherie asked Sheila if we could let her kids live with us until she got her life together, and offered to pay $150 per month for their board and care.

Little Jared and Demi moved in with us. They were beautiful kids, and we loved having them. Valerie and Demi were still preschoolers, but Stevie and Jared were enrolled in kindergarten at Wilson School and Danny began first grade at Assumption Parrish Catholic School. Both schools were within walking distance of home.

The extra income we received for taking in Lorenzo and Jared and Demi helped a lot. It was a tight fit, but we got by just fine. My real estate studies progressed well. At that time, to be eligible to take the real estate examination, I needed the sponsorship of a licensed real estate broker. A sponsoring broker committed to allowing a newly licensed salesperson to deal in activities that required a real estate license under the broker's license.

During the course of a year and a half, Sherie obtained a divorce and married again. Her new husband, Fred Banning, not long out of the United States Marine Corps, seemed to genuinely love my sister and her two kids. I thought Sherie had made a very good choice and time would support my initial impression. Jared and Demi left us to live with their mom and step-father. They were happy, and we were happy for them.

Lorenzo's previously mild dementia became worse. Though only in his early seventies, he mistook Sheila for his ex-wife and began making romantic advances toward her. When it became clear that his fixation toward his granddaughter had become permanent, his children relocated him to a six-patient home for the aged in the City of Hayward, where after a short period he died.

CHAPTER THIRTY-TWO

I began conversing with a few local brokers about sponsoring me. While they all agreed that long hours and hard work were required, each broker suggested substantially different paths to a successful career.

Dick Maciel told me that in order to eventually "find a nickel among the pennies," active salespeople should bank their commissions as much as possible and diligently strive to increase their property holdings.

Hank Deadrich, Sr. said that a salesman who spent five days a week showing property to two prospective buyers each day, and viewing five properties daily could expect to do well. He believed that a salesperson looking at twenty-five properties weekly would, within a month, know the market better than ninety-five percent of his competitors.

Ed Marvin pointed out that a salesperson specializing in residential property could sell those listed by competing firms and marketed through the Multiple Listing Services (MLS). However, Ed told me that salespeople who were able to convince owners to list their properties with them enjoyed substantially higher reliable income potential. He explained that he successfully pursued listings by utilizing the following strategy: He selected a neighborhood in which he wanted to locate a home for prospective buyers with whom he had been working. Often, on Saturday mornings, he started strolling along a block in the targeted area. Inevitably, he came across someone working in their yard, washing a car or otherwise possibly available to speak with him.

In a casual, friendly manner Ed introduced himself and explained his purpose of being there. He said he wondered if the person with whom he spoke might know of someone in the neighborhood thinking of selling their property. Sometimes Ed got valuable referrals resulting in listings. He told me that naturally not every Saturday morning stroll produced a listing; however, each walk helped him become acquainted with potential clients in the canvassed district. Everybody seemed interested in talking real estate—people were so interested in chatting with Ed that he could never walk an entire block on a single Saturday. It wasn't unusual for him to receive a call from someone he met on a stroll months previously, now wanting his services.

I met with those potential sponsoring brokers while in the process of looking for a residential investment property. As usual,

I found myself constrained by a modest budget. I made a few offers which the sellers rejected. I didn't mind though; anything to do with real estate fascinated me, and I continued to learn. In my search to locate a single-family investment property, I became attracted to the Mulford Gardens' district. That older, unincorporated heterogeneous residential community of roughly one square mile existed between the City of San Leandro and the pristine, unspoiled shoreline of the San Francisco Bay.

Prior to becoming a residential subdivision, that square mile of land had been owned and operated as a cattle ranch by Captain John Mulford in the early 1900s. He earned the appellation of "Captain" during his earlier career as a ship captain. In the early 1920s, Captain Mulford obtained a loan from the Bank of America, which he collateralized with the ranch. Hard financial times developed and the bank foreclosed.

Bank of America couldn't find a buyer willing to pay enough to recoup their financial stake in the property, so they subdivided the land into one-acre residential lots. Advertising flyers marketed the lots as "farmettes" and claimed that after planting a garden and investing in a few farm animals, owners could expect to live off the land.

A few industrious folks did indeed manage to survive solely off the bounty produced on their farmette. But the bank couldn't sell many of the acre sites and still owned the majority of the land. They divided the remaining parcels into one-third acre lots and were then able to sell the rest of the Mulford Gardens subdivision.

I discovered Mulford Gardens in 1959. In spite of its relatively spacious lots, tree shaded streets, proximity to the bay shoreline and rural charm, the real estate prices seemed depressed to me. I didn't claim to be an expert, but I observed nascent events in play there that, in my opinion, promised to dramatically cause the value of Mulford real estate to spiral upward.

Several forces were at work that had the potential to create extraordinary investment opportunities. One of those emanated from the high degree of interest in annexing Mulford Gardens to the City of San Leandro. The city's political leaders, developers and residents, as well as many residents of Mulford Gardens saw annexation as the first step toward development of the bay shoreline. However, not all Mulford Gardenites agreed, and the issue became hotly debated. It appeared that those favoring annexation had a slight numerical edge.

Many envisioned that Mulford Gardens—after annexation—would enjoy immediate proximity to the development of a marina complex, replete with a boat harbor, a hotel, high-end restaurants, a championship golf course and spacious recreational facilities. I committed myself to ferreting out an affordable investment property in Mulford Gardens.

While driving through the pleasant thoroughfares of Mulford, looking for real estate signs, I noticed several Ed Marvin Realty signs. I'd met Ed in my search to select a sponsoring broker relative to obtaining my real estate salesman license. I spotted a modest ranch-style house situated on a very large lot, maybe as large as an acre, posted with Ed's sign.

I called his office and made an appointment to view the property. Sheila and I inspected the interior of the home and asked Ed to prepare an offer. Ed had listed the property for $22,500. We made an offer of $19,000, somewhat higher than our comfort level. I justified submitting an offer beyond our budget because I thought the parcel sufficiently large enough to divide into two legal lots.

If the seller accepted our offer and we discovered that we were over extended, perhaps we might find relief by dividing the site and selling one lot. I knew I'd be taking a chance, but I wanted to own that property. Unfortunately, the effort became academic. Ed informed me that the seller had accepted a full price contract brought in by another broker.

Though disappointed, my time hadn't been wasted. I had learned a valuable lesson that would serve me well when I became a licensed real estate salesperson. My perceived strict budget constraints "flew right out the window" when I located a property I really wanted to own. I'd learned that when I would start working in real estate sales, whenever potential buyers might state their upper price limit, I would know to wait until I showed them a property that they really liked before I believed them. At that point, a closer examination of their financial status might be in order. In any event, I knew that I'd never try to influence my clients to pay a higher price than they could afford.

In those days, the real estate licensing process differed from the procedure to which it eventually evolved. When I passed the exam, I received a temporary license. After one year, I had to take another and a somewhat more difficult test, which if passed, resulted in the issuance of a permanent license.

Back then, those examined had to be considerably more knowledgeable than prospective real estate agents tested in later years. The examination I took required that an individual demonstrate his or her ability to clearly set forth in writing, the provisions of a purchase agreement utilizing a specific group of hypothetical conditions contained within the testing material. A licensee needed to know how to draw a legal contract.

The Purchase Agreements (Deposit Receipts) in use by real estate agents at that time consisted of boilerplate language and a large blank space in which the agent drafted the terms reached by the principals. In time, the real estate examinations and the California Real Estate Association (CREA) contract standards were substantially diminished (dummied down). My thoughts regarding the changes are as follows: Attorneys argued that Realtors drafting legal conditions in preparation of purchase contracts infringed upon the privileges existing within the boundaries of their profession. Eventually, the attorneys were able to utilize their influence to bring about the adoption of a clumsy multipage purchase agreement in which the real estate agent input became basically restricted to placing a checkmark adjacent to language drafted by lawyers. Paradoxically, since the advent of what I opine are substantially inferior purchase agreements, lawsuits in the real estate field have proliferated.

For the most part, when I got my real estate salesman's license, real estate brokerage offices were much smaller than would be the case a few years later. When the large franchise real estate operations came onto the scene, those gigantic edifices needed to be filled with licensees.

The number of folks applying to take the real estate license examination began to expand exponentially in California and other states. Prior to the vast increase of applicants, the tests were graded by humans. After all, each exam contained contract preparation language drafted in the words of the examinee.

In order to process the plethora of licensee applications, the examination had to be changed to permit high volume machine grading. Eliminating the requirement of those tested to formulate an agreement written in their own words opened the door to less knowledgeable and perhaps less intelligent agents. The changes in purchase contracts, ancillary documents and license examinations certainly had the effect of filling the halls of the ever-increasing realty franchise operations. However, in my opinion, accommodating the demands of the "legal eagles" and the large franchises didn't serve the public well.

When I entered the real estate business, I thought of myself as a professional. My colleagues and I wouldn't have thought of conducting business dressed in any attire other than a business suit or slacks and sport coat with a dress shirt and tie. Few of us bought errors and omission insurance because we were too damned careful to do anything that would get us sued. In time, it became commonplace to observe agents showing property in jogging outfits. Is it any wonder we were no longer thought of as professionals?

I believe the prevalence of litigation involving real estate licensees responds directly to the diminished skill level of people operating within the industry. That being said, there are many capable real estate agents doing a good job, just not enough of them. When Ronald Reagan served as governor of California, he encouraged the proposition that to become a real estate broker one should obtain a four-year college degree. Because of the efforts of the franchises to open the door to the vast increase of licensees needed to staff their massive offices, Governor Reagan's quest to professionalize the industry didn't reach fruition. Some will argue my contention, citing some states' continuing education requirements. In my opinion, a child of ten could pass the continuing education tests after a minimum of instruction.

PART THREE

A CAREER AS A LICENSED REAL ESTATE AGENT

"a second chance"

CHAPTER THIRTY-THREE

I liked Ed Marvin, and I liked The Mulford Gardens area. At that time, Ed had the only real estate office located in Mulford Gardens. I told him that I wanted to take the real estate salesperson exam and asked if he would be my sponsoring broker. He gladly obliged my request and said that if I passed I would be welcome to work in his office on a part-time basis. Many brokers didn't want part-timers. I passed the test in September, 1960.

At the beginning of October, 1960, I reported for work at Ed's office around five in the afternoon on most weekdays. On weekends I worked all day and some evenings. Ed's sales staff consisted of himself and an elderly, dapper and affable gentleman named Dan Nolan. I instantly knew Dan and I would get along quite well. Ted Meecham rented a desk in Ed's office from which he operated as an independent insurance agent. Ted also had a salesperson's real estate license under Ed's broker's license, but Ted did no real estate business. In time, Ted would quite favorably impact my career.

The Ed Marvin operation occupied a single story, ten by twenty-five foot freestanding white stucco structure under a heavy shake roof. The small, attractive building contained three rooms; a front office with three desks, a bathroom and a rear conference room where the salespeople could converse in private with clients. The building fronted a heavily traveled arterial, in close proximity to three small yet busy strip shopping centers, at the entrance of the Mulford residential subdivision.

I felt excited about reporting to the office, though I didn't know how to get started. It soon became clear that Ed Marvin Realty enjoyed an excellent location. I thought, *Maybe, when I figure out how to do this, I will have a chance of making some serious money.* Ed and Dan couldn't possibly devote sufficient time to successfully deal with the large number of potential buyers that dropped by the office. At that time, the majority of the financing to purchase a home came by way of a government-insured (GI) loan available to veterans, or a Federal Housing Administration (FHA) loan. The FHA financed transactions required a relatively small down payment and GI buyers needed to make no down payment. The interest rate on GI and FHA financing ran less than conventional types of financing provided by banks and savings and loan associations.

Both Ed and Dan were very helpful to me. They let me accompany them as they showed property to prospective buyers. I constantly practiced writing purchase contracts. One Saturday morning Ed asked me to show a residential rental listing to a potential tenant. I showed the unit, and when the likely tenant became an actual tenant and paid the office a twenty dollar rental fee, I received ten dollars. I'd received my first commission. I'd "drawn blood," so to speak, and I saw great potential.

Mom worked as a waitress at the very popular eatery known as Bab's Donuts at Fruitvale Avenue and San Leandro Boulevard in Oakland. Her customers liked her, and she got to know many of them quite well. Whenever the subject of real estate came up, she recommended the services of her son. I let Mom know that each of her referrals resulting in a commission would earn her a referral fee. I told that to everybody.

One of Mom's regulars, Don Milligan, around thirty and recently married, told her he sure wished he owned a home. He had no money, but he had a regular job and as a veteran he could obtain a GI loan. Don and his wife came to the office one evening and I showed them three homes in the Washington Manor area, a popular 1950s subdivision in San Leandro, not far from the office. The Milligans were willing to buy any one of the three homes they had seen. We returned to the office. Just across the parking lot from the office stood a bar called Bill's Rendezvous. While I prepared the purchase contract, Mrs. Milligan wanted to visit the bar for a quick beer. She told Don and me to let her know when I finished preparing the agreement.

They decided to try to buy 1106 Mersey Avenue. Don and Mrs. Milligan signed the offer of $13,250 and a $500 promissory note, which represented their "good faith" deposit. Mrs. Milligan wanted to return to Bill's Rendezvous to celebrate. I thanked her for inviting me to celebrate with them, but declined, telling them I needed to arrange to present their offer to the Mersey Avenue owners. Clearly, Don didn't want to go to the the bar, yet he dutifully followed his little redheaded bride across the parking lot.

I made an appointment with the listing agent, Helen Sproat, to present the contract to the sellers at their home. Helen worked at Manor Realty, a very active real estate office with around twenty agents, located in the commercial area of the Washington Manor subdivision at Manor Boulevard and Farnsworth Avenue. Ed and I met Helen at the Mersey Avenue property the next evening. My first presentation—*damn, pretty exciting stuff.*

Ed had cooperated with Helen on other transactions and they seemed to have a good rapport. He introduced us, and I told Helen how delighted I was to meet her, especially under those circumstances. I liked her and I liked everything about what we were doing. Before we entered the home, we sat in Ed's new Pontiac station wagon and Helen read my contract. The Milligans had made a full price offer.

Many mistakenly believe that the Veteran's Administration makes GI loans, but the loans actually come from non-government lenders. The federal government guarantees those lenders against loss. As stated previously the interest rate lenders could charge at that time on GI financing was less than the rate charged by banks and other conventional lenders. Lenders rectified the disparity between interest rates permitted on GI financing and conventional loans as follows: Sellers of residential property paid a fee, commonly referred to as points, to the lenders making the GI loans. The fee helped to equalize the returns between conventional loans and GI financing.

Before we met with the sellers, Helen said she believed that I'd written a fair offer which she intended to recommend that her clients accept. Even so, she cautioned me not to become overly optimistic because when she listed the property, the sellers told her they wouldn't be interested in a transaction that required the payment of points.

Helen introduced Ed and me to the sellers. They invited us to have a seat in the living room. Ed politely suggested that it might be better to discuss the offer at their dining room table; a smart psychological move on Ed's part. Negotiating face to face at the dining room table is far more conducive to conducting business than in the living room.

The sellers offered us coffee. Helen and Ed declined; they explained that if they drank coffee so late, they wouldn't be able to go to sleep that night. My associates surprised me. We had a selling job to accomplish and we needed every bit of help we could get. Accepting such hospitality or "breaking bread" with the property owners would change the relationship between them and us.

If I acquiesced to the friendly gesture, psychologically I became a guest, rather than a salesperson. Not only would my status become elevated, but my first interaction with my hosts represented the completion of a positive transaction, even if it only happened to be the acceptance of a cup of coffee. Indeed, I did receive the sellers' hospitality gratefully. Once we were seated in the dining room, I recalled sales strategies I learned at Cannon and still used during my job at Standard Register. I refrained from discussing the sales contract until I sensed that the owners felt at ease with me.

My method of establishing a comfortable dialog with the sellers occurred by asking them non-intrusive questions, such as where they might move when their property sold and general comments on subjects of interest to them. I sincerely wanted to gain more information about them. For my strategy to succeed, the sellers had to be doing around seventy-five percent of the talking. If that transpired, I would gain the advantage of knowing more about them which would be helpful when we discussed the sales agreement.

Even at that rudimentary stage of my career, I knew that developing an environment of congeniality served no good purpose if the proposal I presented didn't benefit the sellers. I believed my buyers' offer to be fair, and I felt the time had arrived to begin negotiating. Ed and Helen seemed comfortable with me taking charge of the presentation, which I almost always did from the very beginning of my career. At that point, I refrained from reading the contract to the sellers word for word, as I learned that many agents mistakenly did. The owners would be tense and uncomfortable trying to decipher a legal document, so I made it easy. I knew that what the proceeds of the sale would net them mattered most. After all, if the buyers' proposal failed the money test, discussing the contract legalese would be pointless.

The sellers agreed with my suggestion that it might be helpful if I explained the basics of the offer before laboring over the plethora of details contained in the contract. I didn't even give them a copy of the contract at that point. I quickly prepared a sellers "net sheet" in which I listed each of the owner's expenses and deducted the total cost from the selling price. The sum remaining represented the funds to be received by the sellers when the sale closed. I explained that some circumstances would alter my estimate, such as the cost of potential pest control work (termite damage) and property tax prorations, which varied according to the closing date.

They studied the net sheet as I went over each expense item with them. Then I stopped talking and waited for a response. As expected from my earlier conversation with Helen, Mr. Seller explained that they didn't want a GI financed transaction because of the cost of points that they would have to pay the lender. If they didn't have to pay points, the deal would be acceptable. It pleased me to hear that the only objection came down to the cost of the points. I proceeded to mitigate that single obstacle.

I remarked, "I bet you'll be glad when your property is sold." I explained "I know how you feel having to continually give up your privacy so strangers can look into your closets and judge your housecleaning and put up with all the indignities that go along with showing your home. "

Mrs. Seller remarked, "We haven't relaxed for a minute since our house went on the market. We'll be so relieved when this is over."

I stated that the Milligans had fallen in love with the sellers' beautiful home which is why they offered the full asking price. I used the Milligans name to humanize them in the minds of the owners. I said, "They looked at other homes in the area before deciding they wanted your home. They appreciate what you've done here."

Mr. Seller answered, "The Milligans sound like fine people and we'd really like for them to have this place, Val, but why should we have to pay points?" It went well—he referred to the buyers by name and began to subtlety form a rapport with them. It didn't hurt either that he addressed me by my first name. I moved to nullify the seller's one and only objection—the points. I asked them if they knew in their area most properties sold under either GI or FHA financing, both of which required the owners to pay points. The seller acknowledged that Helen told them that when she listed their property.

I explained the Veteran's Administration—being fully aware of the seller's obligation to pay points on GI loans, made an effort to "level the playing field." It was common knowledge that Veteran's Administration residential appraisers strove to—within reason of course—come in with numbers that enhanced the chances of the applying veterans to acquire home ownership. Additionally, requirements to qualify for a GI loan seemed considerably relaxed compared to other types of financing.

Then Mr. Seller looked at his wife and said, "Hon, actually when you think about this deal, we're really not even paying the points—the Milligan's will be paying them because their offer is more than the property is worth."

She responded, "In that case, we're going to leave our new patio furniture for the Milligans."

The sellers signed the contract and thanked Helen and Ed and me for our efforts on their behalf. Outside, Helen said, "I enjoyed watching you work, Val. I look forward to you selling more of my listings." I sensed that Helen and I would become close friends.

Driving back to the office, Ed commented, "I think you should consider selling real estate full time." If the sale closed, my commission would exceed a month's salary at Standard Register. Right then I loved everybody including the Milligan's, the owners of 1106 Mersey Avenue, and Helen and Ed. I got home and excitedly went over every detail about the evening with Sheila.

CHAPTER THIRTY-FOUR

As time passed, I learned the importance of a real estate salesperson's ability to present offers. I'd sat with agents while they presented their contracts to the owners of my listings, and it amazed me that so many of those agents were utterly inept. Customarily the selling agent rather than the listing agent presented the sales contract. Many times those agents had shown their buyers properties for weeks and finally were able to get a purchase offer signed. Then they often ended up failing to get a fair proposition accepted at the presentation table.

So many agents couldn't seem to understand the intensity of some owners' feelings when they were involved in selling their home. Deciding whether an offer should be accepted or rejected could be an agonizing, confusing experience—even for sophisticated sellers. Frequently, purchase contracts that served the best interest of the seller didn't get accepted, simply because the presenter didn't understand how to sell.

I found that most owners thought the value of their property to be worth more than market conditions dictated. When the seller received an offer under the listed price, yet a very fair offer, the presentation often turned into a battle between the presenting agent and the seller. In many cases, instead of making a strong effort to empathize with the seller's highly charged emotional state, the presenting agent began to point out the property's defects. Such a tactic only heightened the seller's resistance, often resulting in the rejection of a good offer and a terrible waste of an agent's time.

Then when the agent told the buyers he or she couldn't convince the seller to accept their offer, the disappointed potential buyers sometimes lost confidence in the agent and looked for another salesperson. The sellers may have been agreeable to the rejected contract if it had been presented by a more competent agent. You might ask, "How does an agent conduct successful presentations?" At the risk of appearing immodest, I learned to be a very good presenter—so proficient in fact—competitors have paid me to present their contracts. I will tell you how I went about conducting a presentation.

Shortly before meeting the principals of a transaction, I recited the following four-rule mantra:

1. Make the party with whom I am meeting know that I like them. This is easy to accomplish. I learned it at Cannon. A warm, friendly, sincere smile will assure anyone that you like them.

2. Make them like you. Zero in on something about the party that you genuinely admire and pay them a sincere compliment. With a little practice, quickly spotting admirable qualities in people becomes easy. You can comment on how well they maintain their yards, how cute their children or pets are, their choice of automobiles or an endless number of other possibilities that justify a sincere compliment. Sincerity is paramount in such situations.

3. Make them know you are a professional. You must come well prepared to support whatever premise you intend to advance. For instance, if you are presenting an offer to a seller, you need to have written sales data relative to properties comparable to theirs. If the data supports your position, there will be little problem getting an acceptance.

4. Your proposition must be fair and serve the best interest of your client. Do not try to make a sale that doesn't meet your customer's needs, simply so you can receive a commission.

Believe me; putting your customers first will bring you lasting success.

The preceding mantra guides me through the presentation. It's like following a road map. There is a beginning and an end, and I always know where I am.

I simply can't repeat the following too much: Before discussing the subject of our meeting, I conversed with the clients about topics of interest to them. I allowed them to do most of the talking. To deal successfully with people in a sales situation, the more you know about them, the better your chances of success. I can't learn a damn thing about someone while I'm talking.

I heard a presentation line I loved from Ed Brumfield, one of the best real estate salesmen I've ever known. Ed, a distinguished-appearing, soft spoken gentleman, maybe twenty years my senior, presented himself as likable and smooth as a chocolate malt. We met for lunch about once a week. Ed enjoyed being one of the top earners in our industry year after year. I truly enjoyed hearing how he handled various sales situations.

Whenever Ed presented a good and fair offer to a reluctant seller, he asked the seller to picture the offer as a delicious slice of fresh strawberry pie. Even though the pie didn't have as much whipped cream as the seller might like, nonetheless, it was an excellent piece of pie and another one as good might not come along again. I used Ed's line several times with success.

CHAPTER THIRTY-FIVE

Inspired by the Milligan transaction, I continued showing properties both during evenings and weekends. I strung together about four more sales from October 1960 to January 1961 while still working at Standard Register. Letting everyone know about my real estate job paid off. A couple of people at Standard Register listed property with me. Lorenzo Santos, the superintendent of Standard's collating department gave me the listing on his rental house in East Oakland, the home in which he grew up.

Lorenzo inherited the property some years previously and rented it out. He contracted to have an expensive home built in Foster City, and he needed to sell the rental property. In addition to selling the rental house in Oakland, he would soon have to sell the home in which he resided in San Leandro. He hinted that if I did well for him marketing his Oakland property, I could expect to get the listing on his San Leandro home.

When I approached Lorenzo's tenants to arrange to show the home to prospective buyers, they were very disappointed. They had rented the home for seven years. Two of their children attended the public high school just a few blocks away. The thought of having to move distressed them. I sensed an opportunity, so I asked if they would like to buy the home. The idea definitely appealed to the family, but only the husband brought in a check. Qualifying for financing would be difficult. I learned that in addition to the two kids living at home, a single, grown daughter rented an apartment not far away.

The daughter had a good job with Bank of America. I suggested that if she agreed to buy the property in partnership with her parents, qualifying for the financing would pose no problem. I met with her at her parents' home, and she wanted to cooperate. I presented a signed purchase contract to Lorenzo which he happily signed. What a wonderful business. I appreciated the opportunity to help people dramatically improve the quality of their lives, while being well paid to do so.

The Milligan transaction closed, and as Ed handed me the commission check, he pressed me to resign my job with Standard Register and start selling real estate full time.

I let him know that I'd like nothing better. but I had serious financial obligations and had hoped to substantially build up my cash reserves before resigning my full time job. He informed me that he had a savings account with a balance of $1200. He offered to pay me $100 each week until he emptied the account if I would leave Standard Register and come to work at his office full time.

I discussed his offer with Sheila. Clearly, a committed career in real estate would reduce the time I could spend with my family. And clearly, we would enjoy considerably higher income with me selling real estate than in any other field available to me. Several well-meaning friends and family members advised me that a man with family obligations should avoid an occupation in which his income depended upon commissions. It pleased me that Sheila encouraged me to accept Ed's offer. In December of 1960, I submitted my two-week notice of resignation to Standard Register, and the department gave me a pleasant going away party. I'd made some good friends there and looked forward to future associations with them, although I knew they wondered how I would fare in my new venture. It saddened me to know that they would never trade their modest security for the opportunity to reach the heights to which I aspired.

CHAPTER THIRTY-SIX

I gladly invested whatever it took in time and energy to succeed in my new career. Daily, I aggressively showed property to prospective buyers which included relatives, friends and relatives of friends, referrals and office drop-ins. I viewed every adult with whom I came into contact as a potential client.

Belonging to the Southern Alameda County Board of Realtors (SACBOR), the California Real Estate Association (CREA), and the National Association of Real Estate Brokers (NAREB) helped establish my potential to achieve a successful career. Those agencies regularly held seminars and meetings for the purpose of disseminating information designed to assist members to improve their sales ability and help them better serve the public. In an attempt to heighten my chances of enjoying a dramatically successful profession, I attended many such functions and, like a sponge, absorbed every bit of self-improvement information available.

I voraciously read financial success-oriented books and ancillary literature discussing increasing the reader's ability to understand human nature. Interaction with clients served as my "learning how to improve my skill at dealing with people" classroom. I experimented with numerous psychologically-oriented sales techniques just as I had done at Cannon. Some strategies worked well and others didn't. Those that brought favorable results became part of my standard selling repertoire.

A home located in the 1900 block of Juneau Street, a short walk from our office, had been on the market for several months. Bob Burns Realty, basically a two-agent office, had the listing. The vacant Juneau rental house remained unsold until the middle of November, 1960 at which time the listing expired. Ed told me that the owners, Mel and Dee Howard, owned several single-family rental homes in the Marina Gardens neighborhood.

The Howards held title to the Juneau Street property in partnership with Mel's brother and had rented it out for the past few years. When the tenants vacated the property, the Howards decided to sell. Bob Burns represented the Howards when they purchased Juneau, and as often happens in the real estate business, they contacted Bob when they chose to sell.

I had met with Bob Burns a couple of times when I'd picked up keys from him to show his listings. He seemed cheerless, almost morose. Ed mentioned to me that he had heard that Bob had experienced a recent difficult divorce.

As I mentioned earlier, our office was located across a small parking lot from Bill's Rendevous. The Rendevous appeared to me, a bar catering to the community's more serious drinkers, judging from the considerable period of time the bar patron's vehicles remained in the parking lot.

From my desk, I regularly observed Bob visiting the Rendevous. I wondered if his personal problems had interfered with his ability to get the Juneau Street property sold. It didn't seem likely that excessive ingestion of alcohol would permit Bob to work effectively.

I telephoned the Howards and let them know that our office was very close to their Juneau Street property. I truthfully said, "Mr. Howard, I'm trying to locate homes for two young families who wish to relocate in the area of your property." He agreed for me to meet him and his wife, Dee, at seven that evening at their home on State Street.

Juneau Street and State Street were both located in a small residential subdivision known as Marina Gardens. The tract contained approximately three hundred modest homes on streets named after cities or locations in Alaska. Marina Gardens, situated adjacent to the northeast boundary of Mulford Gardens had been developed in the early 1950s. Over the ensuing years, Marina Gardens figured big in my career.

I arrived at the Howards' at seven sharp, just minutes after they got there. When Mel selected the appointment time, he expected they would be home by five-thirty in the afternoon which would have given them time to have dinner before meeting with me. They explained they were unexpectedly delayed getting out of their beauty salon because of customers walking into their establishment just before closing. Mel lamented that they experienced that situation frequently. I didn't know it then but his obvious dissatisfaction with his primary source of income would serve my interest in the years to come.

I offered to leave and come back later in order to give them time to have dinner. They thanked me but insisted on proceeding. As I always did before launching into my listing pitch, I asked for and received a glass of water. Remember why? I'm sure that you recall that it represented a method of elevating my status in their home to a guest, rather than a salesman.

We talked about the Howard's ownership of other rental houses and their proprietorship of Dee's Beauty Salon, and their basic financial goals genuinely drew my interest. Clearly, they were "light years" ahead of me in their quest for financial independence. I hoped that I might benefit from hearing their story. I met their two sons, who were in their early teens, for whom Dee prepared sandwiches while we talked.

Mel and Dee owned commercial property on Marina Boulevard in Mulford Gardens near where that main arterial crossed over the Southern Pacific railroad at the eastern boundary of Mulford

Gardens. Their Marina Boulevard property consisted of a third-acre lot improved with two structures, which originated as single-family homes, subsequently converted to commercial use.

The two buildings were situated in tandem on the parcel and were entirely surrounded by paved parking. The smaller structure at the rear of the lot housed the Howards' beauty salon. The attractive 1300-square-foot building fronting on Marina Boulevard had been recently leased to Farrell and McGovern Realty.

Mel and Dee both styled women's hair. After talking with Mel for a while, I determined that if I didn't know what he did to earn a living, I'd never be able to guess his occupation. With due respect to male hair stylists, Mel just didn't appear to fit the stereotype. I guessed him to be quite capable of performing his job but sick and tired of doing so.

He explained he hoped someday to be able to access the equity in some of the couple's rental properties for the purpose of financing the development of a delicatessen-style restaurant in the building leased to Farrell and McGovern. I think he envisioned himself much happier managing his own restaurant rather than fixing women's hair. Additionally, they figured that when and if the deli began operation, they would lease out the beauty salon business and Dee could retire.

Sitting at their kitchen table, I got on well with Mel and Dee and felt that they were comfortable with me, when their doorbell rang. George, Mel's brother and the owner of one-half interest in the Juneau Street property, had arrived. Mel introduced me to George in a manner that suggested to him that Mel and Dee liked me.

George wanted to know if I really believed I could sell the property in as much as it had recently been on the market for three months and remained unsold. He explained that he needed his share of the equity in Juneau soon. He had contracted to buy a home in the upscale community of Moraga.

I asked all three of them to give me a chance to do a job for them. "Please sign up with me and I promise you'll be glad that you did." At some point in a listing interview, I always simply asked for the listing. Why would I not ask for what I came there to get? Indeed, they gave me a listing at a price for which I felt the property would bring. The next morning, I called Bernie Jacks, who I had been showing properties to in the previous two weeks.

I made an appointment to meet Bernie, his wife, and their two pre-teenaged daughters at the Juneau Street property at six that evening. Around five, I reached Jim Woodard on the phone. I told Jim I had just signed up a listing that I thought fit the needs of his family. He explained they couldn't see the property for a couple of days because he had family visiting. He asked for the address so that he could drive by the house to determine whether he would be interested in having me show him the inside.

That evening Bernie and his family decided Juneau suited them and were anxious to sign a purchase agreement. Later that same evening, just one day after listing their property with me, I met Mel, Dee and George again at the State Street house to present the Jacks' contract. They signed the offer and assured me that if the deal closed according to the terms set forth in the agreement, we would be doing a lot of business together in the future.

Happily, the Juneau escrow closed in just over a month. Bernie thanked me and told me they had tried to find a home working with other agents for months, to no avail. They promised to recommend me to friends in the market to buy a home. True to his word, I received a Bernie Jacks' referral call a few days later. As the years went by, I learned the referral business presented the best opportunity to produce positive results. I worked hard to keep those referrals coming my way.

I loved my career. At first I couldn't spend enough time to help Sheila with the kids very much. She found herself stuck in the stifling role of a young mom with too many kids and not much money. Her happiness meant a lot to me, and I tried hard to convince her that the real estate business would soon make our lives much better.

A few days after signing up the Jacks, I got a call from Jim Woodward. He had driven by Juneau Street and wished to make an appointment to go through the property. When I let him know Juneau had been sold, he expressed disappointment. I promised to find something else he would like. I said, "Jim, really good listings move quickly. I will call you to show you properties that I truly believe will meet your requirements. When I do call you, I suggest you let me show you the property right away so you don't miss out again."

The Howards and I were good for each other. I regularly heard from people referred to me by Mel and Dee, some of which resulted in money-producing transactions. Evidence of my reciprocation was made clear by the fact that every woman in my family sported the bouffant style hairdo so popular with the women that patronized Dee's Beauty Salon. The trust and respect between the Howards and I served us well over many years.

CHAPTER THIRTY-SEVEN

I spent a good deal of time locating owners willing to give me "Exclusive Right to Sell" listings. I continually explored the proposition of working smarter, instead of harder. When Exclusive Right to Sell listed properties sold, the listing agent received a commission even if he or she had not been the selling agent.

Commissions earned from such listings in which the selling agent didn't happen to be the listing agent required a minimal amount of the listing agent's time, thus freeing up the listing agent to pursue new business. The high volume listing agents were generally among the top twenty percent of earners in the business. I relentlessly researched and experimented with various methods of acquiring listings. At that time, my fascination with my dream of financial independence rewarded me with seemingly inexhaustible energy. My work felt like recreation.

The haunting background of financial deprivation combined with the superb selling skills I developed when I worked at Cannon Shoes seemed to steer me along a course that promised to make my cherished dream come true. I knew that to succeed, a person needed to set goals and be convinced that those goals would be attained. I determined a specific amount of money that I needed to acquire to become totally financially independent. I wrote that amount on the back of one of my business card and taped it to my bathroom mirror so that I would be reminded of that magical sum every time I shaved—I shaved every morning. *Keep your goal in your sights at all times.*

Sometimes I thought of my dream as Sheila's nightmare. She had a valid point of view. I couldn't spend as much time with my family as I would have preferred. I continually hoped she would come to understand that what I did, I did for her and the kids, as well as for myself. She resented my long work hours and especially hated the telephone calls I got at home from clients and prospective clients. I just didn't know what I could do about that right then. I concentrated on succeeding in my business, especially at that stage of my career.

I constantly explored numerous avenues of activity that I hoped would result in opportunities, which could lead to profitable repeat business. Each year, Ed bought a second-hand reverse directory from a telephone solicitation company that acquired them at the beginning of each year. The initial price of a directory amounted to around $700. The original buyers used them for a period of six weeks for aggressive telephone campaigns to set up appointments for aluminum siding sales representatives to meet with homeowners. At the end of six weeks, the telephone soliciting companies sold the directories for $100 each to small-business owners like Ed.

Ed made a smart move by buying a reverse directory. It became a valuable tool in the hands of the right person. Reverse directories were so named because as opposed to a standard telephone book, the address appeared first followed by the listed party's name and telephone number.

My first experience using the reverse directory produced results slightly short of miraculous. I had been looking to help a young couple and their two elementary-school-aged children (the previously mentioned Jim Woodward family) locate a home in Marina Gardens. As indicated earlier, they would have bought the Howard's Juneau Street property if it hadn't been sold out from under them. Right at that time no listings existed in Marina Gardens within the Woodward family's price range.

On a Saturday morning during the same week that I sold the Juneau Street property, I opened the reverse directory for the first time ever and turned the pages to the Marina Gardens district. Randomly selected, I dialed the telephone number of Manuel and Marie Gonsalves' home located at 1903 Arctic Street.

Mr. Gonsalves answered, and I explained that I needed to list a home for sale in his neighborhood. When I told him I had been working with a family anxious to reocate in Marina Gardens, he asked me to hold on the line. I heard him say. "Honey, there's a real estate guy on the phone who says he has someone who might like to buy this place."

He came back on the line and asked me if I could drop over right then. The Arctic Street property was located three blocks from the office. I arrived there in five minutes and sat down with Mr. and Mrs. Gonsalves at their kitchen table. When I addressed them as Mr. and Mrs. Gonsalves, it sounded good to hear Mary quickly say, "We're Mary and Manny and you are Val."

As I keep repeating herein, before launching into my listing spiel, I made my usual move designed to be viewed by Mary and Manny as a guest rather than a salesman. "Mary, it's a little warm —may I have a glass of water?"

She answered, "How about a cold Coke instead, Val?" The harmonious environment between Mary, Manny and I progressed well.

Mary had to weigh easily over 300 pounds. She seemed self-confident and considerably larger than Manny. He stood about five feet, five inches tall and probably weighed no more than 135 pounds. Clearly, Mary made the decisions in the Gonsalves family. I wonder why it is that wives who are substantially larger than their husbands are likely to be in charge.

The time came to get down to business. Mary complained, "We've outgrown this house—we have three kids and one bathroom. Val, can you sell this house and find us something that will better fit our needs?"

I said, "Mary, I'm certain I can find just what you want." I took the listing, returned to the office, called my prospective buyers and arranged to show them the Gonsalves property late that afternoon. The immaculate condition of the Gonsalves home made it a pleasure to show. The Woodwards actually liked the location of the Gonsalves property better than the location of the Juneau Street house. The Woodwards weren't about to procrastinate. We left the Gonsalves house and went directly to the office to prepare a purchase offer.

Mr. and Mrs. Woodward quickly signed the agreement for the listed price. Mary and Manny signed the buyer's contract around eight that evening. The utility of the reverse directory as an effective business generator made a very positive impression on me. As a result of that handy tool, in a single day I met the Gonsalves, listed their home and sold it.

The following morning, I showed the Gonsalves three houses that met their needs. A property located on Via Descanso in San Lorenzo particularly appealed to Mary. San Lorenzo is adjacent to and south of San Leandro.

Mary thought that the Via Descanso house had most everything she wanted; two additional factors clinched the deal. The owners had already vacated the house, insuring quick occupancy, and Mary's sister lived just a few blocks away—the sisters enjoyed a close relationship. By three Sunday afternoon, the sellers of the Via Descanso property had accepted Manny and Mary's purchase contract. A listing and two sales within thirty hours made one sweet weekend.

CHAPTER THIRTY-EIGHT

I still looked to buy a rental property and during my daily routine of attempting to view five properties listed by other agents on the MLS, I came across a vacant, very appealing English Tudor in the 700 block of Cary Drive. The home backed up to the halcyon beauty of the San Leandro Creek. The property exuded character.

My find was located within the borders of Estudillo Estates which had the reputation of being one of the best residential locations of San Leandro. The highly desirable prewar subdivision contained around five hundred attractive homes, mostly of either classic Spanish or English Tudor design. Standing in the rear yard, I viewed the towering eucalyptus and cedar trees and the lush foliage along the banks of the adjacent pleasant meandering stream, flowing down from Lake Chabot to the east shore of the San Francisco Bay. That scene created an ambiance reminiscent of a beautiful wooded park. I thought *who wouldn't love to live here?*

The dirty house needed paint, and the planked hardwood maple floors were scarred and stained. Upon entering the steep high-pitched attic, I didn't have to switch on the lights to see, because of the sunlight streaming in through the spaces between the heavy cedar shake shingles. I figured I could get the painting done, hardwood floors refinished and cleaning accomplished economically—maybe even doing those things myself. However, replacing the heavy shake roof might be a budget breaker.

At that early stage of my real estate life, I sometimes fell in love with special properties—Cary Drive fit that category. The MLS information revealed that Ralph Giese, the owner of Ralph Giese Realty had the property listed for $24,950. An FHA insured loan in the amount of $15,500 encumbered the property.

I called Ralph and told him I considered making an offer wherein I would assume the $15,500 FHA loan balance. I asked him if he thought there might be a chance that the owners would be willing to help with the financing by carrying back a second loan. I didn't have enough cash to pay the difference between the purchase price and the FHA loan balance and still have enough left over to make the house rentable.

Ralph couldn't have been more helpful. He explained that he had handled the sale of the property to the present owners around ten years previously. The husband, a United States Air Force officer, had recently transferred to a base in Florida. Purchasing a home in Florida before selling Cary Drive placed the family in a precarious financial position.

The sellers had to make payments on two houses, which they were ill-equipped to do. Ralph surmised that getting cash in hand wasn't of prime importance to his clients; indeed he thought that they might be amenable to helping with the financing to facilitate a quick clean sale. They were aware that their Cary Drive house needed work but were not financially capable of doing anything about it.

The sellers' desperately wanted to protect their credit standing. If their difficult monetary circumstances forced them to stop making payments on the Cary Drive loan, which seemed likely, they risked damaging their credit rating. Failure to meet financial obligations could impede a military officer's prospects of advancement. With high hopes, I drew my purchase proposal as follows: I offered $22,578 and utilized a strategy that I would use many times during my career. When making an offer at less than the listed price, I always submitted an uneven number. I did that for the purpose of giving the impression that very careful consideration had been given to determining the justification of the offering price. Down payment: $2,500 which covered the Realtor's commission (of which I would receive a share) and enough to permit the sellers to pay Ralph back a small loan he had advanced so they could make the last two Cary Drive loan payments.

My agreement proposed to assume the FHA loan and requested that the sellers carry back the balance owing to them in the amount of $5,578, secured with a second note and deed of trust against the property. Said note would bear seven percent interest per annum, interest only payments of fifty dollars per month, principal due in five years from date of origination. I agreed to accept the property in its "as is" condition, thereby releasing the sellers from all liability for needed repairs.

I took the offer to Ralph's office, a converted 1920s bungalow near the east end of Castro Valley Boulevard. Ralph looked a lot like I pictured him while talking with him on the telephone. As we conversed, he smoked a cigarette. Crowned with a thick scraggly head of graying hair he appeared to be in his mid-fifties. He wore a dress shirt and tie, as Realtors did in those days. His pants were held up by colorful suspenders traversing a protruding pot belly. I got the impression Ralph didn't exercise a lot.

After reviewing the contract for a few minutes, I expected him to call his sellers in Florida in my presence. He told me he preferred to present the offer alone. He explained that he could say things to his sellers that he wouldn't be comfortable discussing with them in front of me. He said "Val, this is going to be a tough sell—even so, I believe your contract serves the sellers well. I won't insist but I think your best chance of getting them to accept is to leave and let me do this alone." I didn't feel sure Ralph's strategy worked in my favor, but what choice did I have?

I returned to our office and around eight that evening he called to let me know I would soon be the owner of 720 Cary Drive. I found Ralph great to work with, and I knew our paths would cross again. Over the years, I developed camaraderie with a cadre of guileless, highly ethical Realtors of Ralph's caliber—when possible, we promoted one another's best interests.

When I got home that evening and told Shiela about Cary Drive, she didn't seem very interested. "After all," she stated, "you're the one having all the fun, coming home whenever you like, while I'm taking care of kids alone!"

I understood, but what could I do about it? I hoped that deep down inside Sheila knew that my family came first with me. Maybe she didn't notice, but I spent what little free time I had with her and the kids every chance I got.

Within reason, of course, it has always been my opinion that someone who puts the job first, actually puts the family first. A person who spends abundant time with the family and doesn't excel in the "making a living" department invariably lets the family down when they need that person most. That view isn't often agreed with, but I've seen it happen over and over. I always let my children know I loved them deeply and even though I couldn't be with them as much as I would have liked, I treated them in a manner that I knew would build their self-esteem.

I engaged the services of Jim Slater—a handyman I met through Ed Marvin—to paint, clean and refinish the Cary Drive hardwood floors. Jim's services were reasonable. We could have done a lot more, but I spent just enough to make the property rentable. It pleased me to learn from Jim that even though sunlight shined through the separations between the shingles, the roof might still be serviceable. Jim educated me on the subject of heavy shake shingle roofs. I learned that after a couple of decades of service, cedar shake roof shingles begin to shrink and separate, at which point many people often prematurely replace them. According to Jim, for years after the shingles begin to let the sunlight in, just before the rain arrives, the increased moisture in the air causes the shingles to swell, rendering them watertight.

I considered Jim Slater a valuable resource. Jim, a handsome, likable fellow with beautiful silver hair was small in stature and in his mid-fifties. He seemed to have no lofty aspirations beyond just getting along one day at a time. He had no family, except for his German Shepherd with whom he resided in a rented converted tool shed behind his landlady's Mulford Gardens' home. Jim worked so well that he often wasn't available because of the high demand for his services.

I devised a plan that made Jim readily accessible to me. Some thought of him as borderline retarded and definitely eccentric, yet within the limited boundaries in which he operated, he functioned efficiently. In the early sixties, silver coins remained in circulation in the Nevada gambling casinos. Jim had a childish fascination for real silver dollars. Occasionally, Sheila and I visited the clubs at Stateline, adjacent to Lake Tahoe in Nevada. I always returned home with several hundred dollars worth of Jim's favorite form of money. Assured that his pay for work performed for me would be in the form of his beloved "cartwheels," my projects merited Jim's top priority.

Gil and Viv Harris, a responsible middle-aged couple, rented Cary Drive. They took far better care of the property than I normally expected of tenants. After a year, Gil asked me if I would consider selling Cary Drive to them. I told him I'd be glad to sell them the home, but as it happened, the price exceeded their loan qualification ability by $10,000 or so. But, I knew of a nice somewhat smaller home in the Bonaire district of San Leandro listed for sale on the MLS. I submitted an offer for $16,250 from the Harrises which received acceptance.

Gil applied for a GI loan to finance the purchase of the home. GI loans had begun to take in excess of ninety days to close. The Harrises and I agreed for them to continue renting Cary Drive until they could move into the Bonaire property. I reduced the Cary Drive rental rate and the Harrises permitted me to show the property to prospective buyers during that period.

That arrangement worked well. Gil and Viv kept an immaculate home and their furniture looked great. Cary Drive showed like a model home. By the time the Harrises moved, I'd accepted an offer for Cary Drive that gave us a substantial profit.

CHAPTER THIRTY-NINE

At the time I purchased Cary Drive, I had just turned twenty-six. Being able to buy a property at my tender age in such a desirable location elevated my confidence. Decades later I would buy another creek-side house on Cary Drive—a transaction steeped in irony. In 1958, before I became a licensed real estate agent, as we waited for the sale of our Alameda property escrow to close, we looked to buy a home in San Leandro. The real estate agent we worked with, Bert Kirkpatrick, happened to show us our idea of the perfect home located in the 800 block of Cary Drive.

As Bert escorted us through the home, he introduced us to the owners; an aloof, somewhat unfriendly, middle-aged couple. The wife condescendingly asked me how a couple our ages felt we could afford to buy a house like theirs. I explained we were utilizing proceeds from the sale of our Alameda property to buy in San Leandro. She didn't bother to respond to my explanation.

At $19,500 the listed price severely stretched the upper range of our budget. No matter, we were captivated with the home and in spite of the rudeness of the "lady of the house," we signed an offer for the asking price. Our contract provided for the sellers to carry back a small second loan. The owners quickly rejected our offer. Bert informed us that when he presented the contract to the sellers, they remarked that we were just too young to own a home as fine as theirs.

My feelings were hurt and I believed the sellers unfairly discriminated against us. Looking back from a financial standpoint, I suppose they inadvertently did me a favor. Even so, they still behaved like stinkers.

In 1992, some thirty-five years later, the same property came to my attention again. During that period, California experienced a severe real estate recession. Great Western Saving and Loan Association owned the property and had listed it on the MLS. I knew Great Western could only have acquired ownership of the property through foreclosure. Using my Realtor's lock box key, I entered the vacant house and although it sure didn't appear as pristine as when I looked at it decades earlier, I remembered it perfectly and knew I had to own it.

I considered the property at the listing price of $185,000 a bargain. The house needed work, but I figured fixed up it could bring $285,000. I knew an expenditure of $35,000 or less would get it in top condition. I drew up a cash offer and dropped it off at Great Western's local branch. With my purchase contract I included an extraordinarily high good faith deposit in the amount of $25,000 in form of a certified cashier's check. A large good faith deposit creates a favorable impression with the seller by demonstrating you mean business, yet most bargain hunters put up small deposits. The agreement stated even though I held a licensed real broker's license, I expected no commission.

As always, I agreed to buy the property in its "as is" condition. One thing I had learned long ago is that sellers are sometimes so paranoid of potential litigation that they often accept a lesser priced offer if it contains a release of all-liability clause, especially if the property is in poor condition. I also provided a statement from Bank of America showing I had sufficient funds on deposit to pay cash for the property.

Two days later, I received a telephone call from Great Western telling me although they had received other offers, they liked the clean, all cash, "as is" conditions of my proposal. Even though they couldn't accept my contract in its present form, they were going to hold the others in abeyance and make me a counter offer. They certainly gave me an odd counter offer.

148

I had not asked for a commission credit which I thought would please Great Western. They countered that if I would accept a commission of three percent of the selling price, we had a deal. Talk about someone being unclear of the concept, I signed that agreement so fast—I almost broke my pen. The counter offer put an additional $5,550 in my pocket.

The escrow closed in two weeks, and I immediately began renovation, which included minor termite work, interior painting, new kitchen and bathroom floor coverings and refinishing the hardwood floors throughout. Among the most desirable amenities offered by the property had to be its adjacent proximity to the picturesque San Leandro Creek. The view of much of the verdant natural grandeur flourishing along its banks had been completely obscured by the wild overgrowth of blackberry vines.

I planned to remove the blackberry vines and landscape the unkempt back yard, but I wanted to do something to more dramatically emphasize the definitive rustic beauty of the unique setting. For $10,000 I hired my contractor pal, Larry Barcellos, the owner of Barcellos Construction Company, to build a redwood deck extending out over the creek. The results exceeded my highest hopes. The tranquil beauty of that peaceful setting captivated all who viewed it.

Within a week, after I placed the property on the market, Lou Valez from Century 21 Realty brought me an acceptable offer. Three and a half decades had passed between the time I first looked at that gorgeous piece of paradise until I actually became its owner. When I sold the property, even though I walked away with a $70,000 profit, my greatest source of satisfaction from that transaction had to do with the irony of the situation.

CHAPTER FORTY

Although in some ways taxing, working for Ed brought enormous benefits. When I first started with him, he had the only real estate office in Mulford Gardens and it seemed he knew everyone in the community. Mulford Gardens, giving the appearance of a rural oasis adjacent to bustling city activity, had just been annexed to the City of San Leandro.

Ed's office reminded me of an old-fashioned country store. Mulford Gardenites dropped by daily to discuss happenings in the community and to just plain gossip. Ed, easy going and friendly, always made them feel welcome. Sometimes the locals did get in the way of conducting our routine business activities, but the trade off served us well. Now and then one of them listed their property with us—more so when I came on the scene.

Hungry for business, I considered every visitor a potential customer and treated them accordingly. Since I maintained a relaxed friendly manner, casual visitors never realized that I honed my selling skills every minute we spoke. I don't know how true it is that "practice makes perfect," but I knew I did a lot of business.

At the time of annexation, as I stated earlier herein, Ted Meecham made his living as an independent insurance agent operating his business from a rented desk in Ed's office. Ted also had served as president of the Mulford Gardens Homeowners Association. Based on that fact, the San Leandro City Council appointed Ted to serve as a City Councilman. He represented district six, newly formed to accommodate the addition of Mulford Gardens to the city. His appointment would last for around two years, at which time he would have to be elected in order to continue representing the district.

When I met Ted, I was twenty-five and he was forty-seven years old. It seemed that everyone liked him. He enjoyed his status as a well-established businessman and admired city leader. I was new on the scene and definitely not well established, but Ted treated me as he did everyone in those days, with respect and high regard.

I saw him as a valuable connection, but we were pals as well. Many well-connected business professionals in San Leandro supported him, mostly because of his power and influence on the bustling San Leandro political scene. He introduced me to the City of San Leandro political leaders and many local luminaries. I could never have met so many influential people under such favorable circumstances otherwise. Because of his influence, I did business with many of the people I'd met through Ted. Of course, I always cut him in for a share of the commission. In years to come, long after my association with Ted ended, I continued to derive benefits from my association with people to whom Ted had brought me into contact. When I met Ted, his star shone bright—sadly, in time it faded.

Ted's introduction of me to Judge Jerry Connett proved to be very fortuitous to me and a member of my immediate family. Judge Connett came across as likable and "down to earth" sort of a fellow as you'd ever want to meet. We became very friendly. Every now and then, Jerry would inquire of me something about the real estate market and I'd gladly provide him with the information he wanted. He expressed his appreciation to me for my prompt responses to his requests. What I did for Jerry amounted to very little, but he acted as if I had done something important for him.

I had known Jerry for several years when the police arrested my eighteen year old son, Danny, for possession of an illegal substance. The court sentenced him to serve five weekends at the Alameda County jail known as Santa Rita. He had to check in for his weekend incarceration at the jail no later than five each Friday afternoon. I drove him out to Santa Rita for his first session and waited in line with him to report into the facility.

After a few minutes, a guard gestured for me to come over to where he was standing. He asked me, "Is that your son you are waiting in line with? Do you know what's going to happen to him over this weekend?"

I answered that I had no idea what he meant. He said, "Mister, your boy is small with long blond hair and pretty. While he's in there he's going to be raped. If it were my kid, I'd get him the hell out of here, now."

I thanked the man and relayed to Danny what I'd been told. Danny was terrified and in minutes we headed back to San Leandro. Panicked, I first thought about sending my son back to Missouri to stay with some of my relatives. As soon as I got home, I called Judge Connett. I said, "Jerry, if you think that you owe me a favor, I'd sure like to collect today."

He asked which judge had sentenced Danny. I told him Judge Byrd. Jerry called me back in about twenty minutes. He told me to call Judge Byrd, and gave me his home telephone number.

Judge Byrd said he had spoken with Judge Connett and had come up with a solution. He told me that he had arranged for Danny to serve ten consecutive days in a private room at the Alameda County Hospital known as Fairmont Hospital. He could justify his decision because Jerry had informed him of Danny's diabetic condition. He requested that I let Danny know if he ever came before him again he would "throw the book" at him. I gave my son the message, and as far as I know his days of flirting with illegal drugs came to an end that day.

Two wide thoroughfares, Marina Boulevard and Fairway Drive—gave access through Mulford Gardens to the bay shoreline, and soon-to-be developed San Leandro Marina and Tony Lima Golf course complex, so named for the professional golfer hailing from San Leandro. Coincidentally, I met Tony Lima at a house party in Oakland back when we were teenagers. At that time, I was fifteen and Tony, a year older. He went to Saint Elizabeth High School, and I attended Castlemont High, both schools in Oakland. Tony and I weren't really close pals but we got along alright. Over a period of about a year, we hung out together on weekends with a group of mutual friends. We usually wound up at the weekly Saturday night dance at Spanish Hall in San Leandro.

During the time I hung out with Tony, he enjoyed a reputation as a promising amateur golfer. Neither I, nor our mutual friends back then, had any interest in golf, and Tony rarely talked about it with us. We saw it as a boring game played by elderly rich men. When our group got together our common interest involved trying to pick up girls at Spanish Hall and drinking beer. About a year after I met Tony, he joined the Marines and I never saw him again, except later on television. As a professional golfer he went on to win many prestigious tournaments and became famous before dying in a small-plane crash in 1966. Many years later, I took up golf, but I never excelled at the game. If I had been interested in golf when Tony and I were buddies, maybe he could have helped fix my slice.

CHAPTER FORTY-ONE

In 1961, my first full-time year in the real estate business, I worked hard, put in long hours, and loved it all. Placing people in homes constituted important work. During that year I earned almost four times my annual salary at Standard Register. To put my income into perspective; I sold property to a fellow employed as a senior mechanical engineer for Standard Oil. My 1961 earnings doubled the amount earned that year by my engineer customer. For a former high school drop out with three kids, I felt like a winner.

Sheila did a good job with the kids and I tried hard at being a good dad while scrambling to keep up with my ever-increasingly demanding business schedule. We continued to enjoy family barbecues on many Sundays, played table tennis in the garage and went to drive-in movies on weekends. We welcomed the added income but it sure took a lot of my time to keep the money flowing. On most Saturday nights, our close friends, Dave and Irene, and others dropped by for penny-a-point pinochle or canasta.

I continued to see my career as our road to success and real happiness. Things weren't perfect, but I believed a bright future awaited us. I tried to understand Sheila's discontent, and truly thought that in time I could make up for her difficult years, but the distance between us grew. I felt that surely she would eventually see things as I saw them. After all, I only had our best interests at heart. Strangely, even though I had been blessed with a talent for reading most people accurately, which I figured might be the reason I did so well at selling, she remained an enigma to me. It seemed I could communicate effectively with everyone with whom I came into contact, except my wife.

I'd been in business full-time for only six months when I received a visit from Don Milligan. I negotiated my first home sale to Don and his wife while still a part-time agent just eight months before. The Milligans wanted to sell their home. I only came into contact with Mrs. Milligan briefly for a few minutes over the entire escrow period, and I never got her first name firmly fixed in my memory.

Ironically, circumstances, such as divorce, illness, death, financial ruin and a plethora of other unhappy and catastrophic conditions that plague the human race would bring an abundance of lucrative business to my doorstep throughout my time in real estate. The Milligan property would be easy to sell. They had financed their purchase with an assumable thirty-year, low interest GI loan, which added value beyond the price that the Milligans had paid for the property.

I'd been showing homes to Janice and Bruce Marks for a few weeks. Sheila had attended high school with Janice. Janice, at twenty-six married Bruce in his mid-thirties. He had never been married until he had the honor of becoming Janice's third husband. He came across as a friendly, yet rather serious, mild-mannered and slightly over-weight fellow. He earned his living as a bookkeeper with Samuel Merritt Hospital in Oakland. Bruce had been captivated by the tall, good looking brunette who had two daughters. Physically and mentally, the couple didn't appear to be well matched, at least to me.

Soon after their wedding, they rented a house in San Leandro not far from where we lived. Janice introduced us to Bruce, and their family became incorporated into our social network of friends. They joined us on weekends for card parties, barbecues or table tennis on a regular basis. I liked Bruce and I felt sorry for him. Janice bullied and took unfair advantage of him. She openly flirted with other men, including me. Although I didn't think she would actually be unfaithful, clearly she wanted to intimidate him and erode his self-confidence, and she succeeded.

When Bruce and Janice married, she came into the union financially broke. Her only source of income consisted of modest child support payments from the fathers of her two daughters. Before Janice entered his world, Bruce prudently managed to build up a substantial bank savings account. She couldn't spend his nest-egg fast enough on furniture, clothing, vacations or whatever struck her fancy. He did his best to keep his wife from spending everything they had. She waged a constant campaign to persuade Bruce to spend all the savings and she never eased the pressure on him. He found himself engaged in a losing battle and my heart went out to him.

Janice actually had the temerity to posit that maintaining a savings account defined Bruce as miserly and palpably evil. He did his best to stand up to his ever-nagging wife, but gradually gave in, which gave him an occasional respite from the continual onslaught. I wondered if he ever thought he might have fared better by remaining a bachelor.

I showed the Milligan property to Janice, Bruce and the girls. They liked the house, and the low-interest assumable G.I. loan enticed Bruce. The Milligans listed the property for $16,950. I wrote an offer for $16,000, "as is." I didn't need to order a termite inspection, as a clearance had been issued when the Milligans bought a few months earlier. I presented the contract to the Milligans at the office. They arrived separately. The fellow who drove Mrs. Milligan there waited for her in his car.

When the Milligans learned they would be splitting the net proceeds of approximately $1,800, Don said he felt lucky to be getting any money at all. They signed the contract and left the office. I noticed that Mrs. Milligan and her companion walked over to Bill's Rendezvous. I suppose they wanted to celebrate. I considered for a moment that even though Sheila and I had our differences, we were nothing like the Milligans

The Marks family remained in the Mersey Avenue home for nearly eighteen months during which time Janice gave birth to another daughter. When Janice became pregnant again, they called me to let me know the family would soon outgrow the Mersey Avenue house. They wanted me to sell Mersey Avenue and locate a larger home for them.

Concurrent with listing the Mersey Avenue, I had a sale pending on my listing at 8800 Dowling Street in East Oakland, which my plumber Jake Edwards and his wife, Joan, owned. The Dowling Street neighborhood wasn't all that safe and the Edwards were anxious to get their two pre-teenage daughters into a better area.

By that time, 1964, Sheila and I owned five houses and were constantly involved in various fix-up projects. Jake did our plumbing work. He wasn't inexpensive, but he did efficient, high quality work for us. He gave us excellent advice, which we followed, and he got the job done quickly. Jake became an integral segment of my goal-oriented road to success.

I took the Edwards through a few houses in San Leandro, including the one on Mersey. The Mersey property fit their requirements. The GI assumable loan, which originally financed the Milligan purchase, remained an important selling point. Jake and Joan signed an offer to purchase Mersey for $19,500; one thousand dollars less than the listed price of $20,500. Bruce and Janice split the difference and I presented their $20,000 counter offer to the Edwards, which they found acceptable. So far, when that escrow closed, I would have sold the Mersey property three times in less than two years.

In the meantime, I'd located a lovely single story 1800 square foot home in the Peralta District of San Leandro, which excited

Janice and Bruce. The Peralta District, known to be a fine area located near good schools, was within walking distance of San Leandro's downtown shopping area. Similar to Estudillo Estates, although older, homes in the Peralta community reflected Spanish, Mediterranean and English Tudor architectural influences.

The Peralta home had been listed for $25,750 and after a few offers and counter offers between the Marks and the owners, the parties settled at $24,000. Not long after moving into their newly acquired home, Janice gave birth to a fourth daughter. Expenses, including the down payment to buy their new home, paying for the new baby and buying furniture—all contributed to Janice's goal to eliminate Bruce's savings,

Our two families continued to socialize for a while. Janice decided to go into business making designer clothing. Initially, she tried to develop a customer base consisting of friends and acquaintances. One Friday evening, Janice and Bruce, and the four girls happened to drop by our home as they often did. That particular evening Janice handed me a sports coat, saying she made it for me and named a price; a price double what I would normally spend for such a coat. Damn, I still owned only one pair of dress shoes.

I wondered at the nerve of Janice. *Does she think she can treat everyone as she treats her husband? Who in the hell asked her to make a jacket for me anyway?* I received no advance notice about her making a jacket for me. I didn't like the color—it didn't fit, and I wouldn't wear it if she gave it to me free. Even though I brought home good money, remodeling and maintaining our investment properties and supporting my family left little disposable income.

I politely let Janice know that I'd pass on the jacket and told her that I sure hoped she had someone else my size that might like to own it. Normally, if at all possible, I avoided "burning bridges" but I just couldn't let her get over on me. I knew that because they bought two houses through me I should have acquiesced.

Nevertheless, I watched our money with great care and wasn't about to waste it. Looking back on the "Janice/Jacket Incident," I realize that I might have fallen into the "no-escaping-the-prison-of-poverty-no-matter-how-wealthy-you-become" mentality. Yes … I know … I should have bought the damn thing.

After the sport coat debacle, I never saw the Marks family again. I would miss Bruce; I enjoyed his company. I wished he had shown a little backbone and stood up to Janice occasionally. A few years later, I read in the "San Leandro Morning News" obituary section that he had passed away. I considered that Bruce and Janice were a good example in which the decision maker in the family is often the one totally unqualified to make the decisions.

The Mersey Avenue property just kept on bringing in commissions. In 1965, Jake and Joan Edwards listed the home with me for $28,750. I handled the sale to Phil and Lois Lancaster, a childless couple in their early forties. I stayed in touch with the Lancasters and enjoyed visiting with them now and then. Phil underwent what was at that time a relatively rare open-heart surgery procedure. I grew faint when he described in detail how his medical team worked on his "out of his body" heart. Before the operation, Phil had been so weak he practically functioned as an invalid. After the operation, he experienced a remarkably successful recovery and regained the ability to enjoy a quality of life at a level he had been denied for several years. In 1967, the Lancasters listed Mersey with me for $36,500. I had the property in escrow within three weeks.

The Lancasters sold Mersey to facilitate the purchase of a beautiful new home in the Granada Hills subdivision in Livermore. In 1970, Phil called me. He wondered if I might be interested in buying the Livermore home. He and Lois were divorcing and they needed a quick sale. At the time, I had some severe family problems myself and wasn't up to dealing with property out in Livermore. I suggested they contact a broker I knew near their home that might be better positioned to help them. I rarely turned away business but during that particular time my world had "turned upside down." My emotional state left me little choice. I never heard from the Lancasters again. I hope things turned out well for them.

Returning to July 1961, I continued doing well as a licensed real estate salesman. Commissions came in regularly. But I still remember Dick Maciel's sagacious remark to me back when I went shopping for a sponsoring broker, "in order to find a nickel among the pennies a salesman would be well advised to buy property when possible." We owned our home on Juana and the rental house on Cary Drive. I managed to accumulate money in our savings account at Crocker Anglo Bank, but if I were to buy more property anytime soon, I needed to line up a source for a serious amount of cash.

While making a deposit one morning at Crocker Citizens Bank, I stopped at the manager's desk. I asked him about borrowing money from the bank for the purpose of investing in real estate. Rene Jope introduced himself. He looked to be around sixty and with his deep baritone voice, luxurious white, well-trimmed Van Dyke beard and mustache, he cut a dashing appearance. Graciously, he invited me to have a seat, which I did, whereupon I received some valuable advice. Rene knew that the availability of cash meant everything when it came to buying real estate bargains.

He advised me to borrow whatever amount available to me from any bank I could, whether or not I had an immediate use for the money. Then he said to pay the loan back before it fell due. Generally, such loans came due in ninety days. He went on to say that soon after I paid off the loan, I should repeat the process and try to increase the amount borrowed, and then to continue on in that manner, increasing the size of the loans each time. If I expected to build a substantial unsecured line of credit, Rene warned, I should never be late in paying off a loan.

I learned that banks in which I had no funds wouldn't be interested making loans to me. Rene suggested I open small accounts in several banks. He informed me after a few such transactions, bankers would be as anxious to lend to me, as I would be to borrow from them. Furthermore, as they became comfortable with me, they would encourage me to increase my loan amounts. Before I left Rene's desk, I decided to test the practicality of his theory and I signed a non-secured loan application and necessary loan documents. Sheila came to the bank four days later and placed her signature on the loan documents and $2500 went into our savings account; not a fortune perhaps, but a very promising beginning. Following Rene's guidance the time came when I could borrow $1,000,000 unsecured from Bank of America over the phone.

William Nickerson's book related basically the same information on building a line of credit that I received from Rene. Paraphrasing, Mr. Nickerson wrote that when the bank manager begins to address you by your first name, you know you're on the right track. The morning I received my first loan from Crocker Anglo Bank, Rene approached me and said, "Thanks Val, I'm looking forward to seeing a lot of you."

CHAPTER FORTY-TWO

Neptune Drive in Mulford Gardens seemed aptly named. North from Marina Boulevard to Williams Street, the shoreline thoroughfare was separated from the eastern border of the San Francisco Bay by twenty-one residential lots. All but one of the parcels measured sixty feet in width and 279 feet in depth. Each lot extended approximately 100 feet beyond the shoreline out into the tidelands. The remaining bayside residential parcel located where Williams Street terminated at Neptune Drive differed from the other twenty lots, in as much as it was ninety feet in width, instead of sixty feet wide. Later in my story, the ninety-foot wide lot (12903 Neptune Drive) will come into play, but for now, I will discuss another property on Neptune Drive, situated in the middle of the block.

When still in high school, friends and I sometimes drove through Mulford Gardens to the San Francisco Bay shoreline in San Leandro. Now and then, if we got lucky, girls accompanied us on our bayside visits. Even that far back, I envied the owners of homes on the west side of Neptune Drive. I wondered how anyone ever got so lucky as to live in a home in which a portion of your backyard extended into that gorgeous body of water.

Early one morning in 1961, while examining the latest MLS listings, I found that a shoreline property in the 13000 block of Neptune Drive had come on the market. It had been listed at $19,500. Even though the property included a three bedroom house, I thought the value of the lot alone exceeded the listed price. Rarely did bayside Neptune Drive property come up for sale. Usually ownership changed only through inheritance. I immediately drove to the property. The vacant house, a rather odd looking faux Swiss Chalet design, exuded a rustic charm.

I found no lock box containing a key—no way to legitimately enter the house. Actually, the absence of a key pleased me. I hoped that the listing agent's oversight might favor me by slowing down potential competing buyers. No one would buy a house until seeing it on the inside—except me. I walked to the back of the lot, watched the gulls skimming just above the surface of the sparkling whitecaps, and thrilled to the music of the pounding waves.

What a place to raise my kids. I didn't dare get my hopes up too high, but I promised to do my very best to acquire ownership of that absolutely unique piece of real estate. But I knew I had to move fast, because within days there would be a bidding war for that choice piece of real estate.

I called the listing agent, Bernice Patterson, at San Pablo Realty and told her of my interest in buying the property for my own account. I let her know I had already prepared the purchase agreement and wondered how soon she could set up a contract presentation appointment with the sellers. Bernice asked, "Don't you need to inspect the inside?" I told her that I had been satisfied just looking through the windows. Not wanting to appear overly anxious, I didn't tell her I'd be just as interested if no house existed on the parcel.

Bernice told me that the seller lived out of the area, deep in the Santa Cruz Mountains. She would call him and he would likely drive up to her office to look at my contract during the weekend. Bernice informed me of her extremely busy schedule and that she had no intention to take the time to drive down to, nor maneuver the narrow serpentine roads through the Santa Cruz Mountains to meet with the sellers at their home. Bernice let me know I had to wait until the weekend to meet with the sellers unless I wanted to make the trip without her.

Bernice's hint that I had her permission to present my contract to the seller without her gave me an opening. I acted as if I thought her sarcastic remark represented a serious commitment to let me go alone. To my distinct advantage, our telephone conversation led me to believe that she had no idea what a terrific property she had listed.

I learned from Bernice that the owner, Bill James, a remodeling contractor, had been working exclusively with her for several years. Just recently he and his family relocated from the Bay Area. Bernice confided in me that Mr. James' business hadn't done well in the past few years. He hoped a fresh start in a new location might bring a change of luck. Bernice didn't know me, yet she seemed comfortable to opine she believed the James were simply running away. She also said the sellers owed her money, and she had complete control of marketing the Neptune Drive property.

Although Bernice's candor helped me, I felt the James' interest had not been served well by their listing broker. Bernice clarified that she felt okay with me presenting the contract to her sellers at their home without her. She agreed to call me back when she had been able to arrange a presentation appointment. I received Bernice's call around four in the afternoon. Bill James couldn't meet me until eight that evening. I asked Bernice to let her client know I'd see him at eight. She related to me rather convoluted directions to the James' home that he'd given to her over the phone. I left for my appointment around five, thinking three hours sufficient to allow me to reach my destination on time. After an easy drive down to the Santa Cruz area, traversing the abstruse multitude of unlighted, winding, often unpaved roads to the James' residence gave me a headache.

At last, I reached my destination. Bill James, a balding, somewhat paunchy fellow about five-feet-ten-inches in height appearing to be in his mid-fifties, greeted me from his front porch. I arrived closer to nine than eight. The James' dwelling nestled among tall pines, reminding me more of a summer getaway cabin than a conventional house. Things were a mess. It looked as if they still had a lot of unpacking to do.

I met the rest of the family who appeared thin and haggard. They were congenial enough but from their demeanor I sensed resigned despair. I had left the office in a hurry and hadn't had dinner. Coffee at the table in their cluttered kitchen would have to do to sooth my empty stomach for the present.

Bill James knew the terms of my purchase agreement. Bernice had explained it over the phone and advised him and Mrs. James to sign, which they did with minimal discussion. After signing the purchase agreement, they let me call Bernice from their phone to inform her we were in contract. I wanted to eliminate potential competing buyers.

After the call to Bernice, Mr. and Mrs. James each opened a beer and offered one to me. I politely turned down their offer, explaining I needed a clear head to get back down off those mountains. They laughed at my concern and proceeded to tell me about themselves and the Neptune Drive property. I learned that they had moved the house onto the Neptune Drive lot from another location, where they had built and sold a new house, at a time when their financial future held more promise.

Originally, the James' excitement about the prospects of eventually living adjacent to the bay equaled my own. While busily engaged in conducting and expanding their home remodeling business, Bill spent weekends preparing the Neptune house for his family. Progress went slowly, but within a couple of years the house came close to being ready for them to move into. During that couple of years, however, their business fell into a steep decline and in an effort to expand their operation, they borrowed heavily. Lawsuits over mistakes made by hastily-hired employees and too many slow-paying customers brought them to the brink of insolvency. They hoped to stave off bankruptcy by selling the Neptune property.

I liked the James and regretted the misfortune they'd experienced. I visited with them until midnight. They needed a friendly ear, and I learned about mistakes that I might avoid in my own career. **We can avoid many hardships, if we learn from the experience of others.** I would never meet or speak to the James again and wished the best for them.

We had enough cash—$4000—to make the down payment and closing costs on Neptune. We financed the balance of $15,000 with a thirty-year amortized, seven percent interest loan from Golden West Savings and Loan Association.

In 1961, Golden West Savings and Loan, located in downtown Oakland at the corner of 17th and Harrison Streets, operated as a small, very friendly lender. Some years later the giant World Savings and Loan, not always so friendly, absorbed it. The Neptune Drive transaction may have been the first of many times I would utilize Golden West's services to facilitate purchases of real property for my own account.

Most of the conventional transactions in which I acted as the buyers' agent went through Golden West. Conventional financing involved loans which were not FHA or GI financed. The savings and loans were in hot competition to ingratiate themselves with productive agents. I soon found myself on a first-name basis with the management of Golden West. Their personal representative, Chad Scott, dropped by the office weekly and occasionally invited me to lunch. John Morgan, manager of the Oakland branch, and a prince of a guy, referred to me as their "fair-haired boy." My many years of association with Golden West greatly benefited me. I received preferential treatment until they were taken over by World and when John Morgan retired. After that, in order to get financing from World, I had to deal exclusively with Chad Scott. I experienced a surprising change in my relationship with him.

CHAPTER FORTY-THREE

It was September, 1961, and overall, the gradual accumulation of rental houses loomed heavily in my financial plans. I needed to sell Juana Avenue in order to continue to strengthen my cash position. I called Mr. Santos, the holder of our second loan on

Juana Avenue. I asked him if he might be interested in accepting an immediate $1300 cash payoff to settle our account which had an unpaid balance of around $2100. He responded positively to my offer. He reasoned that he might not be around long enough to collect the full amount owing under the terms of our note.

A discount of $800 didn't represent a fortune, but every little bit helped deliver us toward eventual financial independence. I accomplished the payoff immediately and never mentioned that I intended to sell Juana. If Mr. Santos knew we were going to sell, he needed only to wait and he would receive full payment of the principal sum owing on his promissory note from the escrow when the sale closed.

I always proceeded in that direction, even though in time I could easily pay all cash. Whenever a seller carried back all or any portion of the purchase financing, there existed the opportunity of negotiating a future discount. Such thinking became an integral part of achieving financial independence; my constant goal. As Mr. Santos did, sellers often tired of receiving modest monthly loan installment payments and were happy to settle for an all cash, albeit, discounted payoff amount. Of course, it didn't always work that way, but it did often enough.

I discovered a gold mine of a source for purchasing discounted indebtedness. Private lenders that were in the process of foreclosing on property which secured their loans quite often will assign their interest in a secured loan at a substantial discount. The following is an example of such a transaction. An offer for me to buy the beneficial interest in a secured loan in foreclosure, for half of the outstanding balance owing on the loan, came to me. Three weeks remained until the foreclosure sale date. A little due diligence on my part confirmed that the loan had abundant equity security. If I paid $6,000 for the note, I could expect to receive $12,000 in about three weeks. I accepted the offer and indeed, garnered a 100 percent profit a week after making the deal as the borrower paid off my newly acquired loan in full immediately after I called him to introduce myself.

Surprisingly, the lender, an affluent, active attorney simply wanted to avoid his perceived unpleasantness related to a foreclosure trustee's sale. Actually, the portion of the transaction dealing with the borrower had been simple. He apologized for my inconvenience and immediately after I called him, he dropped off a check at the office of the foreclosing trustee. The attorney who sold his loan to me could have avoided his $6000 loss had he made a friendly call to the borrower as I did. He happened to be a wealthy, but tired man and just took the less troublesome way out. The time came when I met many like him.

We listed our home on Juana Avenue for $17,250. It showed well and we received a full price offer in about two weeks. We had to be out of Juana no later than the close of escrow, but we couldn't move into Neptune Drive yet. It wasn't quite habitable, and Sheila would soon be delivering our fourth child. Her parents invited us to stay with them and their two teen-aged sons until I had Neptune Drive ready for occupancy. Sheila gave birth to our son, Paulie, October 26, 1961, and we moved into Ray and Pat's beautiful home on Louette Court in San Lorenzo.

CHAPTER FORTY-FOUR

Sheila's parents had previously sold their turn-of-the-century Victorian home on San Antonio Avenue in Alameda and moved into an apartment. I had just begun working part-time for Ed Marvin when Ray and Pat listed their home with Justin Realty, a well-established firm in Alameda. I admit that I might have been mildly offended that my wife's parents hadn't given me the listing.

Ed Marvin flatly stated that by not giving me the listing, Sheila's parents had demonstrated an act of family disloyalty. But I understood; Ray had worked his heart out for years to renovate the San Antonio house. They had purchased the property through Justin Realty and felt confident the company would do a good job in marketing their property.

The San Antonio Avenue property had cost Ray and Pat $4000 in 1949. They bought the house in a sad state of repair. It had stood vacant for decades. As finances permitted, Ray worked through every stage of the remodeling process himself and increased the value of the property dramatically.

When they decided to sell, they didn't really know if I could serve them well. They had all their financial eggs, so to speak, invested in the property and they weren't about to take a chance on their green, "wet-behind-the-ears" son-in-law, who had just started in the real estate business and probably didn't know what the hell he was doing. I didn't blame them, and in time I would earn their complete trust and loyalty regarding buying and selling residences, beginning with the house on Louetie Court.

Nearly everyone I dealt with turned a fat profit when they sold, except Ray and Pat. Although I helped them sell quite a few homes over the years, they very seldom realized a substantial profit. Other than the San Antonio Avenue property, they typically bought, and within a short period grew dissatisfied and decided to relocate.

I found excellent deals for them, but they were impetuous, and always sold too soon after buying. Staying in each home a little longer would undoubtedly have produced substantial returns. They did make money, but not nearly as much as they could have if they had exercised more patience. Profit just didn't matter as much to them as it did to me.

I think a void existed in Ray's life. Nothing—moving from house to house, buying boats or motor homes or whatever—seemed to fill that empty space. I believe he searched for whatever eluded him until his death in 2009. The day before Ray died, Steven called me from Ray's hospital room and put him on the phone with me. For a few minutes we spoke and even laughed. I had no idea of the severity of his illness and I joked, "Ray, you know none of us will get out of this alive."

The next day I truly regretted my thoughtless remark. In any event, I felt fortunate to be able to say goodbye to Ray.

CHAPTER FORTY-FIVE

On October 20, 1961, my family, including our brand new son, took up temporary residence with the Drake family. They seemed sincerely happy that we were there. Of course, I loved all my children equally, but each of them touched my heart in a different fashion. Danny, my firstborn, handicapped with sugar diabetes brought about an extreme heightening of my protective nature. Whenever he was out of my sight for any length of time, I worried. As it turned out, my concerns were well founded.

I never worried about Steven. Clearly, he could take care of himself. He came across as strong, very athletic and charismatic. Self-confident, well-liked and popular, he made friends easily. Sometimes, with a kid like him, a parent takes it for granted that they will always be okay. My mistake; as a child, he needed much more from me than I gave him.

I recalled a pleasant Sunday morning in 1957, I was holding Valerie, maybe a month old, in my arms while sitting in the driver's seat of our 1956 Bel Air hardtop convertible. As soon as Sheila and the boys joined us in the car, we would be heading to mass at St. Joseph church. While making funny noises designed to keep her smiling, I looked into those gorgeous blue eyes and fell in love with my baby daughter. I adored her and made a silent promise that I would be the sort of father she deserved. She has always been one of the sweetest, kindest people you could ever hope to meet. I think it didn't happen by accident that she became a registered nurse.

My kids were all very different from each other, which is true I suppose in most households, but perhaps more so in my family. Paulie came into our lives at a time when financial difficulties didn't accompany his arrival, as they did with the others. He brought us pure joy. We gave him all our love and he developed beautifully in response to our affection. Sheila remained unhappy with me much of the time. It seemed we just couldn't communicate with each other effectively, but Paulie's presence seemed to make her life better.

I enjoyed staying with Ray and Pat and Sheila's brothers at Louette Court, and appreciated their hospitality, but we needed to live in our own home. We did a fast job getting the Neptune house ready to occupy, and we moved into our waterfront home in time to host Thanksgiving dinner for relatives and others. Entertaining seemed to be among the things that Sheila most enjoyed. In addition to our parents, Aunt Pauline and Uncle Gene, my Uncle Hobert and his wife, June, plus many folks who had no families with whom to celebrate the holidays, joined us that Thanksgiving day. Many of our guests were individuals we met though our real estate activities. Some worked on our properties, others were customers and a few fit both categories. Our guests obviously enjoyed coming into our home and we were happy to show them a good time.

The demands of the business continued to strain my marriage. I didn't blame Sheila for being moody and cross with me. Our marriage started on a weak foundation and I believe she felt the quality of her life with me came up short. I had goals and she had regrets. I found hope and relief through my real estate activities, and she struggled managing our home and taking care of our kids alone, too much of the time, in her opinion. Maybe someone smarter than me could have forecast severe domestic difficulty ahead, but I wouldn't have believed them—not back then, when I thought I could fix anything.

After we moved into our new home by the bay, things between my wife and I seemed to improve for a while. The house needed a tremendous amount of work, and we were financially able to make substantial improvements. Sheila seemed genuinely enthused about supervising the many upgrades to our home. As my business flourished, it continued to demand more and more of my time. Sheila divided her time between getting the house fixed up and caring for the needs of our children. For a while, she appeared happier which made me happy.

I silently cringed at the planning and execution of a few of her renovation undertakings. She sometimes decided a completed upgrade didn't turn out quite right and proceeded to have it done over. I didn't complain—when she directed her attention toward fixing up the house, it wasn't fixed on the shortcomings of her husband. Additionally, overall she had a great eye for fixing up houses.

CHAPTER FORTY-SIX

Close to the time my family and I took possession of Neptune Drive in 1961, my Uncle Hobert and his wife, June, arrived in San Leandro after a rather circuitous route from Missouri. Hobert, two years younger than my father, lived a rather stable responsible life until my father's death. After Dad died, Hobert's life began to change.

Like all the Barry clan, Hobert had a witty, delightful sense of humor. He and his beautiful first wife, Steva couldn't have children. Steva suffered most of her life with Type I Diabetes. I believe her illness accounted for the fact that they had no children. The childless portion of the union brought them sadness. They were sweet and loving and would have been wonderful parents.

Hobert loved kids. He showered his nieces and nephews, including Sherie and me when we were children in Missouri, with sincere, devoted affectionate attention. We loved all our uncles, but Hobert stood as our favorite by far. I suppose he tried to fill the childless vacuum in his life by drawing Sherie and me and our cousins into his world.

As a youngster I often visited with him and Steva on their serene dairy farm, nestled within a lush half-mile wide valley, bordered by steep hills covered with trees growing around beautiful limestone outcroppings. My uncle's farm, situated in the luxuriant rural topography of the glorious Ozark Mountains, represented a paradise to an eleven-year-old boy. I spent as much time with my Uncle Hobert as I could.

Back then, Hobert instructed me on horsemanship and taught me the delicate skill of adjusting the sights of my single shot, bolt action Winchester twenty-two caliber rifle. Never can I forget that snowy Christmas Eve Missouri morning, with Hobert and me lying on a horizontal tree trunk that extended out over a quiet tributary flowing eight feet below, near the coupling of the James and Finley Rivers, fishing. He had brought a multi-barbed, baitless hook which he attached to a weighted line. From our perch on the tree, he lowered it into the frigid shallow water into a clearly visible school of plump catfish.

Apparently, the extreme cold water caused the fish to be sluggish, and they didn't notice the quiet introduction of our hook into their midst. One by one, we snagged a dozen or so of those aquatic beauties. We returned to the farmhouse, cleaned our catch and recounted the morning's excitement as Aunt Steva fried up the seasoned filets in fresh, home-churned butter. I can't remember enjoying a more delicious breakfast. In a perfect world, every kid has an Uncle Hobert.

Hobert saw my dad as a hero and to him, Don could do no wrong. I never really nailed it down, but after Dad died, Hobert seemed to begin to emulate his deceased brother's lifestyle. He bought a lot in the small town of Nixa and built a house, into which he and Steva moved and soon after sold the farm. He had learned to be a good carpenter as owners of small farms invariably do.

He began earning his living working for residential builders, and soon began building individual homes for people. As he earned a reputation as a highly skilled house builder, he found himself in constant demand, and the money poured in. The story is as old as time; some people just don't handle success well. As he prospered, he started drinking. Not heavily at first—I think he reasoned that lots of folks can drink and still lead functional lives.

That may be true in many cases, but it didn't apply to the Barry brothers.

The population of Springfield, a major city in the southwestern part of Missouri grew.   Expanding industry brought new jobs, and the beauty of the Ozarks brought retirees; both of which increased the demand for new homes. Hobert bought a small tract of land near Nixa and subdivided it into twelve residential lots. By the time he began building homes in his small subdivision, drinking had become a problem. Boozing and chasing women monopolized his time.   Because of his dissolute lifestyle, the admiration and respect he had enjoyed into his late forties had evaporated.

I learned that his marriage of around thirty years ended in divorce in 1959. He lost whatever money he had accumulated and went on a drunken binge that lasted nearly six weeks. Dissipated and out of his mind, he was incarcerated within the confines of a state psychiatric facility in Springfield sometime in the early sixties.

While drying out and striving toward regaining his ability to function, at least sufficiently to survive outside of a mental institution, he began a romantic association with June, his nurse. I don't know what attracted her to Hobert, but I do know she fell completely in love with him. Shortly after his release, Hobert and June married.

He had damaged his reputation to the extent that he needed to leave the area, so the couple headed out west by automobile. Along the way, they stopped now and then to work and replenish their finances. They both found work wherever they stopped; June, as a temporary nurse and Hobert as a carpenter or handyman.

June called me from Ukiah, California and asked if I'd like to see her and my Uncle Hobert. They were on their way to the Bay

Area to visit her two sons who were both in the United States Navy and stationed near us at the Alameda Naval Air Station. Of course, I wanted to see my Uncle Hobert. I knew from my Missouri cousins that he had fallen upon hard times, but I hadn't witnessed his decline in person and decided to withhold judgment until after I knew more about his situation. After all, they were only coming by for a visit.

Seeing my uncle revived happy memories. I remembered how kindly he treated Sherie and me when we were children. I recalled how he patiently taught my sister to drive about the time she turned thirteen. The first night of his visit we talked for hours. I just couldn't get enough of him.

We continually had work in progress on the Neptune house. Living in a house being remodeled presented an inconvenient, yet tolerable mess and nothing new to us. The kitchen floor sloped more than an inch over its twenty foot length, and the soft pine kitchen cabinets, though serviceable, showed their decades of use.

June, very outspoken, came right to the point. "Val, Hob (short for Hobert) is an expert cabinet maker and I know he can make short work at leveling that floor. If you want to advance us enough money to pay a month's rent for an apartment and furnish the materials, he can start tomorrow." *What a deal!* Advancing money though, before the completion of a job, violated one of my firm business rules. I broke my rule; after all, we were talking about my Uncle Hobert.

Hobert performed beautifully. He and June rented a comfortable apartment in a duplex up on Broadmoor, a very nice quiet older community in San Leandro, and he soon found steady work through the carpenters union. His first union job involved helping to construct the Blue Dolphin Restaurant, the first structure built on the new San Leandro Marina Complex, being developed a block from our home. My children grew to love Hobert, just as Sherie and I had when we were kids. He had that same lovable way about him. After building our new cabinets and leveling the kitchen floor, Hobert continued working on the Neptune house on his days off from his union job. Sheila's propensity to re-remodel until she got it just right provided ample work for him.

CHAPTER FORTY-SEVEN

While working in Ed's office, I became aware of a large tract of vacant land generally referred to as the "Charlton Ranch" so designated because of Ben Charlton, a retired new-car dealership proprietor. Contiguous on its western border with the eastern shore of the San Francisco Bay, the roughly 1500 acre marshy parcel's only use was that of a private duck hunting club.

As the population grew, the Charlton ranch was annexed to the City of San Leandro. The usefulness of the ranch as a duck-hunting club diminished. Ed Marvin told me that Ted Meecham, who held a seldom-used real estate salesman's license under Ed, had been approached by Darrell Harmon of the Harmon Construction Company. The Harmons directed their family owned massive home building operation from their main office in Hayward.

Jacob and Grant Harmon had founded their successful and long-established company in Philadelphia in the early 1930s. The brothers had emigrated as young adults from Scotland. Though penniless when they started building homes, they soon experienced spectacular success. When they moved their operations to California, they began developing large residential subdivisions along with major-tenant occupied shopping centers to serve the buyers of their homes. The brothers' wealth probably exceeded their wildest dreams. About the time I met them, they had turned control of their successful enterprise over to Jacob's son, Darrell.

What follows regarding the Harmons and Ted Meecham, relative to Ted acting in the capacity of a real estate agent representing the Harmons and Ben Charlton, in connection to the purchase of the Charlton property by the Harmons, I heard from Ed Marvin. I have no personal first-hand knowledge of Ted's involvement between the Harmons and Ben Charlton.

Ed told me that before the deal closed, Ted fired Ed as his sponsoring broker. Ed thought he did so because Ted didn't want to share the sizable commission he expected to receive from the transaction. The seller and buyers entered into a purchase agreement subject to approval of a rezoning application requesting a designation of a combination of uses, to include single-family homes, apartments, and light industrial and commercial development.

According to Ed, since Ted was a member of the San Leandro City Council, as well as the real estate agent representing a deal involving a rezoning request, a possible conflict of interest arose. It's possible that Ted disclosed his potential financial interest and abstained from voting, and in any event, the rezoning was approved. Escrow closed, the Harmons subdivided the property, and were soon building homes in their subdivision known as Bayside Village.

Even though Ed was no longer Ted's sponsoring broker, Ted used his influence with the Harmons to set up an arrangement between the sales staff at Bayside Village and Ed Marvin Realty. Many San Leandro home owners were interested in buying a new home in Bayside Village but first had to sell their present home. In those cases, Ed and I met with the homeowners and prepared a market appraisal of their property.

When the sellers listed their property with us, we put the listing on the MLS and offered them a guaranty, stating that if their home didn't sell, we would buy it from them at a predetermined price. To demonstrate our good faith and to help the seller, we put up a deposit on their behalf to bind the purchase of their new home at Bayside Village. When the Bayside Village buyer's property that we had listed sold, the deposit came back to us.

Ted had set up a good deal which smoothed out any problems between him and Ed. The Harmons were happy because our guaranty to purchase their buyers' current home ensured that the Bayside Village transaction would close successfully. When we negotiated the sale of the homeowners' previous house, we earned a commission. Although we had to be prepared to do so, I don't recall ever having to exercise our property purchase guaranty.

Additionally, the many homeowners I dealt with relative to the Bayside Village transactions broadened my future client referral base. Bayside Village worked out well financially for all who bought there. So sold on the idea that the homes would increase in value rapidly, I purchased a four-bedroom beauty at 13602 Burton Drive, strictly on speculation.

I suppose our Bayside Village arrangement, in the view of some, worked a little too well. One Sunday morning while I mowed my Neptune Drive lawn, Bert Pennemaker and his family pulled up in front of my home in their new black Cadillac limousine. I didn't even realize Bert knew where I lived. The family looked as if they were on their way to synagogue, but then Bert always looked that way.

Bert headed up the Bayside Village sales staff. He was around forty-five, favorably impressive in appearance and speech, and came across as "satin smooth." He walked over to me, beyond the hearing of his wife and two small sons in the limousine. After a few pleasant minutes during which he complimented me on how well I interacted with their Bayside Village home buyers, he moved toward the point of his visit.

He said, "Val, I've waited to mention this until I knew how you would handle the home purchase guaranty program. I've sold out a lot of large residential subdivisions in my time, and I've never seen anyone manage the buyer's existing home guaranty sales program as well as you have. You're making a lot of money and you deserve every penny."

I appreciated Bert's remarks, and honestly, I agreed. I followed up on every one of his staff's referrals without delay. Additionally, I had set up lines of credit with two local banks to cover me if I needed to move quickly to purchase a Bayside Village homebuyer's property.

Bert edged ever closer to the reason for his visit. He said, "Since you're doing so well, some of the fellows and I have talked it over and feel you might want to kick back some of your profit. After all, your referrals are coming from us. We are already working with a couple of other brokers who are contributing."

I knew about the other brokers. As far as efficient results, which were necessary to accrue the highest benefits to the Bayside Village sales crew, those brokers weren't in my world. In my opinion, the Bayside Village sales staff fared extremely well because of my efforts. Ed and I worked hard to make the endeavor successful for everyone involved. The money didn't just "drop into our laps"—it required tremendous effort to efficiently administer the program. It happened to be a numbers game which, in order to succeed, required that Ed and I meet with many people. A significant percentage of the referrals with whom we met didn't result in profit for us and time spent on the Bayside Village referrals reduced our time spent pursuing other business.

I didn't appreciate Bert looking to me for kickbacks. We did a very good job and Bert's bosses knew of our value to their operation. I'd never say anything to the Harmons regarding Bert's move to chisel me, but he knew if I did, he'd be in trouble. As congenially as I could, I told Bert "Thanks, but no thanks." I called Ed and told him about Bert's visit. Though not sure I'd made the right decision, Ed agreed to follow my lead. He knew we would make good money with or without the Bayside Village business.

For the next month or so, no referrals came our way from Bayside Village. Ted Meecham called me and said Darrel Harmon had asked him why he hadn't seen me around the Bayside Village sales office for the past few weeks. He had received complaints that Bert Pennemaker's other referral brokers were not following up on all the leads given them. I didn't tell Ted about my meeting with Bert in my front yard, but I think he surmised what had occurred. Soon after Ted's call to me, the Bayside Village referrals resumed.

Whenever I had occasion to meet with Bert Pennemaker, he seemed cool toward me. He likely thought that I had contacted the Harmons about his failed attempt to extract unearned compensation from me. No matter though; Bayside Village had just about sold out anyway. But one of the best side-benefits of the Bayside Village experience, of course, turned out to be the large potential future customer base I'd developed.

After the Bayside Village tract had sold out, Ed mentioned to me that Ted had confided to him that his efforts to avoid sharing with Ed a commission disbursement from the Harmon/Charlton land transaction backfired. Ed said that Ted told him that Darrell Harmon promised him that indeed Ted would receive a commercial parcel at the corner of Spalding and Satterfield Drive after the deal closed as compensation for Ted's efforts to bring the transaction to fruition. According to Ed, Ted told him he took Darrell at his word, and their verbal agreement had not been reduced to a written contract.

Ed said Ted told him the following: After the escrow closed, Ted approached Darrell about taking title to the promised parcel and Darrell told him because Ted didn't have a sponsoring broker, Darrell would be breaking the law by paying him a commission. To soften the disappointment, Darrell offered Ted a salaried job working with the new homeowners, helping with their option choices relative flooring, countertops and window coverings, etc. Ted accepted the job offer but didn't last very long, as it required more effort than he wanted to invest and it interfered with his insurance business.

According to Ed, he reminded Ted that if he had remained licensed under Ed, he might have been able to negotiate a binding commission agreement which could have set him up for life. What Ed related to me about what Ted told him and Ted's failure to be re-elected City Councilman probably accounted for the changes I observed in Ted's demeanor. He seemed to me to become bitter and unmotivated. He spent a lot of time alone in Jake Souza's bar. Ted stopped by my office to let me know he had decided to relocate to Southern California to try to start over. I heard he died just a few years later.

CHAPTER FORTY-EIGHT

Early in 1962, my business boomed. Dan Nolan and I occasionally worked as partners. We got on well together and his assistance gave some relief from my crowded schedule, though not enough. In his mid-seventies and suffering with kidney problems, Dan couldn't spend more than a few hours a day in the office. When we took a listing together, he always volunteered to hold our listing open on Sunday afternoons, relieving me of that responsibility. I considered Dan my good friend and valued mentor.

Dan enjoyed a financially comfortable retirement. Making a lot of money didn't really motivate him to keep working. He just didn't want to sit home watching daytime television. Working in the real estate business helped him still feel vital. When they were young, Dan and his wife formulated a recipe for a soft drink at their kitchen table in their little Brooklyn apartment. For most of Dan's working life, he manufactured and marketed their product.

When Dan's failing health led him to sell his business and retire, he and his wife moved to San Leandro to be near children and grandchildren. He had spent years dealing with the stress of providing for and properly raising his six children, just as I did. Although we were of different generations, the similarities of our challenges drew us toward each other.

By mid-1962, I originated around ninety percent of the sales through our office. Ed had never experienced such a high volume of business. Rather than hire a secretary to handle the many follow-up tasks required to close my sales, he decided to stop selling and concentrate on doing the office escrow work himself. The follow-up procedure in the office related to a signed sales contract, consisted of opening an escrow with a title company, locating financing, ordering various inspections and performing the myriad duties related to the overall process.

Subtle differences began to surface between Ed and me. Selling or listing property—the process of obtaining the buyers' and sellers' signatures on the bottom line—represented what made the business work. I excelled at that part of the job. The follow-up tasks were perfunctory, requiring no creativity. I experienced mixed emotions. *Without Ed, where would I be?* But damn . . . he didn't hold up his end. He reminded me of an automobile perpetually running in low gear.

His distracted way of doing business had inadvertently gotten me into some bad situations. In one instance, I negotiated the sale of a property for a couple living in Argentina. They acquired ownership by way of inheritance. I met them at the subject property and took the listing after which they returned to Argentina.

I found a buyer and mailed the purchase agreement to the sellers. They quickly signed the contract and immediately sent it back to me. From that point, Ed took over. Two months after the sale had completed I was in the office alone when the irate seller showed up demanding to know why he hadn't received his money. I explained that I thought his proceeds had been mailed to him. He insisted that had not happened. I called the escrow company, Western Title, and learned that they had mailed the check to us when the escrow closed.

I asked the furious seller to give me time to do some checking and to please return to the office later. When Ed came back, I explained the situation. He followed a routine of tossing unimportant appearing correspondence unopened into a cardboard box in the back room and sorting through it at the end of each month. Evidently he overlooked examining the contents of the box the previous month. He went through all the envelopes, and sure enough, he found the envelope from Western Title containing the seller's check.

When the seller returned, I handed him his check. Ed stayed in the back room, leaving me to explain. Embarrassed as hell, I told the seller exactly what happened. He didn't say a word; he just walked out of the office, disgusted. I felt like a jerk.

Out of self-preservation, I began to do my own in-office escrow work. Ed only got involved in my transactions when little chance existed of him doing any harm. At that point, my workload really became burdensome. The real estate business didn't seem to be quite as much fun as it used to be.

Sometime in 1962, Ed complained to me that since he made very few sales and paid all the office expenses: telephone, advertising, utilities, etc., our fifty-fifty commission split provided him less income than I received. He reasoned that we needed to adjust the commission percentages to compensate for the disparity in our incomes.

I had not forgotten how much my association with Ed had benefited me. Surely, I couldn't disregard the fact that he allowed me full access to his customer base. Whenever I suggested changes that might make the operation function better, he usually agreed. I remembered how he patiently nurtured me as I tried to acquaint myself with the basics of our business. He gave me consideration that likely would not have been available elsewhere.

Calmly and respectfully, I responded to his discontent, telling him I appreciated all he had done for me. I mentioned I knew other brokers paid their top producing agents commission splits as high as ninety percent. Of course, with me producing most of the sales, altering the commission split substantially in my favor wouldn't be fair. I pointed out he had told me himself since I came to work for him, his income far exceeded what it had been in the past. In addition, the fact that he did little work on my deals and he no longer had to make sales himself, I thought he did pretty well. I could see by his expression Ed didn't want the debate to go further.

Even though he chose not to expend the effort needed to create sales on his own, the very active office ranked as his favorite place in the world. He genuinely enjoyed going along with me on listing appointments or sales presentations but avoided the hard, "nitty-gritty" effort of making sales from scratch. He didn't want to do much work but he loved to be part of the action.

As I've indicated throughout herein, the real estate business offered me the opportunity to reach my goal of financial independence. Even though I loved my job, in my heart, it definitely came in second to spending time with my family. A few days after Ed expressed his dissatisfaction that his net income didn't equal mine, I re-opened the subject. I asked, "Ed, what would you think about bringing in another salesman?" I explained my overloaded work schedule prevented me from taking full advantage of all the potential business available to us.

Clearly, Ed needed another salesman. Commissions generated by increasing the sales force surely would elevate Ed's income sufficiently to surpass my earnings. I hoped increasing the sales staff might put an end to his discomforting sulking due to the disparity in our income. Adding a salesman might resolve another problem. The fact that Ed's income almost entirely depended on me made him feel insecure. He tried to keep unreasonable track of my daily activity. Ed assured me that he would go right to work to hire a new salesperson.

Days off from the office were precious to me. Ed's continuous unnecessary calls to my home diminished the quality of time spent with my family. His calls, in addition to those received from customers at all times of the day or night, exacerbated the already strained relationship between Sheila and me.

CHAPTER FORTY-NINE

My reasoning in suggesting Ed recruit a new salesperson led me to the following conclusion: he might be motivated to nurture the newcomer along, as he did me when I first came to work for him. Logic dictated the time Ed might spend monitoring a new agent could decrease his ability and need to concentrate on me. Soon, Ed happily informed me that he had signed up a very promising addition to our sales staff.

The following Monday morning, Ed's new salesman, Ralph Douglas, reported for work. Ed enthusiastically introduced Ralph to Dan and me. Ralph exuded total and likable self-confidence and made a favorable impression on me. A large, well-dressed, fit appearing man around forty with his deep, commanding, yet friendly voice, emitted an aura of success.

After the initial introductions, Ed began to familiarize Ralph with the routine operation of the office. Ed directed his total attention toward his new protégé. About mid-morning, Ed received a call from his wife. He had to leave to attend to a matter at his home. I took the opportunity to get better acquainted with Ralph and invited him to join me for a Danish and coffee at Ronaker's Eatery across the street. We enjoyed a pleasant and informative morning break.

Ralph told me that he and his wife and two teenage daughters relocated from Los Angeles to the Bay Area about a year earlier. Before moving, he worked as a licensed real estate agent selling "recreational" subdivision lots in the Mojave Desert. Many considered such agents to be in the same league as used car or residential aluminum siding salesmen.

Selling real estate in southern California provided Ralph sufficient income to put food on the table, pay the rent and meet the expenses necessary to support his family. But his second and most revered vocation involved preaching the gospel to a small Christian fundamentalist evangelical group in Los Angeles. He would have loved to minister to his flock full time but because of the minuscule size of the congregation, the Sunday morning collections didn't provide enough income to support his family.

A year or so before the Douglases left Los Angeles, a few of Ralph's most devout followers had been transferred by their mutual employer to work at the company's Alameda facility. Ralph maintained close contact with them. When negative publicity began to circulate regarding the money-losing proposition of investing in desert land, Ralph had to find a new way to earn a living. His friends in Alameda encouraged him to make a new start in the Bay Area. The Douglas family left the smog of Los Angeles and headed north. With the help of his former congregational members, Ralph moved into a large older home on Lincoln Avenue.

He conducted regular religious services in his rented home, and his initially small congregation gradually grew. He still needed to earn money from outside sources in order to provide for his family. Even so, Ralph believed his following would rapidly increase to the point he might soon be preaching from a conventional church building with his sole vocation being limited to that of an evangelistic preacher.

Ralph and Dan got off to a bad start which never improved. Dan, a devout Catholic, had lived his seven-plus decades adhering to the canons of his church. Ralph spoke his mind without reservation. One day he stated that the Pope should not be elevated above the status of a regular person. Ralph posited that accepting treatment as a deity represented a serious sin which the Pope had to account for in the hereafter.

Dan, offended, angrily told Ralph what he thought of him and his "holy roller" hillbilly religion. Dan's outburst didn't faze Ralph. He seemed self-assured, to the extent that nothing Dan or anyone could say would penetrate his shield of confidence. Dan left the office whenever Ralph came in, though he didn't need to avoid Ralph very often because Ralph usually could be found out knocking on doors—cold calling in the pursuit of listings.

Door to door canvassing didn't bother Ralph, but it repulsed me. I just didn't have the nerve to knock on strangers' doors dozens of times each day. Ralph worked tirelessly in that fashion over the next three months, and I admired him for it. He must have talked with hundreds of property owners, but his efforts went unrewarded, at least to Ralph. He became discouraged and resigned. I never saw him again, but I hoped his dreams would somehow eventually come true.

CHAPTER FIFTY

After Ralph moved on, some of the people he had met knocking on doors called our office. I figured if he had held out a while longer, he would have been able to develop a steady income stream. He had the right idea; he just didn't have enough patience. I took a call from Mr. Vernon Reynolds late one afternoon. Ralph had knocked on his door around seven in the evening about two months previously. Mr. Reynolds informed me he needed to sell his home on Cedar Avenue located in the Bonaire subdivision in San Leandro.

I met with the Reynolds family that evening. The family consisted of Vernon and Peggy and their four children; three girls and a boy. The children included two teenagers; a boy fourteen and a girl thirteen, plus a seven-year-old daughter named Leslie and a one-year-old toddler. The only name of the kids I can recall is Leslie.

Leslie made a lasting impression. The others looked as if they had slept in the same clothes for a week, or perhaps recently arrived in a trailer from Appalachia. Leslie appeared as if she could have been a child fashion model. Her siblings acted as if they might be afflicted with Attention Deficit Disorder. Leslie, looking a lot like Natalie Wood as a child star, seemed fascinated by her parents' conversation with me. She impressed me as utterly charming.

Vernon, in his forties, looked seventy and very small. I figured he couldn't have weighed more than a hundred pounds. I guessed life hadn't dealt him many winning hands. Peggy looked disheveled and haggard. She had to weigh in at close to five hundred pounds. They presented a clear picture of a couple in trouble.

Peggy, Vernon, and Leslie seemed comfortable with me. The other three kids were engaged in devouring something garlicky and greasy at the cluttered dining room table, seemingly unaware of my presence in their home. A strange family, yet I found them fascinating. Vernon held a well-paying job working as a pharmacist in San Francisco. Peggy didn't work outside the home, or inside apparently, by the looks of things. Her excess weight would have precluded her working at a regular job. While conversing with Vernon and Peggy I found they were the recipients of college educations. I concluded something had gone very wrong for the Reynolds family.

Now, looking back over decades of dealing with dozens of residential properties in deplorable condition, many unfit for human habitation, perhaps I ran across one other property as filthy as the Cedar Avenue house. As I walked across the nasty blackened oak hardwood floors, they were uniformly sticky, resulting from a thick layer of grease. The bathroom linoleum floors were the same. An even thicker layer of opaque grease totally obscured from view the linoleum surface of the kitchen floor. An oily residue also coated the walls and ceilings and every other surface throughout the entire house.

After my first visit with the Reynolds, I politely declined to sit on the furniture on future visits. The grease soaked into my suit when I sat on their couch during our first meeting. As I drove away from that initial encounter, the gooey substance found its way to the front seat of my car. Even though things were getting better financially, I didn't think I could afford to send my suits to the cleaners after every meeting with the Reynolds family.

Vernon explained they had run up credit card debt to the extent their monthly financial outflow exceeded their monthly income. They only owed $3000 on their home. Even in its deplorable condition, the market value left $8000 to $9000 equity in their property. In their opinion the sale of their home would produce sufficient funds to pay off their creditors and help buy a larger home. Vernon said, "Moving my family into another home would be like getting a fresh start in life." Vernon and Peggy were aware that marketing their property in the conventional manner wouldn't work for them. They knew normal people didn't live as they did. They were not about to open their home to the public.

When Ralph Douglas knocked on the Reynolds' door during his quest to secure listings, they invited him in. Vernon told Ralph that they had considered selling but felt ashamed for people to view their living conditions. Ralph assured the Reynolds whoever they chose as their Realtor would likely agree to buy the property, sparing them the discomfort of opening the home to the scrutiny of strangers.

Silently, I thanked Ralph for the good work he had accomplished. I told Vernon and Peggy not only would I cash them out of their Cedar Avenue home, I owned a brand new four bedroom, two bath house in Bayside Village I could put them into immediately. I had just a few days earlier acquired ownership of the house. Originally, I planned to rent it out for a couple of years, then either sell it or move my family into it.

Moments after I told them about my Bayside Village house, they wanted to see it … right then. They followed me in their car to 13602 Burton Drive. Peggy thanked me for inviting the family to ride over in my car and laughed. She asked me "Val, look at me— do you really think you could squeeze us all in your car?" Clearly, they liked me and I genuinely liked them.

They fell in love with the Burton Drive house. Sparkling brand new, it even smelled sparkling brand new. The kids ran from room to room—the teenagers selected their bedrooms. I heard Leslie ask her parents, "Are we really going to live here?"

Peggy answered, "Leslie, honey, say thank you to Mr. Barry, he's going to make this happen for us."

Momentarily, I turned away. It wouldn't be cool to tear up in front of your clients. It wasn't always just about making money. I knew that a power beyond my understanding had put me in touch with the Reynolds family. I told Vernon and Peggy that I would go to my office and draw up the necessary documents which they could review and accept or reject later. I went back to the office to prepare the contracts because I couldn't recall one clean comfortable place to write in the Reynolds home. We agreed to meet at their home at nine that same evening.

Curiously, up to that point the price of either house hadn't been discussed. I realized occasionally some people's lives go so far astray they no longer retain the ability to think rationally. Vernon and Peggy had reached that point. I knew that they would go along with whatever I suggested. Of course, I intended to make money on this deal—yet do so in a fair manner that would truly benefit the Reynolds. If you think I pictured myself playing God, you may be right.

I prepared the pertinent documents to reflect the following conditions: I would pay $12,500 cash for the Reynolds' property which would leave them around $9,000 after paying off their loan against Cedar Avenue. They would pay $25,250 for Burton Drive. Their entire $9000 net equity would be applied toward their purchase of my property. When I purchased Burton Drive, I paid cash down to a new loan in the amount of $18,800 with Great Western Savings and Loan Association.

Reynolds' $9000 down payment toward a purchase price of $25,250 would leave them owing a balance of $16,250, financed as follows: A $2550 portion of the $9000 down payment would reduce the Great Western loan to $16,250 which the Reynolds would assume.

Immediately after transfer of titles to the respective properties I would lend the Reynolds $3500 which they could use to pay off their credit card debt and take care of some of their other expenses. I'd secure my $3500 loan with a promissory note and a second deed of trust against Burton Drive. The second loan would bear seven percent interest per annum, principal and interest payable at $35 per month with the unpaid balance of principal owing to come due in five years.

The Reynolds had bought Cedar Avenue new for about $7500. Selling the property for $12,500 left them with a taxable profit. They were able to defer paying capital gains taxes on the profit when purchasing another home, providing all their equity in Cedar ($9000) applied toward the purchase of Burton Drive, which necessitated the reduction of the Burton Drive Great Western loan from $18,800 to $16,250.

I drew the contracts at the office reflecting the terms described above and returned to Cedar Avenue at nine that evening. Leslie opened the door for me. I found the family gathered around their dining room table aggressively devouring a meal of heavily spiced grease-sodden Mexican cuisine. As I stood nearby waiting for them to finish their dinner—I'm not exaggerating—I spied a dead mouse near the plate of enchiladas that apparently no one but me noticed. When they finished eating, Vernon pushed the dirty plates, bowls and ancillary items related to their dinner to one side of the table. Careful to avoid disturbing the deceased rodent, I laid the documents down for Vernon and Peggy's signatures while explaining the details of my proposal.

They were delighted to sign. Their main concern centered on how they could physically move from Cedar to Burton Drive. I told them not to worry, that at my expense a crew with a large truck would transfer their belongings. I walked out of the Cedar Avenue home that night with a deep feeling of satisfaction. I figured it to be a simple transaction which I planned to close in a couple of weeks. However, the process changed abruptly. Two days after the signing of the transaction documents, I received a call at around seven at night at my home from Vernon. I heard panic in his voice.

I drove immediately to Cedar Avenue and had to park a block away from the house. I couldn't park closer because the street was full of fire engines. Walking toward the house I observed the Reynolds family standing together across the street among a crowd of spectators gazing at the burned out shell of their home. I approached and Vernon said something to the effect that just when it looked as if they were getting a break this had to happen. Responding to emergencies came easy to me. After all, hadn't I been doing that all my life? "Vernon, Peggy, don't worry, this is a minor distraction. You can spend the night at a nice motel up on MacArthur Boulevard which I'll pay for. Tomorrow morning we'll get you moved into Burton Drive." The family looked at me with confusion.

The family received—heretofore practically nonexistent—attention of neighbors. I approached the scorched and water-soaked structure and located the fire fighter who I determined to be in charge. When I explained that I'd soon be the owner of the property, he walked me through the charred remains. He described the good fortune of the Reynolds family. He said that had the fire erupted while the family slept, they wouldn't have survived. As I already knew, he pointed out that prior to the fire every surface of building's interior lay under a coat of grease. For a period spanning years, cooking grease suspended in smoke was carried throughout the house and continued to accumulate.

Apparently, no attempt had ever been made to remove the sticky substance, and the inevitable result occurred that evening.

He had spoken with the family earlier and determined the cause of the fire. Leslie admitted that while the rest of her family ate dinner, she filched a cigarette from her mom's purse and went into one of the bedrooms and lit up. She tossed the lighted match onto the floor from which the fire had erupted, quickly causing the destruction. Paradoxically, the rest of the family thought of Leslie as a little hero because she alerted them in time for them to run uninjured from the inferno.

Things turned out all right. I secured motel accommodations for the family. The next day, I arranged for a couple of fellows who I occasionally hired for odd jobs to rent a truck and move the few salvageable items from Cedar Avenue to Burton Drive. The Reynolds received a large amount of furniture donations from their neighbors and a church they had attended in years gone by. Within a few days, the family became the proud owners of Burton Drive and I took title to Cedar Avenue. Their insurance paid for complete restoration of Cedar at absolutely no expense to me. The homeowner's provision of their insurance policy provided for a cash settlement to the Reynolds to compensate for the loss of their personal belongings. We were all happy with the way things turned out. Within two months, I sold Cedar Avenue for a sizable profit. In addition, I made money on the sale of Burton Drive.

Early in 1964, after the passage of about two years, I stopped receiving the monthly installment payments on the Reynolds' second loan. I attempted to call them but discovered they no longer had telephone service. No payments on my second loan and no telephone—I knew the Reynolds were in trouble. I called Vernon at his job. He said he'd been on the verge of calling but just didn't know what to say to me. We agreed to meet at his home the next evening. When I arrived there, the condition of the house stunned me. They hadn't been living there long enough to duplicate the deplorable state of Cedar Avenue as it had been when I first met them, but they'd made a good start.

Each family member, with the exception of Leslie, looked terrible. Peggy appeared even heavier and Vernon seemed drawn and ill. The teenagers were unkempt and sullen and their odd demeanor toward each other made me suspicious. Severely warped, once beautiful oak hardwood floors had sustained damage beyond repair. The kitchen floor undulated so severely it posed a hazard to traverse. Peggy explained that a year or so ago while she napped in her bedroom one afternoon, her youngest child, tired of playing with the water hose in the front yard, had dragged it into the house. The toddler became distracted and laid the hose down on the kitchen floor, allowing the water to flow all afternoon.

I sat with Vernon and Peggy at their kitchen table and asked if they wanted to level with me. They did. Vernon told me not only were they behind in my payments; they were two months delinquent on the Great Western loan. Great Western informed them foreclosure proceedings would begin soon. Vernon explained for several years he pilfered small quantities of pain killer medication from his place of employment which he and Peggy consumed. At first, the drugs relaxed them and helped smooth the rough edges of their life. Vernon stated he could keep his drug use under control. Peggy couldn't.

Vernon couldn't steal sufficient amounts of pain killers to assuage his wife's cravings. Peggy found sources from which she could obtain illegal drugs. Nothing else seemed to matter to Peggy—satisfying her habit overrode every other aspect of her life including her family, her home and her health. Things continued to deteriorate. When they ran out of money, she began to write checks on a closed bank account. She expected the police to show up at their door any day. As I listened to their sad story, my mind sought a solution. I quickly formulated a plan whereby I could help the Reynolds and, of course, me.

About the same time I sold Burton Drive to the Reynolds, I sold Sheila's parents one of my properties, a beautiful home in Fremont on Russo Drive. They bought the house for $27,500, and financed it with a $4000 cash down payment and a new assumable FHA loan of $24,500. As usual, Ray wanted to move. He wished to move back to San Leandro, closer to friends and relatives. I showed the Reynolds family Russo Drive. In pristine condition, it looked beautiful. They wanted Russo Drive, and they left it up to me to figure everything out.

I did the following: I handled the sale of a home on Clinton Avenue to Ray and Pat. It had a San Leandro mailing address, even though located just outside the San Leandro City limits. I immediately advanced the Reynolds sufficient funds of around $1500 to cover Peggy's bad checks, so she wouldn't be arrested. I personally delivered the money to the bank just to make sure it arrived there okay. I bought Burton Drive for $25,000 in its "as is" condition. Even with the damage to the house, I got a fair buy. The Bay Village properties had increased in value substantially once the tract sold out.

The Reynolds derived enough cash from the sale of Burton Drive to buy Russo Drive for $29,250. They financed the purchase by making a down payment of $5250 and assuming the $24,200 existing FHA loan balance. As I did when I bought Cedar Avenue, I took responsibility for moving the family. Included in the items moved were the same lard filled pots and pans that had been moved from Cedar Avenue to Burton Drive. I fixed up Burton Drive and moved my own family into the home which had been my plan when I bought it about two years previously.

Playing God doesn't always turn out that well. I got a call from Peggy about a year after the family moved to Fremont. Their lives didn't get any better after their last relocation. She called to ask me to attend Vernon's funeral that week. I show up at the funeral and talked with Peggy for a while after the service concluded. She spoke candidly—she hadn't been able to stop using "off the street" illegal drugs. Finally, Vernon died in his sleep from an overdose of painkillers for which he had a legitimate prescription. If the insurance company deemed the overdose accidental, which hadn't been ruled on yet, Peggy would be in line for a substantial settlement. I sure hoped that the decision would go in her favor. I think maybe that it did because I never heard from the Reynolds again. I often wonder whatever became of Leslie.

CHAPTER FIFTY-ONE

Going back to 1962, my financial goals were right on track. Besides our Neptune Drive home, Sheila and I owned several rental houses. Even though we earned substantial income we used much of our money to refurbish our properties, including our own home. I still owned only one pair of dress shoes and only bought my suits on sale, yet we were doing okay. The kids continued to attend parochial school, we drove better automobiles and enjoyed restaurant meals occasionally.

My real estate activity in the latter portion of 1962 and the first half of 1963 still absorbed the majority of my time. The opportunity to do business existed at every turn, and I turned nothing down. I spent quality time with my family—just not enough. The harder I worked building my business, the more time Sheila spent alone with the kids. It remained a troubling issue with her. It seemed to me, that in her mind—because I enjoyed what I did for a living—it didn't count as work. She couldn't understand that if I didn't enjoy my job, I'd be no good at it.

Living on Neptune Drive continually brought delightful experiences. The portion of the bay waters adjacent to the properties situated on the west side of the Neptune Drive existed within a "U" shaped cove. The inlet was bordered by the San Leandro Marina to the south and on the north by a landfill project, which eventually became Oyster Bay Park. Looking out at the bay waters from the mostly windowed west side of our home provided a gorgeous view. Sunny Sunday mornings, the sight of children learning sailing skills, manning dozens of colorful El Toro sailboats, some within yards of our private beach, provided unforgettable memories.

At certain times of the year, strong afternoon winds swept in from the west and whipped the surface of the lagoon into roiling waves which attracted windsurfers, some skilled, others not so skilled. No matter their level of expertise, watching them skim over the angry whitecaps on their surfboards, propelled by their brightly-hued, gale-filled sails brought us hours of thrills.

On clear days, we saw South San Francisco across eight miles of bay. The large variety of shorebirds provided a mesmerizing display of amusing antics. Squawking, combative airborne gulls endlessly competed with members of their flock for morsels deposited along the shoreline. We observed stately wading birds such as egrets, while blue herons patiently stood motionless for long periods poised to spear an aquatic treat.

Sleek, black and white acrobatic terns swooped and dove overhead, protesting our presence. I marveled at their aerodynamic perfection and pondered the theory of reincarnation. I wondered how it might be to return as one of those graceful beauties. Mrs. Barnes, an emotionally troubled neighbor, mentioned to me that her ability to stay out of psychiatrists' offices stayed strengthened because of the time she spent observing the waterfowl show from the kitchen window of her shoreline home. I knew exactly what she meant.

One summer afternoon, from the shoreline of our backyard, Danny, Steven, Valerie and I caught around twenty-five stingrays within a two-hour period. As we mistakenly believed stingrays weren't edible, we tossed them back in the water soon after we brought them ashore. Once on the hook, they put up a hell of a fight—what fun! We owned a small rowboat. Often on warm summer afternoons, the kids and I anchored our boat a few yards off shore and used it as a diving or jumping off platform. We spent wonderful hours frolicking in the briny bay waters. *Could it get any better?* I didn't think so.

Ray Drake, Sheila's step-dad, an avid hunter and fisherman owned a scull-boat which he stored in our backyard and made available to me. The boat had been designed for hunting ducks. The hunter lay on his back in the small shallow craft, out of sight of the waterfowl. He or she silently propelled the boat into a flock of ducks by a twisting motion of an oar protruding through the transom. When the hunter had maneuvered the vessel into its optimum position, the shooter rose and opened fire on his or her prey.

Many early winter mornings, before I got ready for work, I departed from my backyard beach in Ray's scull-boat and rowed out into the bay, about a half mile from the shoreline, beyond the city limits, where I could legally hunt for ducks and geese. Each such morning, I bagged my limit of fat mallards or canvasbacks and returned home. Generally, the adventure took less than an hour. Within a few minutes, I cleaned, packaged and deposited the rewards of my outing into our freezer. Occasionally, Sheila served up a feast of roasted wild waterfowl, heavily spiced and stuffed with onions to obscure the gamey wild taste. If one didn't mind biting into shotgun pellets now and then, the results of my foggy, chilly game-hunting expeditions provided a few pleasant repasts.

I knew people spent large sums to belong to private duck hunting clubs located long distances from their homes. I had difficulty believing their money could buy them a better time than I experienced after launching the scull boat from my backyard. During the year and a half we resided in the 13000 block of Neptune Drive, we enjoyed relatively good times. We gave several house parties and invited friends and family to holiday dinners. I enjoyed entertaining them and Sheila did as well. We got along fine when we were hosting a social event.

From the time we took occupancy of the Neptune Drive home, we had problems with a neighbor. Lance Mangram lived in a home which he had built a few years earlier on a lot he bought through Ed Marvin, adjacent to the north side of our property. Neighbors warned that Lance had mental issues and held hostile feelings toward families with children in our immediate vicinity, even though he and his wife, Faith, were raising two preschool age boys.

Faith Mangram, a sweet woman, came to our home and introduced herself to Sheila. She confirmed that her husband behaved in a paranoid, hostile manner toward neighborhood children. She apologized in advance of his anticipated rude behavior toward our family. We appreciated her early warning. As it turned out, she understated the case.

Various household tasks were routinely assigned to each of our three oldest children. Steven took care of the front yard. One day while watering the flowers adjacent to the Mangram's front yard, a few drops of water (literally, a few drops) landed on their property. Within Sheila's earshot, Lance warned Steven that if he ever again got water on his side of the three-foot high wire fence on the boundary of our properties, he'd make my son real sorry. When Sheila intervened, he repeated his threat and then quickly retreated into his house. Faith stopped by the next day and over coffee expressed her regrets for her husband's outburst. Upset when I learned of the incident, I told Sheila I would speak to Lance. She said, "No, I can handle this with Faith's help. If you get involved, it might make matters worse."

A nice family by the name of Burkhart lived directly across the street from our home. There were three children in their family who resided in the home with their mother. The Burkhart kids, two boys and a girl ranged in age from nine to fourteen. The oldest, Marcy, often babysat our children. My kids adored her. The Burkhart children sometimes played ball in the street. When they did, Lance often called the police. He continually verbally berated them from behind his wire-fence-enclosed front yard. An officer, responding to one of Lance's complaints resulting from my boys and the Burkhart boys playing ball in the street, told me that in a one-year period the department had received 123 complaint calls from our recalcitrant neighbor.

The inevitable confrontation between Lance and me eventually occurred. Pitch dark, I waited in my driveway a few feet from Lance's property for Ed Marvin to pick me up for an evening appointment. Ed pulled his car into my driveway and Lance rushed on his side of the property line wire fence near Ed's car. I stood in the dark just a few feet from Lance—he didn't notice me.

He yelled at Ed, "You son-of-a-bitch, you shined your car lights across my house and now you're going to pay." Stunned, Ed thought that what I recognized from my vantage point as a flashlight in Lance's hand might be a gun. After all the time I had quietly endured Lance's bullshit, my patience ended.

Quietly, I said to him, "Lance, I'm going to ask you this one time only, what can I do to get you to end your hostility toward my family?"

When he recovered from the shock of seeing me so close to him, he said that he would only back off if I moved my front porch and entrance to my house. My front porch had been constructed at the north corner of our house about twelve feet from the front south corner of Lance's house. He demanded that I construct a new driveway, porch and front entrance at the opposite side of my property—at the most distant point possible from his home. Listening to Lance, I wondered if the great deal I got from Bill James on my shoreline home might have had something to do with my nutty neighbor.

I handled the balance of our meeting badly. I said, "Lance, you are as crazy as everyone says you are. If you ever harass any member of my family again, rest assured I will come into your house, drag you out and beat the hell out of you." He fled into his house.

For the next few days, I felt good about myself. I'd put a bully in his place and my two older boys were proud of their dad. I didn't feel quite so cocky, however, when a police officer answering another of Lance's complaints about the Burkhart kids playing ball in the street, knocked on our door and said he'd like to speak with me. While the police officer spoke with Lance, he noticed a shotgun propped up next to the front door. When he inquired about the weapon, Lance told the officer he kept it handy and loaded in case he had to take care of his neighbor—me! The officer told me Lance had a right to keep a loaded gun. He informed me an arrest couldn't be made unless Lance broke the law, which the officer stated he expected to happen eventually.

Shortly thereafter, we moved to a vacant house we owned three blocks away at 12927 Aurora Drive. Just before we left Neptune Drive, Lance planted a bamboo property divider on the property line between his house and ours. Years later, the bamboo "spite" fence as Sheila called it resulted in an extraordinary ironic situation.

Decades passed and the bamboo spread from the property line back to Lance's house. I made sure that the horrendous parasitic growth never got closer to our house than the property line where

Lance first planted it. Over time the bamboo reached twelve or so feet in height. No sunlight could filter through the thick growth to reach Lance's house. A situation existed wherein moisture trapped against the rustic exterior southern walls of Lance's house caused the walls to rot out entirely. He called the mayor of San Leandro and told him that the bamboo *I* had planted was ruining his house. He asked the mayor to prevail upon me to have the bamboo removed. I explained to the mayor the true circumstances, but as a totally goodwill gesture I would make the bamboo disappear; which I did at a cost of $1500. Did Lance thank me? No!

I made a big mistake in how I handled the initial confrontation with Lance. I learned that just because a person has a good reason to lose their temper, doesn't mean the temptation should be indulged. What good did it do for me to threaten him? None whatsoever! Obviously, the fellow suffered from mental complications and my angry threat only made the situation worse. Of course, I had to address his misbehavior firmly, but damn, I should have done a better job.

Lance did one positive thing every year. He went door to door on his block collecting for a charitable agency. I knew most of the people in the neighborhood. Some of the folks he called on while canvassing told me he made a point of letting them know what a low-life rotten crook I was. It would be naïve on my part to deny that his ranting hadn't cost me some business. I strongly emphasize—**People who seriously seek success in business cannot afford the luxury of losing their temper.**

In time, I developed a love of running—running relaxes me and keeps me in good mental and physical condition. Thirty years after my single hostile confrontation with Lance, my running regimen often took me by his home. Whenever I ran past him working or just standing in his front yard, I waved and called out "Hi Lance." He had no idea who had greeted him; he smiled and waved back. He didn't know me, but he still hated me—I felt sorry for him.

CHAPTER FIFTY-TWO

We took occupancy of Aurora Drive in April of 1963 and rented Neptune Drive to Homer Richardson, the pastor of the First Christian Church on Davis Street in San Leandro. Homer and his family, thrilled at the prospect of residing in a bay front home, happily took possession in spite of receiving full disclosure regarding Lance Mangram. In the years to follow—in addition to renting him Neptune Drive—Homer and I did real estate business together and I found reason to engage his ministerial services on more than one occasion.

Years passed and eventually Homer's wife passed away and his children grew up and moved on. He sublet Neptune Drive to a member of his congregation and her family. He remarried and bought what everyone considered one of the most beautiful homes in Mulford Gardens, located at 2327 West Avenue 133rd. Homer and Mrs. Richardson's large, two-story Cape Cod with its heavy shake-shingled roof and white picket fence enclosing a manicured front yard containing the traditional cluster of three white barked birches, situated on a tree-studded, one-third-acre parcel, radiated pure character. I supposed Homer and his bride had found their dream home.

However, I think that once you've lived on the water, you always want to return. An opportunity came along for Homer to buy a home on the bayside of Neptune Drive and he jumped at the chance. The Richardsons needed to sell West Avenue 133rd in order to afford the Neptune Drive home. For years, people had often mentioned to me that if that property ever came on the market, I should let them know. I considered owning just about the most attractive residential property in the community might serve me well. When I told Homer I wanted to buy his home, he said his garbage man had already talked with him and his wife about buying the property.

Homer's garbage man, Stuart Alexander, had recently—upon the death of his father—inherited a large sum of money. Stuart's great aunt emigrated from Portugal to San Leandro in the early twenties. In 1926, she founded the Santo's Linguisa Factory on Washington Avenue. In the beginning, Mrs. Santo's enterprise mainly served a large population of Portuguese immigrants who settled in San Leandro and surrounding communities. Her business expanded and before long, restaurants and grocery stores began buying her delicious linguisa. She operated successfully for many years and upon her demise, her nephew, Herman (Tweedy) Alexander took over.

Stuart Alexander, in his early forties had the reputation of an extremely hard-working, initially very likable fellow. In addition to running the linguisa factory and being employed as a garbage collector for the Oakland Scavenger Company, he actively accumulated residential real estate. At the time Stuart and I competed for the ownership of Homer and Mrs. Richardson's property, I didn't know him personally. I would eventually get to know him well—perhaps too well. I can never forget Stuart for reasons which I will explain later.

I felt Mrs. Richardson favored selling to Stuart. I'd known Homer for several years and we got on well. I believed that Homer held sole title to the Cape Cod property. Even so, it seemed certain that he would acquiesce to his wife's wish to sell to Stuart. It came as a pleasant surprise when Homer informed me he had decided to accept my offer of $212,000. I paid a fair price, yet if necessary, I would have paid more. I considered Homer's decision to sell to me an act of loyalty which I deeply appreciated. In the years to follow, we did more business together. The appearance of success is always extremely helpful to the career of a real estate agent. Ownership of 2327 West Avenue 133rd substantially enhanced my appearance of success.

CHAPTER FIFTY-THREE

In April of 1963, I still worked in Ed's office and my business continued to accelerate. I felt invincible. Early one morning before dawn, I lay in bed imagining and planning an ambitious, improbable goal for the day. The Williams family owned a two bedroom home on a small lot at the corner of Aurora Drive and Elm Street in Mulford Gardens. Bob Williams operated as a lumber broker. He handled sales of out-of-state lumber to various outlets in California.

Bob conducted an efficient family business from his home. His wife, Sally, kept the books, set up appointments for Bob and performed myriad secretarial duties. Bob and Sally's two teen-age boys helped as well. Occasionally, to expedite a rush order, Bob rented a truck and sometimes, with the help of his sons, picked up a load of lumber in Oregon and delivered it to a lumber yard in California.

One morning, Bob came by the office. He mentioned he'd been thinking that if he could find a larger home than the one in which his family then resided, situated on a large Mulford Gardens lot, he might be able to improve his business. Bob explained that if he had sufficient parking space, he might buy a truck instead of renting one and expand the lumber hauling segment of his operation. During summer vacations his boys could handle hauling the lumber. Conducting the brokerage and nascent trucking activity from a more comfortable home would greatly enhance the Williams family enterprise.

A couple of days before, I had taken a listing at West Avenue 134th. The property consisted of an attractive one-story ranch style, 1400 square foot, three bedroom, one-and-a-half bathroom home situated on a one-third acre lot. It seemed perfect for the Williams. Still in bed, after considering the Williams' needs, I thought about Larry and Doris Engleton. Larry and Doris, both schoolteachers with no children, lived in and owned a new home in Richmond.

On a Saturday morning, they drove down to the foot of Marina Boulevard and observed the massive development of the San Leandro Marina. The Engletons considered that Mulford Gardens offered favorable investment potential. On their way from the Marina project they stopped by the office and asked about the Mulford community. I instinctively recognized real buyers when I saw them. As usual, there were several people in the office—no chance to engage in a private conversation there.

Larry and Doris accepted my invitation to go across the street to Ronakers for coffee. I explained my views about the wonderful real estate investment potential in the area. Larry told me he and Doris would love to buy an old dog of a house and make a hobby of fixing it up themselves. I informed the Engletons to expect a call from me very soon. I let them know I would be listing a real fixer on Elm Street, a vacant dwelling that used to be a farmhouse, (literally built around 1910) and moved to its present location about ten years previously.

Mr. Thomas, who lived out of the area, promised to list it with me when he arrived in town in the next few days. Mr. Thomas, an elderly, grizzled cantankerous old bachelor cowboy, moved the house to Elm Street with the intention of eventually modernizing it and taking occupancy when he retired from ranching. He never retired nor modernized the house and decided to get rid of it. A few days later, he did indeed list his Elm Street property with me.

I arose around seven, and mentally refined my ambitious plans for the day. I called Bob Williams around nine and told him about West Avenue 134th. I had that "magic feeling" that skillful salespeople experience occasionally, albeit rarely. I felt irresistible that day. I showed the Williams family the West Avenue 134th property at one that afternoon.

My enthusiasm engulfed the Williams. The place suited them perfectly. We returned to their home and I wrote and they signed a purchase contract, which I immediately presented to the owners, who made a counter offer. They asked that the Williams allow them to remain in the premises one month after close of escrow, rent-free. I went back to the Williams and they accepted the terms of the sellers' counter offer.

To finance the purchase of West Avenue 134th, the Williamses realized they had to sell their present property. I knew I could sell their property to a young couple, Joe and Annie Mendes, whom I'd been showing starter homes. I listed the property for $18,950 and showed it to the Mendes that afternoon. Minutes after inspecting the interior of the house, while sitting in my car, I prepared and they signed a purchase agreement to buy the property for the listed price. They waited in the car while I went into the house and had Bob and Sally sign the agreement.

We still had a financing problem. The Williams needed to close West Avenue 134th in thirty days. The unavoidable necessity of financing the Mendes transaction with a GI loan would take approximately ninety days. The financing complication disappeared when the Williams accepted my offer to lend them the down payment toward the purchase of West Avenue 134th. So far, two sales in one day and I hadn't finished.

Early that morning before leaving my home, I called Larry and Doris at their home in Richmond. I told them about my Elm Street listing. They agreed to meet me at the property at six that evening. Ken said that the Elm Street listing coincided with exactly what he had envisioned, since he and Doris decided to buy a house needing substantial upgrading. While still in the vacant but semi furnished house, we sat on dilapidated furniture, and I prepared an offer which the Engeltons signed.

I met with Mr. Thomas at his sister's home in San Leandro where he intended to reside until his Elm Street property sold. Anxious to sell, but not quite anxious enough to accept Larry and Doris' offer, the crusty old horse trader insisted on making a counter offer. At around eight that evening, after calling the Engletons, I left San Leandro and headed to Richmond to present Mr. Thomas' counter offer. Ed insisted on accompanying me to the Engletons' which I appreciated.

A little disappointed that their initial contract didn't get accepted, Ken realized another opportunity similar to Elm Street might not come along again. The couple signed the counter offer around eleven that evening. I called Mr. Thomas from Ken and Doris' home and notified him of the acceptance of his counter offer. I got home around midnight. Three deals in one day. *Damn, I'm good!*

CHAPTER FIFTY-FOUR

I'd developed quite a following in a short period of time. Ed introduced me to several people in Mulford he had dealt with over the years who were very involved in pursuing their fortunes through investing in real estate. Even though those folks utilized

Ed's services on a hit or miss basis, they didn't consider him "their broker," nor did Ed feel he owed them a degree of special allegiance.

It seemed the people with whom Ed brought me into contact saw no value in maintaining a loyal, exclusive, trusting business association with him. As I hope I've made clear, Ed had many fine qualities, but in my opinion, none that would ever make him or anyone else wealthy. I think it's true with many (certainly not all) real estate agents I've known, the amount of the commission determined the degree of Ed's devotion to his customers. In other words, he never developed a following of loyal customers who would comply with his suggestions simply because they trusted he had their best interests at heart.

He introduced me to the Serianni family. Gabe and Margaret Serianni lived in Mulford Gardens and did quite well buying, selling, building and renting out residential real estate, mostly in Mulford Gardens. The Seriannis' and I fit together perfectly. Before he met me, Gabe worked with any Realtor who presented him with a deal that made sense. I stayed in constant contact with Gabe and Margaret, and in my capacity of a real estate agent, continually negotiated sales to them and for them. Before long, no other agent had a prayer of doing business with the Seriannis' without me being involved.

Gabe and Margaret had two grown children; Dick and Elaine. Dick, a year older than me, did business as a State Farm Insurance agent. We got along well. Dick and I referred customers to each other, which further cemented my relationship with his parents. During the passing years, I perpetually dealt with both generations of the Seriannis.

You will think the following is self-serving language, but the wonderful harmony between the Seriannis' and me existed because of the loyalty I extended to all those with whom I did business. The proposition of attempting to promote a transaction for the sole purpose of getting a commission never became part of my world. If I believed a particular deal offered no real benefit to my client, I stated the facts as I saw them.

Some might believe that my ego demanded that I needed to be considered a "good guy" to all with whom I came into contact. No, I just needed the unequivocal trust of my clients. And more than anything else, I had to be worthy of that trust. I had to elevate my status as an advisor to the point that people, unsure of the true quality of an investment proposition, did whatever I suggested. An agent truly worthy of that degree of trust has to become wealthy. I'm here to say, that my actions warranted such trust because I always tried my best to act in the best interest of my clients.

The Seriannis stayed loyal to me and I to them until the end of their lives. When Gabe died in a hospital in Clearlake, California, I stood beside Margaret and wished him farewell, minutes after he signed the final contract of his life. About fifteen years later, I extended the same courtesy to Dick at Highland Hospital in Oakland, California.

CHAPTER FIFTY-FIVE

Ed introduced me to George and Inez Muno. George and Inez, a childless couple probably as compliant and sweet as anyone I'd ever met, were dedicated to increasing their net worth to insure a comfortable retirement. So far, Ed just kept getting them into bad deals. George, about fifty-seven, worked at the Alameda Naval Air Station and seemed to me to stay a little intoxicated. Inez, a looker, maybe forty-five, worked at the National Can Company in San Leandro and made all the couple's decisions.

Inez made it very clear to me what she wished to accomplish. She wanted to buy a rental house in a good working-class neighborhood. After making a twenty percent down payment, the property had to produce sufficient income to pay the loan payment, property taxes and maintenance costs. After holding the property until George retired, she hoped to be able to sell at a price that would net a fifteen percent profit.

A single family residence located at 2264 Sitka Street, San Leandro listed at $13,950 seemed to meet the Munos' requirements. I promised Inez that if she and George bought Sitka, I would guarantee they could sell for a fifteen percent profit in five years, even if I had to buy the property from them myself. During the following years, the Munos continued to do business with me, long after I left Ed's office.

When George retired from the Alameda Naval Air Station, the Munos listed several properties with me. After the properties sold, George and Inez retired very comfortably in their home state of Arkansas. And yes, I bought 2264 Sitka just as I promised. I think I got it too cheap, but that suited Inez. We said goodbye and I felt proud of my part in helping making their dreams come true. As much as I genuinely liked the Munos, I knew we wouldn't be doing any more business together. As shallow as it might sound, I didn't stay in touch with them. I think of them often with deep affection and if they are still around, I hope they are living the good life they deserve.

As stated earlier, I met many people through Ed, folks like the Seriannis and the Munos who became loyal customers. We all did well. I feel a need to re-emphasize that none of the people Ed introduced me to were his loyal customers. They were simply acquaintances who lived near his office, some with whom he had done business.

In truth, during the time I worked in Ed's office, he made more commissions from folks I brought to his office than I made from people I'd met through him. My enthusiasm and insatiable hunger to succeed encouraged Ed to put me next to as many people as possible. He kept feeding me potential clients, with most of whom, on his own he had little chance of doing business. His referrals resulted in many commissions he would have never received if I were not on the scene.

CHAPTER FIFTY-SIX

In 1963, Ed introduced me to Jack Williams, a likable man about forty-five years old. Jack, a recovering alcoholic, arrived alone in Mulford Gardens from Wyoming maybe five years before I met him. Apparently, Jack's wife couldn't cope with his drinking and divorced him. He came to California in hopes of starting over.

Many small businesses operated successfully in the residentially zoned areas of Mulford Gardens. Because of the recent annexation of Mulford Gardens into the City of San Leandro, zoning violations were often ignored. Jack, with an entrepreneurial spirit and with Ed's guidance, had purchased an attractive ranch style home on West Avenue 136th in Mulford Gardens in 1958. Behind the home situated on the one-third-acre parcel sat three fully stocked greenhouses from which the former owner grew landscaping plants, which he sold mostly to wholesalers.

Jack vainly struggled to make a living from his nursery operation from between 1958 to 1962. In addition to the West Avenue 136th property, Ed had talked Jack into buying an empty third- acre lot at the corner of Menlo Street and West Avenue 138th. Horribly located, eighty feet fronted on West Avenue 138th, a narrow dirt road. The southern 180 foot border of the corner parcel lay a scant thirty feet across Menlo Street from the Southern

Pacific Railroad tracks. No source of water from a public utility company serviced the property—water came from a 100 foot deep well on the site. Immediately adjacent, huge ugly steel towers supporting electrical power lines cast long shadows across the lot.

Jack read that a person could grow rich raising and selling mushrooms. Convinced he would soon make his fortune, he had tons of manure dumped on the site which he believed would make his crop of mushrooms, mushroom him into financial independence (please forgive me, I couldn't resist). The mushrooms didn't survive. Figuratively, one might say Jack's lot stunk. After spreading horse manure over his parcel, it stunk literally, as well. Jack challenged me. "Val, you're as good a salesman as I've seen, but I don't think you will be able find a buyer for this loser."

I responded, "Jack, I suppose the only value your mushroom lot has is something that I haven't figured out yet, but I'm going to do my best for you."

I tried all the standard methods of marketing the lot, including contacting small residential builders. Placing that undesirable piece of land on the MLS and running newspaper advertisements brought no response. I figured that perhaps an owner of one the two contiguous parcels might be interested in Jack's parcel. They weren't.

I refused to give up. I vowed not to let Jack or myself down. Very early one morning, while lying in bed an idea began to form. Often, my best thoughts came to me before I could gather the will to leave the warmth of the covers. I recalled that a young man accompanied by an elderly gentleman had stopped by the office one afternoon some weeks past. They explained the older man— the young man's grandfather—pastored a fundamentalist church from a small rented house on Castro Street in San Leandro. The men introduced themselves as Pastor Gerald Simpson and Howard Simpson, grandfather and grandson respectively.

They experienced problems with their Castro Street location. Religious services, conducted from a property not zoned for such use, attracted complaints from neighbors. The congregation met at their church on Saturday evenings and Sunday mornings which continually created parking problems. They worshiped in a lively, noisy manner, which nearby residents didn't appreciate. Their continued operation on Castro Street seemed tenuous at best, which motivated their visit to our office. Pastor Simpson explained that his church needed to relocate. They couldn't find anything affordable to rent that didn't come with the same problems they were already experiencing. If they owned their church in San Leandro in a location where parking and the noise of their services didn't create problems with the neighbors, certainly their congregation would grow. They had some money— not a lot. The Simpsons wanted to do the work of the Lord and they wondered if I could help them.

The day I spoke with Pastor Gerald and Howard my appointments were stacked one on top of the other. I politely told them I would keep my eyes open and quickly moved on to other waiting clients. Thank goodness, I showed them the courtesy of taking their telephone number. I got out of bed and started planning my strategy. At nine that morning, I called the number the Simpsons had given me.

Howard's wife answered the phone. I explained the purpose of my call and she told me that she would have him call me from work; he managed a service station. A couple of hours passed and he called. Apparently, he had spoken with several agents about finding a church location because he didn't remember me. Happily (for me at least) they still hadn't found anything. He sounded discouraged. I wondered, *where's your faith fellow?*

I told him, "Howard, if you and your grandfather can meet me after you get off work today, I think I have the answer to your prayers." Corny? Of course. At six that evening, not only Pastor

Gerald Simpson and his grandson, Howard, showed up, but so did three or four other members of the congregation.

I met them at the lot. I explained for just a few thousand dollars they could build a small church on the site and expand as the congregation increased. We stood in a light rain which made the horse manure stink even worse than it normally did. I had to raise my voice so they could hear me over the noise of the passing freight train. I stated that the trains didn't run on Saturdays and Sundays so the proximity to the tracks presented no problem. A member of the church group worked for Southern Pacific Railroad and confirmed the accuracy of my statement.

I applied a little reverse selling. "Gentlemen, have you ever seen a more undesirable lot? I don't think I have. You've been dealing with irate neighbors who complain about the noise you make and the parking problems you cause and you're operating from property not zoned for church use." I explained, "as far as parking goes, the only folks parking on the street here will be you and your congregation. Actually, you won't need to park on the street unless it suits you." The size of the lot could easily accommodate a church building and onsite parking.

I said, "There is only well water right now and the lot fronts on a narrow, unpaved dirt road, but I'm sure in the future East Bay Municipal Utility District will bring in water and the City of San Leandro will eventually widen and pave the road. If those improvements were already in place, this lot wouldn't be available to you. Believe me, gentlemen, you will be welcome in this neighborhood. Anything you do on this mess will be an improvement."

We discussed the details at the office. They were more than anxious to make a deal. I asked if they needed to confer with the balance of their congregation before making a final decision. Pastor Simpson informed me that they didn't wish to delay and take the risk of another buyer moving in ahead of them. I thought, *fat chance of that happening.*

The group comprised the elders of the church and they were empowered to enter into an agreement right then and there. They signed the purchase agreement for the full price. I drove over to Jack's. Astonished, I think he actually teared up a little.

Jack said, "Val, this is a small commission deal for you. You should be getting more, but you know I'm practically broke. I'm giving the West Ave 136th property to my cousin. I owe him a great deal. He isn't going to operate the nursery. I want to give you all the plants in the greenhouses. Maybe you can sell some of them and use what's left to upgrade the landscaping around your own properties."

Indeed, I did make good use of the plants he gave me. When the lot sale closed, Jack returned to Wyoming. I never heard from him again.

He had called it right. I didn't receive a big commission for all the effort expended. That didn't matter though. Every time I drove by that corner and saw that cute little church with the large oak tree in front, I thought to myself, *it's there because early one chilly morning while lying in bed, I decided it would be there.* I knew I'd made the right career decision. West Avenue 138th is now an eighty-foot-wide arterial and indeed a public water system services the church property.

CHAPTER FIFTY-SEVEN

I had a listing on three vacant lots on Fairway Drive in Mulford Gardens. I had been actively involved in an extensive remodeling project, which worked out well for me. I thought about trying to get some experience in getting a spec house built. Building a house, speculating that it can be sold after it's built—for a profit—is my definition of a spec house. I talked with a couple of small contractors about building a house on one of the three Fairway Drive lots. The listed price of the lot, added to the projected cost of a new house, exceeded what I thought the developed property could bring.

The idea light bulb in my head went on. The State of California had bought up a plethora of residential properties in the path of the proposed MacArthur Freeway right-of-way and had begun auctioning off the houses in its path. I figured out the most I would likely have to bid to get a nice house, then added the cost to move the house, plus the cost of the lot and the cost of construction required to make the house habitable. I then estimated what price I might reasonably expect to receive for the finished property.

After deducting the estimated expenses from the potential selling price, it seemed that I might expect to net a handsome profit. I approached the owner of the lots and told him I'd like to buy one of his lots myself. I explained what I intended to do if he agreed to sell me the lot. He knew money couldn't be made building new houses on his lots; otherwise, he would have developed them himself. He couldn't see how I could avoid taking a loss if I moved a house onto the lot. I proceeded to buy the lot for the full listed price, minus a credit for the selling commission. Of course, Ed would receive one-half of the selling commission credit.

When I explained to Ed what I planned to do, he insisted that as my broker he had the right to become an equal partner with me on the project. I'd spent considerable time doing due diligence to determine the feasibility of the venture. Ed did nothing, yet he insisted on horning in on my deal. About everything I touched in those days prospered, and in my opinion Ed enjoyed the free ride.

I didn't make an argument because I planned to leave Ed's office soon. I reasoned that if the house-moving deal worked out, perhaps the chance that he and I might part company on good terms would improve. Our ideas in regard to how we should conduct our business seemed as far apart as the distance separating the North and South Poles. Still, I couldn't forget all I'd gained from my association with him. I determined that at a time of my choosing I would end our business relationship on a high note.

Within a week or so of Ed's insistence that he be included as an equal partner in my proposed house relocation project, we attended a Cal Trans house auction in the 100 block of Estudillo Avenue in San Leandro. Of the three houses up for sale by the state that morning, a rustic, single-story flat-top contemporary attracted my attention. It had a pleasing custom architectural design, and I decided I wanted it.

Although I'd never moved a house before, since deciding to do so, I'd done my homework. Comparatively, the design of the house of my choice lent itself to an economical move. The flat-top single story structure would easily glide beneath telephone and electrical power lines. The configuration of the building allowed it to stay in one piece during the move. Most moved houses needed cutting in two pieces, with each piece moved separately, then reassembled at considerable expense after the relocation.

Usually the bidding didn't exceed $2500 to $3000. I noticed several potential buyers eyeing my choice. I wanted to own that beauty so bad I mentally decided to go as high as $5000 if necessary. I loved to participate in real estate related auctions of any sort. Sales resulting from probate auctions in the courtroom, trustee's foreclosures, delinquent property taxes by the county tax assessor and the Federal Deposit Insurance Corporation had all stirred my competitive juices.

The bidding on the Estudillo house started at $250 and at $100 increments the bid quickly reached $1900. At $100 raises, I figured the bidding would soon exceed my feasibility limit. I initiated a bold move and jumped the bid from $1900 abruptly to $3500. If I had heard a bid of $3600, I would then have gone to $5000. If I had heard a bid of more than $5000, I would have "called it a day."

After my bid of $3500, the silence was so profound it seemed to echo. The auctioneer declared me the successful bidder. I spoke with Cecil Titsworth, a house mover who attended all such auctions. Cecil complimented me on my choice of houses. He told me he could move it easily and agreed to do so for $2800. So far, my cost for the house and move came to around $1000 less that my initial estimate.

I hired a contractor who Cecil put me in touch with to construct the foundation. By the end of the next week for $4100 the foundation was completed. Two weeks from the day I bought the house, Cecil and the foundation contractor secured the house to its foundation. By then, I had $10,400 into the project. I thought I'd spend another $5000 making the house pretty, and then put it on the market for $26,500 for a potential profit of $10,000 to $11,000.

Late one afternoon, as I strolled through the building making notes on a yellow pad regarding my plans to finish the house, Lyndon Moore walked through the open front door. Lyndon, a Hayward police officer, not far from retirement lived just a few doors away. His wife of many years had died a couple of years past. Recently, Lyndon had married a woman much younger than him. The new wife didn't like living in the house in which Lyndon and his first wife resided.

Anxious to please his current spouse, Lyndon promised to buy another house. He asked if I would consider selling the property to him in its "as is" condition. He wanted to complete the house in accordance to his bride's taste. I informed Lyndon that I'd be happy to sell the house to him and Mrs. Moore. Not expecting a potential buyer so soon I hadn't settled on a price.

Wanting to make a deal right then, Lyndon asked me if I would accept an offer of $25,000, with a down payment of $5000. He planned to pay off the balance of $20,000 when he sold his home down the street, which he would list with me. Anxious, he agreed to list his property, which included the home in which he lived, plus a rental cottage at the rear portion of his lot for whatever price I thought it would bring. I figured, *this has to be about as easy as it gets. Boy . . . Lyndon really wants to please his new wife.*

He walked back to his house and brought his wife down to look at her potential new home. She couldn't have been more excited. I told them I'd go to the office, prepare the necessary papers, and meet them back at their home in an hour. Ed, when hearing about the deal became as excited as Mrs. Moore. He accompanied me to the Moores' home where we all signed the various required documents. Soon, Ed and I would split a profit of $15,000.

Jim Kerr and his brother bought the Moore listing. Jim, my old friend from Cal Eastern, and the best friend I would ever have, shared my enthusiasm regarding investing in real estate. He and his family entered into many profitable transactions with me during the entire course of my real estate career. The brothers improved and sold the property a year or so after acquiring it. They netted a nice profit which, of course, made me a hero.

It's been a long time ago, and I don't remember the details but I think things didn't go well for the Moores. They made the house livable, but barely. I handled the sale of the property for them to the Sid Green family. Sid worked with me for a few months as a salesman in Ed's office. Not long after the Greens bought the Moores' house, the Greens divorced. Soon after that, Sid died of heart failure. Not everyone involved with the house I moved onto Fairway Drive shared my good luck.

CHAPTER FIFTY-EIGHT

Near the time I planned to leave Ed's office to open my own, Sheila informed me we were expecting. We adored our four children, but we could not see ourselves bearing the responsibility of another child. Sheila, stretched to her limits, lived in a highly emotional state of anxiety. During that period, the majority of the effort required to care for our four youngsters fell to her. Managing my burgeoning business prevented me from giving her much help on the home front. She told me another child would take her to the breaking point.

During that period, except under stringent circumstances, abortions were illegal. A few years previous, the Society for Human Abortion (SHA) had been established in San Francisco. We learned that a board of physicians appointed by the state could authorize a legal fetus termination if the pregnancy didn't exceed thirteen weeks. The board granted such permission only if convinced that the birth of the unwanted child severely compromised the health of the pregnant woman. We presented our case and received permission.

The doctor that delivered our four children accomplished the conclusion of Sheila's pregnancy, as well as affecting a "tubal ligation" to prevent a future pregnancy. Afterwards, I took a bouquet of red roses into her room. She said, "I hope you're happy now that you have forced me to forsake my religion."

I'm fully aware some things can never be made right; maybe we had experienced one of those. We never discussed the subject again.

CHAPTER FIFTY-NINE

I knew I had to operate my business with complete honesty. That decision didn't necessarily come about because of high moral standards or deeply held religious convictions. I had made a non-negotiable commitment to reach financial freedom, and I'd observed those who took moral shortcuts in their business dealings eventually and inevitably ended up on the losing side of the financial equation. In the course of my career, I occasionally found myself dealing with disreputable clients that profited from my association with them. I can honestly say I never permitted my integrity to be compromised by such people.

One Sunday afternoon, a heavy-set man around fifty, wearing glasses so thick they made him resemble a giant owl, dropped by the office. The fellow introduced himself as Gregory Gillespie. He told me he and his associates were looking for real estate investments. He let me know they weren't awfully choosy about what type of property they bought as long as their selection offered profit potential. He leaned out the office door and called to his associates waiting in Greg's new Cadillac to come in and meet me. First Greg introduced me to Victor Berman, a distinguished appearing silver-haired man about Greg's age. Greg told me Victor had a law degree and specialized in real estate law, primarily in connection with Greg's transactions.

Then Greg presented Irene, an attractive redhead, probably twenty-five years younger than her two companions. Clearly, Greg and Irene were romantically involved. The three of them came across as affable and thoroughly charming. They seemed very comfortable with me. Greg, obviously the leader of the trio informed me that he enjoyed a partnership with a well-known used car dealer in San Francisco whose name I recognized because he regularly advertised on television. I believed Greg to be financially capable and wanted to work with me. I assured him he would hear from me before the end of the week.

I called Greg on the following Wednesday and told him about a property I had listed on Marina Boulevard, only a half block from the soon to be developed San Leandro Marina. I told him the property consisted of a modest rental house situated on a multi-family zoned one-third acre parcel. I believed the property sat in the path of progress and within a year could be turned for a nice profit. Greg seemed convinced when I told him, "If you buy this property, and after holding it for four months, if you're dissatisfied with the deal, I'll buy it from you for $1000 more than you paid."

I didn't really know for sure the property would bring a profit; it just made sense to me that it would. Six months after Greg followed my suggestion, I handled the sale of the property to a builder netting Greg a fat profit, as well as earning a nice commission for me and Ed. I had become a hero to the Gillespie group and would soon get to know them a lot better. Greg trusted me completely and followed my suggestions to the letter.

I negotiated a sale to Greg of a one-acre lot zoned for twenty-seven apartment units on Mateo Street in Alameda County just outside the San Leandro City limits. The owners of the parcel accepted Greg's offer of $41,000. I had handled the sale of the parcel to them for $19,000 less than a year before. Greg's purchase contract called for the sale to close in thirty days from the seller's acceptance of the offer.

Greg came up with some excuse to delay completing the sale on time and requested a two week extension. To show his good faith he instructed the escrow company to immediately release his nonrefundable good faith deposit in the amount of $5000 directly to the sellers which they accepted. That experience would teach the owners and me that receiving funds from a buyer before the purchase is completed is a bad mistake.

Greg failed to place the purchase funds into the escrow as promised. The sellers notified Greg they intended to put their property back on the market. Because of his failure to perform according to the terms of the agreement, they felt entitled to keep Greg's $5000 good faith deposit. Victor filed a Suit Pending Notice against the sellers, clouding the title to the property, prohibiting them from selling the property to others. Because the sellers took money from the buyer the court sided with Greg. He delayed closing the escrow for over six months which gave him time to have plans prepared and approved to develop property and arrange construction financing. I learned that abuse of the legal system as described above fit into Greg's normal routine of doing business.

The Mateo Street property had once been part of a large farm. Situated close together on the site were four dilapidated huts that had long ago served as migrant farm workers' quarters. Soon after acquiring ownership of the property, Greg, probably in collusion with a dishonest insurance broker, somehow managed to get the falling down structures insured just as if they were normal habitable dwellings. Prior to the start of construction of the apartment complex, the shacks burned to the ground as the result of alleged vandalism. Greg collected several thousands of dollars from the insurance company.

He hired Gene Deader, a young building contractor, to construct the twenty-seven units he had gotten a permit to build while stalling to close the purchase of the Mateo Street site. When Gene finished the units, Greg and Irene moved into one of the apartments and engaged my services to rent out the others. Greg operated his various enterprises from his comfortable new quarters and enjoyed a nice cash flow from the rentals.

He had convinced Gene to wait for any portion of his contractor's fee until the complex had been finished. For several months after the apartments were built, Greg stalled paying Gene. Finally, Gene understood that Greg never intended to pay him. Gene sued for his money, and the court issued a judgment in his favor. Still, Gene received no money. He foreclosed on the Mateo Street apartments and evicted Greg and Irene. What a great deal for Gene; the cash flow from the units changed his life. Greg's eccentricity had robbed him of a secure income. But he seemed to take the situation in his stride and—always smiling—continued on as if it had never happened.

Sporadically, Greg lived with his wife, Georgia, in their gorgeous hillside Spanish style home in the upscale City of San Rafael. I met them there for the purpose of getting documents signed regarding another real estate transaction. Greg bragged that he hadn't made a loan payment on the home in over a year, and the lender couldn't do a thing about it. He explained that he purchased the home directly from the seller without the services of a Realtor. The owner planned on retiring and wished to carry the balance of the purchase price after receiving a modest down payment so that his interest-bearing loan would provide a secure monthly income. Greg convinced the seller to let him buy the property with an unusually small down payment by agreeing to pay twelve percent interest on the seller's carry back note.

Twelve percent interest exceeded the legal rate and if reported to the authorities, subjected the seller to severe financial penalties. Shortly after closing the escrow, Greg stopped making loan payments to the seller and instructed Victor to file a Suit Pending Notice against the seller preventing him from foreclosing. It could take more than a year for the court to settle such a dispute during which time the intimidated seller likely agreed to an out of court settlement strongly favoring Greg.

Greg introduced me to Max Walker, a small residential remodeling contractor. I sold Max two properties that he improved and sold through me at a profit. I found Max, unlike Greg, to be a man of high principals. Max began working on my properties on a continuing basis. We became close friends. Max had known Greg and his associates for quite a long time and proceeded to inform me of what he knew about Greg.

According to Max, Greg made a small fortune in the used car business in San Francisco, and he hid fruit jars filled with cash in his mother's basement to avoid paying income taxes. Eventually apprehended and convicted of income tax evasion, he spent time in a federal prison. Max told me that Irene was a prostitute that Greg had come across in Las Vegas. Greg lived a fairly lavish lifestyle, dining in fine restaurants daily and staying in first rate hotels frequently. Max informed me that Greg's daily expenses were covered by Irene's activities as a prostitute. Irene had made passes toward me out of sight of Greg. I let her know the attention flattered me, but as a happily married family man I couldn't get romantically involved with her. My ego experienced a little deflation when I learned her motivation likely stemmed from business reasons.

Although my association with Greg had been very lucrative, I realized continuing to work with him wouldn't be in my best interest. I politely let him know my other projects prohibited me from doing business with him. He understood my true meaning and said, "Val, I hope you will still send us Christmas cards."

A few years later, I heard Greg had begun dealing in heroin, and naturally, he tried to avoid paying a dealer who supplied him with drugs. He ended up beaten to death with a claw hammer. I viewed Greg as a victim of a mental condition far beyond my understanding. I never knew anyone more personably likable or more business savvy. He could have easily made a fortune legitimately, but I think he just had a lot more fun doing it his way.

CHAPTER SIXTY

Around May of 1963, I passed the examination for my broker's license. By then, I'd built up a solid referral business. As indicated herein throughout this composition, many of my customers, like me, sought financial independence by way of real estate related investment strategies. Those strongly goal-oriented clients viewed me as a valuable resource. I knew that as long as I stayed committed to their best financial interest, the money stream would continue to flow to me. After all, what did I have to offer them that would establish their loyalty to me and make them want to continue doing business with me, other than my talent, total honesty and sincere concern for their well being?

The time arrived for me to open my own office. As I saw it, Ed planned to scale the financial heights, but on my effort rather than his. I brought in ninety-five percent of the office income, and he took fifty percent. I received little help from him. I figured it would take me twice as long to reach financial freedom as it would if I didn't have to produce his income along with my own.

I personally liked Ed a lot, yet knew I needed to go out on my own. I felt guilty—after all, he gave me my start. I continued to procrastinate, trying to build up my nerve to tell him about my decision to leave his office. Finally, he made it easy for me. One afternoon, he received a call from a party to whom he had sold a property on the 2600 block of West Avenue 133rd some years past. The property, used as a rental since the owners took title, had recently become vacant. The tenant left the small two-bedroom house in a mess. Discouraged by bad tenants, the owners wanted to sell. Ed and I met them at their property that evening around six.

Ed signed up the listing at $16,950, which seemed fair to me. I knew the property would suit Brian and Teresa Orr perfectly. I had shown them several places in Mulford Gardens over the past few weeks. I hadn't been able to find anything that fit their price range. Ed's listing especially met the needs of the Orrs, because Teresa's parents lived just a few doors away and baby-sat the Orr's two pre-school children.

I told Ed I would show the Orrs the property later that same evening, which I did. The young couple signed a full price contract at the office right after viewing the property. They were happy because they believed their search for a suitable home had reached a successful conclusion. Ed observed my meeting in the office with the Orrs. After they signed the purchase agreement, he called the owners at their home in Fremont. He set an appointment for us to present the contract at six the next evening.

We arrived at the sellers' home as planned. They invited Ed and me to sit at the table in the dinette to conduct our business. I cheerfully discussed the contract with the sellers, very confident that they would welcome my buyer's full price offer. That's when Ed, to my amazement, withdrew another purchase agreement from another set of buyers from his briefcase.

Ed's phantom buyers had signed a purchase agreement for $500 more than the listed price. Knowing of the Orr's full price contract, Ed instructed his buyers to come in higher. I felt betrayed —more disappointed for the Orrs than myself. Ed couldn't resist the urge to unfairly hog the full commission, regardless of the questionable ethical behavior. Of course, he had every right to bring in a higher offer, but integrity demanded that he make me aware he had another buyer in tow before the presentation to the sellers. Ed had broken the bond of trust between us. My hesitation to go out on my own no longer existed.

I could and perhaps should have requested that the sellers submit a higher counter offer to the Orrs. Scrapping with my broker in the presence of the sellers didn't appeal to me. I just wanted to get the hell out of there. Ed got his purchase agreement signed and not a word passed between us on the drive back to San Leandro.

When I told the Orrs what had happened, they were furious with me. Certain that I had participated in some insidious greedy profit-driven scheme that deprived them of acquiring their dream home, they ordered me never to call them again. Of course, I would get nothing from the sale of the property, but the Orrs weren't about to believe that.

Actually, years later I wrote another sales contract on the same property. I handled the sale of the property for Karl and Cristiana Minneboo. The Minneboos were the buyers whose offer trumped the Orrs' contract price. The Minneboos, as driven as I to reach financial independence, saw in me a broker who could help make their dreams come to fruition. Over the following decades, the Minneboos bought and sold many properties through me.

Soon after the West Avenue 133rd debacle, I respectfully notified Ed of my decision to open my own office. I felt a little sorry for him. He had never made the kind of money I brought into his office. That, coupled with the fact that he had done very little work in quite a long time, made him feel insecure. He offered to up my share of the commission split or settle for just about any partnership arrangement I chose. I probably could have made a favorable deal with Ed, but I truly wanted to be on my own. We parted company on what I hoped was good terms, not knowing that future events would bring us together again under somewhat different circumstances.

PART FOUR

"exciting opportunities"

CHAPTER SIXTY-ONE

At age twenty-eight I began operating on my own at 14620 E. 14th Street in San Leandro. Vada Hunt, the broker of Hunt Realty, sublet one-half of her office space to me for $42.50 per month. Like me, Vada wanted to keep her overhead low and sharing office space provided an effective method of minimizing expenses. The front portion of the office measured about twenty-five feet in width by fifteen feet in depth. A lightweight, portable, ornate wood filigree structure placed in the middle of the twenty-five foot width of the front area of the office divided Vada's office area from mine. We each had a desk. I bought a nice used oak desk for twenty-five dollars, plus a couple of chairs for visitors. Behind the front portion of the office, on a first-come-first-served basis, Vada and I shared a separate twelve-foot by twelve-foot sitting room containing a couch, coffee table, two easy chairs, a small refrigerator, and an adjacent bathroom.

Jerry Fox, about six years younger than I, became my first salesman and I his first broker. Jerry and I had become acquainted a few years earlier. He would stop by Ed's office when I still worked there. When we met he was still a teenager and a student at Chabot Junior College in Hayward, living with his parents in Mulford Gardens.

While working for Ed Marvin, I had developed a reputation as a young man on the way up the ladder of success and when visiting me during that time, Jerry let me know he wanted to emulate the success he perceived I enjoyed in the real estate business.

I had found Jerry to be an affable kid and I tried to give him some good advice. I explained to him the "twenty percent-eighty percent theory." In every real estate office, twenty percent of the sales staff earned eighty percent of the commissions. Of course, then it followed that twenty percent of the commissions got divided between the remaining eighty percent of the sales staff. I told Jerry, "If you happen to be among the eighty percent, divvying up twenty percent, you aren't earning enough to support yourself."

I explained, in my opinion, eighty percent of the salespeople in most real estate companies didn't really know how to sell, which constituted the reason they didn't make a living. Indeed, I knew how to sell and I learned my skill when I worked for Cannon Shoe Company. I suggested, "Jerry, perhaps before you begin a career in real estate sales, you might be well served to first find work in an industry that offers a comprehensive sales training program."

A few days after I opened my new office, I had a visit from Jerry. He wanted to work for me. Recently married, he hoped to follow my lead and begin his quest for financial independence in the real estate business. To my surprise, he told me he took my advice and went to work as a life insurance salesperson, where he received extensive salesmanship training. Soon thereafter, he passed the state-required real estate salesperson examination, and Jerry and I comprised the ambitious sales staff of Val Barry Realty.

Jerry had learned his craft well. He solicited dozens of his former insurance customers and hit pay dirt. Unbelievably, within a period of three months, he made twenty-two sales: a remarkable accomplishment, which I remember specifically, because—as his employing broker—I had to submit a statement of his income to his wife's attorney after the couple decided to divorce.

I introduced Jerry to my mother's former employer, Lila Maxwell. My mother had worked as a waitress at the Oakland restaurant owned by Lila and her husband. After Mom left the Maxwell's' employment, Lila and her husband divorced. Lila left her marriage with a good financial settlement. She contacted me and let me know she hoped to derive a reliable revenue stream through investing in residential income property. Right at that time, I found myself absolutely inundated with business and asked Lila if she minded if I turned her over to Jerry.

Jerry and Lila got along well. She bought the two houses on Fairway Drive that I had negotiated the sale of to the Kerr brothers for Lyndon Moore. Lila held title to the two houses for maybe three months when I handled the sale of the property for her at a profit and put her into an eighteen-unit apartment complex in Newark. As described above, Jerry enjoyed terrific success early in his real estate sales career. Jerry enjoyed good luck because he made his good luck. He worked prodigiously and earned every cent he brought in. If he continued in that manner, in my opinion he could expect to reach financial freedom in a few years.

Often though, I reasoned that fortune smiled on him a little quickly and perhaps clouded his judgment. His spending habits quickly adjusted to meet his dramatically increased income which is a very common mis-step in the real estate business. For example, one morning he dropped by my house to show off his new gold-colored Chevrolet Monte Carlo hardtop convertible. As I admired his new set of wheels, his wife pulled up in an almost exact duplicate of Jerry's car; hers being a gorgeous cherry red instead of gold. I think Jerry figured if one new Monte Carlo hardtop convertible served him well, two would serve him even better. No matter how much money a person earns, if you spend more than you earn, you are in the process of going broke.

Soon, Jerry spent a lot of time doing what we in the business called "elephant hunting." Elephant hunting occurs when a person spends more time than they can afford trying to make it big on one spectacular deal. And, of course, when a person devotes a great amount of time hunting the elephant, the less exciting transactions that pay the rent and usual daily expenses begin to dry up. I've observed that the typical elephant hunter is under-financed and seldom succeeds.

Anyone who has serious money to begin with can easily make big money. My refined definition of an elephant hunter is a person with inadequate financial resources who chases the big deals. While Jerry worked with me, he invested an inordinate amount of time and effort trying to promote the development of an ice skating rink at the new San Leandro Marina Complex. I would have loved for it to have happened, but it didn't.

A year passed and I decided time had come to open an office in Mulford Gardens. I rented a flimsy one-room freestanding 400 square foot structure with no plumbing and no heating, other than the electric heater I picked up at Ace Hardware. I bought a six by four-foot sheet of marine plywood, painted it blue and glued white plastic letters on both sides which read Val Barry Realty, 510-357-3350. I had Max Walker mount the sign out in front of my new office. If I do say so myself, it looked as if a professional sign company had made it.

The office, located in the 2100 block of Marina Boulevard, was just around the corner from Ed Marvin's office on Doolittle Drive. I knew Ed would be shaken when he learned where I'd relocated. I admit I felt a little strange about my move into what Ed had considered his nearly exclusive territory. I guessed that I'd just have to live with the situation.

Soon, I knew I needed to keep an eye out to eventually find better quarters to work out of. Our crummy work space seemed ice cold in the winter and felt like a sauna in the summer. We had no private conference room, so we tried to schedule meetings with our clients in their homes. Besides we were ashamed to let people see our dreadful headquarters.

In spite of the uncomfortable working conditions, my staff and I did well. I operated in a manner that generated lots of business, all of which I couldn't handle by myself. Any of my salespeople with a reasonable desire to succeed always had clients passed on to them by me. They wouldn't enjoy that amenity in another office which kept them with me.

Notwithstanding the fact that everyone in my office probably made more money than they could anywhere else, I had trouble with Jerry. Even though he didn't bring in nearly as much money as he did when he started with me, he still made a good living. The problem I had with him related to his temper. If someone said something he didn't like, he invariably had to tell the person off. I knew that a quick tempered salesman would not fit well long term into my operation.

It came to a head one summer afternoon. I mentioned earlier that Jerry had handled the sale of the Kerr Property to Lila Maxwell. Lila wanted to move into her new acquisition and had Jerry serve the tenant a thirty-day notice to vacate the premises. The tenant, Jack Paris, a real jerk in my opinion, worked as a bartender at Bill's Rendezvous. Jack knew everyone that frequented the bar. Many of my clientele spent a lot of time complicating their lives in that bar.

When Jerry served the notice to vacate to Jack at Lila's house, Jack let him know that he had no intention of getting out in thirty days. In fact, he said, "I'll get out when I'm damn good and ready, and you can't do a thing about it."

Jerry exploded. He called Jack every dirty name he could think of in front of Jack's family. Jerry told Jack when the thirty days were up he would personally throw Jack and anyone else in the house that day out in the street.

Within a few minutes, Jerry came back to the office. As he explained to me about the confrontation, Jack flew into the office and took a punch at Jerry with his right hand adorned with a set of nasty looking brass knuckles. Jerry, a tough ex-marine ducked

238

and knocked Jack to the floor. I ordered Jerry to leave the office. I told Jack, "Either you sign a statement that you unconditionally promise to leave the property in two weeks, and sign a promissory note for two weeks advance rent right now, or I'm having you arrested for attacking a member of my staff with a deadly weapon."

Jack, who I suspected wanted to steer clear of the San Leandro police department, meekly complied without complaint. He expressed gratitude to me for not reporting him.

That same day, I called Ed Marvin and asked him if he would like to hire my best and most temperamental salesman. Ed had been trying to steal Jerry from me for months and thanked me profusely. I told Jerry about my discussion with Ed. Jerry immediately transferred his license to Ed Marvin Realty. He fit well into Ed's operation. Jerry became a competitor, yet we remained friends over the ensuing years. He stayed with Ed for a year or so, then he moved on, looking for that elusive elephant, I suppose. Eventually, I lost track of Jerry; I liked him and hope he found that elephant.

CHAPTER SIXTY-TWO

Jake and Phyllis Leal, a delightful couple in their mid-forties, for whom I handled the sale of a home to them in Marina Gardens in 1963, became close friends with Sheila and me. One summer afternoon, thirteen-year-old Chris, the oldest of the Leal's three children, suffered a senseless tragedy. Chris and a couple of his pals were hanging out in one of the several open fields adjacent to Mulford and Marina Gardens when suddenly Chris fell unconscious to the ground.

Initially no cause could be observed that explained Chris's condition. One of his friends rushed to the closest house to call for help. Another boy tried unsuccessfully to revive Chris. A fire truck soon arrived. The emergency medical technicians in the fire crew couldn't help Chris—he had died. At the base of the back of his neck, just below his shirt collar, the medical technicians discovered a tiny bloodless puncture. Chris had been shot from quite a long distance. The nearly spent twenty-two-caliber bullet barely penetrated the skin. But it did indeed penetrate his skin and severed the spinal cord killing him instantly.

The police scoured the area looking for anyone who might provide information. The same afternoon of the shooting, officers located two young boys who reported they had seen a boy about sixteen fire a rifle across the field in which Chris and his pals played. That evening officers went from door to door for miles around and learned a teenage boy had been seen carrying a rifle in the neighborhood that day. Police went to the home the boy had ostensibly entered. They confronted and arrested sixteen-year-old Leonard Banks who confessed he had fired the shot that killed Chris.

The Banks boy claimed Chris's death resulted from an unfortunate accident. He said he only wanted to see how close to Chris he could place a bullet without hitting him. At the distance of three quarters of a mile, he had doubted that the bullet would even travel that far. The court ruled that Banks, being a minor, would only be required to be incarcerated until he reached the age of twenty-one. I stopped by the Leals' home to express my condolences. I didn't believe they would ever truly recover. Little did I realize that the grief they were enduring would visit me in a few years.

The Leals had been able to gradually accumulate a nice nest egg which they planned to utilize when Jake retired. Jake carried no excess weight and looked youthful and appeared to be enjoying excellent health. Not so—he suffered from heart trouble and several other health issues. He worked as a truck driver and knew he would have to stop working in a few years. The couple asked if I could make their nest egg grow a little faster so Jake might enjoy an earlier comfortable retirement.

They trusted me, but were timid about taking a chance. I suggested that initially they might make a very small loan to me, which I would use to help finance my own investment strategy. Accepting my advice, they lent me $5000 which I secured with a promissory note secured with a second deed of trust encumbering one of my properties located in the same area in which they lived. They were pretty savvy and knew they could never find an investment that would equal the safety and generous return I provided. After receiving their monthly interest payments right on time over a period of a little less than a year, they wanted to substantially increase their investment account with me, which they did.

CHAPTER SIXTY-THREE

My business continued to grow. Even so, our expenses still devoured most of our income. But clearly, the future seemed to bode well for us. Since I'd started working in real estate, I kept my abundant activities manageable by writing in a daily reminder everything I planned to do on the following day. As I accomplished each task I'd assigned to myself, that item got a check mark in the dairy. At the end of the day, when I had been able to check off every entry, I felt a strong sense of satisfaction. Truly, the success I experienced existed in part as a result of my daily planning routine. I think the cliché goes, **"Plan your work, and work your plan**."

I maintained my long held faith that God favored me by granting me guidance and wisdom. I'm pretty sure that I didn't necessarily deserve all the good that came my way, but somehow I knew it would continue. Occasionally, I experienced good fortune almost beyond belief. It amazed me when I successfully negotiated the sale of thirteen properties in a single month. When something like that happened, I called it "magic time." I didn't converse with others much about that phenomenon, simply because some people might have been jealous and others might not have believed me. Nonetheless, magic time does truly exist in all venues of life. My youngest son Paulie and I attended the Oakland Raiders football games as often as possible. The thrill of watching quarterback, Kenny Stabler, complete a pass to Fred Biletnikoff in a crowd of defenders so thick you couldn't even see Freddie, made the term "magic time" come to mind.

I sat at my desk early one cold and drizzly Monday morning lamenting the fact that I had to operate out of such a decrepit office. I knew those quarters, in the eyes of some, reflected a poor public image of Val Barry Realty. Just then the ringing phone jolted me from my mood of consternation. I answered a call from Mel Howard. You will recall, Mel and Dee Howard owned and operated Dee's Beauty Salon, just across from my office, and they leased the building in front of their shop to Farrell and McGovern Realtors. Mel said, "Good morning, I just drove past your office and saw you sitting at your desk and it dawned on me, I think Val and I can do some good for each other." He informed me that he received notice from Bob Farrell and Ed McGovern that they would soon be vacating his building. Mel asked me if I would be interested in leasing the office.

I contemplated the luxury of not having to utilize the restroom of the Shell Service Station on the corner. Mel and Dee's building in its original state had been a comfortable three bedroom house. Converting the residence to an office amounted to placing large plate glass windows and a sliding glass door at the front of the structure. Additionally, concrete steps a little wider than the sliding glass entry door were installed. The finishing touch involved adorning the entire front of the structure with an expensive light tan stone veneer. I signed a lease that required a $250 monthly payment, which didn't amount to much more than I'd been paying for my one-room ex-lawnmower repair shop across the street. My staff and I happily moved into our office in anticipation of good times ahead.

Soon the news of my new office circulated. Several agents asked if they could join my sales crew. I didn't want to make the mistake of trying to manage too many salespeople, which many brokers did with disastrous results. I limited the number of people working out of my new location to six, including me. My crew included Gay Green and Ernie Cox who were with me across the street. Additionally, Minnie Dutra, Fred Hansen, Dan Nolan and Ted Meecham joined my staff.

Gay lived next door to us on Burton Drive. The real estate business fascinated her. I became the first and only broker she would ever work for. An attractive blond in her mid-forties, Gay impressed everyone she met as charming, sincere and genuine. Frank Green, Gay's husband held the position of superintendent of maintenance at the Tony Lima Golf Course. Frank was a terrific golfer and well liked among the folks who played golf and hung out around the course. Unfortunately, Gay and Frank had little in common. She viewed a career in real estate sales and investments as a way to support herself when the inevitable breakup with Frank happened. In addition to being a steady producer, Gay proved to be my true friend.

I hired Ernie Cox, a grizzled snaggle-toothed, chain-smoking old buzzard in his early eighties, because I felt sorry for him. Ernie had worked for a large construction company as a parts chaser for many years. He had become somewhat of a mascot semi-father figure over the years to the owner of the firm, Jay Dailey.

When Ernie just got too old and confused to conduct the duties of his job satisfactorily, Jay let him go. He suggested that if Ernie obtained a real estate salesman's license, Jay would lean on any of the employees in the firm who were considering buying or selling a home to engage Ernie's real estate services. Jay paid excellent wages, and his people were eager to please him. Until Ernie left my office because of failing health, every now and then his former boss's influence came through for him.

Around sixty-five, Minnie Dutra, a life-long resident of San Leandro, belonged to the large local community of Portuguese ancestry from which she derived a steady clientele. That united and politically dominant group could assure the election of any local municipal candidate they favored. Minnie had worked as a real estate agent locally for many years. After retiring in her forties, she and her husband became the delighted and surprised parents of a baby boy. Eventually, Mr. Dutra developed leukemia and could no longer support his family. Minnie, determined her son would not endure the financial disadvantages that the lack of adequate financial support promised to create, decided to hook up with Val Barry Realty—a lucky break for both of us.

Fred Hansen, an extraordinarily well dressed, paunchy, bald, hard-of-hearing, cheerful fellow had been a real estate agent with E. Jones Realty, a venerable well established firm since the mid-1950s. Fred agreed to join my company if I would provide him with a private office and supply him with a special telephone designed for those with hearing difficulties. He knew a lot about the Alameda County Department of Welfare's housing program by which a welfare recipient could buy a house with only $500 down and secure thirty year low interest financing. I knew Fred would make more than one sale every month and his sterling reputation would reflect well on my operation. Fred looked like a millionaire driving up in his late model gold-colored Cadillac.

Dan Nolan had left Ed Marvin Realty to come in with me. He would have been with me sooner, except we had no bathroom at the lawn mower repair office and Dan, due to his kidney condition, needed frequent restroom access. It pleased me to join up with Dan again. I valued his sage advice and sincere encouragement and most of all, his friendship.

You will recall I met Ted Meecham in Ed Marvin's office when I started there. Ted seldom brought in a real estate deal, but he did pay me a monthly desk fee in connection with the operation of his independent insurance brokerage business. Ted no longer held a seat on the City Council and his former influence in that capacity no longer existed—a situation he found difficult to handle.

CHAPTER SIXTY-FOUR

One morning as I moved into my new office, it shocked me to see that the beautiful light tan, expensive stone veneer on the front of the building had been spray painted with a variety of bright colors. The colors started at the base of the stone and involved the lower six feet of the twelve-foot height of the stonework. Confused at first, I considered it must have been the result of a graffiti attack. I thought, *maybe Mel's insurance would kick in.*

I entered the building and saw Raylene Combs overseeing the installation of new draperies in the room I'd chosen as my private office. Raylene informed me that the chic window coverings were an office-warming gift from her to me. I expressed my sincere gratitude and played down how I felt when she asked me how I liked the decoration she had applied to the rock on the front of the office. I supposed because Mel and Dee and I had such a good relationship, they never mentioned Raylene's handiwork.

I had originally met Raylene and her husband, Seth, one Sunday afternoon when I still worked in Ed Marvin's office. They were an attractive, well-dressed couple appearing to me to be in their late sixties. She, a slender redhead around five feet tall, did most of the talking while Seth, crowned with a head of thick silver hair, standing a little over six feet tall, spoke very little. They stopped by the office and told me they had been driving through the area and were excited by what they had seen. Raylene had been impressed with the large lots bordering Marina Boulevard, situated within a block of the eastern shoreline of the San Francisco Bay.

Seth, friendly yet reserved, let his wife take charge—a role I discerned he had become used to playing. She told me about a large discount retail clothing store she very successfully operated as a single divorced woman for many years on Howard Street in San Francisco. Under the process of eminent domain, fairly recently, the City of San Francisco Redevelopment Agency had bought her store and her other nearby commercial real estate holdings. Seth drove a taxicab in San Francisco. Raylene called for a cab one evening and Seth showed up. He was an excellent driver, a charming escort and before long they formalized their relationship within the bonds of matrimony.

The Combs, both retired, resided on Skyline Boulevard in Oakland in a custom home Raylene designed and had built. She had spent much of her life functioning in the hustle-bustle life of an innovative, aggressive, successful entrepreneur. She dreamed about designing, building and living in her own luxury apartment complex. The San Leandro Marina district (Mulford Gardens) captured her interest. She fascinated me.

Making serious money had motivated her and that appeared to be exactly what she had accomplished. Through her innovation and skill she reached that point in life known as "critical mass," wherein she could financially afford to do whatever she liked. Raylene personified the life I struggled to reach.

She listened intensely while I related the wonderful development I envisioned evolving around the San Leandro Marina shoreline and golf course complex. I dreamed to be part of all that promised to happen there, and I could tell she shared my enthusiasm. She wanted me to come up with something for her. She told me she knew I could help her accomplish her goal and she wouldn't be talking with other Realtors. I asked the Combs to give me a few days to do a little investigating, and I promised to get back to them within the week.

I could find nothing listed for sale on Marina Boulevard but that only worked in my favor. Dan Nolan and I had bought a little house situated on a third-acre lot in the 2600 block of Marina Boulevard from an out-of-the-area owner a few months previously. I continually contacted out-of-area owners. Often they were eager to sell and quite easy to deal with. Greg Gillespie owned a property adjacent to ours which he had bought recently through me. Greg agreed to list his property with me, and Dan and I would be glad to sell ours for a nice profit.

I showed the sites to Raylene and Seth and she signed the purchase agreement so fast I thought she might break my pen. We closed the escrow in a couple of weeks and she engaged the services of Charles Winkler, the architect who had helped her with the house on Skyline. I referred Raylene to a couple of reputable builders and she began the city approval process. The house on the lot that Greg Gillespie sold Raylene looked to be quite a nice building. I contacted the owner of a vacant lot a couple of blocks away from the property Raylene had bought from Greg.

247

The owner agreed to list his lot for sale with me. I negotiated the sale of the lot to Raylene. She had the house she bought from Greg moved onto the vacant parcel. I put Raylene together with the same contractor I used on Fairway Drive (remember the Fairway Dr. move on) to build a new foundation and get the house ready to sell. I then wrote a purchase contract for the property on which Raylene's house had been moved, which she accepted.

In about six months, the Combs moved into a stunning 3200 square foot manager's apartment (a duplicate floor plan of her home on Skyline Boulevard in Oakland) in Raylene's newly built twenty-five unit "top of the line" apartment complex, a half block from the developing San Leandro Marina Complex. The deal worked out well for a lot of us. Dan and I made a good profit on the property Raylene bought from us. Greg Gillespie did very well on the property he sold to Raylene through my Realtor services. I earned a commission on the sale of the vacant lot to Raylene and another commission in connection with the sale of the property on which Raylene's house was moved.

The series of transactions described in this chapter leading to the construction of Raylene's apartment complex occurred when Dan and I still worked in Ed Marvin's office and he received a commission from every transaction. Raylene seemed delighted with me and we would do more business. I guess it is clear that properties Raylene acquired through my services went solely into her name as her separate property.

CHAPTER SIXTY-FIVE

Perhaps my dogged level of commitment to succeed in my real estate career is somewhat revealed by the manner in which I worked through the following transaction: I felt fortunate obtaining the listing regarding the sale of the Riley family home. The spacious, tree-studded, well tended grounds reminded me of a picturesque park. Sitting in the middle of that tranquil setting stood a good-looking ranch-style house, exuding character. The Riley's, independently wealthy, listed the property realistically and let me know they would not negotiate their price. The listing offered a real opportunity to enhance my business. Mrs. Riley belonged to that large Portuguese ancestry population I mentioned previously so prominent in San Leandro. If my service impressed the Riley's sufficiently, I knew additional referral business would follow.

The real estate market had fallen into a stubborn downward cycle—full price purchase contracts were rare. Realtors are obliged to present all offers. Within the first month of the listing we had presented three offers below the listed price to the Riley's which they rejected. I believed that exceptional property would bring the full asking price. Gay held the home open on a Sunday and a married couple initially spent around forty-five minutes looking it over. Gay learned the wife and husband were both foreign born. The wife was a gregarious, busty blond from West Germany and her husband had emigrated from Taiwan.

Clearly, the Mrs. wanted to buy but the husband remained noncommittal. After a heated debate out on the patio, Mrs. Chew seemed to prevail. Gay had the pair sign a full price purchase contract and accepted a $1500 good faith deposit check which would be deposited into my trustee account. A contingency stipulation within the agreement involved the buyers' ability to acquire a thirty-year loan for eighty percent of the purchase price, with said financing bearing five and three-quarters percent interest. Gay assured them currently the loan they needed could be obtained through the lender we normally used.

The agreement provided for the sale to be completed in thirty days from the date the sellers signed the purchase contract. The husband insisted on placing the loan with a company of his choosing. I reluctantly agreed to his demand that he alone be allowed to pursue a lender—which proved to be a mistake. The sellers accepted the offer that evening and we opened escrow the next morning.

We soon learned two things that put us on edge. Mr. Chew didn't get around to contacting a lender for more than a week. Mrs. Riley let us know that if the sale didn't close within the thirty days as provided in the contract, her mother had decided she wanted to buy the property. If Mrs. Riley's mom bought the property per a client exemption agreement made when I took the listing, we would receive no commission. I called the Chews and let them know we needed to complete the sale within the next two weeks. Mr. Chew admitted his lender couldn't place the loan for less than six percent interest, and he damn well wouldn't pay more than five and three-quarters percent. After wasting precious days Mr. Chew finally gave me the go-ahead to locate a lender that would grant a loan in compliance with the conditions of the purchase agreement.

No luck. Five and three-quarters percent financing no longer existed. Had we been free to go after the needed financing at the beginning of the escrow, we would have nailed it. Now we couldn't locate anything below six percent. I called Mr.Chew. He told me they didn't want the property if they had to pay more than five and three quarters percent interest. Discouraged, but not ready to give up, I tried a different approach. When Gay had the Chews sign the purchase contract, she got both their work numbers.

The following morning, I called Helga Chew (she had asked me to call her Helga). I knew she wanted the property and didn't give a damn about a quarter of a percent higher interest. I quietly explained the numerous advantages of owning the property and if she let the deal die, how difficult it would be to locate something she would like as much. I called Mr. Chew again—I didn't feel at liberty to call him by his first name—and basically repeated what I had minutes before said to Helga. He coldly said he would talk it over with his wife after they got home from work. He instructed me to call around eight that evening.

That night Mr. Chew told me they had decided to pass on the property. They wished to drop by my office the following afternoon around six to pick up their good faith deposit refund check. I talked the situation over with Gay. We had put a lot of work into bringing that sale to fruition and now it looked like all our effort amounted to a big waste of time. Gay mentioned what a difficult time she had getting Mr. Chew to sign the purchase agreement, even after the couple decided they wanted to own the property. She commented that she thought Mr. Chew had a phobia about signing documents. Her remarks gave me an idea. I pondered how I might use Mr. Chew's eccentricity to my advantage.

When my supercilious, ultra-conservative buyer and his wife arrived at my office, I had my big trustee account check book wide open and in plain view on my desk. Mr. Chew could see I'd already written the deposit refund check still attached to the checkbook. With a friendly smile I greeted the couple courteously and let them know that in order to officially cancel the transaction, they needed to sign a few routine documents. Mr. Chew's eyes narrowed defensively at my mention of the requirement. Gay had been right—the man hated signing.

I presented a perfunctory escrow cancellation form in addition to a document assigning their right to buy the property to me. Mr. Chew's eyes narrowed even more when I placed the documents and my pen in front of him on my desk and said curtly, "Please sign here."

Angrily, Mr. Chew blurted out, "Why in the hell should I assign my position to you—you're trying to take advantage; we're damn well buying this property whether you like it or not."

I sincerely apologized for attempting to enhance my position at their expense and had them sign a less daunting financing contingency removal form. We called the Chews' lending agent and let him know his clients were agreeable to a six percent interest rate. The sale closed within the allotted time—we collected a well-earned commission and everyone seemed happy, especially Helga.

CHAPTER SIXTY-SIX

In 1966 the money poured in. I drove a late model Cadillac (the Realtors weren't into Mercedes yet.) We dined in good restaurants and paid for the kid's orthodontic work in cash. As a matter of fact, everything we bought, other than real estate in which we were heavily invested, we paid for in cash. Sheila efficiently took care of the prodigious amount of bookwork required by our prolific business activities.

She belonged to a women's club wherein the ladies met every month, which resulted in quite a few ancillary social engagements that included the husbands. She served as an active Cub Scout den mother, and the boys seemed to love her. In spite of our busy schedules, we enjoyed a pleasant social life. We hired Mrs. Nagy, a matronly lady who came in each Monday to clean house and prepare a week of delicious frozen dinners. We hadn't exactly arrived yet, but we were sure on our way.

I knew our life had to get much easier soon and things would come together between us then. Wherever we had a disagreement, which happened often, I found myself apologizing, and she let me know she didn't love me. I just couldn't believe she meant that, yet maybe I should have. In the early days of our marriage we professed our love for each other often. After all, aren't husbands and wives supposed to be in love? I wondered sometimes *had Sheila's feelings toward me really changed or had she just stopped pretending.*

The following situation didn't happen often but it seemed typical of circumstances that strained the well-being of our marriage. I arose early Saturday morning. That night we were hosting a house party to which many of our closest friends were invited. The get-together had been planned for weeks. That event meant a lot, especially for Sheila, and I knew I had better not screw it up.

A couple of weeks earlier, I had been introduced to a very likable middle-aged couple, Armon and Mitzie Hanks, at Ray and Pat's home. The couples socialized together frequently. The Hanks both worked and earned an above average income. Armon explained and grumbled that much of their money went to pay income taxes. They lived in a rented apartment, had no children, and consequently, no tax deductions.

I suggested that they might be well served by considering the purchase of a house plus a duplex complex of which many had been built in Mulford Gardens. They could live in the house that I felt sure would suit them better than the apartment in which they presently resided. The duplex would provide income and a write-off to reduce their state and federal tax obligation. I asked, "After all, why not let the government help you pay for whatever real estate you might acquire?" They were intrigued. Armon enjoyed tinkering and maintaining his own property appealed to him. They wanted me to find something for them, which I promised to do.

The type of property I described to the Hanks didn't come on the market frequently. A lot of folks had the same needs that they had. I found only one such property for sale in Mulford Gardens. Pete Simmons, a real estate broker I respected, had the listing. I called Pete Friday evening and he told me the sellers had just accepted an offer. I knew the Hanks would have liked the property. I asked Pete to let me know if anything happened to his deal.

He called me at nine Saturday morning and informed me that the buyers of his listing had a sudden death occur in their family and had backed out of the purchase agreement. He said, "Val, you should move quickly on this because others will jump on it when they learn my listing is back on the market."

I called the Hanks and they seemed excited. I asked Pete to call his sellers and set an appointment for me to show the property to my potential buyers at noon. I had to move quickly because our party guests would be arriving around seven that evening.

As I showed one of the duplex units, I noticed another agent escorting clients through the house. The Hanks liked what they saw. At my office, they signed an offer not far below the listed price. I called Pete and asked him to set up an appointment for him and me to present the purchase contract to the sellers. As the Hanks left, I told them I'd let them know the sellers' reaction as soon as I had an answer. About three, Pete called and let me know

254

he had a presentation appointment for us at the sellers' home at six. I was cutting it close, but I had to go ahead. I called Sheila and told her I'd get there as soon as I could. She hung up on me. I understood how she felt. I wished she understood how I felt.

The sellers were congenial, but they decided to counter at a price midway between the listed price and the initial offer. I called Armon and Mitzi and headed for Alameda. They would pay the price the seller had agreed to only if they could have possession of the house the day the escrow closed, which of course required me to draw another counter offer.

I called Pete from Alameda and he said the seller would be home all evening and to just meet him at their house. At eleven, I drove back to present what I hoped would be the final counter offer. Rain poured down. I sure hoped Sheila and our guests were having a good time. The owners signed the last counter offer after a protracted period of discussion. I called the Hanks from the sellers' home and let them know they were in contract. I walked through our front door at one o'clock Sunday morning. As Willie Nelson would say, "The party's over."

Sheila gave me the silent treatment for days. I knew she thought of me as a selfish, thoughtless bastard. To her, my behavior wouldn't have been any worse than if I had spent Saturday night at Bill's Rendezvous. Of course, I felt bad ... real bad. I should have been at the party. My absence embarrassed my wife and caused her considerable discomfort. I'd try to make it up to her; there would be other parties, and I would be there.

I looked at the situation as follows: My efforts brought in a few thousand dollars. Had I waited and not acted as I did, I would have run into competition which could have ruined my chances of making the sale. I served the best interests of my clients which served my family's best interests as well. Among other things, the commission helped insure that our kids would get the balance of the orthodontic work they needed and served to keep them in Catholic school.

I always tried to figure out how to widen my services in order to maintain a steady, ever increasing stream of income, not subject to any one of the capricious nature of the various segments of the real estate market. I observed many real estate agents whose annual income fell short of meeting their needs in spite of the fact they knew how to sell. They simply hadn't prepared themselves to adjust to the vagaries that governed the success of their chosen career.

When the income from your profession ranges between feast and famine, eventually famine emerges victorious. I tried to invest sufficient time and effort required to develop a large number of skills to deposit in my repertoire of services. Whenever some component of the real estate business faded, inevitably another moved to the forefront. I endeavored to profitably take advantage of whatever segment of the industry became available to me at any time. My synthesis of several service components gave birth to an all-encompassing mode of activity that guaranteed uninterrupted productivity.

Shortly before moving into the 2108 Marina Boulevard office, I completed a course on real estate appraisal at Chabot Junior College. When I became able to run my business out of more spacious quarters, I made good use of the appraisal course. I knew General Electric and Alcoa Credit Corporations were in the business of financing home improvement projects. They secured their loans with promissory notes and deeds of trust that encumbered the properties being improved. I knew the properties had to be appraised as part of the loan approval process.

Both companies responded favorably to my offer of service as a fee appraiser. They both said the heavy volume of their business required the services of more than one appraiser and they seemed pleased I had called. I committed to do one trial appraisal and if they weren't entirely satisfied with my work, there would be no charge. I dropped by each company—they were both located in Hayward. I met the managers and received my trial appraisal assignments.

I designed an especially easily understandable check-off list identifying the characteristics of the properties, and included two Polaroid photos of the houses and a list of same neighborhood comparable properties that had sold within the last six months. I inserted the informational material, along with my estimate of reasonable market value of the subject property into an attractive clear plastic folder. My appraisals appeared very professional. Both credit companies were favorably impressed and paid my fee, comparable to the amount charged by VA and FHA appraisers.

I had entered the appraisal business and I loved it. I did as many appraisals as I could handle and still have time to accomplish my other activities. The appraisal assignment requests came in steadily. They took about ten hours of my time each week. As far as I knew, no other active general brokerage Realtor enhanced their income by doing part time appraisals. Occasionally, an owner of a property I appraised, with whom I had become friendly, referred me to friends and relatives who utilized my other real estate related services.

Generally, providing property management services didn't appeal to me, but as a courtesy when asked to handle someone's rental property, I did so and I received frequent requests. I saw an opportunity to establish a reliable source of steady monthly income by aggressively soliciting a substantial clientele of rental property owners. Minnie Dutra and I discussed the matter. She agreed to head up a first-class rental property management division.

We did some advertising and made a lot of solicitation calls. In a short time we had more than a hundred accounts netting a little over $5000 a month which Minnie and I split down the middle. As

I stated earlier, I didn't like to manage rentals, but Minnie did, so Val Barry Property Management Services served us well. When one of our owners decided to sell, who would you imagine got first chance at the listing? In time, many renters decided they preferred to make payments on their own home, rather than on their landlord's property and often sought our help.

I always liked the hard money real property loan brokerage business. I learned the basics of hard money lending in Ed's office. It worked like this: If a property owner in need of a loan had substantial equity in their property, yet had poor credit, I could help them. I located a person looking to grant a relatively high interest loan, well secured by a promissory note tied to a deed of trust which encumbered the borrower's real property. If the borrower had sufficient equity in the securing property, the lender couldn't lose. Poor credit-rated borrowers were generally unable to obtain financing from conventional loan sources such as banks, etc. That foolish policy deprived conventional lending institutions of a lot of business. No matter, their short-sightedness served me well.

Acting in the capacity of a loan broker, which a licensed real estate broker could legally do, I arranged the loan from the lender to the borrower and received a hefty commission from the borrower. You might wonder where these private lenders were found. They came from all walks of life. If your reputation defined you as a reliable broker, lenders sought you out. Many of them were older retired people who looked to safely increase their income. But they were attracted by more than just money. Dealing with the loan broker and receiving installment payments from the borrowers made them feel they were still an important component in the game of life.

Many of my private lenders were like family. I never arranged a loan for a lender that I feared making myself. If a borrower went "bad" and the lender had to protect their capital by foreclosing, I made sure my lender always got their money back in full. If the lender just didn't want to go through the foreclosure process, I bought the loan at its face value and handled the legalities myself. That seldom happened. Occasionally, yet rarely, a foreclosure had to be initiated and most private lenders, knowing they were financially well-secured, weren't put off by the process.

Surprisingly, I experienced foreclosure situations in which an owner had to sell the securing property to save his/her equity. Then sometime later that same borrower asked for a loan on another property and the same lender gladly granted another loan. Every promissory note contained a provision wherein the borrower had to pay a late payment penalty if the lender didn't receive the monthly payment within fifteen days of the due date. Mrs. Van Gundy, a lovable, grandmotherly octogenarian, and one of my long-time private lenders, always insisted that I bring her borrowers who would likely make their payments late each month. She loved collecting those penalties.

Don't make the mistake of believing that all hard money lenders are greedy wolves—although some indeed are—who are out to benefit no one except themselves. I admonish you not to consider all hard money borrowers hapless victims on the wrong end of the money equation, being quick-sanded into financial ruin, although some are. Conventional lenders hampered by credit rating constraints simply cannot help those who are in a temporary currency crunch, facing ruin absent a quick infusion of cash. Often the hard money lender, sometimes in the form of a sweet old grandma, comes to the rescue, making a nice bundle of monetary honey for herself while helping a temporarily strapped family get back on their feet. It isn't the banks of America that keep such families from being tossed out of their homes; no, it's hard money lenders.

Often, a small—and occasionally a large homebuilder needed an interim loan to get a proposed project to a point where construction could begin. The nascent development hadn't progressed far enough to qualify for a regular construction loan. Getting the project to that point had tapped the builder out. Mighty Mouse, better known as the hard money lender would save the day. It tickled the grateful builder to pay a premium interest rate and loan broker commission. The profit realized by the developer when his or her enterprise—saved by grandma hard money lender—reached fruition, could make the cost of the temporary financing seem like a pittance. That situation happened constantly.

Why did the hard money brokerage business have such a ghastly reputation? The answer to that question never varied; it fell under the heading of "conflict of interest." A party would ask the loan broker to arrange a loan. The broker appraised the potential borrower's proposed securing real estate. If the property failed to have sufficient value to safely secure the requested loan, legally the broker had to advise the lender accordingly. If that happened, the broker received no commission.

So, what would you think some brokers might be tempted to do in such a case? Bingo! Right on . . . they falsely inflated the appraisal value of the property and collected a nice loan fee and the lender had been duped into making a bad loan. Soon, such brokers were out of business. As I stated previously herein, that never happened with me. When I arranged a loan, if it went bad, I either bought the loan from the lender or I bid the property in at the foreclosure sale at a price that made the lender whole. In such a case that lender stayed mine for life. Because of the enormous liability potential in connection with arranging hard money loans, in my office only I acted in the capacity of a loan broker.

CHAPTER SIXTY-SEVEN

While alone in the office early one Monday morning, Tom Santos and his pretty wife, Sandy, stopped by the office looking for a home in the area to rent. The couple appeared to be in their mid-twenties. They explained they rented an apartment in a pretty rough neighborhood. Tom and Sandy looked to relocate mainly because they did not wish their two children, a five-year-old boy and their four-year-old daughter, attending school in the area in which the family presently resided.

I handed them a rental application and asked them to fill it out. When Minnie arrived, I planned to give her their application form. As the Santos' filled it in, they told me a little about themselves. Tom had been employed as an automotive body and fender mechanic for several years. Sandy worked as a secretary for the Kaiser Foundation in Oakland. I asked, "How is your credit?"

Tom answered, "I guess it's pretty good, everyone seems willing to let us charge."

My following question had become a mantra with me, "Why not buy a home instead of renting and paying for someone else to own the home you're living in?"

Tom showed interest; he asked, "Do you think we could really buy? We have bills, you know."

I inquired further and told them I believed them to be excellent candidates to become homeowners. Then I discussed the many advantages of owning over renting. I asked, "Do you have time now to let me show you a home I think you might like?"

They seemed glad that I took an interest in them. I planned to show them a house that Dan Kerr bought from the U.S. Navy Surplus Housing Department in Alameda and moved to West Avenue 130th. Dan purchased the lot through me to accommodate the move. He had just put the finishing touches on his project and planned to list it with me in a day or so.

As I showed the Santos the property, Sandy said to me, "Val, if you can make this happen for us, let's do it."

Even though I didn't have the property listed yet, Dan and I had already established a price. I wrote a purchase contract which the Santos signed and Dan gladly accepted. Dan had made the house like new and the property and the buyers easily qualified for a new FHA loan. The family took possession in time for Billy, their little boy to start school at Garfield Elementary, a block from their new home.

Tom earned extra money by doing auto body work at his home on weekends and evenings. He did good work and I referred customers to him. We stayed in touch and as time went by I became a little disappointed at the changing course the Santos' life took. Tom explained to me that they met Robin and Jack Hendrickson, a married couple, at a free love rally in Berkeley. Tom found that lifestyle appealing and Sandy went along with him.

The two couples developed an intimate relationship, which progressed to the point that the Hendricksons moved in with the Santoses. I told Tom that I didn't mean to sound judgmental but what he said saddened me. He assured me they had never been happier. Actually, Tom had always seemed a little rough around the edges, but Sandy didn't seem suited to that lifestyle.

The story got more bizarre. I ran into Tom at the neighborhood Shell Station and he let me know the two couples had driven down to Tijuana, Mexico. While there, Tom and Sandy divorced, as did Jack and Robin. Tom then married Robin and Jack married Sandy. The four of them returned home and continued living in the same house. In time, Jack and Sandy moved and took Tom and Sandy's children. I never saw Sandy again, but I did see a lot of Tom and Robin.

A year or so passed and one day I received a call from Tom. He wanted to set up an appointment with me. He arrived at my office on a Harley Davidson motorcycle. He let me know he and Robin had agreed to try to buy Sandy's interest in the West Avenue 130th property. He wanted to know if I would make a second loan to him and Robin to finance the purchase of interest in the property. He asked if I would also handle the necessary paperwork to accomplish the transfer of title.

Residential real estate in the area had gone up in value considerably and certainly sufficient equity existed to justify a loan secured with a promissory note. Actually, Tom wanted to borrow more money than he needed to pay Sandy. I asked him how he planned to use the extra funds, and he quickly changed the subject. No matter, I didn't need to know.

Tom and Robin made payments on my loan for the next five months. After that the payments stopped. They didn't answer my letters. I received a notice from the lender who held the first loan encumbering the property. The first loan had gone into default, thereby placing my loan in second position in jeopardy. I had no choice other than bringing the first lender's delinquent payments current and then initiating my own foreclosure process.

If the foreclosure hadn't been cured in about a hundred and eleven days from the date of the filing of the Notice of Default, the property would be sold to satisfy the indebtedness. I heard nothing from the Santos. Shortly thereafter, I read in the Daily

Review Newspaper their home had been raided by the San Leandro Police. Tom had been arrested and charged with manufacturing methamphetamine in his garage. I checked with the police department and learned Tom had been incarcerated in the Santa Rita Jail in Dublin, about a thirty-minute drive from my office.

I drove out to Santa Rita for a visit with Tom. Not having seen him in several months, his emaciated appearance disturbed me. He seemed glad to see me and candidly told me about the circumstances that brought him to his unfortunate state. He explained that it started to go wrong when he and Robin's recreational drug use evolved into full blown addiction. Robin, a registered nurse had access to drugs when she still worked in that profession, which she no longer did.

Things reached the point when neither of them could hold a job. Part of the money they had borrowed from me went for living expenses and some for a purpose hard for me to understand. Tom explained that he had begun making mechanical repairs from his home for a motorcycle club by the name of the Satan's Warriors. He didn't actually belong to the club, but he sure wanted to. They told him joining the Warriors didn't happen easily; he had to prove his worthiness.

Five of the Warriors had been arrested on suspicion of murdering three members of a rival motorcycle club in central California. Supposedly, the killings resulted from disputes between the two clubs regarding control of drug marketing territories. Tom and Robin saw the situation as an opportunity to ingratiate themselves with their heroes. They put up a portion of the money they borrowed from me to bail out the jailed bikers. Tom's new friends also prevailed upon him to turn his garage into a dope manufacturing facility, which landed him in Santa Rita.

Tom didn't hold back; he told me the funds I lent him and Robin only covered the cost of bailing out three of the five accused murderers. They signed another note and deed of trust encumbering their home in favor of Chuck Marks, a bails bondman which resulted in temporarily freeing the remaining two bikers. I told Tom, I'd try to find a buyer for his home before he lost it in foreclosure. But I let him know the house had to be vacated immediately. After all that had happened, I couldn't sell it with anyone occupying the property. He understood and asked me to explain it to Robin which I promised to do.

Before I met with Robin I called Chuck Marks. I met Chuck at "Marks," his upscale restaurant in Fremont, a twenty-minute drive from San Leandro. Chuck came across much differently than I had expected. I found him friendly and likable, and I believe he thought the same of me.

When someone didn't have the cash to pay his fee for arranging bail, and if the party owned property, Chuck took his fee in the form of a securing note and deed of trust against their property. The amount of the note exceeded the usual amount of the fee had it been paid in cash. In such cases, Chuck often sold the note and deed of trust discounted by an amount sufficient to net him his customary fee. He offered to sell the Santos loan to me and I accepted his offer.

Chuck had done well as a bails bondsman, but it was a nasty business, to which he would have liked to say farewell. He seemed to be too nice a guy to earn his living as he did. He had opened his beautiful restaurant in hopes that it would soon provide a financial escape from his present occupation. He invited me to sit at the bar and have lunch with him. I gladly accepted the invitation and enjoyed the delicious food.

Incidentally, Chuck did end his bails bond career, but not as planned. A few years after the Santos transaction, a murderer's bullet ended his life in his office late at night. The authorities never apprehended his killer. He dealt with some pretty rough customers.

I arrived at Robin's around three that afternoon. Walking up to the front door, I noticed a few Harley Davidson bikes, which didn't surprise me because Tom had begun concentrating on fixing motorcycles. Robin answered the door and invited me in. After the usual niceties, I began to explain the unpleasant facts to her. In a week, her home would be auctioned off via the foreclosure process on the steps of the Alameda County Courthouse. She would then face immediate eviction. Robin, a tough little gal, gave me some hard looks.

I proceeded to let her know if she would be out of the house over the weekend, I would delay the foreclosure sale and try to find a buyer for the property for enough to pay off the first lender and me, and hopefully leave something for her and Tom. After I'd thoroughly explained my position, I noticed I had gathered an audience. About a dozen biker types surrounded me and they didn't look real friendly. Robin said, "These are some of the Satan's Warriors motorcycle club, Val."

She pointed at a guy who must have weighed over three hundred pounds and he didn't look fat. She introduced me to Marty Trainer, the vice-president of the local chapter of the biker club. I knew of that guy from my meeting with Chuck Marks. Trainer was one of the accused killers Robin and Tom had bailed out. Trainer didn't look like he wanted to shake hands with me. I tried to relax as much as I could; I hoped to leave there alive and I knew I'd better not look scared.

Then something unexpected occurred: The bikers backed away and went about whatever I suppose they were doing before I arrived. They said nothing to me, nor did I address them. Robin explained the house had come under "biker's law," which she told me meant she had to sleep with any of those guys anytime at their convenience. With due respect to Robin, I think she'd never been happier, and I figured Tom to be honored. Well, Robin and the bikers vacated the house over the following weekend, taking all the household furnishings. I found a buyer for the property who paid enough to clear the loans, net me a commission and leave a couple of thousands of dollars for the Santos.

After my encounter with the Satan's Warriors and Robin that afternoon, I wondered how I had avoided being physically attacked. Those guys' normal mode of behavior operated within a world of violence. I wouldn't have had a chance to protect myself had things turned ugly. I think I eventually figured it out. My visit amounted to me doing what I had to do in the course of conducting my business.

I had let Robin know exactly what steps she and Tom needed to take in order to salvage any vestige of value remaining in their home. She heard no criticism or blame from me as to the conduct that led to their difficulty. I think the bikers determined I had no intention of making any judgments; rather my job involved making the best of the existing situation.

Surprisingly, to some degree Tom and Robin eventually pulled things together and bought another home through me. Their continuing ups and downs and bizarre lifestyle could fill a book, but there isn't room to tell their whole story in this one.

In keeping with the absence of violence by the outlaw bikers toward me as described above, I will discuss here my thoughts on a type of deadly attack that occurs daily throughout the United States. Reports of lethal mayhem associated with foreclosures, evictions, postal workers, libraries, attorney offices, often involving terminated employees and a plethora of other venues are commonplace. Real estate offices are prime locations for fatal confrontations which I suppose aroused my interest in the subject.

In the course of almost any human endeavor, circumstances will develop in which someone is jilted, divorced, sued, fired or otherwise brought to personal distress. The occurrences of such events, which are inevitable, sometimes result in homicidal consequences. I believe in most cases the underlying reason producing murderous conduct has nothing to do with the initial action being levied against the perpetrator of bloodshed.

Informing tenants that eviction must be carried out due to nonpayment of rent, or whatever other move must be accomplished in order to gain control of an untenable condition, will not result in deathly retaliation. What will get you killed are gratuitous expressions of personal hostility and insults leveled against those who are being taken to task because they've failed to meet their obligations.

The fellow that can't make his house payments knows the bank has no choice other than initiating foreclosure. Naturally, he won't be happy about his family being put out on the street. However, usually the situation or any similar proposition will be accepted relatively peacefully because no matter how regretful, the process is totally in keeping with what is expected in such cases. But anyone who thinks he can forego common courtesy and get away with adding to someone's misery by indulging in the luxury of verbal abuse might end up paying the ultimate price for such foolishness.

CHAPTER SIXTY-EIGHT

Around 1970, the residential real estate market entered a steep downturn. Lots of folks faced financial problems and were forced into foreclosure. Those were sad and hurtful times for a lot of people. In Alameda County, foreclosure trustee auction sales are generally conducted on the county courthouse steps at 1225 Fallon Street in Oakland.

I found myself to be the successful bidder at a couple of the foreclosure sales and soon turned my acquisitions for a quick profit. But such opportunities quickly deteriorated. The dramatically increasing bidding competition became so aggressive that a few times I saw properties sold on the courthouse steps for more than they would bring on the regular market. People bought foreclosures thinking they would make a profit and ended up losing money. Actually, the ancillary expenses related to the foreclosure process often sucked any potential profit out of such transactions. No matter, I knew a ton of money could be made by a smart operator in the distressed property market, and I intended to figure how best to do that.

I puzzled as to why many homes in which existed ample equity were sold at foreclosure auctions. I pondered why the owners didn't just sell their properties on the open market, rather than losing their equity in foreclosure. In fact, my curiosity led me to contact some of those folks to try to learn why they just hadn't sold their property. My investigation enabled me to discover a valuable lesson about how human nature can prevent people from acting in their own best interest.

The consensus of what I learned from people who allowed the equity in their home to be vacuumed away through foreclosure revealed the following: Most told me the trauma of the threat of losing their home so paralyzed them, they simply took no action whatsoever, which led to total loss.

I set out to develop a program to reduce the overwhelming distress connected to the potential loss of a family's home (many times in such situations, indeed a family is involved). Foreclosures begin when the trustee named in a deed of trust has a Notice of Default (NOD) published in the legal notices section of an authorized newspaper. The process from beginning to end takes about one hundred twenty days.

If I discovered a NOD property located in an area in which I'd like to own, I sent a form letter to the owners. My communication mentioned nothing about buying the property. Such owners received many offers from people wanting to buy their property. Those unfortunate owners who couldn't bear the thought of giving up their homes were the people I hoped to link up with. I stated that I'd seen their NOD, and I'd like to make them a loan at a reasonable interest rate that would allow them to keep their home.

Rest assured, those folks had received no other correspondence offering the possibility of a loan to save them from losing their home in foreclosure. Boy, did I figure it right. A plethora of calls came from people who wanted to talk about getting a loan to pull their home out of foreclosure. I met with the callers. Many owed so much that I just couldn't help them. But some did have enough equity to justify a loan sufficient to cure their foreclosure. I became well acquainted with those owners and because I'd saved them, at least for a while, most listened to my sound advice.

Some repaid the money I'd lent them as agreed, which represented good business for me. A few borrowed enough to resolve their financial dilemma for awhile, but their money mis-management propensities soon put them back into financial hot water. Again, in many cases, because I'd been able to bail them out temporarily, they trusted me. They generally either sold directly to me or utilized my services as a Realtor to market their home. If I bought the property myself, and if they wished, I allowed them to rent the property from me for one year, during which time they had a marketable option to buy the property back from me. Did it work out well? You bet it did; I became so busy I had to give up my appraisal business in order to keep up.

In a few instances, insufficient equity existed to justify making a loan but still there was some equity. To such properties I offered and permitted the former owners to rent back from me and gave them a one-year option to buy the property back at a price equal to six percent more than I paid. One Sunday morning I met with a couple in my office in their early forties. Although they were well along in foreclosure, they really didn't owe a lot on their home in Washington Manor.

The couple, who seemed to be intelligent, offered to sell the property to me at a price they knew to be substantially below market value if I would give them a forty-day option to buy the property back at a price slightly higher than what I paid. Additionally, they would be permitted to live in the property during the forty-day option period. I had them sign a sales agreement which stated they were aware they were selling their property below market value and that they had set the price. I happened to be very busy at that time; too busy in fact. The lot alone had to be worth more than what the couple asked. I didn't even bother to look at the property. I closed the escrow a few days later.

The forty days went by and I heard nothing from the sellers. In about two months, I went to the property—I'd never seen it before. I knocked on the door and got no answer. Newspapers and advertisements strewn about the place convinced me the house was unoccupied. I left and came back with Jim Slater, my handyman, in the afternoon. Jim got us into the house and we found it to be completely vacant. The utilities were off and the kitchen had been gutted down to the two-by-four studs. I tried to locate the sellers; I even contacted the police department. They couldn't be found. I never heard from the sellers again. I had a new kitchen installed and sold the property for a nice profit. I could only figure that the sellers had thought they had put one over on me by selling me a house in which an apparent remodeling project had been abandoned.

CHAPTER SIXTY-NINE

Starting with my experience as a thirteen-year-old newspaper delivery boy, I developed the ability of being an effective collector of money owed to me. I had observed that otherwise capable entrepreneurs often ended up in bankruptcy because they were lazy collectors. I recall taking over the management of a fourteen-unit residential rental complex. In the capacity of a Realtor, I had handled the sale of the property to the current owner. When Cy Graham, probably the kindest man I have ever known, acquired ownership, the demonstrated past reliability of the tenants gave assurance that he had entered into a prosperous venture. The rental rates were a little less than the competition which should have had the effect of encouraging full occupancy.

Cy called me a year or so later, lamenting that less than half his tenants were paying rent. At the time he took over the complex it produced sufficient income to meet the loan payments and all expenses related to the complex and still provided ample cash flow. Now, in order to meet the financial obligations necessary to avoid foreclosure, he had to make up the shortages from his diminishing savings. What should have been a gratifying experience had become a sleep-robbing nightmare.

"Cy, how did this happen?" I asked. He told me that when a tenant explained that more pressing financial situations made it impossible to pay the rent, he just couldn't bring himself to demand payment. Over time, other tenants understood that they could play the same game and they took full advantage.

Eventually, to save his floundering enterprise, Cy reluctantly and apologetically demanded payment. The delinquent tenants accused their former benefactor of greedily trying to exploit them. Ignoring the past kindness their landlord had extended, they banded together and offered an obscenely unfair compromise. They agreed to resume making payments only if Cy would forgive past due unpaid rent. They also demanded that the rent rates be decreased to an amount less than those set forth in the rental agreements they had originally signed, even though they were already below normal market rates. If Cy refused to accede to their demands, they threatened to initiate a rent payment strike and encourage the few paying tenants to join.

What a mess . . . the stress and depression Cy had been enduring showed on his face. I agreed to take over management of the complex on the non-negotiable condition that he would have no further contact with the tenants. I knew that in the beginning some of the rebellious tenants would try to reach him to circumvent my authority, which indeed they did. True to his word, he informed the tenants who approached him that he had turned total control of the complex over to me. I placed in motion a plan of action.

I sent collection demands to all the delinquent tenants except two and initiated the process to evict the two tenants who had influenced the others to shirk their obligations. Those two had three days to bring their unpaid accounts current in order to avoid getting kicked out. Four days later, both brought their past due rent to my office. I refused reinstatement for the one I considered to be the prime trouble maker. The already floundering rebellion ended when the other tenants watched the Alameda County Deputy Sheriffs remove the initial instigator and his family from their very fairly priced comfortable apartment.

Some of the tenants hadn't paid for nearly a year. Although they were willing and able to resume regular monthly payments, they simply didn't have the money to pay their entire past due rent up to date all at once. I negotiated a compromise requiring that they sign a promissory note covering the back rent which provided for reasonable monthly payments including principle and interest. A failing operation rebounded to prosperity, and I felt deep pleasure observing the return of Cy's sense of well-being.

Ironically, the kindness Cy had shown his tenants earned him their hostile rejection while my no non-sense control resulted in their respect and cooperation. Over the following years, I earned a monthly management fee which Cy gladly paid. Eventually, his health began to fail and he decided to sell the fourteen units as well as other property he owned. Naturally he chose me to represent him as his Realtor and upon the sale of the properties I received a handsome commission.

CHAPTER SEVENTY

I didn't spend as much time with my kids as I wished, but when with them I liked to think that we spent quality time together. We subscribed to Reader's Digest, and I liked to sit with the three older ones in our living room and have each of them read aloud the stories they selected themselves. The kids seemed to enjoy this activity and I knew it did them good. Each of them discussed the issues set forth in the articles. I encouraged them to express their thoughts succinctly and confidently.

Danny, curious about everything and bright as a shiny new dime, always seemed to have some fascinating project in the works. He found a dead frog and placed it in a sunny spot for a couple of weeks. The sun dried the little frog corpse into a hard shell, retaining all its original features. Danny and I painted the mummified amphibian a lustrous white with green eyes and ruby red lips. That unique work of art still remains an attraction.

Another time he gathered scraps of hardwood leftover from one of his mother's eternal home improvement activities. We configured the richly textured pieces into the form of a ten-inch high cross with a mahogany base and glued a little framed likeness of baby Jesus and Mary onto the front of the cross, creating a truly beautiful religious artifact.

Paulie belonged to the Cub Scouts and wanted me to help build a miniature car to enter into the annual local Cub Scout Pinewood Derby racing event. We started with a rectangular block of wood about two inches square and six inches long. We painstakingly carved the piece into an aerodynamically shaped, sleek little speedster. After the wheels were attached, it looked as if it zoomed along at a hundred miles per hour, while sitting still. We painted it gold and entered the contest and won first place. We built another a year later and finished in second place.

For a long period, almost every Sunday, Sheila and the kids attended mass at St. Felicitous Church. I opted out, so I could spend the time at my office catching up on paperwork and planning my schedule for the coming week. More accurately, being at mass to me was tantamount to performing stoop labor in the hot sun for eight hours. As I've made clear, no one has more faith in a benevolent God than I, but I'm no fan of institutional religion.

Nonetheless, those days I sensed trouble on the horizon regarding the status of my marriage. I understood Sheila's complaints and tried to mitigate them. In any event, I decided to start going to church on Sundays with her and the kids. It didn't quite work out as I expected. She said that because she had taken the children to mass for years without me, my turn had arrived. The kids and I would do the church thing while she slept in.

Okay, *I'll do what she wants, but I'll do it my way*. I tried to make Sunday worship fun, or at least less boring. Often, we attended different churches. Believe me, there is variety between Catholic houses of worship. My kids and I enjoyed viewing those differences first hand. St. Louis Bertrund's in Oakland entertained the congregation with uplifting modern music. If we wanted to see a lot of really old people, we attended St Mary's Immaculate Conception in West Oakland. Practically the entire congregation of Our Lady of the Rosary in San Leandro consisted of Philippine extraction. I think we were the only whites among a sea of black faces at St. Benedicts in East Oakland. You get the idea; we didn't entirely cure the boredom, but it helped. After mass we headed for Jerry's Pancake House on MacArthur Boulevard in San Leandro, which we enjoyed immensely. Some Sundays Sheila joined us for pancakes.

CHAPTER SEVENTY-ONE

I'd been involved in the "stop the foreclosure" routine for a couple of years. The activity paid well, but I had grown tired of dealing with the misery lack of money gave birth to. Not all, of course, but a large percentage of the people who faced severe financial adversity arrived in that sad state as a result of irresponsible behavior. Their problems were often tied to drug use, either legal or illegal or both, excessive drinking and sometimes just old fashioned stupidity. Those sad lives wore me down, and I had to get away from them, at least for a while.

Probate sales began to draw my interest. They didn't involve the misery which accompanied foreclosures. It worked like this: The administrator or executor of the estate of a deceased or incapacitated party placed the subject property on the market. Upon acceptance of a purchase contract, the agreement proceeded to probate court wherein the probate judge usually approved the proposed transaction. However, the system provided for other potential buyers present in the court to overbid the initial contract with an opening bid starting at a set percentage above the first contract presented to the court.

For a while I followed the probates fairly closely. If someone overbid an accepted agreement, the broker who prepared the original contract received a commission, as well as the broker representing the overbidding buyer. Sometimes brokers were not involved but most times they were. Even if the successful buyer happened to be a broker acting on his or her own behalf, the court usually approved a commission credit to that person. I knew I'd made a good deal when the probate judge approved my overbid on a well located residential property on Dowling Street in San Leandro. Dowling Street is a great location, and it surprised me that I had been the only over-bidder, and that I bought the property at such a bargain price.

As I left the courtroom that morning, a fellow approached me in the hall and introduced himself as Dale Hansen. Dale informed me he had observed the transaction involving Dowling Street. He wanted to know if I would assign my "right to purchase position" to him right then for a fast profit. I couldn't resist his offer of a ten thousand dollar profit for ten minutes work which really hadn't been work at all. Dale handed me a check for ten thousand dollars and we made an appointment to meet in my office that afternoon to accomplish the relatively simple paperwork. Coincidentally, Dale, a licensed real estate agent, soon transferred his license to my firm. He wanted to accumulate ownership of single family rental homes in San Leandro. I quickly sold him two of my properties in stable blue-collar locations in San Leandro at prices beneficial to us both. Thus, Dale and I began an enduring profitable association.

I submitted a purchase contract on a probate sale on Beveloqua Street in San Lorenzo. An attorney in Hayward, well into his nineties, handled the disposition of the estate. He administered the estate of a couple who had occupied the home until they died in their late eighties. The only heir, also quite elderly, lived on the east coast in some sort of a care home. The attorney and the heir just wanted to get through the business of selling the contents of the estate as quickly and as uncomplicated as possible. Simplicity and speed, rather than the amount of financial proceeds seemed to be the overriding motivating factor in the transaction. I made my deal indeed simple—all cash immediately with no contingency inspections. I hoped to close the escrow while the attorney and the heir were still alive. The court approved the purchase; I surmised there were no over-bidders because the attorney had done nothing to market the property.

My . . . what a sweet deal. I didn't just buy a piece of real estate—every bit of the personal property including furniture, two automobiles, a television set and kitchen ware— everything— right down to linens and clothing were mine. I immediately sold the cars and some of the furniture and donated a lot of clothing and hard-to-sell items to Goodwill. The furniture I didn't sell complemented the furnishings in my office. My step-father always enjoyed exploring the properties I acquired. He discovered a homemade, fully-stocked bomb shelter under the Beveloqua Street house. I rented the house out until eventually Cal-Trans bought the property to accommodate the widening of the adjacent freeway. Because of the nature of the transaction—a forced sale for the public good—I sold at a handsome tax-deferred profit.

CHAPTER SEVENTY-TWO

We've arrived at the latter part of 1968. The agents in my office brought in a steady commission income. If I took a listing, I just passed it on to one of my sales staff I could depend on to service it effectively. I tried to avoid showing property myself to prospective buyers anymore unless I owned the property or the potential sale promised an unusually large commission. The rental management area of my operation did well and took very little of my time.

The enjoyable and profitable loan business continued to grow. I arranged loans for lenders and often made secured loans for my own account since the principals on both sides of that activity were always happy about getting exactly what they wanted. Sometimes borrowers for whom I arranged loans eventually got themselves into financial circumstances in which they became lenders themselves, which pleased me immensely.

Because I'd been able to build up a good line of credit, whenever someone needed to sell fast, I had the ability to accommodate that need. Good buys came my way regularly. Occasionally, I fixed up a property and turned it over right away. Other times I just added a new acquisition to my portfolio of rentals. I'd learned the value of a good fix-up crew. They stuck with me because I paid them well, and sometimes I even bought a property I might barely break even on, just to keep the guys working.

I didn't have to hustle to find clients as I needed to do in the beginning. Way back, a very wise and wealthy broker told me an active, truly honest agent would build up a dependable referral business in less than three years. I could confirm what he told me to be true. With a loyal and ever-increasing clientele base, I had all the business I could handle. I found myself on a first name basis with numerous bank executives eager to provide unsecured financing upon my request. Sheila and I owned several income-producing properties, as well as interest bearing secured notes. I'd been elected to serve on the board of directors of three property owners associations. I enjoyed substantial community respect, unaware of what the future held.

An interest in building began to attract my attention. I listed a Mulford Gardens vacant lot on Fairway Drive zoned for two houses. I arranged a sale of the lot to my mother and step-father. Of course, I disclosed to the sellers my relationship to the buyers. That didn't matter to them at all. They were getting full price and a very good price at that. Late in 1968, I made my parents an offer to buy the lot from them. They netted a substantial profit.

Not long after I bought the lot, what I hoped would happen, did happen. Fairway Drive served as one of two arterials accessing the "Jewel of the Bay," an enhancing term often used to identify the San Leandro Marina and Golf Course Complex. To encourage high-quality multi-family residential development along the corridor leading to the ambitious shoreline project, the city rezoned Fairway Drive to O-PUD. That zoning classification permitted higher density complexes in exchange for increased city and community architectural control. I got to work doing all I needed to do to put the property to its highest and best use.

CHAPTER SEVENTY-THREE

During the early sixties, the potential of a multifamily residential development generated a great deal of interest. That held true all over the City of San Leandro but especially in Mulford Gardens, due to its spacious lots and proximity to the anticipated ambitious development of the shoreline. The Mulford Gardens zoning designation didn't permit high-density residential development and many of the community residents wanted to maintain the status quo. Even so, the city fathers favored some rezoning to permit increased residential density in the area. Many of those who unsuccessfully tried to stop the annexation of Mulford Gardens to the City of San Leandro aggressively opposed any and all changes the city tried to promote in Mulford Gardens. Most of those resisters operated through the Mulford Gardens Improvement Association (MGIA).

There were parcels as large as an acre on the most westerly block of Marina Boulevard which led into the huge developing San Leandro Marina and shoreline golf complex. Many of the houses fronting the street were of substandard construction and not well maintained. They detracted from the entry of the Marina, much to the chagrin of those involved in promoting the benefits of the so called "Jewel of the Bay."

Not long after annexation, the city rezoned that westerly single block of Marina Boulevard to a classification designated as R-3, which permitted the construction of an apartment for each 1200 square feet of land. Under R-3 zoning, as long as the developer met setback, side yard and height limit requirements, neither the city nor the community had the right to impose any architectural controls. The MGIA fought in vain to stop that change in zoning classification.

They were right to oppose R-3 zoning but wrong to oppose *any* rezoning classification. Rezoning that block served the interest of the entire community. The MGIA might have been wise to have worked with the city to negotiate for a change in zoning that would have given the officials and community a reasonable amount of control over the development of the land. I believe they resisted any higher density whatsoever, never considering—at least in that instance—that they fought a losing battle.

In my opinion, the majority of property owners who favored annexation welcomed the city's involvement in Mulford Gardens. Prior to becoming a part of San Leandro, lax county code compliance monitoring had resulted in much of the area being developed in a sub-standard manner. Many held out the hope that with some rezoning, strict building standards, and a modern sewage disposal system, Mulford Gardens would gradually become a more desirable place to live.

Initially, after annexation of Mulford Gardens, property owners requested permission to build multifamily units on their spacious lots. A tremendous amount of community demand for the city to rezone the area to permit higher density residential construction was juxtaposed against a vociferous stand by the MGIA to limit development to minimum density. The city officials, in my opinion, instead of having the fortitude to ignore the angry opposing factions and actually do the best thing for the area and the entire city, took the expedient way out and enacted a compromise rezoning. The new zoning designation permitted all the standard third-acre lots to be developed with three units in the form of one house plus a duplex. Architectural oversight controls and building standards were basically minimal. The city's action failed to support the best use of the property and basically pleased no one.

Mulford Gardens' property holders continued filing rezoning applications to accommodate construction that better met their needs. The process worked as follows: The applicant presented his or her rezoning request with the city planning staff that studied the proposal and worked with the applicant and, in due course, submitted a recommendation to the Planning Commission. At a Planning Commission meeting the commissioners discussed the matter within the auspices of a public hearing forum. In that setting, people expressed their opinions regarding the proposal. The commission then passed the matter on to the City Council with their recommendation. The City Council then conducted a public hearing along the same fashion as the Planning Commission. The Council either rejected or approved the application.

During the Planning Commission public hearings involving properties located in Mulford Gardens, members of the MGIA, one after another, advanced to the podium facing the Planning Commissioners. The MGIA members stridently voiced their opposition to any rezoning request. They repeated the process at the City Council's public hearings. Generally, only the applicant spoke in favor of the application. I frequently attended those public hearings and observed that Mulford Gardens' property applications at the City Council level were always denied. In time, owners who wanted to develop their properties beyond the existing zoning status became discouraged to the extent that rezoning applications were rarely submitted.

The Planning Commission consisted of six members. Each member held their position through appointment by the Councilperson representing the district in which they resided. Often, the merit of the change of zoning request had little to do with how the Council voted. As indicated previously, the applicant or sometimes the applicant's representative spoke in support of the request and a half dozen or so MGIA members demanded rejection of the application.

I determined that the six council members and the mayor, all elected to their positions, took the politically convenient way out and voted with the majority of the speakers. The dynamics of the process fascinated me. If a person could succeed in getting a rezoning application approved, the value of the subject parcel would increase dramatically. Until I left Ed Marvin's office, because of the lack of privacy, I often overheard rezoning applicants come to the office to plead their position to Ted Meecham. I listened, learned and planned. I believed I had some good ideas on how to proceed to get property rezoned that I had not noticed anyone trying, which I would attempt to implement when it served my purpose.

As I recall, the MGIA officers and some members maintained their resolve to fight any rezoning in the community whatsoever. There existed no constructive dialogue between the city officials and the MGIA. However, a zoning classification being utilized in other areas of San Leandro, many would have liked to see implemented in Mulford Gardens, excepting the MGIA officers. That zoning designation was entitled Planned Unit Development (PUD).

PUD permitted submission of an application for the development of as many units as the city officials and neighboring property owners agreed would serve the interest of the community as well as the developer. The neighbors, developer and the city planning staff conferred to implement construction and design features to insure minimal impact on the privacy of adjacent property occupants. Allowing the developer more leeway regarding the number of units that could be built made the project financially feasible to support higher quality and aesthetically more pleasing construction.

CHAPTER SEVENTY-FOUR

Among the unusual personalities I've known, Everett Peters definitely belonged in the "eccentric character" category. I met Everett, a sixty year old bachelor, in 1961. He lived in the house of his birth on 51st Avenue in Oakland, California His mother shared the home with him until she died at an advanced age.

Everett, a bald, short, stocky, fast-talking, high-pitch-voiced fellow, qualified as the consummate entrepreneur. He bought and sold about anything he sensed might turn a profit. Mainly, he purchased dented cans of food from canneries and resold them to restaurants throughout the San Francisco Bay Area. Some of his other enterprises included marketing industrial diamonds and speculating in cemetery plots.

I represented Everett as a Realtor in connection with his acquisition of residential income property. Though highly talented in matters of business, Everett seemed socially inept to the point of being childlike. I came to understand how Everett became rich. He displayed brilliance at accurately determining the potential of any investment opportunity presented to him. If a business proposal made sense to him, he never ever hesitated to invest.

We developed a mutually beneficial rapport with each other. He trusted me and I did my best to help advance his financial interests. On one hand, Everett could be the ideal client. On the other, he could be a nightmare. Although generally a pleasant person, he lacked the ability to empathize. Everett expected anyone he dealt with to be available twenty-four hours a day. Suspending business on Christmas or after midnight seemed ridiculous to him.

I recall when Everett, in the process of evicting a family with several children for non-payment of rent, exhibited a remarkable lack of good will. The scheduled date to remove the family from Everett's property fell on Christmas eve. The Alameda County Sheriff moved the eviction date to the day after Christmas. Everett, dumbfounded, couldn't understand. He held no animosity whatsoever toward the family, but he believed delaying their removal, no matter the reason, constituted a violation of his civil rights. When I explained how it would look to evict a family on Christmas eve or Christmas day, he simply stared at me, puzzled.

We enjoyed inviting people with no families to share Thanksgiving and Christmas dinner in our home. On one such occasion, Everett met Ruth, a single woman in her late fifties. She had spent her life with her father until his recent demise. Extreme religious fundamentalists, Ruth and her dad made their living for many years selling religious tracts. After dinner, Everett, attracted to Ruth, invited her to see his home and she accepted.

According to Everett, his visit with Ruth went well until he showed her his bedroom. When she saw a picture of a voluptuous nude blond above his bed, she informed him she would not return to his home until a portrait of the Lord hung over his bed. Eager to please, Everett invited Ruth back, assuring her that he had complied with her admonition. He failed to understand her distress when she viewed the likeness of Jesus hanging beside the voluptuous blond.

Everett's brief marriage to a professional wrestler is included among my favorite memories of him. The union ended when she threw him through his living room plate glass window. I recall the time an owner of a "serve yourself, all you can eat" type restaurant arrived an hour late for an appointment with Everett at his restaurant. While waiting, Everett retaliated by eating eighty pieces of chicken. I'll never forget the time he insisted that I bring my family to his home to enjoy a treat he had prepared for us, which turned out to be a refrigerator vegetable crisper full of lime Jell-O with particles of old lettuce and other bits of vegetation suspended within the gelatinous mass. I explained I sure wished he had called us before we had eaten breakfast.

Diagnosed with cancer in 1968, Everett refused to take time from his numerous business operations to receive treatment. When the cancer spread to his liver, he entered the Southern Pacific Hospital in San Francisco. He called from there to let me know he would be delivering $40,000 in cash to me the following day, his share of the down payment toward a lot he and I were buying. He mentioned he had the cash at his home.

I didn't see Everett the next day. He passed away soon after he called. He is buried in his favorite plot (he owned several) in Colma, a small town adjacent to San Francisco, consisting entirely of cemeteries. Next to Everett in a plot he had given her lies Dorothy, a former high school girl friend. His will stipulated that in the capacity of a Realtor, I would handle the sale of all his real property. Additionally, he appointed me to dispose of all his personal property. Upon liquidation of his estate, the cash went to the Shriner's Crippled Children's Foundation.

I never found Everett's industrial diamonds or the $40,000 he intended to deliver to me. A huge, gaudy, bright-gold-painted fireplace that dominated Everett's living room seemed to hold special significance to him. A sterling silver picture frame on the mantel held a photograph of his beloved mother. A small florescent light attached to the top of the frame illuminated her visage. Slender vases on each side of the picture held fresh orchids.

A couple of years after Everett died, Jim Slater, my handyman who also worked for Everett occasionally, asked me what I had found in the safe hidden under Everett's hinged fireplace hearth. While painting Everett's living room, Jim had observed him placing a small black metal box into the safe. Everett once showed me a small black metal box half-full of diamonds. I couldn't answer Jim's question because before he told me about seeing Everett place the black box into the safe, I had no idea that the hidden safe existed.

CHAPTER SEVENTY-FIVE

When I bought the lot on Fairway Drive in 1968 from my parents under its O-R zoning designation, I could have built two houses on the site. Developing the parcel with two houses might have brought a little profit but not much. From the offset I had planned on trying to get my lot rezoned O-PUD. If such a rezoning application met with success, contingent upon city and community approval, I might have been permitted to construct a higher density residential complex on the parcel. As I mentioned earlier, a lucky break came my way. I didn't even have to apply for the rezoning. To enhance the probability of attractive residential development along one of the two roadways leading to one of the entrances of the ambitious shoreline project, the city leaders rezoned Fairway Drive to O-PUD (outer-residential planned unit development).

At that point, no planned unit development projects had ever been accomplished in Mulford Gardens because such zoning didn't exist there. An O-PUD development would have to be approved by the Planning Commission and City Council exactly the same as a rezoning request. I knew the MGIA officers wanted no part of O-PUD in Mulford Gardens and would vigorously fight any such development project I might submit.

Rezoning—or in that case, getting an O-PUD submission approved in Mulford Gardens—would not happen easily. Time after time, I'd seen rezoning proposals turned down because the applicant failed to understand the dynamics of the process. He or she mistakenly believed the merit of the project should determine whether or not a rezoning request would be granted. Whenever a request for rezoning occurred, everyone knew if it gained approval, the value of the subject property rose. Few admit the truth, but I've found that human nature abhors anyone benefitting financially as a result of the approval of a change of land use application. I'd observed from the moment of such a submission, applicants faced an array of resistance—sometimes openly and often times subtly—aligned against them.

For years, I'd quietly created a situation in which much of the resistance one might face when applying for a change of permitted land use could be weakened; not eliminated— weakened. In the course of my normal business activities, I often had occasion to deal with the San Leandro planning staff. I had genuinely made friends with Norm Wisebroad, the head of that department. We shared an interest in nostalgic collectables. Whenever I stopped by, we usually spent some time discussing our collectable hobby and other mutually interesting subjects. I believed that when I eventually showed up with a reasonable change of land use request, I'd have Norm's support.

In my opinion, the initial land use approved by the city for Mulford Gardens since annexation had not served the area well. I don't think there existed a single apartment or duplex unit in the entire subdivision that had more than one bathroom. I agreed with a remark by Mrs Audrey Albers, a prominent officer in the MGIA, that what she observed being built in Mulford Gardens reminded her of rabbit warrens. I hoped that the recent reclassification of some areas of Mulford Gardens to O-PUD would bring about positive changes in the quality of new residential construction in the community.

I met with the planning staff and explained to Norm Wisebroad that I wanted to build a seven-unit apartment complex on my Fairway Drive parcel. I planned to construct six spacious two-bedroom apartments, plus one three-bedroom unit, far superior to any other I knew of in Mulford Gardens. The landscaping would be low maintenance and create the ambiance of a tranquil park-like setting. I planned to provide ample covered parking for the tenants and their guests. I wanted the parking area to be obscured behind beautiful stone walls. I knew if I built what I described to the planning staff, I'd attract just the type of tenants I envisioned occupying my creation.

I proceeded to consult with Charlie Mullins, an apartment-complex designer in Hayward, whose building concepts I'd admired for years. Charlie immediately grasped what I wanted. When I met with him the following week, he had completed drawings beautifully transferring what I'd pictured in my mind to colorful architectural renderings. I submitted Charlie's work to the San Leandro planning staff. They made some suggestions which I readily agreed to have Charlie incorporate into his design.

The staff accepted my O-PUD application and with their recommendation for approval submitted my proposal to the Planning Commission. The Commission scheduled a public hearing. I garnered my forces which I knew I needed to have in place to have any chance of convincing the commissioners to vote in my favor. I knew from attending several such public hearings that I could expect four or five people from the MGIA to speak against my project.

Based upon past experience they would be confident of their ability to scuttle my undertaking. I knew if I developed my lot in accordance with the details set forth in my proposal, a trend would commence that promised to enhance the prospects of superior quality development of the abundant vacant land in Mulford Gardens. I also knew that would mean nothing to my opposition. I intended to surprise them.

Sheila enthusiastically served as a Cub Scout den mother. The parents of several of the boys in her den were members of the MGIA. They appreciated Sheila's interest in their children. Both Danny and Steven were active in the Boy Scouts and each had paper routes in the community. Our family enjoyed living in Mulford Gardens. We supported community projects and seemed to be well liked there.

The MGIA clubhouse, where the general membership and officers met and conducted the business of the association, was old and required constant maintenance. I volunteered to install a badly needed new floor in the clubhouse bathroom. I didn't pay someone to install the floor; I did it myself. The members expressed gratitude for my contribution. The president of MGIA, Herb McDaid, presented me with a new toolbox he made for me. Notwithstanding my cordial relationship with the group, I knew they would oppose approval of my Fairway Drive project. However, I suspected I might escape the vicious attacks I'd seen others endure.

I contacted several Mulford Gardens property owners and explained if my O-PUD proposal reached fruition, others would follow my lead and property values in the community would surely rise. It wasn't a question of whether or not the large amount of vacant land in Mulford Gardens would be developed. It definitely would be developed; it was vital to the quality of living in Mulford Gardens as to *how* the land would be developed. I knew O-PUD projects with its city and neighborhood controls would serve the best interests of Mulford Gardens.

I enlisted six of the property owners with whom I conferred to speak in favor of my application at the Planning Commission public hearing. The commissioners registered surprise at the number of people at the podium requesting a recommendation to the City Council for approval of my proposal. Prior to the hearing, each commissioner received numerous letters urging their support of my submission. Naturally, all such correspondence came from folks I had contacted. Each letter bore the signature of a different Mulford Gardens property owner and every letter had been composed by me. If you ask someone to write a letter of support, they may or may not find time to write. If you write the letter and ask them to sign it, you will invariably receive a favorable response. The commissioners were taken aback; they weren't used to getting correspondence of support for land use changes in connection with properties in Mulford Gardens.

The commission sent my application on to the City Council with a favorable recommendation. The MGIA opposition didn't quite know how to react. They felt certain they would prevail at the City Council public hearing, but they didn't. Everything I did in preparation for the Planning Commission public hearing, I did more of for the Council hearing, and I won. I had perfected a highly successful strategy that I would repeat many times.

A year or so before I acquired the Fairway Drive lot, I bought a block-long vacant parcel on Doolittle Drive, just a few hundred feet down the street from my Fairway Drive property. My intuition told me I should own that beautiful parcel. Relative to its zoning designation, I paid too much and the monthly loan payments on the portion of the purchase price the seller carried back were pretty high. The man from whom I bought my property, Manuel Ferreira, a man in his seventies, had owned the parcel for many years. For some time he had anticipated achieving a zoning reclassification that would permit the construction of a twenty-two unit apartment complex, which he planned to have built and do the managing himself.

About six months before I purchased his lot, Manuel had plans drawn and applied for rezoning. What he wanted to have constructed on his property made good sense and based on the merit of his proposal, his rezoning bid should have been approved. He hired a well-known local attorney to speak on his behalf at the city's required public hearings. The MGIA opponents of Manuel's application dominated the hearings and his dream of many years went down in defeat.

Manuel and I were friends. Discouraged, he came to me and asked if I might be interested in buying his lot. He trusted me and offered to carry back the majority of the purchase price. Despite his unfortunate experience, and the fact that he wanted too much, I needed to own that property and foolishly paid Manuel's price. Until my recent Fairway Drive good fortune, I figured buying Manuel's property had been a mistake.

CHAPTER SEVENTY-SIX

My Fairway Drive building plans were soon finalized. Golden West Savings and Loan provided the financing of the construction of the seven units. The City of San Leandro issued a building permit. I entered into an agreement with William Drinkward, a contractor who had been supervising regional shopping center projects for a large commercial building company for fifteen years. William had just started contracting on his own. Karl and Christana Minneboo, wonderful loyal clients who were striving for financial independence—just like me—introduced me to William.

William and his wife, Alice, were close friends with the Minneboos. The couples emigrated from Holland soon after the Second World War. Both Karl and Bill escaped from Nazi concentration camps, and both families carried the emotional scars of that period. Karl assured me that venerable old world craftsmanship would show in William's work, and indeed it did.

If that project went the way I thought it should, perhaps at long last I would be able to demonstrate to Sheila that the hardship we'd endured would soon bring to us the pleasurable stress free life I'd dreamed of for years. When those beautifully designed units were completed and rented, the total amount of our passive income would support us handsomely. If we decided to stop working for a while and just enjoy life; well, that would be just fine. I looked forward to the freedom of doting on my four wonderful children and convincing Sheila that it had all been worthwhile. Things between her and I lately hadn't been that great; even so, I felt sure that I could soon repair our deteriorating relationship.

But for the time being I had a demanding business to run and a seven-unit luxury apartment complex to build. We broke ground and as construction began, I found myself fully engaged in moving the project toward the fulfillment of my dream of financial freedom. Although Drinkward coordinated and oversaw the progress of the work, I became an integral part of the construction process as well. My experience in the multi-faceted real estate business had brought me into contact with many residential building trades people.

Perhaps my background better equipped me to quickly get together with sub-contractors than William. Once he and I agreed upon someone to accomplish a specific step in the construction process, his supervisory skill kicked in. My job required I make sure that sub-contractors were always available, and we never experienced down time because we hadn't scheduled the progression of the work in a timely decision. An element in assisting with the birth of a quality building that would serve the needs of people for a period beyond my expected lifetime, made me understand the significance of my efforts.

Unless a person has been involved in such development, one would never realize every single feature—no matter how minor—of the project had to be considered, compared and analyzed before finally decided upon. Choices of light fixtures, colors, style of address numbers and dozens of other items are constantly weighing on the mind of whoever is charged with such responsibilities. There is always a governing budget to deal with and if the endeavor is to be financially feasible, cost constraints must be obeyed.

After my other daily ongoing real estate-related activities were handled, I did whatever I could to help William. Sheila and the kids pitched in, and they were good. Late every afternoon we piled up the debris, such as scrap lumber, sheetrock remnants and all other litter left by the workers that had accumulated on the site during the day. My family loaded it into our trash-hauling old pickup truck and carted it to the city dumps. We paid the kids well for their excellent work. They felt good about what they did, and I think Sheila loved that part of the job. Strange ... other families went waterskiing and camping and mine made dump hauls. I wonder if my kids realize the work they did back then has a lot to do with the success they enjoy today.

CHAPTER SEVENTY-SEVEN

I guess things were just going too well. The framing had been about completed and construction of the roof would soon begin when a legal notice was posted on the front of the skeleton of the building. What a shock—the MGIA had filed a lawsuit against us and the Alameda County Superior Court had issued a temporary injunction ordering us to halt construction. We had to stop all work immediately. At a future date, the court would decide whether or not we would be obliged to tear down what we'd constructed to date, or if we would be permitted to finish the project. The action came as a total surprise and sent me reeling. If the MGIA had their way, this would be a severe career setback. I'd served on their board of directors and recently installed a new linoleum bathroom floor in their clubhouse. The tired cliché came to mind, "With friends like these, who needs enemies?"

The suit alleged I had violated the Mulford Gardens' Conditions, Covenants and Deed Restrictions (CC&Rs), originally recorded in 1927. I'd handled the sale of a lot of properties in the area and knew every piece of real estate in Mulford Gardens to be encumbered by the same restrictions. A vast number of those properties didn't conform to the CC&Rs. Ironically, most of the homes of the officers of the MGIA failed to comply with the conditions they were trying to force upon me. Additionally, the city enacted zoning requirements under which dozens of Mulford Gardens' sites had been developed ignoring the restrictions.

A bad time indeed, but not nearly as bad as what would soon be coming my way. I contacted attorney Bruno Brunzell. Bruno successfully handled a similar suit filed by the MGIA against Ray Olsen, a builder, friend and future customer. Smooth and articulate, Bruno inspired confidence. He assured me he thought my chances of prevailing against the MGIA were good, but he couldn't make any guaranties. He said some judges seemed to hold a bias in favor of homeowner associations pitted against developers. Our success or failure depended upon the quality of the preparation of our case. Clearly, I had to come up with documentation that supported our position, and Bruno's responsibility mandated him to convince the court to rule in our favor.

I went to the Alameda County Courthouse and bought several two-by-three foot copies of the original plat map of the 1927 Mulford Gardens subdivision. I then used crayons to color each lot depicted on the subdivision map. The color Red identified lots developed with non-conforming buildings. Yellow indicated lots having structures that violated the front and rear yard and or side yard setbacks according to the requirements set forth in the

CC&Rs. Green indicated lots in compliance with the CC&Rs. Less than ten percent of the of the lots qualified to be colored green.

To be able to prepare the maps required me to drive through the entire subdivision and make copious notes. I drafted a comprehensive letter explaining the details of my results for Bruno to submit to the court. To get the map documentation ready took thirty hours, during which time I didn't go to bed.

The case aroused a lot of interest. I expected a packed courtroom. As I left San Leandro heading for court, my car just stopped. Feeling like an exhausted wreck, I got out of the car to look for a phone booth so I could call someone to get me to the court. A friend driving by spotted me; he stopped and agreed to drive me. I thanked him profusely; he said "no problem, that's where I'm headed anyway." It seemed the trial had turned out to be the Mulford Gardens social event of the year. Not an empty seat remained in the room.

The plaintiff's attorney presented his case, leaving me worried. Bruno took over. He submitted and explained my maps which were easily understood with the help of my letter of detailed explanation. I was the only witness Bruno called. I testified just short of two hours. Before the judge rendered his decision, he angrily chastised the MGIA's attorney for bringing that matter into his court. Of course, he ruled in my favor. Thrilled and happy? Yes, but right then, I just wanted to go home and sleep.

In order to get the court to issue the preliminary stop work injunction, the MGIA had to put up a security bond. The bond encumbered the one-acre parcel owned by the MGIA on which the association's clubhouse stood. The bond insured that if I prevailed in the legal matter, I could collect from the MGIA an amount commensurate with any damages I might have incurred as a result of the work stoppage. I knew at least one couple had cancelled their membership in the MGIA in hopes of avoiding personal liability related to litigation I might initiate against the group.

The MGIA's officers endured mounting criticism from the association's members for foolishly placing the beautiful park-like property in jeopardy. The board of directors had moved against me without thinking. They had to worry about the consequences of their senseless act. They needed to worry; I sure had, and indeed they had damaged me. Nevertheless, I decided not to try to collect on the surety bond. My kids loved our home in Mulford Gardens, and a good percentage of my income came from that community.

In the real estate business, acquiring a few enemies couldn't be avoided, but creating them on purpose made no sense. I let the MGIA officers off with no fanfare. Although they did not openly thank me—it was important to them to try to save face—I knew some of them felt truly grateful. Two of the officers eventually became important investors in my loan business, and as far as they were concerned, I could do no wrong.

The MGIA never supported my projects because the association existed to stop real estate developers within the boundaries of Mulford Gardens. Their aggressive opposition against my projects had diminished significantly. Actually, I believe if they had adopted a policy of working with developers instead of fighting against every proposed project, the area would have fared far better than it did. It's important to point out here that some of the MGIA membership and officers were open to reasonable negotiation regarding development of the community, just not enough of them.

I wanted to make up for the construction time lost during the litigation process. I devoted more and more of my workday to the Fairway Drive project. I liked being on the job site. Whatever William needed to keep the progress flowing, I tried to be on hand to help. As the need arose for various items, I went on my way to the building suppliers. I didn't want William to waste his time being a parts chaser. I constantly looked for bargains. I found a terrific buy on linoleum at Conklin Brothers Flooring in Hayward. At night, after the other workers went home, I installed the linoleum in seven kitchens and fourteen bathrooms. That gorgeous complex shaped up to reach fruition at far below budget.

CHAPTER SEVENTY-EIGHT

Early one morning, as I proudly finished some last minute cleaning and accomplished a few touch-ups near the front of the completed Fairway Drive Project, a fellow in his mid-fifties pulled up in a flashy, late-model Cadillac convertible. He approached confidently, carrying what appeared to be rolls of building plans. He greeted me with a friendly smile as he introduced himself as Bud Mayer. In time, Bud turned out to be one of the most interesting and confusing characters that ever crossed my path. Initially, he impressed me as pure "blue suede." Bud complimented me on my beautiful complex. He told me he had been watching our progress since we broke ground. He knew all about my legal problems with the MGIA and had even attended the trial. Bud told me he thought I did a brilliant job in the courtroom. I began to like him.

Bud got to the reason for his visit. He explained he held an option to purchase four lots on Doolittle Drive, just three blocks away. All the work necessary to obtain building permits to construct a four-plex on each of the lots had been accomplished. We walked to his car and he unrolled the building plans on the hood. I liked what I saw. Bud had no money and no credit established to finance the purchase of the lots and construction of the four-plexes. He explained that if I would put up the cash to purchase the lots and qualify for construction financing, we would build and sell the units and split the profit.

Naturally, I had knowledge of current building costs. I liked the price of the lots. The numbers looked good. I asked Bud not to take offense, but I had to let him know that the only person in the world I trusted happened to be me. If he agreed to put everything in my name and allow me to have the final word on all decisions, we had a deal. He laughed at my forthright position and we shook hands.

Boy, had Bud set it up right, he already had a contractor in place—Lawrence Ramos, as well as a construction lender—Golden West Savings and Loan Association, my favorite lender. Within thirty days, we broke ground on the Doolittle Drive four-plex project.

Bud loved everything about building. He made endless suggestions to the contractor and his crew while strolling the building site, always with a set of plans under his arm. He managed everything related to the physical construction of our buildings. The part of the job that Bud enjoyed held little interest for me. I directed my energy toward controlling expenses and making sure our financial goals stayed in focus. We worked well together. This began the first of many ventures that made us both a lot of money.

About that same time, I decided to apply for rezoning of the parcel I bought from Manuel Ferreira. By then I knew the routine well. I repeated all the steps that worked so well on Fairway Drive. Despite their recent defeat, the MGIA geared up to oppose me. They had stopped Manuel, and had committed their efforts to do the same to me. This time a new strategy came into play. The battle between the MGIA and my property reclassification request became concentrated in the *Letters to the Editor* section of the *San Leandro Morning News*.

Letters from the MGIA leaders urging denial of my application, juxtaposed against more letters supporting the PUD type of development I promoted in Mulford Gardens, appeared in the paper daily. In order for a letter to be published it had to be signed by its author. All the letters supporting me had been signed by different Mulford Gardens property owners, and they were all drafted by me. The City Council unanimously approved my zoning request. I had effectively impeded the MGIA's control over how the area might develop, and I continued to do so. I initiated my own and supported others' projects that promised to enhance the quality of living in Mulford Gardens.

CHAPTER SEVENTY-NINE

Although Sheila had been a wonderful helpmate relative to the Fairway Drive Project, she seemed clearly disenchanted with me. Whenever we had a disagreement, she coldly informed me she no longer loved me. I didn't believe her—I guess I should have. After we argued, I always apologized and tried to make up, which got me nowhere. At that time, she found reasons to be away from home a lot. She attended cosmetic parties occasionally and met with a group of lady friends at their homes a few nights each month. Additionally, she attended evening classes at Chabot Community College with the hope of eventually becoming a teacher, which pleased me immensely.

She volunteered as a teacher's aide working with troubled elementary school children. Those activities seemed enjoyable to her, and I happily supported them. One night just after she left for her evening class at Chabot College, a visiting relative remarked to me that it seemed odd that a woman would wear perfume to attend night school. I thought nothing of the comment until a few months later.

I still took the kids to church most Sundays, and Sheila continued to refuse to go with us. When she and the kids went on outings, she often excluded me. We had been friends with Martin and Carol Benz since we married. They had married about the same time as us. The Benzes, near our age, had a slew of kids, two more than we had. Martin had worked at the Alameda Naval Air Station from the time we had become friends. He had been elected as a union steward and eventually rose to a high level officer in the union. Something went wrong, and Martin lost his position in the union.

The family ended up living in the mountains in northern California. The story I heard indicated they were receiving public assistance, which stopped when the welfare department discovered Martin earned money by carving and selling wooden depictions of various animals. Early one Sunday morning, Sheila took the kids and drove up to visit the Benzes. I would have enjoyed going with them, but she made it clear she didn't want me along. I received that sort of treatment quite frequently. Even so, I still believed I could soon put things back together between Sheila and me.

About nine that evening, my family arrived home from their visit with the Benzes. Sheila wanted to have a talk with me immediately. That pleased me—unless absolutely necessary, she hardly ever spoke with me anymore. Clearly upset, she informed me our good friends were in terrible circumstances. Martin didn't earn enough to feed his family—they were hungry. They couldn't get welfare and didn't have anyone else willing to help. Sheila acted friendly toward me for a change. She asked me to help them.

I took that as an opportunity to put my relationship with my wife back together. Actually, I felt blessed by being in a position to help. But primarily, by being of service to Benzes, I hoped to earn the gratitude of my wife. Whenever I did something that benefited others, I never played hero. Trying to come off as "Daddy Warbucks," (the wealthy benefactor in the Orphan Annie stories) didn't suit me. I tried to understate any charitable acts in which I engaged. In a day or so I had formulated my plans. I asked Sheila if Martin and Carol could visit with us. They came to our home that night.

Sheila had prepared plum jam from fruit harvested in our backyard orchard. She offered Martin and Carol slices of toast spread with her jam. They accepted and quickly devoured the pleasant treat. They unashamedly emptied two jars of the jam. I felt sad for them and laid out my plans to help them get back to a normal life. I had talked with Bud and also Lawrence Ramos, our contractor on the Doolittle four-plex job.

Lawrence agreed to put Martin to work on our project starting the next Monday. The Benzes' tired old station wagon fell apart. Not long before that I had bought two cars and three trucks from the estate of my good client, Everett Peters, who recently passed away. I signed over to Martin and Carol the pink slip to an International Harvester pickup truck in excellent condition. My good friend Gay Green owned a nice, vacant three-bedroom rental home in a good location in Hayward, which—as a favor to me— she rented to the Benzes.

Martin thanked me for what I'd done for his family. Still, he wondered if I might be willing to do one more thing for them. He asked for a cash loan to help them restart their lives. I agreed to make the loan, and Martin and Carol signed a Promissory Note which named Sheila and me as the beneficiaries. The note called for them to make small monthly payments which Martin assured me they could handle easily from the proceeds of the job I'd arranged for him. I didn't really feel good about the loan request. I thought it a little nervy. No matter; I'd pleased Sheila, which to me loomed important. Sadly, I learned that the wretched state of the Benzes' lives before I helped them was exactly where they deserved to be. I'm talking about Martin and Carol, not their children.

CHAPTER EIGHTY

For a very short period, Sheila and I got along better. The seven units on Fairway Drive rented quickly. Our combined investments produced sufficient passive income that if I chose to retire, I could do so. Certainly, at thirty-six years of age I had no intention of not working, but a very pleasant change of our lifestyle seemed possible and I moved quickly to make that happen. I thought two weeks on a houseboat on beautiful Lake Shasta—fishing, swimming, barbecuing, and exploring the hundreds of miles of shoreline inlets and coves—promised to be a swell way for our family to start reaping the rewards of our sacrifices. I mailed the rental deposit to reserve our luxury houseboat two-week getaway.

I tried very hard to please Sheila, but she distanced herself from me more and more. The time she spent away from home increased. She met with the women in her ladies club much more frequently. She was a notary public primarily for the purpose of notarizing documents related to transactions occurring in my office. She began performing notary services for people I didn't know, away from our home or office. The notary sessions lasted for hours. Her cold attitude toward me and even the kids, and her long absences confused me. Even though I felt uneasy, I still believed that we could be happy together. After all, the hard times had passed—now we could begin the type of life we'd worked so hard to achieve.

One summer Friday evening, Sheila seemed very edgy. She started behaving in a manner that appeared to be intentionally geared toward irritating me. Moments after I voiced a mild complaint, she angrily bolted from the house and sped off in her car. I had no idea what I did to upset her so, because I had been trying hard to get along. She didn't come home, which of course worried me.

At around two in the morning our phone rang. I heard Martin Benzes' voice on the line. He surprised me when he told me that Sheila and Carol had gone out together, as they often did. He didn't know what they did, but based on what had happened in the past with Carol, he had his suspicions. I listened as Martin talked about some of the details in connection with his long troubled marriage. Before he hung up, he said if he learned what our wives were up to he would let me know. He asked me to return the favor.

I got up around eight the next morning after a sleepless night. Sheila hadn't come home. I didn't know what I should do. I wondered if she had gotten into an accident and if I should call the police or hospitals. Then "out of the blue" Margaret Phillips, a friend and neighbor, who lived directly across the street, called and asked me over to have a cup of coffee with her. Margaret, Carol and Sheila had been pals for a long time. I knew Margaret regarded me highly, and I suspected that she had more on her mind than just having a cup of coffee with me. I accepted her invitation.

I liked Margaret and if I hadn't been so distressed, I would have enjoyed visiting with her. A few minutes of small talk passed before she settled into the real purpose of her invitation. She said, "Val, isn't it just awful the way Sheila and Carol are acting?"

I nodded my head affirmatively pretending I understood. She proceeded to inform me how disgusted she felt that my wife and Carol were running around with truck drivers who were friends of Carol's before she and Martin had moved to the mountains. In fact, according to Margaret, the reason Martin had demanded that they move was to get Carol away from those guys. I felt like I'd been shot, but I acted as if I knew the whole story. I thanked Margaret for the coffee and the conversation and with an aching heart, made my way home.

The shock of that day didn't end there; more misery followed. I'd known Sheila for twenty years. She kept meticulous written records of every significant thing she did. If what Margaret and Martin had told me constituted the truth, I had a hunch that Sheila had probably secretly reduced her activity to writing. I opened a dresser drawer where she kept a lot of her written material and observed a lump under the paper lining at the bottom of the drawer. I lifted the lining and found both sides of a sheet of typing paper filled with the written events of a part of my wife's life that I never knew existed. Whoever coined the term "the husband is last to know" must have been thinking about a guy just like me.

To describe my feelings as heartbroken is a monumental understatement, but strangely, I felt no anger. I figured a lot of what had happened to be my fault. I could never really give her what I thought she needed—an easier life. Although close to doing that, it seemed my time had run out. Even at that very early juncture, I knew my marriage had ended. No amount of counseling would ever put it back together. My tortured mind kept asking: *How could she have ever done this to our family?*

Sheila called and started to give me some excuse about why she didn't come home the night before. I might have believed her before I found out how she had been truly spending her time. *What a sap I'd been.* I told her what I'd learned and let her know I'd be going to my mom's for a few days until I could arrange to move into one of the new apartments Bud and I had just about finished. She expressed no remorse, which didn't surprise me. I told her we could get together shortly to sort out the details necessary to go on with our lives. I felt scared, hurt and alone.

CHAPTER EIGHTY-ONE

My world exploded in my face. Clearly, our marriage had undergone difficulty, yet until that painful day, I had never envisioned divorce. Absent an offense commensurate with what had happened, I could have never left Sheila. Strange, although still legally bound together, in my mind I no longer had a wife. Pride destroyed, my emotions seemed trapped within a raging tidal wave. I knew the hurt had to last for a very long time, but I preferred heartbreak to living a lie. I knew one thing for sure; no one would ever touch the deepest depths of my heart again as Sheila had.

When I moved into my parents' home for a few days, I explained to them what had happened. Mom didn't excuse Sheila's behavior, but she railed at me to keep my marriage intact for the sake of the children. I understood her feelings, but I just couldn't make a life with a woman I couldn't trust. My step-father had very little to say, but when we were alone, he quietly said, "Val, if you do go back to her, you'll never be able to hold your head up again." His words reminded me of the day he influenced me to marry Sheila about eighteen years before.

Sheila and I saw things differently. The value system to which I'd devoted half my life meant nothing to her. Overnight it seemed all I'd so carefully planned for my family had taken an abrupt detour. I agonized in my futile attempt to understand why this had happened. Nothing I'd ever endured hurt like that. My wife didn't just burn bridges, she blew them to smithereens. In my grief, I recalled the poignant words of John Greenleaf Whittier, *"Of all the sad words of tongue or pen, the saddest are these, it might have been!"*

For the past several years, my self-confidence had soared. Egotistically, I'd considered myself the "boy with the golden touch." I didn't feel that way any longer.

No matter what had happened and regardless of my emotional devastation, I couldn't hate my wife. Sheila took the situation in her stride; she just didn't seem to give a damn. I still loved her, not romantically, but as the mother of my children and as a mate who had faced life's vagaries and vicissitudes with me for eighteen years. I contemplated the effect it might have on our kids if I filed for the divorce.

Her frequent absences from our home, while sowing her wild oats, had damaged our children. I knew if I stayed with Sheila they would have been hurt even more. When a man sues for divorce, I believe the wife's reputation is soiled far more than if the woman brings the action. I had to be divorced. Sheila understood my reasoning and agreed to initiate legal proceedings.

To minimize gossip, we decided to select an attorney not located in San Leandro. Sheila engaged the services of attorney Jerry Hanford, who operated out of Oakland. Because of our business background, Sheila and I knew the importance of insisting that Jerry make a firm commitment as to what he would be charging for handling our almost-friendly divorce. He told us because of our apparent civility toward each other, and because I didn't intend to contest the action, his fee would be $650.

We explained to him that in our experience, in the course of business-related activities, we had observed that some attorneys arbitrarily increased their previously agreed to compensation and that would be entirely unacceptable to us. He assured us that he would keep his word. He asked that we give him a list of our assets, which we did, and he protested that we could afford to pay him more. Sheila insisted that he stand by his commitment or she would move on. He could see he had to keep his word or lose the business and coldly agreed to represent her for his initial quote of $650. Perhaps because of the sour start, the attorney did not serve us well. I believe his ineptness delayed the final decree far longer than necessary.

PART FIVE

SINGLE

"a strange new world"

CHAPTER EIGHTY-TWO

Do you recall that loan Sheila and I made to the Benzes? According to the terms of the promissory note they signed we should have been receiving monthly payments, but none came. I'd written a couple of very friendly letters to Martin reminding him of his obligation but hadn't heard back. I reminded Sheila that I'd agreed to that loan simply to please her, and I damn well intended to collect. I expected her to help enforce payment and if she wouldn't, I thought she should absorb the loss by herself.

Sheila placed some of the blame for her behavior which led to our breakup on Carol. She assured me she would totally support whatever I had to do to settle the matter. I think Sheila tried to contact Carol and received the same non-response treatment I got from Martin. If either of them had asked for some sort of an adjustment on the repayment requirements set forth in the promissory note, they would have been accommodated. Clearly, the Benzes had no intention of doing the right thing.

By now, Martin had received an inheritance from the estate of his deceased parents, and he and Carol had purchased a home in Mulford Gardens through Ed Martin's office. Ironically, they bought a property that I had handled the sale of three times since I began my career as a real estate agent. You might recall the property located on Elm Street that I first negotiated the sale of to Larry and Doris Engleton for Mr. Thomas, the colorful old cowboy who had the house moved onto the lot.

In the course of planning how to proceed to enforce payment of the loan, I asked Ed about the details of the sale of the Elm Street property to Martin and Carol. Ed told me he secretly loaned them

$2500 to help them qualify for a loan to finance the purchase of the property. Ed told me that Martin refused to repay the loan. Martin took the position that if Ed tried to enforce payment, Martin threatened to file a complaint with the California Department of Real Estate charging Ed with failing to disclose the loan he made to the Benzes in a transaction in which Ed received a sales commission. Ed had trusted him, and Martin ran true to form. I felt sorry for Ed; he trusted the wrong person, just as I had.

I talked with Eddie Ramos, my attorney and friend, who handled mundane legal matters for me occasionally. I asked Eddie to write the Benzes and tell them if acceptable arrangements couldn't be negotiated regarding repayment of their indebtedness to Sheila and me by a certain date, he would take the matter to court. That date passed with no response. Eddie proceeded to file an action against the Benzes. Amazingly…instead of contacting Eddie to amicably reach some sort of settlement, the Benzes hired an attorney to defend their refusal to pay.

The case had been scheduled to be heard by Judge Robert Byrd, a person with whom I had a friendly relationship. On the morning of the hearing, Sheila and I waited outside the courtroom while Eddie conferred with the opposing attorney to see if the matter could still be resolved absent further litigation. He returned looking perplexed; he maneuvered me beyond Sheila's ability to hear. Eddie said, "When you hear their strategy, you may decide to take the loss and just walk away from this."

Eddie explained what Martin planned to testify to in court. What Eddie said made me momentarily speechless— then angry. Martin claimed I had agreed to forgive his debt in return for him gathering information about Sheila's adulterous conduct and report to me what he learned. Further, he threatened to reveal in court everything he knew of Sheila's misconduct. Of course, Martin believed he could embarrass her as well as me because Carol had told him about the secrets she and Sheila shared and the things both of them had done. Carol told Martin everything; he wouldn't leave her, no matter what she did.

I told Sheila what Martin had planned. Even though she knew me well enough to know my pride would never permit me to hire anyone to spy on my wife, the prospect of being exposed and even lied about in public terrified her. I said, "Sheila, neither of us could ever look ourselves in the mirror again if we let this go unchallenged."

She answered, "Alright, I'm leaving it up to you."

Martin had miscalculated; I knew I could tear him up in court. Eddie listened to my plan and agreed to follow my lead. He possessed the ability to translate the strategy I formulated adeptly into courtroom parlance.

I wrote out a list of blunt questions encompassing who, when and where to put to Martin when Eddie got him on the stand. When the court went into session, Judge Byrd announced that he knew me personally. You may recall that Judge Byrd had allowed Danny to serve ten days at Fairmont Hospital rather than Santa Rita Jail. He asked the lawyers if they would like him to recuse himself from hearing the case. Both attorneys answered no, but I noted the expression of concern on the face of the Benzes' attorney, and I knew that a point had already been scored in my favor.

Eddie rammed my questions down Martin's throat and before the interrogation ended, it became clear his lies had backfired and his scheme had collapsed. I took the stand and after both attorneys finished with me, Judge Byrd asked, "Mr. Barry, did you ever agree to pay the defendant for obtaining information about your wife and passing that information on to you?"

I answered, "Absolutely not." Judge Byrd informed us he would consider the matter and render his decision in a few days.

As Eddie, Sheila and I descended the steps outdoors leading away from the court complex, the Benzes' attorney sidled next to Eddie. I overheard him say, "Ed, obviously Judge Byrd will rule in your clients' favor but it won't do them any good. The Benzes aren't working; they will soon be filing bankruptcy and their property is homesteaded."

His remarks would boomerang and smack him right in his smug face. I knew for a homestead to be of any effect it had to be recorded in the same county as the location of the subject property. A Homestead exempted any legal action jeopardizing a judgment debtor's home in the amount of $75,000 above the loans encumbering the property on the date that the Homestead recorded. If the Benzes' Homestead recorded before the issuance of my judgment, we might never be paid. A Homestead constituted a method of avoiding paying a legitimate debt and consequently was frowned upon by potential issuers of credit. Therefore, at that time, Homesteads were never filed until the property owner faced imminent danger of being on the losing end of a court issued judgment, or in other words, until the Homestead became needed.

I figured the Benzes' attorney most likely had prepared the Homestead. Not knowing whether or not his clients would prevail in the case, he probably tossed the document into his desk drawer with the intention of filing it with the county if his clients lost. Still on the courthouse steps, I asked Eddie to call the court clerk later that afternoon and ask if Judge Byrd could issue his judgment by the next morning and permit Eddie to pick it up right away. Eddie looked at me, puzzled by my odd request. I said to him, "Please Eddie, just do as I ask, I will explain later."

Around five that afternoon, Eddie called and told me that Judge Byrd agreed to accommodate his request, and I could pick up the judgment at Eddie's office at ten the following morning, which I did. I delivered the judgment to the County Recorder's Office and had it officially recorded. It turned out I had figured it right; the Benzes' Homestead recorded two days later. As my judgment went on record first, the Homestead could not interfere with my right to move against the Benzes' property to collect my Judgment Award.

I immediately ordered a thirty-day Sheriff's sale on the Benzes' property. When the Deputy Sheriffs posted the Order of Sale on their front door, in a panic, Martin called their attorney, who I felt certain had told him their home had been homesteaded, rendering me powerless to go against them. Their lawyer quickly called Eddie, who then called me and asked, "Val, what the hell are you doing, you're going to get into trouble; that property is Homesteaded."

I answered, "Yes, Eddie, their Homestead recorded *after* my judgment recorded, thereby giving my judgment priority."

Eddie hung up the phone, did a little reviewing, conferred with the opposing attorney, called me back and asked, "Val, please explain to me how you pulled this off."

A couple of days later, Martin called me. He apologized for lying about me in court and pleaded with me not to force the Sheriff's sale of his home. Actually, I felt sorry for him. I told him if he would lift his Homestead, I would total the value of the time I'd invested in trying to collect the debt. I figured adding the value of my collection time to the Judgment Award, which included my attorney fees, equaled the amount of the Benzes' indebtedness to Sheila and me.

I prepared an interest-bearing Promissory Note which would be secured with a Deed of Trust encumbering the Benzes' property. Martin and Carol signed the documents, and I recorded the Deed of Trust with the Alameda County Recorder. I required that Martin have the loan documents approved by his attorney before the transaction consummated. The Benzes gratefully accepted my terms.The property sold shortly thereafter, and the escrow company paid off the Promissory Note plus interest. My experience with the Benzes' emphasized my belief that people involved in legal matters should not solely rely upon their lawyer to do all the thinking.

Only for a brief period did I feel victorious over the Benzes. I recalled that a time existed when they believed their future loomed bright, and they had enjoyed a high degree of self-respect. Somehow the continual painful blows life dealt them robbed Martin and Carol of self-esteem and reduced the couple to an existence of mere survival. Their plight brought a profound sense of sadness to me, and I silently hoped better days lay ahead for them.

CHAPTER EIGHTY-THREE

Even though I struggled to pick up the pieces of my life, I never criticized or talked bad about Sheila. Any argument I had with her ended with the divorce. In time, she wanted to discuss reconciliation. I quietly reckoned she had come upon "the grass isn't necessarily greener" syndrome. No, I just didn't want to live like others I knew who were together out of convenience, even though a bond of trust no longer existed between them. My business had brought me into contact with couples with assets comparable to ours who were guilty of unforgivable infidelities. They refused to end their marriages because they couldn't stand the thought of dividing their wealth. Maybe Sheila had walked out with the better half of our holdings; it didn't matter, I'd make it back in time.

I daily endured a continual stomach ache and I discovered a bald spot on the back of my scalp which I guessed resulted from stress. Engaged in the midst of two risky multifamily apartment complex building projects, I didn't have the luxury of wallowing in depression. Appearances had to be kept up. It had taken years of positioning the operation of my business so that it functioned well. Even though terribly distracted, I had to be very careful. I'd watched others in similar situations lose everything.

Notwithstanding the fact that my business did alright, I worked a lot fewer hours than I had before the breakup. I traveled to Mexico for a few days' vacation three times within the period of a year. By myself, I'd fly to San Diego, stay there overnight and drive to Ensenada and Rosaria, and just sort of lose myself before returning to San Diego and flying home. I used that time to try to figure how to get my life together. I'd heard that time healed all wounds. I sure hoped that saying held true.

No matter that I operated adrift on a sea of disarray, I instinctively knew that my eventual recovery depended somewhat upon my degree of success in business. I had no intention of joining those poor souls I'd watched who had allowed unfortunate circumstances—similar to what I'd experienced—rob them of the will to remain financially viable. As always, Taylor Abercrombie's long ago admonition: **"Val, a poor man must do things in a poor way,"** remained a continual guide.

Although not even close to attending to my business obligations as diligently as before, I truly excelled in one area. The results of my activity directed toward remodeling and building were indeed gratifying. Responsibility for the physical aspects of remodeling and erecting the buildings fell to my contractors. My ability to plan and coordinate all functions of the progress of construction exceeded even my own expectations. For example, from the day we broke ground to construct twenty-two residential apartment units on the parcel I bought from Manuel Ferreira, to the day we rented them out, took slightly less than ninety days. My awareness that such phenomenal ability could bring riches far beyond what I'd ever envisioned in the past, fired my imagination. Circumstances surfaced though that dampened my dream of acquiring wealth in the hundreds of millions of dollars.

CHAPTER EIGHTY-FOUR

The divorce harmed the kids, even though I spent as much time with them as I could. I had season tickets to the Raiders football games, and I took eight-year-old Paulie to every home game. After each game we practiced passing and catching the ball at Marina Park in San Leandro. In the years to come he played on the Hayward High School championship football team. I tried my best to convince his mom to let him live with me, to no avail.

Danny graduated from Pacific High in San Leandro and eventually moved in with me. He operated business from space number twenty-three at the Alameda Flea Market, formerly the Island drive-in movie theatre in Alameda. During the week he scrounged collectibles and general merchandise which he sold on weekends.

I never worried about Steven. He came across as capable and totally self-confident. It seemed that he made friends with anyone he met. I had such confidence in Steven that I made the mistake of not paying close enough attention to him. Sometimes he lived with Sheila and sometimes with me. He pretty much did as he wanted.

Valerie and her mom just couldn't get along. They were two temperamental gals. Valerie ran away from her mom's home twice. My thirteen-year old daughter and I had always gotten along beautifully, and Sheila reluctantly permitted her to live with me. Raising that girl brought me sheer joy. Occasionally she'd get obstinate, but she always came around, I think because she knew I wanted only the best for her.

Naturally, because Valerie lived with me, I spent more time with her and had more influence over her than I did with my other three kids. The results of my troubled childhood and failed marriage plagued me with self-esteem issues. Therefore, driven to help my children develop a high degree of self-worth, I regularly endeavored to try to steer them into positive situations.

When Valerie reached the age of fifteen, I insisted that she enroll in modeling school. I wonder if she realizes how much of the grace and charm with which she carries herself to this day emanated from that experience. When she turned sixteen, I prevailed upon a friend, the owner of a hotdog stand, to give her a part-time job. She loved serving and bantering with the hotdog customers. She developed skills there that, decades later, continue to serve her well. I'm proud to know that my kids have always enjoyed a healthy sense of self-confidence.

I started dating. I'd never looked at another woman romantically during my eighteen-year marriage, and at first dating felt awkward, but I got over that. I had no intentions of ever getting married again and made my position on that subject very clear. Numerous opportunities existed to live with some of the ladies I dated, but I let them know of my dedication to raising my daughter and I wouldn't put her in that environment. Even so, I did my best to show the gals a good time and had no problem maintaining relationships. I liked women; I just didn't entirely trust most of them.

Even though I found my life to be far from perfect, I looked around and counted my blessings. Mel Howard, my office landlord decided he wanted to start and operate a delicatessen in the building I leased from him. His decision shook me, but he had told me years ago that would happen. To help finance his enterprise I bought two of his rental houses—one in Marina Gardens and the other in Washington Manor. He gave me a terrific deal, perhaps to help me feel better about making me move. I relocated in a former barber shop in the Ideal Market strip shopping center, absolutely the best commercial location in Mulford Gardens.

Finally, things had settled down. Every segment of my business prospered. I enjoyed being a dad. I did well socially and even played golf once each week. Sheila sold her Mulford Gardens home that had once been *our* home. She bought a nice place in Hayward where she had a beautiful swimming pool installed. She owned and managed her own kitchen remodeling business that she had recently acquired at a bargain price. We were congenial to the point that she actually invited my family and me and sometimes my friends into her home on special occasions. On top of that, she remarried. She seemed happy, which pleased me. All and all, things seemed to be going my way again, but I suppose I should have known by then that life could be full of unpleasant surprises.

CHAPTER EIGHTY-FIVE

Events occurring during the summer of 1973 are recorded permanently deep within the recesses of my mind. Sharon Martinez, a real estate agent licensed with Carter Realty, had listed a property located just blocks from my office in an area in which I'd been accumulating rental properties for some time. I wrote an offer on Sharon's listing. The owner accepted the offer and during the course of the transaction, Sharon and I got acquainted.

Not long after that she found a buyer for a property in Mulford Gardens I had listed and we presented the offer together. Sharon charmed my sellers into accepting her contract. She had a friendly sense of humor, and we got on well together. I asked her for a date, and she coolly informed me she was married.

A few weeks passed and Sharon dropped by my office. We exchanged pleasantries for a while until she informed me her husband had left her. The couple had decided to divorce. Furthermore, she wanted to know if I would still like to date her. We went out together a few times and enjoyed each other's company.

On a Sunday, sometime in July 1973, she held a home open up in Bayo Vista in the San Leandro Hills. I picked her up as she closed her open house, and we went to my house, where I introduced her to Valerie. We relaxed and visited for the next few hours. Sharon liked Valerie which pleased me. At around eleven, I took her back to her Bayo Vista listing where she had left her car. We enjoyed the view from my car for a short while, and I walked her across the street. She got into her car and I kissed her goodnight through the open window and headed back home.

The next morning I arrived at my office and found an Alameda County Deputy Sheriff waiting for me. He informed me that the bodies of Sharon and her husband had been discovered in her station wagon in Castro Valley (which is just a short distance from Bayo Vista) at six that morning. Those words left me dumbfounded. He told me they had determined that Sharon's husband had parked behind her car in Bayo Vista. He got into her vehicle and hid on the floor behind the front seat. They found evidence that while he waited for her, he drank coffee and loaded his revolver. I became clearly aware that when I opened the car door for Sharon and kissed her good night, I had kissed a woman within three feet of her estranged husband, likely holding a loaded gun.

Sharon then drove with her husband to Castro Valley Boulevard. She appeared to have been fatally shot in her car around midnight, only a half hour or so after I had left her in Bayo Vista. Three shots to the face ended her life. Her husband had apparently stewed over what he had done until around four or five in the morning and turned the gun on himself.

What a tragedy; in a moment of jealous anger, the man murdered a beautiful human being he surely loved, and before the sun rose, succeeded in orphaning their children. I served as a pallbearer at Sharon's open casket funeral. Surprisingly, no visible evidence existed that indicated her life had ended as a result of three gunshots to the face. The mortician who prepared her body for the occasion was indeed an artist. As I gazed at that woman, beautiful even in death, filled with despair and anger, I wondered, *why people behave in such a ghastly fashion.*

CHAPTER EIGHTY-SIX

About three weeks after Sharon's death, from which I still reeled, I returned to my office from a meeting at around two in the afternoon. I felt pretty good about the appointment I had just finished at a client's workplace, in which I had signed up a very saleable listing. As I walked through the door, it puzzled me to see Cathy, my son Danny's girlfriend, and my secretary seated next to a standing California highway patrolman. Cathy stared at me forlornly. I asked her, "What's going on?"

The officer said, "There's been an accident involving your son." Cathy softly said to me, "Danny is dead."

They explained, yet I couldn't understand. Danny and Cathy had driven out to my sister's home in Livermore that morning to pick up a car my sister had given Danny. Unexpectedly, the car wouldn't start so they decided to tow it back to San Leandro behind Danny's pickup truck. They had no tow bar so Danny used a rope that he had in his truck. Cathy sat behind the steering wheel of the car being towed, and Danny drove the truck.

They proceeded along Interstate 580 toward San Leandro with no difficulty until they reached Castro Valley, well over half way home. Cathy noticed Danny trying to wave at her in an apparent effort to give her some sort of a signal. The truck sped up abruptly. The sudden acceleration caused the towing rope to snap apart. The truck catapulted out of control and crossed the center divider into the oncoming freeway traffic. The first collision caused Danny to be thrown from the truck where several cars struck him. Incredulously, I reacted to the description of the accident by asking Cathy, "I understand, but how is he now?"

You will recall that I explained earlier, Danny suffered from Type I Diabetes. I believe the energy Danny exerted, regarding the unexpected necessity to tow the disabled car, had the effect of lowering his blood sugar level to the extent he suffered an insulin reaction, which caused him to lose control of the truck. Insulin reactions come on suddenly and when Danny realized his situation, he tried to signal Cathy— too late, of course.

CHAPTER EIGHTY-SEVEN

The loss of my first born changed some elements of my life forever. Often, when I read about the death of a child, even though I don't know the family, I send them a letter of condolence. I've received wonderful, comforting responses to such letters. Prior to the events that occurred during the summer of 1973, no matter what painful blows fate dished out, I refused to succumb to depression. That mindset no longer held true. For the next year and a half, even though I kept my business running—albeit a whole lot less efficiently than before, I played a lot of golf, ran around more than I should have and spent a little too much time in bars. The one responsibility during this troubled period that kept my full attention involved raising my daughter.

During that period, I did only as much as necessary to manage my business. Don't misunderstand; I didn't need to worry about going broke. My income from rentals, promissory notes and loan broker commissions which required little time and effort, kept me financially healthy. To explain my mindset at the time, I owned a nice house in Milpitas that had been vacant for more than a year. I just didn't have the energy or interest to get it ready to rent. My negligence of the Milpitas house didn't represent the only responsibility on which I had slacked off. I put practically no effort into growing my business since losing Danny.

I dated Janet Gomes, a good-looking gal who seemed to fit well into my disoriented lifestyle back then. Janet rented a house from me at 2445 Esser Avenue in San Leandro. She regularly used marijuana and didn't have to try very hard to get me to join her. I'd never seen her intoxicated but she loved to spend a lot of time in bars with me in tow. Neither happy nor unhappy, I just sort of drifted along, not quite ready or even knowing how to deal with my underlying state of dissatisfaction.

Divorced at that time, Janet had five daughters from two former husbands. The girls ranged in age from three to eight and included two sets of twins, one set from each husband. Valerie loved Janet's delightful girls, which figured high among the reasons that kept me in that relationship. The girls adored Valerie, and a sense of family existed between them. But without expending the energy to really think the situation through, I knew it couldn't last.

Janet and her girls attended church every Sunday at the First Presbyterian Church on MacArthur Boulevard in San Leandro. She told me her minister, Pastor Robert Laird, enjoyed a reputation as a highly-respected hypnotist. Janet said he occasionally worked with people who needed surgery but couldn't tolerate anesthetics. Pastor Laird had the ability to place some such people into a hypnotic state, enabling them to be operated on absent pain-killing medication. Janet begged me to go with her to Pastor Laird's beginning weekly evening class, designed to teach people how to improve the quality of their lives through the process of self-hypnosis. To me the idea seemed ridiculous, but to please Janet, I agreed to go with her to at least one session.

Janet's pastor impressed me favorably. He came across as friendly, relaxed and reassuring. That first evening, he instructed the class on how to place themselves into a state of self-hypnosis, which we did, or at least I did. He suggested while in that condition we envision our lives as we wished them to be, and imagine doing the things that could produce the desired results. I did as he suggested and experienced an almost overwhelming sensation of self-confidence. I felt a surge of my old energy and seemed almost ready to start living again.

The next day, I drove out to inspect my house in Milpitas that had been vacant for a year. I made a list of what I needed to make it rentable, and that afternoon I scheduled one of my best handymen to accomplish the needed repairs. Minnie, my rental property manager, had the place rented by the following Monday. I no longer drifted aimlessly and again engaged in the lifestyle that had worked so well for me before my divorce and the loss of my son.

After completing Pastor Laird's first program on self-hypnosis, I enrolled in another one sponsored by the San Leandro School District. As much as I liked and respected the Pastor, I needed to move on. I hoped that Janet might continue attending her Pastor's classes, but I realized that the lifestyle to which I needed to return, would not fit with what she wanted from me. I decided it best that I remove myself from her life in the friendliest manner I could construct.

Actually, I did Janet a favor by breaking off with her. In a few months, Valerie and I received an invitation to her wedding at the First Presbyterian Church to be conducted by Pastor Laird. I met and liked Janet's husband and sincerely wished the couple the best. Soon after her marriage, Janet called and asked me to consider selling her and her husband the house she rented from me. She told me they could finance the purchase with a GI loan available to her veteran husband. It pleased me to accommodate her request.

CHAPTER EIGHTY-EIGHT

After my divorce and the events of the summer of 1973, although once again I became very ambitious, my financial goals did not remain as astronomical as they once had been. I believe financial independence is necessary to achieve true joy in life. But money isn't everything; it's only part of the story.

In 1975, all facets of my real estate career prospered. I didn't have to chase business; it came to me through loyal clients and ever-increasing referrals. Regarding my loan business, I'd built up a backlog of lenders and borrowers that continued to expand. At the time, I did some lending of my own funds and collected excellent interest. But I contained the majority of my lending activity within the capacity of a loan broker for which I received commissions for arranging loans. In time, circumstances permitted me to alter the procedure to my distinct advantage.

There existed absolute beauty in the diverse activities residing under the umbrella sheltering the scope of my services. I may have negotiated the sale of a property which entitled me to be paid a commission when the transaction closed. Often, if for some reason that buyer couldn't secure financing from conventional sources to complete the purchase of the property, I might be called upon to arrange a loan which earned me another commission. Usually such monetary arrangements provided for a three to five year balloon payment due date. When the unpaid balance owing on the loan came due, and the borrower needed me to arrange a new loan, another commission came my way. If the borrower decided to sell the property, instead of refinancing, often I handled the sale and received a commission.

I continually purchased properties for my own account; many in very poor condition. Sometimes I sold that type of real estate for a small mark-up to a party with aspirations of fixing it up and reselling for a profit. In such transactions, if my entrepreneurial buyer could make a substantial down payment, I provided the financing and collected a commission. Upon completion of the fix-up, of course, the owner listed the property with me which provided me with another commission.

In 1973, Louis Sanda, the father-in-law of Raylene Combs' granddaughter, bought a vacant lot on the west end of Fairway Drive, a block from the San Leandro Marina. Louis knew nothing about the area, but Raylene's enthusiasm about the area inspired him to take a chance. Louis didn't appear to be interested in emulating Raylene by building on his property. His lot appeared well located for a small condominium project. I'd never been involved in the development of condos, yet I wanted to be.

I knew what Louis' lot cost him, so I made him an offer to buy it for a higher price than he had paid. I met with him in his appliance store in the City of Richmond. I found him to be a very likable person, and it pleased me when he agreed to sell to me. No one had built condominiums in Mulford Gardens yet, and several people thought I could be making a mistake.

The lot could easily accommodate four units. The Rombough Construction Company had recently completed a three-unit rental complex in the area that I found very appealing. Until his untimely death, Jeffery Rombough ran the company. Upon Mr. Rombough's demise, his wife, Phyllis, took over the operation of the firm. She proved to be a capable building designer, as well as an efficient general contractor. Her twenty-two-year-old son, who while still a child had started working in the family business, took charge of construction.

Mrs. Rombough designed a complex consisting of four three-bedroom, two-bath units divided into two separate buildings. Each unit featured a one-car enclosed garage, in addition to a covered carport. The owners would share a kidney-shaped pool surrounded by a pleasant patio area. Phyllis had done a beautiful job. That block on Fairway Drive had already been rezoned PUD so I didn't have to go through the rezoning process. The neighbors quickly approved the proposal, and the city issued building permits.

Surprise, surprise . . . the only group in opposition happened to be the MGIA officials, but their protests got them nowhere. Notwithstanding the fact that I often found myself at cross-purposes with the MGIA, I always knew the community benefitted from their existence. I can honestly say that in spite of our differing views, I genuinely liked every member.

As construction of the units progressed, I started looking for buyers. Marge and Al Basuino lived in Bayside Village, not far from my project, in a home they purchased through me three years previously. Before Marge and Al bought in Bayside Village, I handled the sale of their home in Marina Gardens. I suggested they might do well to buy one of my new condominiums. Among several potential benefits, the thought of no longer having to deal with yardwork strongly appealed to them. Additionally, envisioning their enjoyment of the pool and lovely community patio, more or less sealed the deal.

The Basuinos expressed gratitude that I had thought of them. I listed their Bayside Village home, guaranteeing to buy it myself if it failed to bring the price at which we put it on the market. I didn't need to exercise my guaranty, as the Basuinos' home sold within two weeks. Construction of my complex hadn't yet been completed, so we negotiated an Occupancy Agreement wherein Marge and Al could rent back the Bayside Village property from the current owners until the Basuinos could take possession of their new condo.

Much to the surprise of several people, including me, all four of the units sold before completion. What a mistake: I never again sold a house or condo before construction had been finished and I'd had a chance to really test the market. One person, Dick Miller, found a buyer for the unit he had under contract to purchase from me. One week after Dick acquired title from me he closed the sale to his buyer. He made as much profit on the sale of his single condominium as I did on all four units.

CHAPTER EIGHTY-NINE

I think sometime in 1967, I had rented one of my houses in Marina Gardens to the Taveras family. The family included Frank and his wife Beth, both in their mid-thirties, and their two children; Will, around fourteen, and Angela, maybe a couple of years younger. The Taveras were an attractive, wholesome family. Frank worked as a tool and die-maker and received a salary sufficient to allow Beth to stay at home to devote her time and energy to raising the children. They seemed to be the "All American Family." Frank coached the kids' soccer teams after work and on the weekends, and Beth functioned as a truly "hands on" mom.

The Taveras' rent always arrived a few days before it came due. They took care of my property as if they were the owners. Frank delivered the rent one afternoon and I invited him to sit and talk a few minutes. I said, "You know, Frank, I feel guilty taking your rent. I'm not going to give it back to you, but maybe I can do something better for you." I used a line I often employed, "Why are you buying a house for me when you could buy one for yourself?"

He wanted to hear more. By the end of the week, I'd negotiated the sale to Frank and Beth of an attractive, three-bedroom, two-bath home on Oahu Avenue in Bayside Village.

About four years had passed since the Taveras had purchased their Bayside Village home through me, when I got a call from Beth one afternoon. She sounded cheerful and told me she needed to talk with me. She asked if I had time to stop over that afternoon; she would explain why when she saw me. A little confused, I wondered why she couldn't tell me what she needed over the phone. I arrived and found her alone in the home. Beth's appearance had changed considerably since I last saw her. She still looked pretty, but clearly something more than the few passing years had taken a toll. Surprised, at only three in the afternoon, I detected the odor of alcohol on her breath.

Beth told me the relationship between her and Frank gradually deteriorated, and they had decided to go their separate ways. They wanted to sell their home and wished to list it with me. As Beth showed me through the house, I asked her about the shattered glass sliding door leading from the family room to the patio. She explained that a bullet Frank fired toward her had struck the door. She pointed out other bullet holes in the living and dining room walls. She said Frank could have easily killed her if he'd wanted; he only intended to terrify her, and he did. I felt disappointed and surprised at what had happened to what I had once considered the ideal family. Well, maybe not all that surprised; after all, I'd had some personal experience with a deteriorating marital relationship.

That evening I saw the Taveras at their home a little after nine. At their request, each appointment after my initial meeting with Beth occurred in the home between nine and midnight. Frank insisted on listing the property about five percent higher than I suggested. It didn't really matter as they truly wanted to sell. I knew, after a reasonable passage of time, I could convince them to accept a fair offer. Unless I felt a seller to be truly motivated, I generally avoided taking overpriced listings.

About a week later a tragedy happened on Oahu Avenue, just a block from my listing. Four members of the popular Reardon family had been discovered shot to death in their beds in the wee hours of Wednesday morning. The victims included Mr. and Mrs. Reardon and two of their three children. At the time of the shootings, a third child, a sixteen-year-old boy visited with relatives out-of-state. The killer or killers executed the family dog as well. A stunned and frightened community struggled with the overwhelming question as to what sort of a monster could have committed such an act.

Frank asked me to hold the house open on the following Sunday, which I agreed to do. I started the open house at one and planned to stay until four. At my suggestion, the family left me alone in the house so that potential buyers would feel free to candidly ask questions and express their feelings about the property. The weather cooperated and the home showed well— the bullet damage had been repaired. Several potential buyers dropped by throughout the afternoon until around half-past three when the activity slacked off.

About that time, Will—Frank and Beth's eighteen-year-old son —showed up. Will had been on hand when I'd taken the listing. Each time I tried to engage him in conversation he practically ignored me, almost to the point of rudeness. I gave him a friendly greeting, and as usual, he responded with a sour nod. Not ready to give up on him quite yet. I asked him if he knew the Reardon family. Suddenly I had his rapt attention. In a flash, his demeanor transformed. That kid came alive. He told me he knew the family well and spent a lot of time in their home. Will and the Reardon boy who had escaped the massacre because of his out-of-state visit, according to Will, had been best friends for years.

I left the Taveras' home a little after four. As I rounded up my "open house" signs and drove back to the office, I couldn't get over my encounter with Will. I felt glad to see Gay in the office. She and I had a close relationship and what I said to her I knew I couldn't say to anyone else. She asked me how my open house turned out. I told her it went fine, but explained I wanted to run something by her that happened there. I related my conversation with Will, and told her, "You know Gay, I believe Will Taveras murdered the Reardon family." She looked at me like she thought I might be a little crazy.

On the following Wednesday morning I got a frantic call from Beth. She told me the police came to their home that morning with a search warrant. They took Frank's thirteen guns and several other items and arrested both Frank and Will Some of the items taken—and the arrests—had something to do with a rash of burglaries that had occurred in the area recently. Beth asked if I knew how she might get them bailed out. I gave her the number of my bails bondsman friend, Chuck Marks. A few minutes later she called me back; she had scheduled a meeting with Chuck at the jail in an hour and asked me to join her.

I met Beth at the Police Department lobby. She told me Chuck went into another room to arrange bail. We talked a few minutes, and I saw Chuck entering the lobby; he motioned for me to walk over to him. Apparently, he wanted to talk with me away from Beth. He told me he could post bond for Frank, but Will had to remain in custody. What he said next related to my Sunday afternoon conversation with Gay. The police suspected Will had murdered the Reardon family. I drove back to the office, and Beth waited for her husband.

Beth called me a few days later and told me Will had confessed to the murders. She said Mr. Reardon suspected Will belonged to a burglary ring that had designed some sort of a universal garage apparatus capable of opening any electronically operated garage door. Such a device may have been used in the numerous recent neighborhood burglaries.

Apparently, Mr. Reardon had announced his intentions to pass his suspicions on to the San Leandro Police Department. To keep that from happening, Will ostensibly murdered the Reardon family that tragic predawn morning. As the coroner extracted two different calibers of bullets from the bodies, speculation as to the possibility of two killers abounded, but only Will had been charged. Each of the victims' bodies turned out to be discovered in their beds, as if they had been shot in their sleep. It seemed likely if only one shooter committed those murders, at least one of his prey might have been disturbed by the gunfire and left their bed. Indeed, I believed another killer existed, and I thought I knew his identity.

During that hectic period I still had the Tavares home listed for sale, but the emotional distress of the family precluded it from being shown. I got a call from Beth asking if I could drop by for a meeting with her and Frank that evening. I arrived at nine per Beth's request and found the atmosphere of the house and its occupants forlorn and without hope. The stress of the terrible turmoil Frank and Beth endured, on top of their already distressed marital relationship, reflected in their dispirited faces. I felt sad for them and wished I could do something to ease their despair.

They explained that they had been getting nasty threatening telephone calls and mail placing the responsibility for the murders on them. They could no longer live there. Frank asked, "Val, I know you are always buying houses . . . will you buy ours?"

I knew Will's ghastly behavior had stigmatized the house and if I did buy it, finding a buyer might be difficult. I explained that to Frank; he understood and told me to name my price. Of course when I bought property, I always looked for a bargain. But I also knew this family trusted me. I had to be fair.

We agreed upon what we both considered a fair price and closed the escrow in two weeks. The family couldn't get away from there fast enough. Will's punishment required he serve four twenty-eight-year consecutive sentences; one for each murder he had been convicted of committing. Frank and his young daughter relocated to Bakersfield where Frank had grown up and where his parents still lived. Beth left for Idaho. She had friends there. I never heard from Frank again, but Beth called me frequently. After a year or so, she fell in love and married a long haul-truck driver.

Heartbreak followed Beth to Idaho. She called me one evening and told me her husband had been killed. While parked on a rain-soaked highway shoulder, his truck slid down an embankment into a large drainage ditch. The truck settled upside down into the rain-filled channel. The vehicle wedged in so tightly into the channel that Beth's husband couldn't open the doors to escape, and he drowned.

After doing a little cosmetic work on the Oahu house, I put it on the market. In about a week, Gay brought me an acceptable offer from a divorced Chinese lady with two children. She agreed to pay all cash, which meant the sale could close in just a few days. We made an appointment for Mrs. Wu to sign the final closing papers in the office at five o'clock. At that meeting, for the first time, I met Mrs. Wu and her two charming young children, a boy and a girl. Mrs. Wu barely spoke English. Her children did some interpreting for us. Clearly, she felt that owning the Oahu house constituted a blessing to her and the children.

As we finished having Mrs. Wu sign her closing documents, a troubling thought occurred to me. I didn't know if Gay had made her aware that a convicted murderer had lived in what would soon be her home. No legal obligation existed to reveal such information; after all the murders did not happen in the home. Morally I knew what I had to do. I explained the situation slowly to Mrs Wu. At first my words confused her, but when she realized the importance of my statement, she tersely responded with, "We no buy!"

I saw no point in trying to get her to reconsider, so I told Gay to make arrangements to refund Mrs.Wu's good faith deposit.

CHAPTER NINETY

Jake and Phyllis Leal introduced me to their close long-time friends, Bob and Janet Joaquin. Bob and Janet wanted me to do for them what I had done for the Leals. Bob and Janet both worked— he as a school custodian for the San Leandro School District and Janet as a bookkeeper for a local construction company. The nature of the Joaquins' employment and middle class lifestyle, coupled with their unpretentious demeanor, failed to divulge the impressive extent of their financial wealth. They explained the basic source of their affluence derived via inheritance. Just prior to the 1929 stock market crash, Bob's father had accumulated a fortune buying equities that had risen in value quickly. Just before it all went so bad, he sold his stock holdings and bought gold—a fortuitous move for which his heirs were deeply grateful.

Impressed with their trusted friends' recommendation, the Joaquins invested a substantial sum with me. As I did with the Leals, I borrowed their money for my own account for the purpose of financing my own ever-expanding investment portfolio. I generally no longer acted in the capacity of a loan broker for lenders other than myself.

I lent funds I'd borrowed at a higher interest rate than the interest I paid. In such transactions, the borrower paid me a commission even though I made such loans with my own funds. The investors that lent funds to me knew that I lent those funds at higher interest rates than they received from me. The situation made them feel comfortable because my substantial net worth offered them a sense of heightened security.

Assets left to Bob Joaquin and his sister, Irene Dunaway, by their father included two houses located in the exclusive and highly desirable Gold Coast area of Alameda. I looked at both properties; one on St. Charles Street and the other on Paru Street and found them both to be in excellent condition. The family decided to list the homes for sale with me. I placed the properties on the MLS and immediately started getting calls from Alameda Realtors. Julie Summers with Gallager and Lindsey Realtors brought in an acceptable offer on the Paru Street home. My initial impression of Julie was positive with her instant likability and classy good looks. The escrow went well, and she impressed me with her high degree of professionalism. The property on St. Charles took a little longer to move, and it also sold through a Gallagher and Lindsey agent.

Although Julie and I found ourselves attracted to one another, we happened to be involved with others. Even so, we met late one night in the cocktail lounge of the popular and very elegant Blue Dolphin Restaurant, overlooking the harbor at the San Leandro Marina. We had that one date, and discovered a strong romantic chemistry existed between us, but again . . . it didn't seem to be the right time.

Nonetheless, what Julie told me fascinated me. She, with her family, had moved to California from Missouri, and as a child lived in the same area as my family in Richmond. She and her sister attended Washington Elementary School in Richmond, as I did. Many of her unfortunate childhood family experiences paralleled my own. She impressed me and I wished I could see more of her. I felt comfortable with her; as if I'd known her for years instead of months. Still, at that time we went our separate ways, managing to stay in touch by phone over the next few years. Little did I know then what lay in store for us.

Julie and I were soul mates; we just didn't know it for a while. Both of us had engaged in a struggle to overcome obstacles visited upon us early in life that sometimes obscured our vision. Wounded vanity obscured my emotional vision. As I alluded to earlier, the circumstances which brought about the end of my marriage left me feeling pretty worthless. Attracting women helped restore my level of self-confidence, which sadly I felt I needed to experience over and over. It didn't work for anyone to become romantically involved with me, because I couldn't begin to honestly commit based upon my innate lack of ability to trust. I needed psychiatric help, but I just hadn't figured that out yet.

CHAPTER NINETY-ONE

I met Robert and Emily Richards when they contacted me to view a beautiful home I had listed in Mulford Gardens on West Avenue 133rd, one of the most desirable locations within the community. They inspected my listing and wanted to own it. I prepared the purchase offer which the owner quickly accepted. As soon as I opened an escrow on the West Avenue 133rd transaction, Robert and Emily wanted to list their home with me in the elite Bayo Vista district in the San Leandro hills.

The Richards had three children, a boy and two girls ranging in age from five to eleven. Both Robert and Emily exuded palpable charisma. I found myself spending more time with them than the conduct of our business actually required, but they seemed to genuinely like me and made me feel at ease. Robert, a nationally known baseball player had recently retired from that profession. Emily, the typical blond trophy wife so often married to famous athletes, told me she and Robert married upon her graduation from a well-known eastern college. Prominently displayed on a table in their home I observed a large glossy photograph of her when she received her college homecoming queen crown. The spread between their lives and mine constituted an incalculable distance and left me somewhat in awe of them.

I got their Bayo Vista home sold, and the Richards moved to Mulford Gardens. I continually received calls from Emily with various mundane questions, a common experience with people with whom I'd done business. One day Emily called and asked if we might meet in a local coffee shop to discuss the details of a real estate tax assessment notice that had arrived by mail. She informed me that Robert couldn't attend the meeting. The call puzzled me. I told her I had a very busy schedule that day, but I'd be happy to drop by their home to look over the assessment around six that evening. She explained that she preferred to call back the next day and reschedule.

The next afternoon, while I worked alone in the office, in walked Emily. She told me she needed to talk with me and wondered if I could meet her somewhere where we might be alone. I said I had an appointment with clients in a half hour. I didn't expect anyone else to be in the office until they arrived so I figured we could visit alone there until then.

Emily caught me off guard as she told me that her marriage had ended, and that she and Robert agreed to go their separate ways. I thought, *why is she telling this to me?* I just didn't believe what followed. She declared she loved another man. I started to express my surprise because to me, she and Robert seemed so happy and well suited to one another. But, before I finished my sentence, Emily stated, "I'm in love with you, Val."

The thought that this homecoming queen married to a nationally known professional athlete had fallen in love with a high school dropout seemed bizarre. Even though I didn't believe her, I felt flattered and my crippled male vanity soared. With mixed feelings I told her this must end immediately, and I politely asked her to leave my office which she did. Sure, the prospect tempted me, but the memory of Sharon Martinez still haunted me. A day or so later, Robert stopped by the office and confirmed his departure for Tokyo in a few days in pursuit of a promising business opportunity. Before he left the office, he said he and Emily were divorcing.

Looking back on Robert's last visit to my office, I sometimes wondered if he knew more than I thought he knew. I pondered the question—would his true purpose of dropping by involve giving me his tacit approval of a romantic relationship between his wife and me? I guess I will never know the answer, but in any event, Emily and I dated steadily for the next two years, and on and off for an additional couple of years. We learned from each other; I found I could operate comfortably on a social level in association with women that once I would have felt totally inferior to. I believe I influenced Emily about how people must function to survive in the real world.

Relevant to accommodating their divorce settlement, Robert and Emily listed their Mulford Gardens home with me. I quickly found a buyer, and Emily had to locate a place to live for her and the children. You will recall Mrs. Wu had just backed out of buying the Oahu home because a murderer had lived there. I had the vacant house ready to move into. I asked Emily if she had reservations about buying a home at a very advantageous price that had recently housed a killer. I showed the home to her and the kids and they loved it. Maybe a stigma had attached to the property in the view of Mrs. Wu, but not to Emily. She couldn't pass up such a bargain.

A short-lived lavish income, so typical within the world of professional athletes, often lured its prey into a lifestyle that ended in financial ruin. I believe Emily and Robert temporarily fell victim to that paradigm. When I first met Emily, even in the face of dwindling resources, she seemed to believe some innate obligation required daily expenditures at the mall of her choice.

However, by the time we went our separate ways that had changed. She had adjusted her living standards to fit comfortably within her financial parameters, which expanded dramatically as a result of her entry into the realm of a successful real estate agent. Her good fortune pleased me, except when she tried to steal my clients, which happened often.

CHAPTER NINETY-TWO

I continued to buy more property, primarily single family homes in good working class neighborhoods, which I either sold for a small profit right away or rented out with the intention of reaping a much higher gain in time. I enjoyed access to abundant amounts of cash available from private lenders, bank lines of credit or my own growing reserves of capital. Many good buying opportunities came my way because of my ability to make instant decisions, and my financial ability to move on a deal with lightning speed.

Among my best moves toward making advantageous property acquisitions, entailed enticing other Realtors to serve my interest. I didn't think I'd seen anyone else using this ploy, but it sure worked beautifully for me. If I located a property I'd like to own that was listed by another company, I asked the listing agent to consider me his or her client. I had him or her prepare and present my offer to the seller. As a Realtor, one half of the commission belonged to me, but I insisted that my share be paid to the listing agent. My purchases constituted all cash transactions in which I relieved the owners of all requirements to accomplish any repairs whatsoever. Not many buyers like me came along, and I continually had a half dozen or so former competitors on the lookout for good buys for me.

Sometimes if a deal is too good, it can blow up in your face. Remember Bud Mayer, the fellow I partnered with to build the four four-plexes on Doolittle Drive in San Leandro? Well, Bud operated as an aggressive entrepreneur to whom I continually lent money to finance his multitude of real estate related activities. Sometimes I sold him property, sometimes I bought property from him, and occasionally I partnered with him in a joint venture. Bud made me think of a hound dog constantly following the scent of any situation promising a chance of a profit.

One morning around eleven, I got a call from Bud. He phoned from the annual auction in which the office of the Alameda County Tax Collector sold tax defaulted properties to the public. Bud told me that he had been the winning bidder on a single-family home in San Leandro he thought I might like. He gave me the address and the amount of his accepted bid. I knew the area well—I already owned other homes in the same neighborhood. Upon acceptance of his bid, Bud had to put up a deposit for the property to be held until the auction process ended later that day, at which time he had to pay the balance of the purchase price in full.

Bud explained that even though he had been the winning bidder, he didn't have the cash to complete the purchase, and he didn't want to forfeit his deposit. He asked to borrow the money to complete his purchase from me, or sell his position to me for $4000. Without even looking at the property, I knew buying his position served my best interest. I also knew that had been Bud's plan from the outset. I picked up a cashier's check from Bank of America made payable to the Alameda County Tax Collector on my way to meet Bud at the Alameda County Courthouse complex, the location of the auction. I easily substituted my name for Bud's as the buyer, paid the purchase price and gave Bud a check for $4000. I thought I'd made a good buy.

As I left the courthouse, Bob Brown, a San Leandro Realtor and a fellow I liked very much, stopped me. I think I'd seldom ever been at a public property auction that I hadn't seen Bob—the process fascinated him. He had observed the transaction between Bud and me and the official from the Tax Collector's office. Bob asked me, "Have you talked with the man who owned the property you just bought?"

I answered, "No Bob, I've never even seen the house. I'm going by there now to see if anyone is living there, and if they are, to make arrangements to get possession."

Bob said, "When I read the property would be auctioned off, I dropped by to talk to the owner about maybe buying it myself. After talking with the owner, I decided I wouldn't get near this."

Bob explained that the eighty-four-year-old owner lived alone and seemed mentally incompetent. Other than delinquent taxes, which only amounted to $1500 or so, he owed nothing on the property. He simply didn't know enough to pay the property taxes for five consecutive years, at which time ownership of the property passed to the Alameda County Tax Collector. According to Bob, and I feared him to be correct, in addition to buying the property I'd also bought a headache. I thanked Bob for the information and headed out to look at my new acquisition and formulate a strategy.

I pulled up in front of the property located in the blue collar Davis Tract district. Situated on an attractive wide corner lot, the house had a pleasing architectural design. Yet, when I observed the run down condition of the property, I figured maybe I hadn't got that much of a bargain. But no matter; I liked the neighborhood, and it fit into the category of the type of property I tried to accumulate. I knocked on the front door and saw a large, older, white-haired man through the glass panel next to the door. He peered at me and frantically gestured for me to leave. I called out to him to please open the door so we could talk. Well, that didn't happen, so I pondered what to do next.

As I stood on the porch, I spotted a fellow doing yard work across the street. I crossed over and introduced myself. I let him know my purpose for being there and asked if he knew the gentleman who lived in the house. He did and he told me he had known Bernard Perkins, the occupant and former owner, for many years. I asked the neighbor if he could tell me a little bit about Mr. Perkins which he seemed glad to do.

He told me Mr. Perkins and his wife had purchased the home new in 1948. After Mrs. Perkins died some years ago, Bernard became a heavy drinker. For decades he had been reclusive and hostile to his neighbors. A couple of years ago, he got into a dispute with a neighbor and attacked him with a garden hoe.

The terrified victim of Bernard's ire called the police, which resulted in Bernard's arrest. Charged and convicted of assault, Bernard had been incarcerated in Deuel Vocational Institute in Stockton, California. The man telling me the story didn't know the length of Bernard's sentence, but it didn't really matter as things turned out. Due to his advanced age, he served his time in a very low-security facility. After a couple of months behind bars, one day he simply walked away from prison, returned home and no one bothered to come looking for him. I asked if he had any relatives I might contact. I learned of a niece who turned out to be Bernard's sole living relative. My talkative and helpful information source introduced his wife to me. She had the niece's Texas telephone number.

I returned to my office and called Bernard's niece. I told her what had happened and wondered if she might be interested in coming to California to assist her uncle. Absent some sort of financial compensation, she had no desire to help. Apparently, ill will existed between her and Uncle Bernard and they hadn't communicated for years. When she retired from the Army and brought her non-Caucasian groom to visit, ugly words were exchanged, leaving no hope of reconciliation. I wondered, *what the hell do I do now?*

I contacted the Alameda County Health Department and explained the dilemma to them. I went to Fairmont Hospital and met with County Health Nurse, Maria Paris. She seemed friendly and sincerely concerned. She promised to consult with her superiors immediately, and she promised I would hear from her in a day or so, and I did. She had scheduled a staff meeting for the same week, which she informed me I needed to attend.

When I showed up for the meeting I joined seven or eight people including Nurse Paris. There were other nurses, doctors and administrators in attendance. I learned that the same day I first met Nurse Paris, she visited Bernard. It surprised me he let her enter the house along with an Alameda County Deputy Sheriff. Based upon Nurse Paris' assessment and the circumstances of the situation to date, the staff had developed a plan.

They wanted me to evict Bernard. The plan provided that when the Deputy Sheriffs removed Bernard from my property, the Health Department needed to take official custody of him because they deemed him unable to care for himself. The group dashed my hope that the County could just take Bernard from the house without any further involvement from me.

I explained that evicting an eighty-four-year-old widower from the home he had lost for non-payment of property taxes, resulting from his mental inability to understand, happened to be something I wanted nothing to do with. They expressed sympathy for my plight. However, they made me understand I really had no choice. They asked me to be very careful to avoid media involvement. They may as well have advised me to stop the tide from coming in.

On the morning of the eviction, I went to Leona Drive and met the deputies in charge of removing Bernard from the property. Merle Etherton, my handyman, came to disable the front door lock in the event we were refused access, which was what happened. Of course Nurse Paris joined our little group. Merle got the door open, and the deputies entered the house and placed Bernard in handcuffs to reduce the chances of him sustaining an injury in the event he forcibly resisted removal. *How did I ever get into this?*

The word "ghastly" understated the condition of the interior of the house. The foul stench of excrement coupled with rampant filth repulsed me and the others. The toilet appeared to have been used daily, long after it became inoperable. Other than a half empty bottle of gin on the kitchen table, no other nourishment existed on the premises. Obviously, that sad story had played out over several years. I turned my head to hide my emotion when Nurse Paris quietly said, "Val, you haven't harmed Mr. Perkins, you've rescued him."

Before the Health Department could place Bernard into a medical facility, a certain amount of legal minutia had to be accomplished. Following the eviction, the deputies delivered Bernard to the Twin Palms Hotel on "B" Street in Hayward. In order to accommodate situations as described herein, when incapacitated people awaited placement into an appropriate medical facility, the County had a contract in place with Twin Palms Hotel to provide such individuals temporary lodging.

A couple of days passed, and I received a call from Nurse Paris. She let me know Bernard had been placed into Fairmont Hospital. She explained that on the evening that Bernard checked into Twin Palms, he spent a considerable amount of time in the hotel's street-level bar. Unfortunately, around midnight he fell off a barstool, which resulted in a broken ankle. His injury led to a hasty admittance into Fairmont.

After a little time at Fairmont, away from booze, and receiving good nutrition, Nurse Paris said Bernard looked much better than he had on the day he left his home. I asked Nurse Paris for permission to visit him at Fairmont. She accommodated my request. I spoke with Bernard and found him to be friendly and cheerful. He didn't understand the reason for my visit or how we happened to be associated and that worked out fine for me.

The County authorities placed Bernard into an excellent home for the elderly in Oakland. The care and genuine loving attention Bernard enjoyed there gave hope that the remaining years of his life might pass in contentment and peace. What made that happy ending possible? Notwithstanding the fact that Bernard lost his home as a result of failing to pay his property taxes, he was actually financially well off relative to his needs. He continued to receive a generous monthly income from his pension plus his social security payments. And remember; his delinquent property taxes amounted to only around $1500. The balance of the money the property brought at the tax auction belonged to Bernard. What initially looked to be a disaster for him turned out to be a blessing.

Although Bernard appeared happily settled in, my part of the story soon got nasty. Immediately after gaining possession of the property, my contractors got busy doing their thing. In a short period, I transformed a nearly uninhabitable mess into one of the most attractive homes in the area. However, word that an eighty-four-year-old senile widower had lost and been kicked out of his home for non-payment of property taxes, soon caught the attention of the media. The manner in which the media presented the story infuriated the public. People envisioned the classic tale of the greedy real estate mogul stealing the home of the helpless widow (widower in this case). Angry, outraged citizens picketed the office and personal residence of the Alameda County Tax Collector.

Misinformed accounts of the events that transpired appeared in the newspapers every day for weeks. A woman walked into my office, stood in front of my desk and declared she just wanted to see the bastard that had stolen an elderly widower's home. She turned and walked quickly out, with me trailing, asking her to stay long enough to hear the whole story. She refused to listen. Film on television news showed the property in its pristine condition after I'd spent several thousands of dollars bringing it back to life. The misleading implication led the public to believe that I took title to the property in its fixed-up state.

Letters to the editor mostly denouncing me and the County Tax Collector showed up in the local newspapers daily. The Office of the Tax Collector and I were sued by the State of California. The state asked the court to reverse the tax sale. I filed an answer to the suit to avoid a Default Judgment and waited. I granted a television interview in my office to Jennie Burns from Channel Two News. She treated me fairly and gave me ample time to explain exactly what happened. I told her, "Generally, people considered Bernard 'slipped through the cracks' and the system failed him. Not so—the system served him well; compare his life now to when he lived at Leona Way."

Off camera, Ms. Burns said, "You may be right, Val, but you will never convince anyone that it's proper to put handcuffs on an eighty-four-year-old man in this sort of a situation."

I answered, "I don't disagree with you Jennie, but please remember ... I didn't place Bernard in handcuffs."

The Grey Panthers, a group that advocated for the elderly, called me for a telephone interview. Initially the lady conducting the interview displayed somewhat of an "attitude". But as the discussion progressed, and she learned more about Mr. Perkins, she softened and we concluded on a friendly basis. Time passed and the State of California lawsuit died for lack of timely follow-up.

Various groups constantly tried to figure out how to get title to the property, ostensibly for the benefit of Bernard, yet sought to have the title vested in their name. I received a call from a local newspaper reporter who had covered the story for weeks. We talked about various aspects of the situation. I told her, if any one of the groups looking to acquire ownership of Leona Way sincerely wished to help Bernard, I had a proposition for them. I would sell them the property at well below market value if they would enter into a binding agreement that any profit they gained from the sale of the property had to be paid to Bernard. The offer stipulated that they had to sell to the highest bidder within ninety days after they acquired title to the property. No one took me up on my offer. My proposal redeemed me in the eyes of a lot of critics—not all, of course.

I never saw Bernard after that visit to Fairmont. I like to think that his remaining years went well. The experience taught me a lot about people. Surprisingly, some of the letters to the editor printed in the newspapers favored my position. Actually, some calls I received came from people who wanted me to explain how they might do what I did.

Cecile Babcock, an attorney in Oakland, wrote a wonderful long letter of support which appeared in the Oakland Tribune. I called her and thanked her for her thoughtful words. A year later, I bought a property from her on Billings Avenue, located just a few blocks from Leona Drive. She had taken title to Billings in lieu of a legal fee. I did well on that purchase. If not for the Bernard Perkins deal, that transaction might never have happened. However, I think if I ever get the chance to buy a property in a tax auction lost by an elderly widower, I'll let someone else take advantage of that opportunity.

CHAPTER NINETY-THREE

Around 1980 something happened that pleased me immensely. Ed Marvin's daughter, Virginia Thacker, had been working as a Red Carpet real estate agent for Ed and his partner, Michael Rogers, for the past few years. Back when I made the choice to open my own office, I remembered her as as a tall, gangly, rather independent fifteen-year-old kid. She called me one morning and asked if she might stop by the office to talk with me. I wondered, *Now what does this girl want to talk with me about?*

She had grown into a tall, slender, blond beauty. She told me that even though her dad and I sometimes competed fairly aggressively, he had always respected and admired me. I doubted that, but I enjoyed hearing it anyway. After a few minutes, she told me what brought her to my office. Her dad had slowed down a lot in the last few years due to health problems including heart trouble. Michael had more or less taken charge of running the Red Carpet office. Virginia didn't like how Michael managed the operation of the firm. She believed he favored some agents over her. She wanted to know if I would consider letting her come to work in my office.

Of course she could come to work in my office. To have the daughter of my prime competitor in Mulford Gardens leave his office to join my staff shaped up to be a real coup. That beauty would dress up my office and might bring a clientele following with her.

Virginia produced a good amount of business, especially during her first year with me. She worked well with certain types. Confused young couples experiencing marital problems flocked to her. With those types she often, by de facto, expanded her role as a real estate salesperson to that of a family counselor. As time passed, her operation became more and more narrowly confined to fit that venue.

One day she asked me if I might consider allowing her dad to come to work in my office. Oh boy . . . would I. Ed and I had our differences, but I liked him a lot. In spite of some health issues, I knew he still had ambition. He would fit well into my operation. Although Red Carpet had never given me a lot of competition, with Ed in my office I felt Red Carpet would cease to rival me in Mulford Gardens completely. He never knew it, but because of my start with Ed, there had been times (not many) when I stayed away from clients I could have easily taken from him.

Well, Ed did indeed come to work as an independent broker at Val Barry Realty. He took on the unofficial role as office manager, which made him happy and certainly benefited me. Just the same as back when I worked for him, he arrived very early at the office each morning and prided himself on leaving late. All the others in the office followed Ed's suggestions, except Virginia. She always resisted his well-meaning suggestions, and Ed wouldn't cross her.

The "old time" Mulford Gardens property owners were impressed that Ed and I got back together. There seemed to be something wholesome about that arrangement. Eventually, Virginia and I disagreed about how a particular situation should be handled. I couldn't give in to her, nor could she give in to me. The matter got resolved by her going back to work with Michael at Red Carpet. I gave her a nice farewell lunch, and I hoped we parted friends.

Ed stayed with me for several years until his wife passed on and his health gradually dissipated. The day before he died of brain cancer, I visited him at his home. He knew his time had about run out, yet didn't seem to mind a lot. I brought him a box of See's nut-filled chocolates and he seemed to really enjoy the several pieces he ate and insisted that I join him. Even though Ed and I never conducted our business in the same manner, I learned a lot from him. When we disagreed on how situations should be handled, he generally went along with me—not always though. In any event, I'm grateful fate brought us together. Had I not met Ed, I sometimes wonder how things would have gone for me.

CHAPTER NINETY-FOUR

I had a tendency to open my office early, before any of the other agents or my secretary arrived. During my time alone, I planned my day and often engaged in self-hypnosis which continually served me so very well. On one such morning in 1980, Julie Summers dropped by; she had never before been to my office. We had that one short date in 1975, and we'd visited over the telephone occasionally, yet an attraction existed between us from the time we'd met. Nothing serious had developed between us because we always seemed to be involved with others. Julie explained she had business nearby and just stopped in to say "hello."

I looked at her, and boy . . . did I like what I saw. She reminded me of a beautiful model the way her slender body moved so gracefully inside her chic, form-fitting dress. Strangely, I suppose the fact that she didn't try hard to look sexy made her so sexy. We chatted about a variety of subjects, all of which might have bored me had I been talking to someone else, but visiting with her I found our conversation fascinating. While I thought about how best to go about trying to line up a date, she gave me some very serendipitous information.

She mentioned that she and her twenty-one-year-old daughter, Joan, planned to leave the next week for a short vacation in Honolulu. Coincidentally, I was too, but not for a vacation; I'd be there on business. Phyllis Leal's mother, Angelina Reposa, lived in Honolulu. Some years back, Mrs. Reposa and Phyllis' father Raymond, lived in and owned a home in San Leandro on Juneau Street, just two blocks from Jake and Phyllis Raymond passed away, and the time came when Mrs. Reposa wanted to move back to the little house in Honolulu where she and Raymond had raised Phyllis and their other two children. When she left for Hawaii, which she always considered her true home, I rented out and managed the Juneau Street house for her.

When the Juneau Street tenants vacated the house, I suggested to the Leals that as the residential real estate market had experienced an unusual upturn in value, it might be a good time to sell the property. Phyllis called her mom in Hawaii and passed on my recommendation. I followed up with a call to Honolulu. Mrs. Raposa agreed to give me the listing but only at a price I knew to be too high.

When I told her what she could expect realistically, she responded negatively. I didn't argue with her. I'd been around long enough to know that no matter how effective I might have made my point, I couldn't get a contract signed over the telephone. I sent her the overpriced listing, which indicated what she expected to receive.

Jake and Phyllis cleaned and painted the interior of the Juneau Street house, and I started showing it to prospective buyers. Whenever anything needed to be done to the house, the responsibility fell on Jake and Phyllis. Notwithstanding, Mrs. Raposa's insistence that I find a buyer who would pay her price, her daughter and son-in-law wanted the property sold. They knew for that to happen, Mrs. Raposa had to take less than she wanted.

Within a couple of weeks, I located a buyer willing to pay a fair price for the property. Again, I knew I couldn't get a contract signed over the telephone, so I decided to present the offer in person. I told Jake and Phyllis I needed their help. I asked them to fly to Honolulu with me at my expense. They enthusiastically accepted my proposition. I considered my risk. If Mrs. Raposa refused the offer, I stood to lose money. On the other hand, I wanted to do this for the Leals. They had often demonstrated their friendship and continuously recommended my services. It pleased me to stand the expense of their round trip flight to and from Honolulu, no matter what Mrs. Raposa decided.

I told Julie that inasmuch as she and her daughter's stay in Honolulu coincided with mine, maybe we could book in at the same hotel and spend some time together. She cheerfully agreed, which made me happy. My business trip promised to be a vacation trip as well. Jake and Phyllis planned to stay with Mrs. Raposa and return to California a week after my departure from Hawaii. I instructed my secretary to make hotel and flight reservations. That seemed simple enough, but complications arose.

According to Emily Richards, my temporary secretary, our flight left out of Oakland at 1:40 Monday afternoon. At around noon, Emily drove the Leals and me to the airport. Once inside the terminal, I discovered I'd been given the wrong information. Our flight had been scheduled to leave San Francisco International Airport at 1:40—not Oakland. I tried to call Emily at the office and got no answer.

I then frantically called Virginia Thacker at her home and asked if she could pick us up and take us to San Francisco . . . fast. I told her, "Virginia, if you make this happen, I will be in your debt, big time."

My being in Virginia's debt appealed to her. Ignoring speed limits and uneasy passengers, she dropped us off at the San

Francisco International Airport with practically no time to spare. I didn't know if we could make our flight. I tried to give Virginia twenty dollars for gas. She responded with, "No thanks, Val, you said *big time,* remember?" I knew what that meant. When I got back she expected me to hand her a commission deal.

We checked our bags with the Red Caps on the terminal curb and raced toward the gate where our plane would depart in minutes. Believe me, at San Francisco International it's a long way from the terminal entrance to where the flights leave for Hawaii. It felt hot and humid as we rushed to reach our gate in time. Jake had barely recovered from open heart surgery. When I noticed his face turning blue, I told him to please slow up, and I jogged ahead. Maybe I could get them to hold up the flight for a few minutes. When we boarded our plane with no time to spare, I thought my stress had ended, but I figured wrong.

Jake and Phyllis made that trip often. They enjoyed reducing the tedium of the journey by watching an in-flight movie, which I planned to do that day as well. Although the film appeared throughout the aircraft on overhead screens, passengers who wished to hear the dialogue had to rent earphones that the flight attendants passed out. The Leals, on previous flights, had gotten away with not returning their rented earphones.

Now when they traveled by air they used those purloined hearing devices to avoid having to pay to enjoy the film. Jake slipped me a set and instructed me to put them on after the flight attendants had distributed earphones to those who wished to rent them. I really didn't wish to do that. I didn't mind paying, but Jake insisted, so I went along.

About a quarter through the movie, I noticed a flight attendant glaring at me. I couldn't figure it out until I noticed the difference between my earphones and the other passenger's earphones. I had red ones and everyone else, including the Leals, who sat a few rows ahead of me, wore blue ones. I quickly removed my red earphones, while the look on the stewardess' face made me feel like a real jerk. I never mentioned it to the Leals, and I guessed I'd never know if I had been the victim of a practical joke or if if the Leals just didn't notice the difference.

When we arrived in Honolulu, I picked up a rental car and dropped the Leals off at Phyllis's mom's house. We felt a little tired and agreed to discuss business the next the morning. Mrs. Raposa insisted I join them for breakfast. I checked into my room at the Kahala Hilton and called Julie. I met her and Joan in the hotel lobby. I met Joan and discovered, just like her mom, she radiated beauty and charm. We went to dinner and later, dancing.

Next morning, I met with the Leals and Mrs. Raposa. Before discussing the Juneau Street transaction, Mrs. Raposa served a true Polynesian-style breakfast consisting of a variety of delicious exotic fruit, all picked in her backyard. I presented the contract and to my surprise, she just asked me, "Where do I sign?" I figured because I had brought her daughter to her, I had earned her full cooperation.

Julie and I spent the rest of the week together, and I sure hoped she had as much fun as I did. I didn't see much of Joan as she had cultivated a group of musician friends and enjoyed spending most of her time with them. It truly amazed me that Julie and I had so much in common. We both came from hard times and had very similar goals. She gave me a feeling of security and maybe I had the same effect on her. We took in the sights of Honolulu and on Saturday morning we flew back to California together. We talked every minute of the flight, and I experienced a feeling that I thought could never happen to me.

CHAPTER NINETY-FIVE

My association with Bud Mayer produced a never-ending source of income. He continued to develop investment opportunities which he needed me to finance. Bud didn't mind paying the hard-money interest rates I charged because I came up with the money he needed fast. Additionally, as I've said before herein, guys like Bud figured the interest they paid to fund their projects paled in comparison to the potential profit they hoped to gain. Every deal Bud entered, he wanted me to go into with him as a partner. Occasionally, I did, but not often.

Anytime Bud and I became partners, I set up a situation that put me in complete control. I could do that because I always provided the financing and he trusted me. Even so, with Bud as a partner, I had to be very alert. For instance, when we built the four-plex on Doolittle Drive that I discussed earlier, he located a buyer for one of our buildings that he told me nothing about. Then he offered to buy me out at a price substantially less than what his secret buyer paid him after I sold my interest to him.

In that case, Bud reaped a fat profit, some of which came at my expense. I could never deal that way with a partner. It seemed to me that he utilized such tactics in every partnership in which he became involved. In most such cases, some very hard feelings developed. I explained to Bud when he worked against the interest of his partner, he couldn't expect that person ever to do business with him again. Not so in my case—after the four-plex deal, the interest I charged him on following projects increased substantially. He understood my reasoning and didn't protest. I know this is trite, but in real estate speculation "The Golden Rule" equates to the fact that the one with the gold makes the rules.

The State of California anticipated eventually constructing a new freeway through the Hayward hills. Over a period of several years, Cal Trans—the agency in charge of acquiring ownership of the properties in the path of the proposed freeway—proceeded to buy such properties through the process of eminent domain. The right of a governmental agency to expropriate privately owned property is utilized under the following conditions: Whenever a situation develops in which it is deemed that for the good of the public, ownership of certain property is needed by the government, the power of eminent domain takes precedence over private property rights.

Well, years after acquiring ownership of miles of private property, the state decided that the shape of the economy dictated no freeway would be constructed through the Hayward hills. Therefore, Cal Trans proceeded to auction off the properties, one by one, to the public. Cal Trans held their on-site auctions on every non-holiday Wednesday. After a property sold, the auction advanced to the next property along the once-proposed freeway route. I enjoyed the bidding process and attended as often as I could.

One morning, after unsuccessfully bidding on a nice three bedroom home on Mozelle Court, which sold for more than its true market value, I leisurely strolled behind potential buyers or those just observing the action to the next property. By the time I got there, the bidding had already begun. The vacant parcel consisted of about three acres. A flagpole stood alone on the property, making me believe the land might have in the past accommodated a school. I observed two bidders fighting it out, and I knew both of them—Bud Mayer and Doug Fredriqui, a successful residential developer. I nodded to them. I knew nothing about the property, but I figured those savvy guys did.

I followed the pattern I often did when I saw knowledgeable investors engaged in such a contest, I entered the bidding process. I figured it could turn out to be a great buy or someone might pay me not to drive the price up. It had happened before. Bud moved beside me fast and said, "Let's not fight each other on this, Val. How about let's go in together?"

I said, "Alright, I'll do the bidding for both of us."

Bud knew how to win at an auction. Fredriqui offered one hundred thousand dollars, upping Bud's previous bid by two thousand dollars. Bud whispered to me, "If the price is going to go up only in two-thousand-dollar increments, this will take forever to reach two hundred thousand, which is about what the site is worth. Jump your offer to one hundred forty thousand, and let's see what he does."

I called out . . . "One forty!" Fredriqui stared at me, smiled and walked away.

When you won the bidding contest at a Cal Trans sale, you actually bought a ninety-day day option to purchase the property. At the site of the auction, the successful bidder paid the auctioneer ten percent of the purchase price. The balance owing then had to be paid no later than ninety days from the date of the initial transaction. If the balance did not get paid within that time, the optionee forfeited the ten percent option fee. Bud and I each paid seven thousand dollars and left with our option form drawn in both our names.

Two days later, I met Bud and a fellow from Tri Tel Corporation, with whom Bud had previously done business, for lunch at Emil Villas. After a pleasant repast, Bud told me that Tri Tel had offered us $60,000 for our $140,000 option to buy the Cal Trans site. Of course, I immediately accepted the deal.

Bud, sure of my decision, had already instructed the Tri Tel official to bring two separate certified checks to our lunch appointment. I signed the option assignment and collected my check before our lunch guest had time to change his mind. I didn't mind that Bud received $2500 more than me; he earned his commission. I figured for twenty minutes work I had been well paid.

CHAPTER NINETY-SIX

Byron Alba, an electrical contractor, whom I often made short term secured loans to, referred me to Patrick Cooper and his brother, Jeff. Byron subcontracted for Patrick and Jeff, general home remodeling contractors who worked mainly on houses in San Francisco. I received a call from Jeff explaining that he and Patrick wondered if I might be able to make them a loan similar to the loans I had been making to Byron Alba. After talking with him for about fifteen minutes, if what he told me held true, I figured indeed we could do business.

Jeff and Patrick wanted to meet me in the cocktail lounge of the Holiday Inn near the San Francisco Airport which they felt in that quiet environment they could better explain the somewhat unusual ramifications of their business. I met the Cooper brothers in the hotel lounge and instantly liked them. I sipped a diet coke while they explained over a carafe of chardonnay the fascinating circumstances of their operation.

Jeff and Patrick had learned that a large number of elderly people lived in homes in upscale neighborhoods in San Francisco which they had owned for several decades. The value of those homes had multiplied many times since they had been purchased by their long-time owners. The Coopers also discovered that many of those old-timers had no children and had outlived their heirs. Even though the value of the properties reached very lofty heights, their owners didn't have funds to modernize their homes, or even properly maintain them.

The Coopers advertised their home remodeling services in the San Francisco newspapers. They received a lot of calls from elderly San Francisco homeowners because their advertisements offered substantial discounts to senior citizens Patrick's estimates to upgrade such homes seldom got accepted because the owners simply couldn't pay for the improvements. After one such pricing session, the owners, Colin and Kate Howey, expressed palpable regret they just didn't have the financial resources to accept Patrick's bid. The Howey's asked Patrick if he could figure out a way to help them.

At that particular meeting, Patrick posited a proposition that had been playing in his mind as he had prepared his bid. He offered to completely modernize the home and buy it for a price substantially less than its current market value. He wanted the Howeys to carry the purchase price and receive monthly loan payments from the Coopers. Patrick and Jeff agreed to rent the house back to the Howeys.

The amount owing on the loan carried back by the Howeys for the Coopers would adjust each month reflecting the monthly rent owed to the Coopers by the Howeys. By paying the rent in that manner, no out of pocket rental payments had to be made by the Howeys. The Coopers proposed to pay the Howeys a monthly interest payment on the Howeys' property loan. They could then enjoy the rest of their lives in a modern home and receive a steady monthly income.

The Patricks and Howeys consummated the deal which delighted all parties to the transaction. The quality of the selling octogenarian's lifestyle improved dramatically as a result of

Patrick's brain-child. Upon the expected demise of their elderly tenants in a few short years, the Coopers anticipated extracting a huge profit by selling the property for far more than it had cost them. The Coopers felt they had constructed a magnificent business paradigm, which they named Benevolent Ventures.

Unexpectedly, Colin died within three months after the Coopers bought the Howey property. Kate Howey went into an assisted care home. Under the terms of the purchase agreement, the Coopers sold the property. After paying off the Howey loan, Patrick and Jeff walked away with what they thought of as an "astronomical" profit.

Within a few months, the Coopers had replicated the Howey purchase a half dozen times. In order to keep every aspect of each transaction "squeaky clean," they took in a minor partner, Andy Whitman. Andy, a retired certified public accountant, had helped the Coopers manage their books and tax return preparation for several years. Whitman had the Coopers' complete trust, and he paid all the bills related to each of the Benevolent Ventures transactions. The profit from the Howey deal went into an account on which Andy wrote checks.

Another one of the Benevolent Ventures' sellers requested that their loan be paid off because they—as had Mrs. Howey—needed to go into an assisted care facility because they could no longer manage housekeeping or food preparation. Of course the Coopers gladly accommodated them. The property sold and again the amount of the profit astounded the Coopers and Whitman. The net proceeds from the sale went into their mutual account.

Blinded by the tremendous profit gained from just two property sales, the Benevolent Ventures' partners' lifestyles took an abrupt and unwise change. They misunderstood the reality of their situation. Of course with patience, the potential of their business promised to make them millionaires. They just didn't seem to understand that potential millionaires and actual millionaires are not quite the same. The Coopers and Whitman happily began spending money as if they had already reached their long term financial goals, which they had not.

Patrick bought a new Rolls Royce to keep up with Jeff, who had recently purchased a new Ferrari. They each bought 6000 square foot homes adjacent to Pebble Beach Golf Course with unobstructed ocean views. They hosted friends, relatives and customers at the most expensive restaurants and paid for their guest's lodging and travel expenses to the best Las Vegas shows. Naturally, their Benevolent Ventures bank account soon went dry. In order to pay for the completion of remodeling the homes per their agreement with the elderly folks whose homes they had purchased, they needed to borrow money fast.

In some cases, Patrick and Jeff had been able to convince their geriatric sellers to allow their loans to be placed in second position to a conventional bank loan. Most sellers cooperated. They did so, because they believed that their cooperation would enable the Coopers to fulfill their obligation to accomplish the needed renovation to the house they expected to live in throughout their twilight years.

The funds the Coopers easily obtained from the banks went toward the remodeling projects as well as paying for their financially out of control, lavish lifestyle. Soon they needed more cash. The Coopers learned that most banks did not want to make second loans and the few that did make second loans seemed to take forever. In time, they borrowed second loans through a hard money loan broker, namely me. Their attraction to me emanated from my ability to very quickly arrange financing.

I arranged two separate loans to the Coopers on properties in which I believed sufficient equity existed to provide adequate security. Ed Marvin, who made the loans, thought he might eventually have to foreclose. No matter, he knew one way or another he had made well secured, safe investments. After a few months, the Coopers stopped making payments to Ed. He delayed taking action—he liked the Coopers and hoped he might be able to avoid foreclosing. We both called and wrote the Coopers but received no response from them.

Ed started the foreclosure process on both loans. He acquired ownership of one of the properties which he sold, and he got back all he had loaned, plus interest and a small profit. The Coopers sold the other property before they lost it in foreclosure and out of escrow paid Ed off in full. For the Coopers and Andy Whitman, their beautiful dream became a horrible nightmare.

But the suffering they endured paled, juxtaposed against the anguish experienced by the elderly folks who had sold their properties to the Coopers. Not receiving payments, the banks holding the loans against the properties initiated foreclosure proceedings. When title to the properties transferred by way of foreclosure to the banks or individuals who had bought them on the courthouse steps, the new owners began eviction proceedings against the aged occupants of those dwellings.

One of the new owners removed the elderly couple occupying his property and deposited them into a motel. Then he notified the police what had happened. The old folks couldn't understand the tragedy consuming their lives. Another person being evicted from the home he had resided in for over a half century, keeled over dead. The police arrested Patrick and Jeff on a variety of charges including fraud and elder abuse. Although an arrest warrant had been issued against Andy Whitman, it never reached fruition because he disappeared from sight shortly after he had drained the Coopers' and his mutual bank account.

Andy eluded apprehension, and it appeared that he had absconded to a country in South America. Patrick served three years in San Quentin, probably one of the toughest prisons in California. Although Jeff spent only a short time in jail, his period of probation lasted several years. After Patrick served his sentence, he and Jeff reunited and went back into the contracting business but just couldn't make a go of it. Today Jeff gets by working as a handyman and Patrick gives customer assistance in a well known home improvement outlet.

I've seen the Coopers' story repeated numerous times, one way or another during my career. In my opinion, Patrick and Jeff never intended to engage in a single dishonest act. I believe their crime stemmed from their lack of knowledge regarding money. Once an unusually large amount of funds came their way, they thought of themselves as independently wealthy, and adjusted their lifestyle according to their mistaken beliefs.

Actually, their guilt stemmed from stupidity rather than dishonesty. Initially they had a wonderful idea that truly could have served the needs of their elderly clientele beautifully, if only the Coopers had known enough to proceed prudently. Any smart entrepreneur aspiring to reach financial success might be wise to consider intelligently emulating the Coopers' initial operation. But, for the fact that I'm a little "long in the tooth," I might be tempted to try it myself.

CHAPTER NINETY-SEVEN

I lived in a very attractive home on Maracaibo Way in Marina Faire, a property which I had recently acquired in a trade with the Patridge family, for one of my former rental properties on Neptune Drive in Mulford Gardens. As far as houses went, the Maracaibo home looked much more attractive than the one in Mulford Gardens. Although older and smaller than the Maracaibo home, the Neptune Drive house sat on a full third of an acre lot.

Pat Patridge earned his living as a welder. Because of relaxed zoning enforcement in Mulford Gardens and ample space, Pat had plenty of room to take evening and weekend welding jobs on the side of his home. The trade had enabled the Patridges to double their income. I derived great satisfaction working with people in that manner.

Even though I enjoyed the Maracaibo home, I continually searched to find something in Mulford Gardens—just blocks away —that might justify the inconvenience of moving. Marina Faire consisted of an attractive newer sub-division in which the beautifully landscaped and immaculate homes attested to abundant community pride. Still, I preferred Mulford Gardens, with its pleasant shaded avenues. I liked driving or walking those streets lined with mature Maples, some so full and tall that they formed an overhead canopy that blocked the sun. I cherished the heterogeneous character of that district.

The events of my life had motivated me to move far too often since reaching adulthood. The next time I relocated, I intended to stay awhile. So, wherever that next nesting place might be, it had to be special. An opportunity I never expected to happen . . . happened! I got a call from Bob Joaquin. You remember the Joaquins—the charming family who gave me the Alameda listings and then invested the proceeds from the sales of those properties into my loan business? Bob asked if I could stop by their home that night, which I did.

Bob and Janet lived at 12903 Neptune Drive in a beautiful house they had custom built just a few years ago. Their gorgeous property boasted a ninety-foot frontage on the San Francisco Bay shoreline. The magnificent view paralleled the one I enjoyed a few years back when I lived with my family in the 13000 block of Neptune Drive, which Sheila acquired sole ownership of as a result of our divorce settlement. Ever since we moved from that charming bay-front abode, I'd always longed to live beside the calming tidal waters again.

I believe the Joaquin home ranked among the finest in Mulford Gardens. Shoreline real estate generally never came on the market. Although Bob didn't tell me why he wanted to see me, I looked forward to meeting with him and Janet. A visit with the Joaquins always made me feel good. Bob ushered me to the back of the home, into the attractive spacious rumpus room with rustic beamed vaulted ceilings and a wall-to-wall brick fireplace. The melody of the surf striking the rocky beach, just a few feet from where Bob invited me to sit, enhanced the ambiance of that comfortable nesting place.

It surprised me to see Dixie Townsend, Janet's eighty-six-year-old mother, who owned and lived in her home next door, seated in the big easy chair across the coffee table from me. As Bob and Janet explained why they asked me there, their mood seemed somber; not at all jovial and cheerful as I had expected. Bob told me that a few days ago, while he and Janet had been at work, Dixie watched television in that very room as she often did. She heard the doorbell ring and opened the door to find a young black man on the front porch.

The man told Dixie he came to see Bob, which momentarily put her at ease because she figured if he knew Bob, he must be alright. Dixie told the fellow that Bob and Janet were at work. He held a paper of some sort and handed it toward Dixie and asked her to please just give it to Bob when he came home. As Dixie reached to take the paper, suddenly the man violently shoved her back into the house.

She fell in the entry hall, he grabbed her and held a knife to her throat. Terrified, she listened as he told her if she quietly did what he told her, he wouldn't kill her. He took a rope from under his jacket and bound Dixie's hands and feet. He grappled her into the hall closet and ordered her to remain there. Dixie stayed in the closet until discovered by Janet around five thirty that afternoon. Bob and Janet had specific items, mainly jewelry and cash, they thought were well hidden in the home. It appeared the home invading mugger knew exactly where the valuables were. He took them and nothing else. Apparently he completed his work in minutes and had all afternoon before the police could be notified.

Bob said, "Val, we just can't stay here any longer. We're moving to our vacation home on the San Joaquin River, just north of Tracy. We're leaving immediately and Dixie is going with us." He went on to say, "You have always told me how much you like this place. I don't know, after what happened here if you are still interested in owning it, but if you are, it's for sale."

I thought, *Oh boy, how should I handle this?* I experienced mixed emotions. I felt disturbed about the unpleasant circumstances that brought this opportunity to me but delighted that I had a chance of owning that gorgeous property.

I went to my car and returned with my briefcase containing purchase contracts. I gave Bob and Janet my estimate of the market value of their property. I tried to come in at the high range of potential value. No bargain hunting that evening; I really wanted to own the property. Bob and Janet looked at each other and said nothing for an uncomfortably long period. Finally Bob said, "We don't like your offer, Val." I asked myself, *Oh damn, have I blown this?*

Bob continued, "You know we consider you our friend, there's no way we'll let you pay that much. I think we'll be happy with …" and he named a price fifty thousand less than my estimate of value.

Maybe I'd lost my marbles, but I told them, "You're right, we are friends and friends deal fairly with each other. What if we split the difference?"

Bob and Janet looked at each other again for a moment and Bob said, "I figured you to come back with something like that, now will you draw the contract? It's getting late and we have another matter to discuss with you."

I prepared the purchase agreement, we signed it and Dixie asked me, "Would you like my place as well?"

I couldn't believe this. I'd been trying to buy something on the water for years with no luck and tonight two precious shoreline properties came my way. Yes, indeed …. *I'm in the right business.*

Dixie explained that the next guy that tried to assault her wouldn't have such an easy time of it and she showed me a pistol that she now constantly carried in the breast fold of her dress. Dealing with her basically repeated what I had just done with her daughter and son-in- law. I made her a verbal offer, she countered, reducing my proposal by fifty thousand. Again, I asked if we could meet in the middle which made her very happy.

Our transactions closed in a week. Bob and Janet invested their sales proceeds into my loan business. Soon after selling Maracaibo, I took possession of what I believed to be the most desirable home in Mulford Gardens. I've told this story many times and I think I'm rarely believed. Actually, I'm not quite as generous as the preceding might lead one to believe. It's just that a guy in my position doesn't want to get too terrific of a deal. It isn't good for the reputation.

CHAPTER NINETY-EIGHT

Early Saturday morning on December 3, 1983, as dawn broke, and while still in my warm bed sleepily staring out my window, I noticed an unusually high wind-driven bay surf. I loved to lie in bed and look out the window at the rain and the bay. Not yet disturbed, I thought, *I've never seen a flood here, but that saying about "there's always a first time for everything" might be true.* Soon, agitated, angry, higher-than-normal tidal waters trespassed over the bayside embankment. My backyard became inundated. The high tide and strong incoming wind and gale-level torrents of rain arrived together, and I didn't know what might happen.

The back portion of my shoreline home had recently been converted to a cozy bachelor apartment. It became my favorite part of the house and where I spent the majority of my time. It never mattered before, but the fact that my little apartment had been built on a ground-level slab two feet below the rest of the house, gave me cause for concern that morning. Water in the backyard continued to rise. Wind and rain increased and surging whitecaps informed me that I should move my furniture to the higher part of the house, quickly.

By 10:00, two feet of water surged over my back yard and the floor of my apartment. The little house next door I bought from Dixie, built right at the shoreline, got pounded by the raging surf. I waded through water surging above my knees to help my tenant, Terry, move his belongings from the house out in front by the street where the water was only inches deep. As I approached Terry's house, a ninety-mile-per-hour gust of wind blew me off my feet.

Before we emptied Terry's house, the raging tide tore it from the foundation and carried it in pieces into the front yard. By now a dozen or so official city vehicles with flashing yellow lights traveled up and down Neptune Drive. Those municipal workers could do nothing beyond moving piles of leaves and floating debris off the storm drains in an effort to keep the street from flooding. A crowd of friends and relatives arrived to try to help and to enjoy the spectacle of the "hundred-year flood."

To most folks living on the bayside of Neptune Drive that day represented a tragedy. Used to dealing with the unexpected, the whole bizarre scene took on a comical turn to me. My home was on the last residential lot at the north end of the block. The fierce wind blew across the incoming tide in a northeasterly direction. A thirty-foot high pile of debris consisting of small boats, ripped away piers and hundreds of storm-driven articles, had been deposited on my portion of the shoreline. For weeks, other Neptune Drive waterside property owners sifted through the trash in back of my house looking to recover salvageable lost personal property.

In keeping with my philosophy of looking for the good in every situation, I decided to build a home next door in place of the one destroyed by the flood. I dealt with a Sausalito architect who specialized in designing waterfront homes. I played with the thought that, *maybe I could convince Julie to move into this home with me.* I wanted it constructed in a manner that took full advantage of its adjacency to the bay.

My architect knew exactly what I wanted. His plans depicted a double front door that opened to an eight-foot wide hall extending from the front to the back of the house. Upon entering through the front door, one immediately experienced a dramatic bay view. That central hall led to the rear portion of the home, which contained the living, dining and family rooms, each with a huge sliding glass doors accessing a deck the width of the house overlooking breaking waves.

Notwithstanding the fact that everyone who saw the impressive architectural renderings liked them because of the memory of the devastation from the recent storm, the building approval process proved to be unnecessarily tedious. In addition to going through the City of San Leandro Building Department, I also had to get permission to build from the Bay Conservation Development Commission. Naturally, I wanted to build a house that could successfully withstand the ravages of a storm even more powerful than the one we had recently experienced. However, the precautionary extremes required of me made no sense.

Even so, in the end I understood that in order to build this house I had to do exactly what the governing bodies demanded. The requirement that I had to build a foundation designed to rest on four-foot wide cement pilings poured over steel and sunk twelve feet into the ground represented stupidity beyond belief. If I had planned to construct a multi-story apartment complex such underpinning would have still been excessive.

I hired Larry Barcellos, owner of Barcellos Construction, to build my house on the bay. I utilized Larry's services for two reasons; he did good quality work and he regularly borrowed from me to finance his various building projects.

As far as the quality of that building went, Larry—as usual—did fine work, even though the progress moved slowly. His sluggish momentum, coupled with the building department's inordinate conditions made me wonder if I'd still be around when Larry completed my house. It took five months to finish, and it made me proud that it turned out even better than I'd envisioned. I mentioned earlier that I considered Julie and I might move into my new home together, but that just didn't jell. So I stayed next door and rented it to a gay psychiatrist. With the exception of one heterosexual couple over the years, all the tenants have been gay.

I had plenty of room to build another house on the lot, but as much as I liked Larry, I needed to find a contractor that moved a little faster. I had plans drawn and started getting bids. Julie, by then, had gone into business for herself. She owned eleven real estate offices and had in excess of a hundred sales agents working in her company. She operated out of her main office, a gorgeous Victorian mansion in Alameda. In addition to converting the building in which her headquarters functioned into its present commercial use, she continuously upgraded and restored turn of the twentieth century multi-family residences in Alameda.

Julie introduced me to a contractor by the name of Steve Woodworth who had handled a number of her remodeling ventures. He looked over my building plans and submitted a bid to construct the four-bedroom, three-bath house with a four-car detached garage as depicted in my drawings for $175,000. For that period of time, Steve's proposal might have been a little on the high side. Even so, I seriously considered signing with him.

Just before making a commitment to have Steve Woodworth build my house, my old pal, Bud Mayer invited me to have lunch with him and Steve Jaca, a contractor he had been thinking of hiring. Steve—a young, likable and obviously knowledgeable fellow—and I immediately liked each other. He told me he had heard I granted loans very quickly, subject to satisfactory security. I told him about the house I hoped to build soon. The plans happened to be in my car, and he asked to borrow them for a few days.

Two days later he called. He wanted to meet for lunch again. We got together at a seafood restaurant in San Lorenzo, just fifteen minutes from my office. As it turned out, Steve had transformed a large vacant space situated within in a small shopping center, into the beautiful restaurant in which we had lunch. The owner came over to our booth, and I could tell he respected Steve, which made me think he liked what Steve had done for him. I realized exactly why Steve wanted to have lunch with me there.

We enjoyed a delightful meal and carefully concentrated on getting to know each other. Steve, around twenty-nine, hadn't been on his own for more than a couple of years, but he'd worked steadily in the construction business for a decade. I got the idea he'd learned his craft well. He struck me as the type of guy who had a good future.

After we finished eating and the waitress cleared the table, he said, "You will think I'm out of my mind, but please hear me out before you come to any conclusions about what I'm going to tell you. You mentioned you were disappointed at how long it took to finish the last house you had built on Neptune. If you give me the job, I'll complete your house in thirty-six calendar days from the date I break ground."

I thought, *what has this guy been smoking?* He read my mind and said, "For every day I go over thirty-six days, I'll reduce my contract price by one thousand dollars. So if I'm a little slow, it works in your favor."

"What's this going to cost?" I asked.

You will recall, Steve Woodworth, the contractor Julie referred me to had agreed to build the house for $175,000. Steve Jaca said, "The price I'm about to give you will pay for my crew and subcontractors, but I will make nothing. I want to impress you and if I can pull this off, you might become a good source of financing. I've needed to hook up with someone like you since I began contracting. Give me a chance; you will be glad you did."

I repeated, "How much?"

As he presented me with a contract, he answered, "I can do the job for $75,000."

I didn't believe he could build my house in thirty-six days and he sure couldn't do it for $75,000. However, though I didn't mention it—if he failed to deliver, I could afford to make adjustments, which I figured, within reason, I didn't mind doing.

Remember, I lived right next door in the home I bought from the Joaquins to where Steve planned to work his magic. The morning construction began, I couldn't believe what I saw. At least a dozen men worked on the job, with every man diligently dedicated to his assigned task. Within five days, framing had begun, with even more workers moving quickly and efficiently. They reminded me of a colony of ants or a swarm of bees moving in unison to accomplish a shared goal.

Steve efficiently coordinated the various components of his construction team. He paid the men well, more than they could expect elsewhere. He quickly terminated any employee or subcontractor unwilling to meet the Jaca Construction Company's elevated standard of performance. I stopped by the job one day just after lunch and observed him summarily firing two of his crew in full view of me and everyone else on the job-site. He explained to me within earshot of the others that those two men reported back to the job ten minutes after their lunch break ended. Steve went on to tell me he had no room in his operation for anyone not entirely committed to the goals he had set for his company. By firing those two fellows so openly he had clearly reiterated to the other workers what he expected of them.

True to his word, he had the final inspection report in hand thirty-six calendar days after construction began. He had accomplished something I had never seen before, and whenever I tell that story to anyone, they don't believe me. When I asked him how he came out financially, he told me he did fine. I knew he had to lose money, but I also knew in his frantic rush to finish my house, he had no idea how he did. A few days later, he commenced construction on a duplex for me at 2323 West Avenue

133rd, also in Mulford Gardens. He gave me a good price, but I made sure he would make money on that project.

Naturally, it seemed as if everyone now sought Steve's services. He had other construction projects going, yet he turned in another stellar performance for me. Forty days after his crew commenced work on my duplex, I had potential tenants inspecting my finished units. Steve's talent could not be denied, but I foresaw future problems. In his frenzied zeal to complete those projects at breakneck speed he made inexcusable errors.

For instance, on my duplex undertaking, Steve's superintendent ordered more twelve-foot-long four-by-twelve-inch beams than the job required. Of course, that sort of thing can happen now and then as a result of poor planning. Normally such excess material got used on another job or returned to the supplier for credit. On Steve's jobs, no one paid attention and expensive material got hauled to the dumps or the workers took it for their personal use.

I loaned Steve $40,000 so he could secure a contract to build an apartment complex in Hayward. He paid me back as agreed, but clearly, Steve's fast but sloppy operation faced serious problems. I told him, "Steve, I'm sure someday you're going to become a multi-millionaire but unless you wise up, I think you'll have to go bankrupt a couple of times first." We parted friends and went our separate ways. I'm not sure whatever happened to Steve, but one of these days, I think I'll try to find out.

CHAPTER NINETY-NINE

In early 1984, the Federal Deposit Insurance Company (FDIC) announced they would be auctioning off thirty acres which Bud Mayer brought to my attention. The property being sold constituted part of the assets the FDIC had acquired from a failed bank. The acreage consisted of four separate parcels situated within the Seven Hills subdivision in Union City. I thought of the area as a "blue collar" working class community and my favorite type of investment property. Bud wanted the two of us to attempt to buy the property as equal partners. If our bid succeeded, he wanted me to lend him his share of the purchase price. Again, subject to us submitting the winning bid, he agreed to secure what he owed me by giving me an interest bearing promissory note, secured with an encumbering deed of trust affecting other property he owned.

It presented a good opportunity for me for the following reasons: The deal offered very promising profit potential. I didn't mind lending Bud money—the loan would earn good interest. In this sort of a proposition Bud made the ideal partner. He loved to work on developing raw land. Whenever I entered into an alliance in which I put up all the money, which happened frequently, the joint venture agreement provided that I make all final decisions.That condition served my partnerships well because I have always been good at project management and little valuable time was ever wasted arguing over how any situation should be handled.

You might wonder, as many deals in which Bud involved himself, why he continually borrowed from me instead of using his own funds. Bud rarely had cash. He made lots of deals—some good and some real losers. Bud operated as an inveterate gambler; he took chances a normal entrepreneur would never consider. Some of his ventures made loads of money, but the bad ones ate up the profit from the good ones.

In my view, Bud suffered from an extraordinary addiction to the excitement of the real estate game. If a venture went bad, he took it in stride and if one turned out successful, he quickly risked the profit on whatever came his way next. I recall sometimes advising him to stay clear of some harebrained scheme which, in my opinion, could only lose. On more than one occasion he answered, "Val, you know I'm a gambler, but thanks for the advice anyway." Notwithstanding Bud's bent toward taking unwarranted risks, in some areas of business, he probably ranked among the smartest men I've ever known.

The conditions of the auction required that sealed bids be submitted to the FDIC on or before a specific date. The envelope containing the amount of the bid had to include a good faith deposit in the form of a cashier's check for ten percent of the bid. The winning bidder had to pay off the balance of the purchase price in cash within ninety days of the date of acceptance by the FDIC, or forfeit the deposit.

Bud and I had just finished breakfast at Emil Villa's. Emil's enjoyed the reputation as the favorite gathering place of the area's vibrant world of real estate investment operators. I've lost count of the number of deals I helped hatch in that pleasant establishment, just as I did that morning. In charge of preparing our written bid, I told Bud how much I wanted to offer. The amount I mentioned disappointed Bud and he felt we should go higher. I countered with, "If our bid gets accepted, we will have made a great deal."

Bud asked me, "Tell me, Val, if you owned this land that we're trying to buy what's the lowest price you'd take for it?" I thought carefully for a minute and silently came up with a number five times higher than the amount I said I'd offer. That wise old fox didn't have to say another word. I filled in the bid sheet and doubled the amount I had planned to submit before his wise counsel.

When the FDIC opened the envelopes containing the bids, it surprised me that there were only three bidders including us. As they announced that Mayer and Barry had won, for a second I contemplated how many great opportunities I'd lost to others because I didn't construct my offers more realistically. Bud appreciated it when I acknowledged my gratitude for his guidance.

We took full advantage of the ninety-day period between the FDIC's acceptance of our offer and the time we had to pay the balance owing to complete the purchase. We met with the Union City Planning staff to determine how they would allow the property to be developed. Oh my ... had we run into a hornet's nest! A fellow named Mr. Grimer, the head of the department, expressed open hostility. We just wanted to know how best to proceed in order to gain city and community support in our effort to make our thirty acres productive.

Mr. Grimer's attitude seemed to indicate he thought we got too good a deal, and he intended do everything within his power to cause problems for us. The nasty little jerk couldn't begin to conceal the extent of his jealousy. No matter—Bud and I both had experienced the ways of envious, petty bureaucrats. Such people lacked the courage to stray beyond the security cocoon of officialdom, and some—as this fellow did—strove to compensate for their deflated egos by making life hard for people like Bud and me.

Let me quickly point out that I believe such miscreants are very much in the minority. I've had the pleasure of working with planners whose guidance and assistance have immensely benefitted my projects and the communities in which they served. And in all fairness, we did come across some such cooperative and very intelligent individuals within the Union City Planning and Engineering Departments. Even so, there are enough of the second-rate ones around to cause the needless delays and impediments, resulting in exorbitant costs, and who actually scuttle some potentially beneficial developments or create substantial unnecessary expense to consumers. Regardless, even though Grimer may have been a headache, he had been right about one thing, we did make a great deal and our venture promised to fly high.

As mentioned previously, our thirty acres consisted of four separate parcels. One fifteen acre site fronted Mission Boulevard—a main arterial—for approximately fifteen hundred feet. Another six or so acres fronted on Monaco Street, situated amongst homes built several years past within the Seven Hills subdivision. One isolated two-hundred-foot-wide site ascended gently up from and at a right angle to Monaco Street for a distance of around six hundred feet. That piece appeared to be a dry creek bed and I believed it to be worthless because of the likely very high development expense.

Finally, there existed a six-acre parcel accessible only by a narrow access road off Riviera Drive serving a small municipal children's playground. Although that gently up-sloped parcel provided an excellent view of the San Francisco Bay, I doubted that it could be of much value because we needed permission from Union City to widen and use their narrow access road in order to develop that plot. The way things stood, I didn't think we could count on the Union City officials to make such a generous accommodation to us.

Bud and I decided it served our best interest to concentrate on getting the Monaco Drive property subdivided into residential building lots. The property permitted only agricultural use, so before we could do anything about getting a subdivision approved, we needed to apply for rezoning. The city may not have been willing to cooperate with us with alacrity, but ultimately they would likely have to acquiesce because single-family homes were the only practical use of the land. Concurrent with the Monaco rezoning and subdivision process, we went about trying to find a buyer for the fifteen acres on Mission Boulevard.

Getting approvals to rezone and subdivide Monaco proved tedious and time consuming. Because of the continuing lack of cooperation from the chief of the Union City planning staff. It seemed for each two steps we moved toward our goal, we had to go back a step. Sure, he could delay us; he just couldn't stop us. We couldn't devote full time to the Union City project; both Bud and I had to attend to our other burgeoning business affairs.

Although we made halting, but reasonably steady progress in Union City, my deadline for paying the balance of the purchase price owing to the FDIC fast approached. Right then, my involvement in so many house remodels, property purchases and making loans, my cash reserves had become temporarily depleted. I had even utilized my line of credit with Bank of America. Oh, I could raise the money for FDIC in time if I had to, but only at considerable expense, so I decided to employ a different tactic.

I called Michael Black, the person heading the FDIC's department in Oakland. He had conducted the auction from which we acquired the right to buy the Union City property. I liked Michael; he had been very helpful to me. We had become friendly to the extent he seemed sincerely interested in my business operations in general.

He had indicated that after the Union City transaction concluded he wanted to talk about using me as a Realtor to market some of the other real property assets under his control. I called him and asked if I could drop by his office around three-thirty that afternoon. He told me he looked forward to seeing me. I wondered if he'd feel that way after hearing what I had to say.

For years, I'd been continually involved in self-hypnosis. I believed my activity in that subject had contributed substantially to the success I enjoyed. A little after noon, I drove down to the San Leandro Marina. I headed for the most westerly parking lot and pulled into a space near the water's edge. I sat in my car looking out over the whitecaps, and I placed myself into a deep self-hypnotic trance.

I carefully visualized every likely aspect of that afternoon's upcoming meeting with Michael Black. I deposited the idea into my sub-conscious mind that I could persuade the FDIC to extend the time I had to pay the balance owing on the Union City purchase for an additional three months. As impossible as my proposition seemed, and indeed it seemed completely impossible, I believed that I couldn't fail.

A few minutes before three, I walked into Michael's office. For perhaps twenty minutes we chatted about several subjects that had nothing to do with the real purpose of my visit. Finally, I told him I needed the FDIC to extend my payment date for three months. At first he acted incredulous. He asked if I just didn't have the money. I told him, of course, I had the money. I said my request had nothing to do with my ability to pay. Not for a moment did I lose my congenial manner as I made a calculated move to place Michael on the defensive.

I asked, "Michael, when you advertised the Union City acreage for sale, did you know that after a hard rain the Mission Boulevard parcel develops a large pond that can't drain naturally and takes weeks to evaporate?" Michael said he knew nothing about the problem. I respond with, "Don't you think you should have obtained a geological report before marketing the property?"

The ponding situation in fact did exist, but the FDIC clearly marketed the land on an "as is" basis. Michael knew that, but he made no mention of it. Beyond any doubt, I knew a psychic power emanated from my sub-conscious that day that could not be denied.

He protested that giving us an extension of time didn't seem fair to the other bidders. I said nothing as he continued talking. Finally he said, "I don't have the authority to grant this; I'll have to call my superior in Washington DC, which will have to wait until tomorrow. Because of the time differential, his office is closed."

I said, "Surely, Michael, you must have his home number."

He didn't answer; he checked a list of numbers from his desk drawer and called his boss.

The two of them discussed the situation at length, reiterating a number of arguments I had heard from Michael before he made the call, plus a few the supervisor came up with. They concluded their lengthy conversation and Michael hung up the phone. He turned to me and said, "I have good news. My director says we can grant the extension, but you will be required to pay twelve percent interest on the principal still owing."

I answered, "No thank you, Michael, I'm not asking you to lend me money on which I would be obligated to pay interest, I simply am requesting an additional three months to pay off the balance owing on the property."

Exasperated, he placed another call to his director and conveyed my position. I didn't know what exactly transpired between them, but when he finished the conversation he turned to me and with a friendly smile said, "Okay, Val, I don't know how you did it, but your request is granted."

When I told Bud what happened, he hardly believed me. He gave me a sincere compliment for what I'd gained for our partnership. I think it may have been the first time and certainly the last time I ever heard Bud compliment anyone. Within the next two months, we sold the Mission Boulevard fifteen acres to a group of Taiwanese investors for twice what we paid for the entire thirty acres. We paid off the FDIC a little earlier than expected. Michael Black seemed delighted and proceeded to give me a listing on a subdivision consisting of nine vacant lots in Hayward, for which I negotiated a sale to Bud.

I loathed the necessity of selling the Mission Boulevard parcel as I knew its potential value far surpassed the amount Bud and I sold it for. But selling it made all my other endeavors financially viable. It's said that "no one ever went broke taking a profit," but I've seen plenty of guys, including big and small operators alike, go broke by overextending themselves. Even so, I cringed a little when I learned the Taiwanese group sold the land they bought from us a year or so later for twice what they paid for the property. I cringed again when I heard that the fellow who bought the site from the Taiwanese, doubled his money when he sold it to the group that actually developed the property with residential condominiums. I guess it's all in the timing.

Bud and I ended up with nine approved building lots on Monaco. Bud wanted to have manufactured houses delivered to the lots and placed on foundations we would have built. I determined we could finish a manufactured house for about half the cost of constructing a conventional built home of equal or lesser quality. Oh boy … everyone fought us on that idea. I heard that our nemesis in the Planning Commission actually publicly stated he thought we would make too much money if we developed our lots with manufactured housing. *Oh well, if it was easy, everyone would be doing it.*

The Seven Hills Homeowners Association (SHHA) opposed us because they equated manufactured housing with units you might find in a trailer park. Bud and I asked if we might be allowed to present our position at a scheduled SHHA meeting. Forty-two homeowners attended the meeting. Assessing them as hostile to Bud and I understated the situation. I told the group I genuinely appreciated their position and showed them an attractive architectural rendering of the unit we wanted to place on the first lot we developed. The drawing looked a lot better than the homes in which those SHHA members resided. Still they didn't seem convinced.

I explained in a courteous manner that our lots had been legally zoned for single-family dwellings and if we chose to place factory built units on them, neither the city nor the homeowners could stop us from doing so. However, we wanted the goodwill of the community. I asked that they allow us to develop one lot with a factory manufactured unit without instituting legal obstacles that might delay our progress. Then, if the results didn't satisfy them, we would build out the rest of the lots conventionally. One of the homeowners attending the meeting served as a Union City Planning Commissioner. He believed we had offered a fair proposition and the group voted to allow us to proceed without interference.

We finished that unit and, indeed, the only complaint came from a SHHA member who lived across the street. She said our building put the existing houses in the neighborhood to shame. You know, it's pretty hard to please everyone. Our first house sold quickly and we did quite well financially. Other small builders approached us about buying our remaining lots. I figured we could make nearly as much profit selling some lots rather than developing them and save ourselves a lot of time and trouble. We quickly negotiated with Golden West Homes to buy four more units from them. We sold three of the lots to Ray Olson, a builder

I'd done business with before. However, that transaction caused some friction between Bud and me.

Bud also owned a roofing business known as M & M Roofing— M & M stood for Mayer and Mitch; Mitch being Bud's partner in the business. M & M Roofing had recently installed a roof on a new twenty-unit apartment complex Ray had constructed.

Ray demanded people with whom he did business do exactly what they were supposed to do. After installing the roof on Ray's building, M&M neglected to remove roofing debris from the construction site. Ray called Bud and gave him three days to clean up the mess. Bud didn't really take Ray seriously and forgot about the deadline. When Bud received the check for the roofing job, he discovered a substantial sum had been charged to M&M to cover the cost of Ray having the roofing debris mess dealt with. It angered Bud that Ray didn't give him more time to take care of the problem.

Following the roofing debris debacle, I asked Bud if he would mind if I offered to sell four lots to Ray. Bud knew Ray had the ability to pay all cash which many small builders couldn't do. Notwithstanding his recent disagreement with Ray, Bud urged me to offer our lots to Ray. I made the call on Thursday afternoon while Bud sat across my desk from me. Ray expressed his interest, and I showed him the lots around six that evening. He promised to give me an answer the next day. Before he made a final decision, he wanted to show the lots to his two sons, his potential partners, if he decided to go on the deal.

On Friday afternoon, Ray called me. He wanted our lots and agreed to pay our asking price. He planned to develop the lots with factory manufactured houses. He agreed to list the properties with me when they were completed.

Ray asked me to bring the necessary paperwork to his home that evening. I put him off until the following Monday morning as

I had plans for that night and the weekend. I told him I'd call Bud and get his verbal agreement to our potential transaction.

I called Bud and told him what Ray had decided. I said, "Bud, I know you don't like Ray so I need to know we're together on this because if it's okay with you, I'm going to call Ray and tell him we have a deal." Bud assured me that we had a deal. Even though I didn't need to call Ray, I did anyway. I confirmed our Monday morning appointment.

Sunday evening, I received an urgent call from Bud. He told me to forget about selling the lots to Ray. For a couple of weeks, he had been trying to sell them to a group from Santa Cruz. Right after we confirmed our verbal agreement with Ray, he called the guys in Santa Cruz. They wanted to beat Ray's offer. I told Bud we couldn't do that, we'd given our word. Ray trusted us, at least he trusted me. Livid, Bud asked me, "What do you think Ray would do to us if our positions were reversed?"

I explained it didn't matter what Ray or anyone might do. "If our commitments are no good, then we are no good."

I knew Bud thought he had a crazy partner. I reminded him because I'd put up every cent that had gone into the project, I made all final decisions. He didn't like it but knew he had no choice.

A small builder, Mr. Singh, bought the remaining lot adjacent to one of the parcels on which Bud and I had placed a manufactured house. Mr. Singh planned to construct a conventionally built house on his site. Because going the manufactured housing route went so much faster than standard construction methods, we completed our home a couple of months before Mr. Singh had expected to finish his house. In order to market our property, a fence needed to be constructed between Mr. Singh's property and ours. Of course, in order to market his property, he as well had to have a have a fence in place separating our properties.

I asked Mr. Singh to split the cost of building the fence we both needed. He coldly explained to me that I had to have the fence right then and he wouldn't need one for a couple of months. He had determined that if I went ahead and built my fence, he wouldn't have to build one. In my opinion, his course of action lacked accepted ethics, but he obviously thought he had me at a disadvantage, and he did.

A couple of months later, Mr. Singh and one of his employees began building a house in a nearby city. They dug a deep trench to accommodate the sewer line from the street to the house they had under construction. It had rained steadily over the past few days. While Mr. Singh and his employee worked in the trench, its sodden walls suddenly collapsed, burying the two men alive. The media reported that the earthen walls of the deep trench failed due to a lack of adequate support. Not adhering to legally required safety measures proved to be a fatal mistake.

I mentioned earlier that I assumed that the two-hundred-foot by six-hundred-foot dry creek bed site situated at a right angle to Monaco had no value. In that type of situation it paid to be in partnership with Bud. He figured that we could fill in the creek-bed, build a short cul-de-sac type street and produce seven build-able lots, each with a bay view. Bud secured a bid for the project from Brian Sullivan, his partner in another one of his numerous enterprises. The cost to create the lots came to about half what they could sell for.

I continually lent construction money to Ben Chalwa, a house builder from India, who came to the U.S. through Canada. He seemed genuinely impressed with what we had done with our former dry creek bed. Ben very much involved himself in the local community of his compatriots who had replicated his path from India and settled in this country. He said he could sell six of our lots to members of that tightly knit group, and he did. For his service, we transferred free and clear title to the seventh lot to Ben.

Bud, as usual, ran true to form. He asked me to sell my interest to him in the six-acre parcel overlooking the children's playground. That meant he had found a buyer for the property. I figured he wanted to buy me out cheap, and then resell my share of the site at a substantially higher price than he paid me. I never did that to Bud, but it didn't really matter. As a serial hard-money borrower, he supplied me with a steady, dependable income. If he made a profit at my expense, so be it. Gaining approval from the city to build a street to the basically landlocked site promised to be a long and arduous process. I took Bud's offer and sure enough as soon as we closed, he sold the six acres to his secret buyer.

The Union City project had worked out very well. The money I made there enabled me to expand every part of my multi-faceted operation, especially buying improved properties and making loans. As equal partners on the Union City venture, Bud earned as much as I did—actually, a little more, figuring the Riviera Drive deal. He became very excited about a new undertaking he visualized could make his lifelong dream of reaching financial Utopia come true.

Brian Sullivan's primary contracting activity involved replacing soil that had become polluted from gasoline leaking from underground service station storage tanks. He removed the faulty storage containers and adjacent contaminated soil, replacing them with new storage tanks and clean soil. The entire undertaking cost plenty, so much so that many stations required by law to remove the tanks and the surrounding fouled ground, never went back into operation. Disposing of the degraded soil represented the most daunting expense.

Brian convinced Bud—who didn't require much persuasion—he could design and build a machine capable of washing and making oil polluted soil totally and inexpensively reusable. Bud and Brian negotiated an equal partnership in the venture. Of course, as Brian needed to devote most of his time on the project, it fell upon Bud to pay Brian a salary. In addition, Bud had to cover the cost of the expensive mechanical devices necessary to comply with Brian's design.

Soon Bud fell too deep financially into the project to withdraw funding. The only chance he had to come out whole required him to stay with the project to the end. Actually it seemed to be a pretty good deal for Brian; he had a steady income and reasonable job security.

Early on, I watched a television program in which a major chemical company tried to develop a soil cleaning process. The design of their dirt washing machine looked very similar to what Bud and Brian had constructed. They couldn't make it work. When I explained to Bud about the national company's disappointing results, he reminded me again that he liked to picture himself as a gambler.

In any event, it turned out to be a losing bet. All of Bud's Union City profits and a lot more went into the defunct dirt cleansing apparatus. Bud couldn't even sell the various expensive pumps and other parts used in building the so-called "Dirt Machine" because Bud said Brian had moved it where Bud couldn't find it. I truly felt bad for Bud but as crazy as it sounds sometimes I thought he enjoyed losing.

One afternoon, as Bud and I traveled in my car, he explained to me about a series of financial mishaps he had created that threatened to put him out of business. Although he rarely followed my counsel, he consistently sought my advice when he experienced such problems, which happened often. I listened and determined his situation seemed hopeless; I just couldn't think of a solution. Finally, I said to him, "Bud, I really don't know what to tell you. Maybe you just need to pray for help."

After a minute or so of silence between us, Bud responded with, "Do you really think God could figure this out?"

CHAPTER ONE HUNDRED

As illustrated herein, a key to the business success I continually enjoyed lay in the fact I didn't tie myself to just one or two areas in which I totally concentrated my efforts. This chapter discusses a specific transaction within an area in which I enjoyed investing my time and money occasionally. With some folks whom I found compatible with my way of thinking and with whom I'd done business, a high degree of mutual trust between us had evolved. For such people, I had in place a standing offer.

If any of those parties became aware of a situation in which a property could be purchased that had potential to produce substantial profit, I bought it. I provided all funds to purchase and do whatever necessary to make the acquisition capable of selling for the highest profit. Usually, the so called "finder" could only become involved in such an undertaking if dealing with a very experienced operator with substantial cash and a proven ability to move with speed.

When the property sold, I disbursed one half of the net profit to the party who brought the opportunity to my attention. In any such proceedings, no written contracts existed between the finder and me. Written contracts are constantly disputed. In that type of deal it had to be done my way or not at all. Even though I considered suggestions from my verbal partners, I made all final decisions. I have been involved in many such ventures and all have concluded happily. Could I really be trusted with such power? The answer is absolutely . . . yes!

To be eligible to belong to this special group, my potential partners had to pass my secret test of character. If you want to know how someone will treat you if they should gain some advantage over you, "just observe how they behave toward people they don't have to be nice to." That formula measuring a person's basic nature has served me well over the years.

Lyle Stanton qualified as such a partner. He told me of a property in Montclair on Saroni Drive scheduled to be sold in foreclosure in about a week. Lyle had done his homework and became baffled by what he had discovered. The only loan encumbering the property happened to be a very old one that had been paid down to a principal balance of only around thirteen thousand dollars. That just didn't make any sense. The strong demand for residential property in Montclair kept the prices high. Lyle had knocked on the door and the owner told him politely, but firmly that he permitted no one other than his family to enter the home.

I said that Lyle had done his homework and indeed he had. Somehow he learned where Mr. Winters, the owner, worked and that he held a supervisory position. My instincts told me I should try to reach the owner on his job. I made the call and the receptionist put me through to his office. I hoped he would talk with me when he learned the purpose of my call. He answered his phone and seemed reserved but congenial with me. He told me that only I, in reference to that subject, had called him at his work. Otherwise, he had been inundated with letters and door knockers like Lyle, and he had told them all he didn't want to talk with them. I'd been in the business quite awhile, and I began to get an idea of the dynamics of the situation.

I stated, "Mr. Winters, I sure don't want to be a bother to you, but I think I can give you some valuable advice, and I promise it won't cost you a penny."

He responded with, "If you want to come to my home, forget it."

The unstated reason for his resistance became even clearer to me, and my experience guided me. I asked if I might stop by his office that day during his lunch. He invited me to come by his workplace anytime between eight in the morning and four in the afternoon, Monday through Friday. I met with him at two that afternoon. He asked if I minded sitting outside on the steps of a side entrance to the large building in which he worked. He didn't want anyone in the building hearing the content of our discussion.

Mr. Winters surprised me. I guess I thought I'd meet a defensive beat up fellow unable to cope with the financial calamity facing him. No, I found him to be a nice looking, well dressed, reserved but friendly man. Surely he must have had some degree of capability to effectively respond to that looming crisis. After all, he supervised a fairly sizable business operation. I explained to him by taking no action he risked a large amount of the equity he had accumulated in his property. I'd learned from Lyle that Mr. Winters had two teenage children, a boy and a girl. As diplomatically as possible I pointed out to him that if he didn't seek help, he jeopardized the security of those two kids.

Then, I broached the very sensitive subject that I believed accounted for the reason he refused to move to protect the substantial financial interest in his home. I said, "Mr. Winters, I'm going to say something that might make you angry, so angry that you may want to end this meeting immediately. If that happens, I will leave and not bother you again. Sir, I'm guessing your home is disgustingly filthy inside, so bad that you can't bear for anyone to see the deplorable conditions in which you and your children are living. Believe me as awful as it might be, I won't be shocked, —I've probably seen worse. Please trust me and let me help you. I know just how to help you, and I promise to make it easy for you and your family."

The way in which he looked at me through moist eyes and said nothing let me know I'd figured right. He told me he would prepare his kids that night and meet me at his home at ten the following morning. I thanked him and told him Lyle would be with me, to which he didn't object. The next morning Lyle and I arrived right on time in a driving rainstorm.

Mr. Winters opened the front door and a foul—*very* foul—odor overwhelmed my olfactory senses. Lyle and I stepped inside and saw a beautiful blond-haired girl of about fifteen and a tall handsome boy, maybe a year older than his sister. Mr. Winters introduced Lyle and me to Gwen and Jack, and, like their dad, these two impeccably dressed kids seemed reserved but not unfriendly.

The contrast between the pleasant occupants and the revolting condition of the house confused me. When I told Mr. Winters that I'd probably seen worse, I'd been mistaken. I concealed my shock at what I saw. I saw a two-foot depth of stinking, rotting, raw garbage, relieved only by narrow trails that provided accessibility to the various rooms. The refuse on the floors of the bathrooms and kitchen appeared to be about half as deep as on the rest of the street level floor. As we walked through that gloomy, almost surreal setting, Mr. Winters explained when his wife died ten years before he stopped paying for garbage removal, which resulted in cancellation of the service. Since that time, he and the kids continued to dispose of the garbage and any debris right on the premises.

He said he didn't know why he let that happen. When he lost his wife, he stopped thinking clearly. For the first couple of years after Mrs. Winters passed away, the family deposited the garbage in plastic bags which they placed into the attached garage, accessible from the kitchen. When the bags of garbage filled the garage to the rafters and much of the house, the family no longer bothered to bag the garbage and disposed of it loose throughout the home. I opened the door from the kitchen to the garage and indeed found it stuffed full of bagged garbage. The sound of rustling movement within that filth made me aware that rats resided there.

We saw three bedrooms on the street level floor, one for each member of the family. The bedrooms had just as much raw garbage in them as the other rooms. I observed a sleeping bag lying on the filth in each bedroom. Again, it astounded me that an attractive clean-cut-appearing family could live in such a vile environment. The ample amount of furniture included a baby grand piano which I thought may have been played, because surprisingly, the garbage didn't touch it. The wood portions of the rest of the furniture throughout appeared raw and grainy. I guessed acid emanating from the decaying waste in direct contact with the furnishings had removed the original finish.

Gwen told Lyle and me if we needed to look downstairs, she had to accompany us. She promised to keep the dogs down there from attacking us. We followed her down the twenty or so steps. When the dogs heard us they began barking explosively. If I thought the stench upstairs rivaled any offensive smell I'd ever experienced before, I learned differently. The stink that assaulted my nostrils as I descended the stairs, exceeded anything I'd ever encountered. About halfway down, Lyle whispered, "I'm sorry, Val, I'm going outside, I'm getting sick."

About two steps before I reached the bottom, Gwen said, "Please wait here until I move the dogs into another room." I saw two large German Shepherds still barking excitedly but obedient to Gwen's commands for them to move into an adjoining room. She shut the door securing the dogs and told me to inspect at my leisure as she headed upstairs. I stood in at least six inches of dog feces. Obviously, the animals always remained inside the house and no one ever cleaned up after them. I wondered how many years it took to accumulate so much dog crap. My inspection of the downstairs took less than a minute because if I remained down there longer I'd have to join Lyle.

I thanked the family for allowing us into their home. Mr. Winters and I agreed to meet at his office at nine the following morning. Actually, I had the paperwork I needed to wrap up the deal stored in my car. But what I wished to say to Mr. Winters, I thought might be more comfortably addressed in private. And I didn't relish spending any more time in that house right then. Before Lyle and I climbed into my car, we took off our wet raincoats and put them into the trunk—they reeked of the filth we had left minutes before.

A couple of hours before my appointment with Mr. Winters I mentally rehearsed how best to deal with him. It's strange, in similar situations I usually called the person with whom I dealt with by their first name. Instinctively, I felt that addressing Mr. Winters by any name other than Mr. Winters could blow the deal. I knew I had to treat him with the respect he received as a supervisor at his place of employment. Even though I had to take complete charge of the situation, I could not make that obvious to him.

That afternoon he invited me into his office and asked his secretary to bring us coffee and to hold his calls until I left. Watching him operate so efficiently, one would never guess how dysfunctionally he conducted his life outside that place. I presented him with a purchase agreement which promised to net him substantial cash and still leave room for a fair profit for Lyle and me. Part of my service included arranging—at our expense—to have whatever furniture he might want to keep moved to a rental home or apartment to be located for him by Lyle. Anything he didn't want to keep would be our responsibility to remove from the premises.

I explained I expected the transaction to proceed as follows: First he and I needed to sign the purchase agreement. Ordering a preliminary title report came next. After the title company report guarantied his legal right to sell, he could collect advance funds—

prior to closing—to pay rent on his new residence. Additionally, at that point he would receive money to buy new furniture. I didn't think he wanted much of the furniture in the house. Surprised he asked me, "Do you offer such broad services often?"

I responded with, "Yes, people facing foreclosure encounter tremendous stress—I consider it my job to help reduce the level of stress."

Lyle located a new, never occupied condominium situated close to the Winters' home. The slow market made it difficult for the builder/owner to sell the last unit of his four unit complex. He accepted a rental application from Mr. Winters. Even though a credit report revealed the foreclosure in progress, the condominium owner learned Mr. Winters held an important position in his company and had been employed there for many years. Additionally, a personal interview convinced the owner that the Winters' family promised to make good tenants. I advanced more funds and the family went on a furniture shopping spree.

I hired Larry, a fellow who did handyman jobs for me, and his three cousins to move the few items the Winters' wished to retain to their condo. He agreed to remove the garbage and everything else from the house as well. Before Larry saw the house I warned him that I'd given him a nasty job. He assured me that he'd probably seen worse, and he and his cousins needed the work.

Early that miserable wet Monday morning, Larry and his cousins met me at the Winters' house. When they looked inside they didn't like what they saw. They walked back to their pickup to confer, and I sensed a problem brewing. After a few minutes Larry came back into the house and said, "Val, you told me that you'd given us a dirty job, but this is too much. The guys are afraid they'll get sick working in this filth. I'm sorry, but we're going to pass."

Quickly I pondered, *damn, they're here and I'm not going to find a better crew.* I knew I couldn't change their minds unless I resorted to some sort of clever manipulation. Well, I didn't like to openly admit it, but manipulation came easy for me. To accomplish all that I had set out to do in my life, I had to be an effective manipulator. I said, "Larry, I see your mind is made up, and I won't try to change it. But, you know I feel bad, it's a shame you fellows have driven such a long way in the rain this morning for nothing. So that it won't be a total loss for you, how about just moving the piano over to the Winters' condo for three hundred dollars."

Larry responded, "Sure Val, I'm sure the guys will go for that."

Compared to the very heavy piano, the garbage and the furniture weighed very little. I figured after they wrestled the piano down the steep porch steps in the rain and into the condominium, moving the rest of the junk might not seem too bad.

That's exactly how it worked. After the piano, everything else looked easy. It took a week to finish the job. It cost over four thousand dollars to remove all the garbage and dog manure and I thought I got a bargain. When I asked Larry to use more rat poison he said, "I have to buy more, they eat it as fast as I put it out." Well, we closed the deal, made the house look like a model home and sold for a nice profit.

A month or so later, I got a call from Mr. Winters. He told me a Montclair area broker wrote him and told him that he had been cheated. He called that broker and told him that I did a lot more than save him from losing it all in foreclosure. He went on to say I had figured out how to communicate with him when others couldn't and because of me, his family truly enjoyed life for the first time in years. I thanked Mr. Winters for his thoughtful words. I never saw the family again but when I think about the Montclair deal, I feel good.

CHAPTER ONE HUNDRED ONE

I had access to abundant cash for investment purposes. If the equity in a potential borrower's real estate provided sufficient security for a requested loan, I always made the loan. In the late eighties, we had entered into a vicious real estate recession, and several Realtor friends and associates who experienced difficult times came to me in pursuit of badly needed fast financing. I heard from many such people and their stories seemed pretty much the same. I haven't the inclination to write about all of them here, but in this chapter I will discuss two such people fairly typical of that group.

As my daughter, Valerie, and I waited for a booth at Emil Villas for an early morning breakfast as we often did, Harry Murray, the owner of Murray Real Estate, also waited and asked if he might join us. Valerie said, "Of course, Harry, it will be our pleasure."

She had worked as an escrow officer and knew Harry, having been involved in the escrows of some of his brokerage transactions. Harry enjoyed his reputation as a fascinating, witty and thoroughly entertaining fellow and somewhat of a legend in the residential real estate business.

When I started as a real estate agent, Harry had more properties listed for sale than any ten agents combined. He went door to door through a neighborhood and invariably ended up with five or six listings in one day; more than most agents obtained in three months. Harry wore thousand-dollar silk suits and drove Lincoln Continentals when both of my suits cost a total of a hundred and fifty dollars, and I got around in a five-year-old Ford. I never forgot that whenever I wrote an offer on one of Harry's listings, we presented it together to his sellers and he treated me with sincere respect and sold hard to get my contract accepted.

As Valerie and Harry and I savored our breakfast, Harry mentioned to me that a property he owned would be sold in foreclosure in four days. He explained the pressures of his business and a variety of problems had worn him down, and he had let matters slide. When his agents walked out on him, he threw his hands up and got on a plane to Ireland. It sounded like Harry's life went pretty much into the dumps. I liked the location of his property soon to be sold in foreclosure. When he told me what he owed on it, I knew he had enough equity to justify me making a loan to stop the foreclosure.

Harry followed me to my office. I called the foreclosing trustee in Los Angeles to find out where we could take a cashier's check in the Bay Area to cure the foreclosure. I'll never forget the name. Bob Mallard was the guy I spoke with on the telephone. The sadistic little jerk played games with me. He said he didn't have time to give me that information.

I explained that time had just about run out, and we needed to know what to do. Clearly, the guy relished having a perverted good time at what he considered a loser's expense. Harry took the phone from me. He said, "Mr. Mallard, I've talked with you before, and I know where you are. Either you give Mr. Barry what he is asking you for or I will get on a plane to Los Angeles now, come to your office and blow your brains out; your choice, sir. I have terminal cancer and it really doesn't matter much to me."

The tone of Harry's voice sounded deadly serious. He handed the phone to me. A moment of silence passed and another fellow came on the line. He politely gave me the information I needed. Sorry, the story didn't end well. Harry got the foreclosure sale date wrong. The property sold on the Alameda County Courthouse steps the next morning. I'm estimating his carelessness cost him at least twenty thousand dollars.

Several of Harry's properties had loans in default. I lent him enough money to cure the payment delinquencies. I secured my loan with a promissory note and a blanket deed of trust which encumbered all his real estate holdings. Title reports showed some outstanding deeds of trust on his properties securing promissory notes which he swore he had paid off. When a loan has been paid off, it is the responsibility of the borrower to record a Deed of Reconveyance (DOR) signed by the lender with the County Recorder.

It didn't surprise me that Harry had failed to record DORs because it happened often. He asked me to contact the lenders he had paid-off and clear the situation up for him. He didn't think those people, all private individuals, wanted to hear from him personally. He admitted he'd burned some bridges with some of those folks. I agreed to Harry's request because I knew what to do, and I knew helping Harry had to lead to good business for me.

I contacted Harry's paid-off lenders and learned that, indeed, he really had burned some bridges. When he paid them off, it happened only after the loans had gone long past due, and he had responded only to repeated threats of foreclosure. His attitude had been rude and arrogant. None of those creditors agreed to cooperate with me by simply signing a DOR. Legally, they could have been forced to comply, but Harry hadn't time to enforce his legal rights. I apologized for his behavior and offered them a modest financial contribution in appreciation of their cooperation which resolved the matter satisfactorily.

Harry had a fair amount of equity in his properties and if he felt so inclined, he might have been able to rebuild the fortune he once enjoyed. I'm no psychiatrist, of course, but I figured the pressure he dealt with in better times finally caused some sort of a breakdown. It didn't seem likely that he would ever really put it back together. He couldn't make the payments on my loan, and I sure didn't want to foreclose on him. We arrived at a mutually satisfactory number, and I bought his properties. We remained good friends.

As mentioned earlier, Julie Summers owned eleven real estate offices. She had a lot of new agents manning those offices, and many of them could use some help in acquiring listings, the life blood of our business. I introduced Julie and Harry and he agreed to go out with a few of her agents and teach them something about convincing owners to list their properties with them. Maybe Harry didn't perform as well as he once did, but he still fared better than most. I think Julie's agents profited from their association with Harry, and he earned a few dollars as well.

I ran into a lot of guys like Harry. They scrambled as I did to acquire properties which they hoped would lead them to total financial independence one day. But as the number of assets increase, the program can become very hard to control. If extremely effective backup management techniques and capable bookkeeping personnel are not part of one's operation, the vagaries associated with the business have a tendency to burn a person out. One setback leads to another and then more and more. In time, discouragement sets in and many such operators just want to live a less complicated life, which is where I often came in.

Before Ed Marvin came into my office, his partner, Michael Rogers—a fellow I liked a lot, had done very well. I admired Michael. I thought of him as an honest, hard-working Realtor. He owned several single family homes of the sort I always liked to acquire. Initially, I thought he might make it big. Close to the same age, we had a lot in common. Michael lost his wife— but not as I lost mine; his wife, Barbara, died of cancer at around age forty-two. She left him with two kids to raise.

Michael called me. He wanted to talk about obtaining a loan, fast. I stopped in at his gorgeous office that same day. I noted his office seemed much larger and fancier than anything I could ever need and I knew it to be also larger and fancier than anything he needed. The overhead must have been a real burden. He explained he had made a bad mistake. He went "elephant hunting" and got himself into a financial disaster.

He borrowed heavily against his real estate holdings and invested the money with a contractor who claimed to have an "in" with the federal government that promised to lead to many highly lucrative federal contracts to build housing for military personnel. I couldn't count how many times I'd heard that tired story. Well, instead of making a fortune, he lost one and he needed help to stay afloat.

I made the loan he requested which brought him some relief. Michael fought hard to keep his sinking financial ship afloat but eventually it just didn't seem worth the struggle. He owned around thirteen properties, besides his home, and a couple of notes secured with deeds of trust. One day we figured his equity in those assets, and I agreed to buy everything except his home. He felt glad to be out from under the burdensome debt and although it took a couple of years of maneuvering, I gained a notable profit. I'd enjoyed a reputation of being good at handling such situations and more and more people in similar situations came to me for help.

Often, I thought about fellows like Harry and Michael and others I will write about later. I tried to figure out just exactly what went wrong. Those guys appeared right on track to reach lofty financial heights, yet somewhere along that serpentine trail things just sort of fell apart. I guess the best I could figure they just got tired and lost that razor sharp entrepreneurial edge.

As the saying goes, maybe they stayed at the circus too long. I hoped that would never happen to me. I always thought a protective aspect of my life lie in the fact that I continued maintaining unassailable faith in the benevolence of my creator. I enhanced my trust in God through continual self-hypnotic activity which served me well. Strong spiritual belief, plus dedication to mental and physical fitness achieved through my addiction to long distance running—which I will address at length later herein —bolstered my resolve to avoid the traps that ensnared so many with whom I dealt.

CHAPTER ONE HUNDRED TWO

In the late 1980s and early 1990s, as I continued my never-ending quest to own more property, the landscape for such activity changed in a pleasant manner. Much of the real estate I held or had owned and sold had come my way as a result of someone's financial distress. I began to come across relatively financially comfortable sellers. Getting the most money for their property took second place to accomplishing a fast, clean, cash trouble-free sale, which I did well.

When I first started selling real estate back in the early 1960s, I ran across Eddie Schmucker, a young fellow a person just couldn't help liking. Eddie reminded me a little of myself. Like me, he started a family quite young. Anyone around Eddie for a while knew that even though he didn't have much of a formal education, his innate, far above-average level of intelligence, natural charm and irrepressible ambition would take him far. Ed trusted me and I trusted him. I made investment suggestions which he readily accepted when possible. I felt delighted and proud of the progress I helped him achieve when one of those damn vagaries that occasionally show up in life, hit Ed hard.

Besides his income-producing avocation of buying, fixing up and selling cars, Ed held a regular day job as an auto mechanic. One day, while maneuvering an engine block suspended by a chain attached to a moveable, overhead hoist toward a solvent tub, the chain broke and the engine block fell on his leg. Ed lost that leg and his life changed forever. Before long, he and his wife divorced. I saw him now and then, and he did alright. In fact, he really did well, just not the same as before his accident.

A few years passed and I got a call from Ed. He asked me if I could come to his home in San Ramon. He had something he wished to discuss with me. His beautiful home impressed me. Ed told me that for his own personal reasons, he wanted to hide his assets. He said I ranked as one of the only people in his life he trusted. He wanted to know if he could put his home in my name for the time being. Touched by Ed's confidence in me I couldn't turn him down.

A year or so went by and Ed stopped by the office one day after he got off work at the Navy Base in Oakland. He explained his elderly mother wanted to live near him. He asked me to find something in San Leandro with two houses on one lot, one for his mom and the other for him. I had Carman Holder, my current property manager and star salesperson, start looking for what Ed needed.

Before long she found exactly what he had requested. Ed had plenty of cash to pay for the property Carman had located for him. When I say Ed had the cash, I mean just that; he kept large amounts of cash in a shoe box under his bed. He wanted to sell his San Ramon property, though he didn't have to sell it to be able to afford San Leandro.

Ed asked me to appraise the San Ramon property, which I did. He told me he didn't want to list it. He wanted me to buy it from him. I said, "Ed, you'll be much better off to list it with me. San Ramon is pretty far away from my regular area of operation and the house is too expensive to rent out. It wouldn't produce enough rent to bring a fair return for the cost to buy the property."

He wouldn't be dissuaded, he said, "You don't understand, I really don't want to list the property. I want you to buy it. Now how much will you pay me?"

When I told Ed what I would pay, I figured he'd decide to list with me or maybe ask me to leave. Ed told me, "It's a deal, Val, on just one condition. I want you to hold the San Leandro property in your name, just as you have been doing here."

I mentally classified Ed as one of those people just not interested in getting the highest dollar amount for their property. Like other sellers I met in those days, he agreed to take less money for his property for the convenience of a clean, trouble-free cash deal. Ed wished to receive his sales proceeds in cash. I would have been glad to accommodate Ed, but the escrow company only disbursed money by check.

A few days before we closed the sale, Ed called me. He let me know he'd been talking with his neighbor who told him he would pay me a fifteen-thousand dollar profit for the property. I told Ed that I was making a nice commission on the San Leandro deal. I wouldn't charge him anything to handle the sale from him to his neighbor so he could make that extra fifteen thousand dollars. He laughed and said, "Forget it, Val, I'm selling to you. If you want that fifteen thousand, you can sell the property to my neighbor when you own it."

I closed my deal with Ed and a few months later, I got a call from him. He said, "I'd like to talk with you about lending you some money. I think it would be good to earn some interest for a change."

I responded with, "Glad to hear you've been thinking about what I suggested, Ed. How about meeting at Burger King on Davis Street for lunch, and I'll let you know how it works."

After we finished our Whoppers, Ed handed me a large manila envelope, stuffed with cash. "How much is here, Ed?" I asked.

"Exactly two hundred thousand," he answered. I quickly took Ed to the Bank of America on Marina Boulevard and Merced Avenue, just a few blocks from my office and where I did most of my banking.

I gave Ed a receipt and deposited his two hundred thousand into my account. Not surprisingly, the large cash deposit of that amount triggered an Internal Revenue Service audit. The government wanted to know where all that cash came from. I told them, which brought an audit down on Ed. I felt very much relieved when he came through his audit with no problems. Ed only wanted a promissory note, no recorded deed of trust. He wanted to keep his business as private as possible.

When I think of folks whose selling decisions were not reached based upon the amount of money their property would bring, I recall the Wilkins family. Sometime back in 1969, I negotiated the sale to Ivan and Marge Wilkins of a small home on a third-acre lot in Mulford Gardens in the 2300 block of West Avenue 136th. Ivan and Marge had the house moved to the rear of their large lot. They made it very comfortable with Ivan, a skilled carpenter, doing most of the work. Upon finishing and refurbishing the house, they took occupancy of it with their five-year-old daughter, Kathy. After moving to West Avenue 136th, the Wilkins listed their home on Marina Court with me, also located in Mulford Gardens but on a relatively small lot. The Marina Court home sold quickly.

Over the following two or so years, the Wilkins family designed the home of their dreams. The house they intended to build on the front portion of their West Avenue 136th property promised to include every amenity they had ever desired in a home. Ivan wanted a huge, attached, four-vehicle garage with the roof rafters built at a height to accommodate a motor home if he ever decided to acquire one. Madge needed a laundry room large enough to serve as a hobby room as well, and a formal dining room plus a spacious rumpus room with a wall to wall fireplace. Three full bathrooms insured no one in the three-person family would ever be denied immediate access to such facilities.

They had that architectural beauty constructed with Ivan providing much of the carpentry, which helped make it affordable. When they finished their elegant creation, the family took possession and rented out the home they vacated at the rear of their lot. The gorgeous landscaping included a fruit orchard irrigated with well water. It seemed that they lived in a home situated in a picturesque park. I thought I resided in the most beautiful home in Mulford Gardens. After seeing what the Wilkins had created, I didn't feel so sure of that anymore. When Kathy finished college and got a good job, she bought and moved into a condominium in the popular Seagate subdivision, just blocks away from her mom and dad.

One afternoon, I received a call from Marge. She asked if I could come to their home the next morning. As I enjoyed coffee with Marge and Ivan, who had recently retired, they explained why they had asked me to drop by. Marge told me Kathy's company had offered her a very desirable position that required her to relocate to the eastern part of the nation. She just couldn't turn down the advantages of the new position. The Wilkens had always been an extraordinarily close knit family. Marge and Ivan decided to relocate to be close to their daughter.

Marge wanted me to buy their home and Kathy's condominium. I told Marge and Ivan I might buy their home, but due to the current severe real estate recession, I'd been called upon to lend out a lot of my capital. The price I could pay had to be less than what I thought it would bring if we just placed it on the market. Even in that depressed market I told them I thought their showplace property would move fast and bring a higher price than I could pay. Marge wanted me to make them my best offer. Again, I emphasized that if they would just let me list their property on the open market, they would get a higher price.

Marge mentioned that they had another property lined up to buy in the east and would like to settle up with me right away. They wanted to show me Kathy's condominium. When we got there, Marge asked how much I could pay for Kathy's unit. As before, I told them what I believed it should sell for if placed on the open market and what I thought I could handle—again a significant difference.

I could tell for this family getting the top dollar for their properties took second place to expediency and convenience. I asked them to discuss what I'd advised. "Take a couple of days, think it over carefully and call me back," I said.

Two days later, Marge called and said that a decision had been reached and asked me to drop by their home. When I got there, she stated, "Val, we trust you. You have always been honest with us, but we can't take your advice this time. We'd like you to buy our property and Kathy's condo as soon as possible."

Very strange I know, but I ran into a lot of similar situations back then.

CHAPTER ONE HUNDRED THREE

It should be clear by now that I've met some fairly strange characters during my years in business, but perhaps none stranger than Christina and Troy Cannon and Mercedes Gallardo, Christina's sister. I met Christina and Mercedes sometime in 1973. Christina looked around forty-four and Mercedes a year or so older or younger. Christina, a licensed real estate sales person worked under the broker's license of Beverly O'Brien, a successful Realtor operating out of a Hayward office.

Our first meeting occurred when Christina and Mercedes dropped by a house I owned and held open in San Lorenzo one Sunday afternoon. Christina, short and fat, brimmed over with enthusiasm.When she smiled, she exposed a mouth full of rotten, stained, broken teeth. Her clothing looked like Goodwill rejects. Mercedes appeared just as disgusting as her sister. Both women wore bad wigs and smelled as if they hadn't bathed in weeks. They spoke in harsh staccato tones and in torrents of verbiage in which they tried too hard to express their thoughts effectively.

Nonetheless, I treated them with respect and thanked them for stopping by my open house. When I mentioned I owned the property, Christina asked if I minded if she concentrated on getting the property sold for me. Although I thought it highly unlikely, I mentioned I'd be delighted if she successfully negotiated a sale for me.

To my surprise, the following afternoon Christina called and informed me she had located a buyer and requested an appointment to present an offer. The sisters arrived at my office in less than an hour. Christina's purchase agreement pleased me, and I didn't hesitate to sign. The sale closed within thirty days and thus began a series of transactions between Christina Cannon and Val Barry Realty that spanned two decades.

Their dreadful appearance and sickening odor narrowed their scope of potential clients, which in a way worked in my favor because they did indeed devote a lot of time and effort to getting my properties sold. Of course, the same reasons that caused others to reject Mercedes and Christina sometimes put me off as well. Still, I admired them, and in spite of their shortcomings, they regularly closed sales. Because I tried to look beyond their handicaps, they seemed irresistibly drawn to me.

Beverly O'Brien, Christina's broker operated her business as a very capable, stern, "by the book" boss. She made sure that her agents paid close attention to the highest standards of professional conduct, notwithstanding appearance and hygiene in Christina's case. Few brokers permitted someone as unorthodox as Christina to work under their licenses. Christina knew that she had to stay in Beverly's good graces. She behaved exactly as Beverly dictated and in those early years all went well between Christina and me.

Beverly's husband, Alex, worked as a general contractor specializing in the construction of houses and apartment complexes. A developer offered Alex an advantageous contract to build a large number of apartment buildings and homes in Southern California. The developer's proposal included the provision that if Beverly relocated her real estate sales operation to Southern California she would be given exclusive "right to sell" listings on the finished properties. Beverly accepted the offer.

Beverly told Christina that she had to transfer her salesperson's license to another broker. No other broker agreed to hire Christina, including me. Although I liked them, my small office could not tolerate Mercedes and Christina's ghastly body odor. Whenever they came into my office, most of my staff found an excuse to leave. As soon as Mercedes and Christina left, I or a staff member thoroughly sprayed the office with room deodorant.

Beverly didn't leave the Bay Area for about a year which gave Christina time to prepare for the State of California Real Estate Broker's test. She obtained her broker's license and opened a small office in Castro Valley. Under her new license, she soon listed a six-patient elderly-care home in San Lorenzo.

A woman in her late eighties suffering with cancer owned the care home. Due to her medical condition and advanced age, she needed a fast sale. I showed the property to a couple I had been working with who wanted to buy a care home. My clients liked Christina's listing. The same day my clients saw the property, I prepared an offer which Christina and I presented to her seller that evening in the owner's dining room.

Christina showed up at the presentation with Mercedes, which I considered completely unprofessional. I had never observed Christina and Mercedes separated from each other for more than just a few feet so Mercedes' presence didn't surprise me. Not only did Mercedes accompany her sister to the presentation, but another person came with them. Christina introduced a man in his twenties as Troy, her and Mercedes' brother. Troy appeared well groomed and neatly attired in a three-piece, expensive double-breasted suit. His bearing and appearance stood in stark contrast to his sisters. Christina explained that as soon as Troy acquired his real estate salesperson's license, he planned to work for her. She thought it good experience for him to observe our presentation.

The seller, Christina and I progressed through the details of the purchase contract while Mercedes and Troy observed. Troy seemed austere and didn't connect with the seller and me whatsoever, yet appeared pleased when the seller signed the contract. I didn't know exactly why, but I didn't like him. Generally, though not always, my first impressions of people tended to be accurate.

The purchase agreement provided for the sale to close within forty-five days. Around thirty days after acceptance of the contract, Christina asked if I could figure a way to complete the escrow early. I explained that even though the buyers and I wished we could speed up the closing it just wasn't possible. In order to provide all the documentation required by the state and county relative to the transfer of title to a licensed care home, we needed the full forty-five days per the contract.

Christina didn't want to let it go at that, she asked if she and Mercedes might drop by to discuss the matter in person. Thirty minutes later she walked into my office. My secretary and a couple of the sales people worked busily at their desks. Christina

412

asked me to talk with her and Mercedes in their car. Mercedes sat in the back seat with a small scruffy looking dog. I settled in the front passenger side and Christina positioned herself behind the steering wheel facing me.

Somehow, by their demeanor that morning I sensed our relationship moving into a new phase. Those two odd women had learned to be extremely skillful at accurately discerning human nature; likely a trait necessary for their survival. They seemed to perceive my genuine interest in them. I liked them in spite of their eccentricities. They had been secretive regarding their family's lifestyle or history. However, on that day they decided to act on their belief that I might be one of the only people, perhaps at that time, the only outsider they trusted enough to take into their confidence.

I couldn't help but notice the bandage covering Christina's left hand. When I asked what happened, she hesitated before answering and her eyes grew moist. She said, "That's what I want to talk to you about, Val." She started off by telling me that Troy, the fellow she introduced as her brother was actually her son. She went on to tell me that she lived with Mercedes, Troy and Mercedes' and her elderly mother, Shelly, in a rented house in Castro Valley.

Christina explained that as the only person in the family capable of earning a living, and that none of the others had ever held a job, she considered Cannon Realty a family enterprise. At the time she acquired her broker's license, she incorporated the business. She appointed Troy the president of the corporation. Christina acted as the vice-president and Mercedes, the treasurer. Troy did no work whatsoever, yet he considered his position as the corporate president bestowed upon him the right to be totally in charge of every aspect of the operation, including complete control of the income. He warned Christina and Mercedes to expect punishment if they failed to obey his orders to the letter.

Troy sat Christina and Mercedes down and informed them he had looked at a collectible pistol at the Traders Gun Store in San Leandro. He wanted the pistol and instructed Christina to hand him $1300 to buy the object of his desire within five days. After paying house rent and fixed living expenses, Christina couldn't comply with her son's demand. For her disobedience, Troy ordered her to position her left hand against the door jamb of the back door to their home. He slammed the door on her hand twice and, of course, broke it. To avoid potential trouble with law enforcement, she decided to forgo medical treatment. To hide the swelling and bruising, Mercedes bandaged Christina's hand. Troy selected his mother's left hand because she wrote sales contracts and signed checks with her right hand.

Practically all the money Christina earned, other than basic living expenses, went to Troy. He wore expensive tailor made clothing while his mother, aunt and grandmother dressed in rags. Christina and Mercedes feared Troy, but they didn't hate him— they adored him and loved to please him. Christina and Mercedes' sole purpose in life centered on pleasing Troy and surviving.

Every day of the week, the family dined in expensive restaurants. At the time of my meeting with Christina and Mercedes in their car, presently under discussion, their social life consisted of interaction with the restaurant personnel. Their servers and maitre d's always received generous tips. Naturally, their magnanimity earned them elaborate attention from the restaurant help which gave the family a desperately needed sense of importance and acceptance.

At one of the fine restaurants they frequented, the Blue Dolphin on the San Leandro Marina, Troy became enamored with Dianne, one of restaurant's waitresses who served the family regularly. Dianne, in her mid-seventies looked every day of her age. Bizarre but true, their brief courtship culminated in a Reno wedding chapel. When anyone inquired about the age difference, Troy wryly explained his passion as an antique collector.

Troy moved into his wife's condominium in Hayward. It didn't take him long to persuade her to take out a second loan on her home. Of course, he took control of the loan proceeds. Due to health issues, Dianne retired from her waitress job. She soon found herself relegated to the status of Christina and Mercedes. One day someone observed Troy slapping Dianne just outside Christina's office. The witness called the police who placed Troy under arrest.

The police contacted Dianne's family who picked her up and took to their home. Troy showed up a few days later at the condominium and had the misfortune of encountering Dianne's teenage grandson, who gave Troy the beating he so richly deserved. Dianne's son threw Troy's clothing outside on the ground. Dianne's grandson told Troy that if he ever showed up there again, he could expect the next beating to be worse. The marriage soon ended in divorce.

Christina, Mercedes, Shelly and Troy just didn't function in the world in the same manner as the rest of us. It's hard to believe but they never registered or insured their regularly driven cars. What's more amazing is that they got away with it. For some mysterious reason, based on paranoia I suppose, they most always paid their house rent through an attorney instead of directly to their landlord.

Mercedes revealed to me a jolting departure from normality on a day when she needed to talk to someone outside her strange family. She told me her mother passed away in the car one afternoon as Christina drove to and from their various destinations. Christina, Mercedes and Troy, who were also in the car, didn't know what they should do. Instead of reporting the situation to the appropriate authorities, they just propped Shelly's dead body up in the back seat of their old Cadillac limousine and carted her corpse along on their daily rounds. This went on for days until decomposition prompted them to turn the body over to a San Lorenzo mortuary.

As I've mentioned earlier, Emil Villa's Hickory Pit Restaurant in San Leandro had the reputation as a favorite gathering place for real estate people. I had lunch there several times each week. The place always drew a crowd—especially at lunch time—and often if a couple sat at a booth that would accommodate four, an invitation might be extended to share seating. One particularly busy lunch period at Emil's, Guy Madison and his daughter Vera, both Realtors I liked and with whom I had dealt, asked Bud and me to join them in their booth.

Our conversation drifted back and forth regarding our current activities. We swapped stories and Guy said what he wanted to tell us next didn't qualify as pleasant mealtime conversation. However, because the subject weighed so heavily on his and Vera's minds, he decided to tell us anyway.

Guy described certain conditions in connection with a rental house he owned in Castro Valley. He explained he had received complaints from people living near his house regarding a sickening odor coming from the residence. When he contacted his tenants, they told him the neighbors had lied to him. When Guy informed them he needed to inspect the interior of the home, they informed him he could enter the house after they vacated sometime before the end of the month.

What Guy discovered in the empty house shocked him. The toilet had obviously been stopped up for a considerable period. It had been filled solid with feces which overflowed onto the floor. When the privy could no longer accommodate additional human waste, the bathtub served as a toilet. It appeared that the condition had existed for years.

The foul odor impregnated the interior surfaces of the house so thoroughly the sheetrock had to be replaced, and still, traces of the stench remained. I inquired of Guy as to the location of his house. His answer let me know Christina and her family had been his tenants. That catastrophe simply resulted from unreasonable paranoia. When the toilet originally stopped up, all that needed to be done involved nothing more than calling Guy or a plumber.

Christina operated her business out of an older office complex building in Castro Valley. Dr. Jerome Wiggams, a lonely, elderly, retired and widowed medical doctor owned the building. As usual, Christina adeptly spotted Dr. Wiggams' vulnerability. Christina, Mercedes and Troy lavished attention on their office landlord. They made him feel welcome and encouraged him to visit the office daily.

It didn't take long for Christina to winnow information out of the doctor substantiating that he had several hundred thousand dollars deposited in a bank savings account earning minimal interest. Troy lied, telling the basically senile doctor he functioned and prospered as a knowledgeable licensed investment counselor.

Directing their collective charm toward Dr. Wiggams, Christina, Mercedes and Troy convinced him they could assist him in investing a good portion of his savings account funds into a lucrative trouble-free venture. They informed him of an attractive apartment complex that might be acquired at quite a bargain if they moved quickly. The trio assured the doctor the investment opportunity offered a steady cash flow as well as establishing a substantial income tax "write off."

The finishing stroke, removing any iota of resistance, came when Christina and Troy promised—for a small fee—to handle every facet of the management of the complex. To get things rolling the doctor agreed to Troy's suggestion that he write a check to Cannon Realty trust account for a half million dollars.

Troy immediately forced Christina to transfer Dr. Wiggams money to his account. Then he left Christina and Mercedes to fend for themselves. Troy joined an art deco club and passed himself off as a wealthy patron of the arts. The good doctor's money flowed like water down the toilet under Troy's control. At a cost of $8000 he hosted a party in Oakland in a restored 1930s vintage movie palace for an art enthusiasts' group which he courted.

Every morning Troy awoke next to a gorgeous young redhead who lived with him on his rented opulent houseboat in Sausalito. After donning her black uniform, she chauffeured him around the Bay Area while he luxuriated in his leased stretch limousine. Troy knew nothing about handling money and soon he pissed away the stolen half million and serious trouble came his way.

Within a short period after Troy absconded with Dr. Wiggams' money, Christina and Mercedes abandoned the office. Unable to contact any member of Cannon Realty, the doctor reported to the police that he had been swindled. As a result of his thievery, Troy spent two years in prison.

Because Troy terrified Christina into giving him the money, she didn't face criminal charges. However, the California Department of Real Estate scheduled a public hearing in San Francisco resulting from a complaint lodged against her by Dr. Wiggams. Revocation of Christina's brokers' license seemed likely. Christina and Mercedes pleaded with me to speak on Christina's behalf at the hearing. Christina quietly and emotionally explained to me that the history of her clan had been riddled with incompetency and failure. Her acquisition of a real estate license accounted for the most notable achievement ever accomplished by any member of her family.

The depth of her anguish touched me and my heart went out to those two disadvantaged women. I had experienced some difficult times in my life but nothing equal to the challenges they faced daily. Up to that point, my transactions involving Christina had served me well. I viewed her as a positive factor in my business.

The sisters looked so tattered that I presented them each with a new jacket I bought for them at Mervyns Department Store. I figured it might serve them well to wear the spiffy looking coats to the hearing. I guess my motivation for such generosity emanated from an uncomfortable feeling of guilt because things went so well for me and so bad for them.

I probably made a mistake, but I did appear at the hearing and described in detail the satisfactory dealings between Christina and me that had transpired over the years. I felt good to see and hear other people speak in support of Christina. Those who testified in favor of Christina included satisfied clients and other real estate agents. Paradoxically, Dr. Wiggams, who had lodged the complaint, didn't show up at the hearing. I think Christina received some sort of disciplinary action, but she retained her license. I noticed neither Christina nor Mercedes wore the coats that I had given them. I suspected they took them back to Mervyns for a refund.

When Troy had paid his debt to society and was released from prison, he wanted to live with Christina and Mercedes and they wanted to live with him. That presented a difficult proposition because at that time Troy's mother and aunt lived in their car. They utilized restaurant and service station restrooms to accommodate daily bodily functions.

Christina and Mercedes lived in their car, but Troy couldn't bring himself to reside there with them. The trio had a fairly well-to-do aunt, Viola, who owned a nice duplex on 35th Avenue in Oakland. Apparently, some sort of mental impairment ran in the family because the aunt, in her own fashion, seemed as nuts as Christina, Mercedes and Troy. She lived in one of her duplex units and for years had kept the adjacent apartment vacant because she didn't want anyone living in the same building with her.

Viola had resided alone for decades and felt the insecurity that so often accompanies aging. Christina, Mercedes and Troy pleaded with Aunt Viola to permit them to move into the empty apartment. After all, they posited, family members should help one another. Reluctantly, their aunt agreed to permit them to take occupancy of the vacant duplex unit.

After her nieces and grand nephew settled into their new accommodations, Aunt Viola refused to give them any privacy. Her constant presence in their apartment unnerved them. She demanded they shop for her grocery items daily and never stopped screaming at them. One day Mercedes and I tried to have a telephone conversation while hysterical screaming in the background made it nearly impossible to hear each other. Mercedes explained the cacophony I heard represented her aunt's normal mode of verbal communication, and it only stopped when Viola went to bed.

One night, the usual verbal assault resulted in physical retaliation. Troy wrestled his great aunt to the floor just as the police arrived, who had been summoned by concerned neighbors. The officers warned Troy he faced arrest for domestic violence if they had to come back. Terrified he might end up being incarcerated again, he quickly decided the three of them needed to relocate without delay.

Troy found a job as a telemarketer, the first time he had ever been employed. Christina earned a steady income managing some apartment complexes located in Hayward and Oakland for Nick Milian. They begged me to rent them a vacant house I owned in Marina Gardens. I did rent to them even though I knew I shouldn't, but I remembered a passage in the First Testament wherein Jesus allegedly said, *"As you do unto the least of these, you do unto me,"* and it seemed that Christina, Mercedes and Troy might qualify as "the least of these."

After a year, Troy lost his telemarketing position. He applied for and received welfare assistance. Apparently, during the period Troy lived it up with the money he swindled from Dr. Wiggam, he developed a liking for cocaine. Christina and Mercedes knew of his addiction. When Troy worked, his income combined with what Christina gave him, supported the use of his drug of choice. Even though the welfare checks didn't match what Troy had made while he worked, Christina, because of her earnings from Nick Milian could give Troy enough money to maintain his habit. She simply did her best to avoid a revisit to the brutality her son had inflicted on her in the past.

Sadly, the respite from the travails engineered by Troy that Christina and Mercedes had known neared its conclusion. Now that Troy no longer spent time working for a living, he demanded to be allowed to accompany Christina and Mercedes on their daily rounds as he had done in the past. He maneuvered to again take control of the finances which Mercedes and Christina, even though terrified of him, refused to permit. He knew of the substantial income from Milian and that his mother still earned sales commissions occasionally. She did her best to keep Troy in the dark regarding her income as he became ever more threatening.

Mercedes and Christina got away from Troy long enough to meet me at my office to explain their dilemma and ask for help. They wanted me to rent the two of them a house. If I agreed, they would scheme to move without Troy knowing where they had gone. Christina said that she had the ability to subsidize Troy's rent to me each month. Her contribution combined with his public assistance income would enable him to remain in my Marina Gardens house.

Christina made good money and was certainly financially capable of accomplishing her proposal. Of course, I suspected that it could all go bad; nonetheless, I rented the sisters a house I owned on Tulsa Avenue. One evening, while Troy met up with acquaintances who shared his fondness of pharmaceutical substances, Christina and Mercedes succeeded in making their escape to the Tulsa house.

For a while, all went as Christina had predicted, but in time Troy stopped paying any portion of the rent on the Marina Gardens home. Christina paid the full amount of rent for Troy for a couple of months. When rent stopped coming in, I had him served with a notice which commenced the eviction process. Paranoia remained a constant mindset in the family, especially with Troy since his time in prison. Any development threatening to put them into contact with the law terrified them. The same day Troy received a Pay Rent or Quit Notice he put his belongings in storage and vacated my house. Actually, applying his security deposit toward his rent made me come out financially whole on the deal.

I think Troy lived in his car for a while until somehow Christina made contact with him. She made the lamentable decision to let him move into the Tulsa Avenue house with her and Mercedes subject to his agreement to abide by certain conditions. He would be permitted to spend his public assistance money as he wished. Christina committed to pay for their living expenses, including dining in their favorite restaurants daily. Additionally, she pledged to give him $200 every week. His part of the arrangement precluded him from trying to take control of the money she earned or physically abusing her or Mercedes, ever. Violation of the terms set forth by his mother and aunt meant immediate abandonment.

Things went well for about a year, until one month I didn't receive my rental payment. I called the telephone number I had for Christina and learned it no longer existed. I dropped by the house and discovered the electricity had been turned off. A neighbor saw me looking around the property and informed me my tenants had moved out a couple of weeks previous.

The next day, Lee Wirt, my property manager at that time, had to get our handyman to disable the front door lock so we could gain entry to the house. Normally she had a key to every rental house she managed, in case of an emergency. Not so with Christina, Mercedes and Troy; driven by their paranoia, they had installed their own lock and, of course, didn't give us a duplicate key. Their inconsideration necessitated us enduring the expense of a new lock and the cost of installation. The condition of the house disgusted me. I guess I'd seen filthier places but not many.

About a year and a half passed before I heard from Christina. She called and asked if she and Mercedes could have an appointment to talk with me about something important. My anger had long subsided, but I did ask, "Christina, why do you think I should give you the time of day after the way you left the Tulsa house?"

Her response brought a smile to my face. She said, "You know, Val, I only want to see you so I can make more money for you."

She told me they couldn't call me when they moved out of the Tulsa house; their mobile phone service had been cancelled because they couldn't pay the $3000 bill they owed at that time. She reminded me that by moving out as they did, they saved me the expense of evicting them. Christina tried to convince me that maybe I should be the one apologizing.

More out of curiosity than anything else, I agreed to see them. They arrived at my office in ten minutes—they had called me on their cell phone from two blocks away. I noticed their hygiene hadn't improved. I imagined Lee or Carman probably had the room deodorant spray handy. Christina wanted me to consider making a loan to Nick Milian. She explained Nick owned six four-plex apartment buildings in Oakland and a sixty unit apartment

423

complex in Hayward. He wanted to borrow $90,000 which he proposed to secure with a promissory note and a second blanket deed of trust. I told Christina before I made a commitment I'd like to meet Nick in person.

She explained I could join her and Mercedes and Nick that afternoon for lunch at the Black Angus in San Lorenzo. I met them, but I lied when I said I'd already eaten lunch and I'd settle for coffee. The ladies smelled so bad I couldn't eat at the same table with them.

Christina always hinted that she and Nick had a romantic relationship. When I met him I knew she had lied. Nick, a handsome, likable and articulate fellow didn't seem likely to be attracted to Christina. I wondered how in the world he got involved with her. I would come to understand that mystery at another time. Nick didn't behave rudely, but he seemed a little cool toward me which confused me until I learned the reason why some weeks later.

He explained he and his elderly parents, with whom he had a very close relationship, lived in one of his apartments in the Hayward complex. The money Nick hoped to borrow from me would be used to do some renovation to his buildings to prepare them for sale. After they sold he planned to buy a home which he and his parents would occupy. Tired of being a landlord, he wished to go back to doing some architectural work, sort of on a semi-retirement basis. Although it sounded as if Nick had a good plan, when I think back on that conversation, I'm reminded of the line from John Steinbeck's novella entitled, *Of Mice and Men*, "the best laid plans of mice and men, oft go awry."

The next day Christina showed me Nick's properties. I had no interest in lending on the units in Oakland—the neighborhood looked so bad I didn't even get out of the car to inspect the buildings. Nick had acquired ownership before the blight set in.

He should have sold years before—holding on too long in a negatively transitional area is a common mistake.

I liked the Hayward property. I told Christina to let Nick know I would lend him $60,000 gross instead of the $90,000 he requested and my loan would only encumber his Hayward complex. The escrow charges and my broker's commission would be deducted from the $60,000 in escrow. Nick agreed to my commitment and the escrow closed in about a week.

I supposed Nick had given Christina a fee for her part in helping him get the loan from me. It seemed at that time, notwithstanding the usual complications of their lives, that Christina, Mercedes and Troy's relationship functioned well. Christina explained they rented a comfortable home in San Lorenzo owned by Nick. She had recently negotiated the sale of the property to Nick by convincing him in a year he could sell and net at least a $10,000 profit. I thought she had figured correctly.

I bought a duplex located in Hayward at a foreclosure sale held on the Alameda County Superior Courthouse steps in Oakland. I hadn't seen the inside of the building before buying it. The person who owned the property still occupied one of the units and hated the foreclosure process. The foreclosing trustee advised it unsafe to try to gain access to the interior of the premises before the sale. I thought the trustee gave good advice because who knew what an irate owner might do in such a case?

In any event, the situation worked out well for me. Because of the lack of opportunity to adequately inspect the duplex, I had no competition. As the sole bidder, I acquired ownership at a bargain price. I went right from the courthouse steps to my new acquisition. Mrs. Ryan, the former owner, a very distraught middle-aged woman, answered my knock on the door. Politely, I explained my reason for being there. Then I listened patiently to a long and complicated story. It always interested me as to why people ended up in such situations. Knowing the details of every such circumstance served as a valuable learning experience.

Mrs. Ryan told me when she quit working for health reasons, she made a deal with her daughter and son-in-law. They agreed to make the bank loan payments on the property in return for taking occupancy of the vacant unit and receiving a deed from her for one half interest in the duplex. They moved in, made only one payment and vacated the apartment about two weeks before the trustee's foreclosure sale. I sincerely sympathized with Mrs. Ryan: she had kept her part of the deal, but her daughter and son-in-law let her down, and subsequently I acquired ownership of the property.

When Mrs. Ryan finished her story all the anger had drained out of her and only resignation remained. She asked if she could have until the end of the week to move out. She planned to move in with her sister in Stockton. She said I could take immediate possession of the vacant unit next door. She moved out as agreed, and I geared up to make the property salable.

It took a little while for me to figure out why portions of the floor in the apartment Mrs. Ryan occupied had numerous one inch in diameter holes drilled through them. I discovered that instead of repairing or replacing the severely leaking roof, Mrs. Ryan's son-in-law drilled the holes in the floor so that the water coming in from the leaking roof flowed out of the apartment through the holes in the floor. After I completed the renovation, Christina negotiated a sale of the duplex for me to a large Filipino family who occupied both units.

Christina and Mercedes, and occasionally Troy, by then stopped by my office regularly. I mentioned earlier Christina possessed an uncanny ability to discover and exploit weaknesses in people or situations. When Christina and Mercedes resumed frequenting my office, I found myself extremely busy, temporarily understaffed and, I guess, somewhat careless.

426

For several weeks during that period, whenever my nineteen-year-old secretary, Patti, presented me with checks that needed my signature, I relied upon her to verify the validity of the bills we paid. I had gotten into the bad habit of signing checks without reviewing the bills myself. Christina noticed my vulnerability as quickly as a vulture spotted road kill.

One day, I happened to notice a check payable to the classified ad department of the Oakland Tribune. I did have an account with the Tribune, but hadn't advertised with them in at least a year. Many Realtors get into serious financial problems by permitting office staff to call in newspaper ads on their own. I had an arrangement with any newspaper company with whom we had an account that they could only run ads I had placed with them personally.

Patti checked with the Tribune. They told her the ad had been placed on my account by Christina Cannon. We discovered Christina had advertised several of her listings on my account. She represented to the Tribune that I had agreed to be responsible for the ads she called in.

I called the classified ad department at the Tribune and explained the situation. The manager promised to immediately review my account and get back to me right away. I contacted Christina and calmly informed her I knew what she had done. I didn't raise my voice or lose my temper, which I believe scared her more than if I had started yelling at her. When I told her to expect a visit from the Sheriff's Department, she screamed to somebody with her, "He's going to kill me."

Just before I dialed the Sheriff's Department, I received a call from the Tribune. The manager of the classified ad department with whom I spoke earlier apologized for erroneously billing my account. He informed me that I could pick up a certified refund check at the paper's cashier's department for the full amount I had paid for Christina's ads. Additionally, for my inconvenience, I received a generous free advertising credit. Maybe I should have, but I didn't report Christina to the Sheriff's Department or the California Department of Real Estate, but I did carefully examine the checks I signed from then on.

Normally, I received my loan payments from Nick Milian by mail. However, one morning he personally delivered the payment to my office. Alone in the office, I invited him to sit and talk. He explained he expected to pay off my loan soon because he had a sale pending on his sixty-unit apartment complex as well as his properties in Oakland. I knew Christina would receive a large listing commission.

Sadly, I learned both Nick's parents with whom he had always been associated in various businesses had recently passed away. As Nick and I visited, we found we liked each other. He apologized for acting so aloof when I met him with Christina and Mercedes at the Black Angus. He explained the reason for his attitude. Christina told him even though I could lend him the money he needed, I operated dishonestly and he shouldn't trust me. She promised to protect him from me.

After Nick and I talked for a while, he realized Christina lied to keep him away from someone who might weaken his dependence on her. Indeed, he became far too reliant upon her, and he went on to tell me why. He described the circumstances that led him to an addiction which seriously detracted from the efficiency of how he managed his business affairs.

For many years while in his twenties, Nick and his parents owned a successful upscale cocktail lounge in Berkeley. During the time the close knit family operated their bar and before they sold it, Nick became an architect, a profession at which he prospered. He bought and sold and held various residential income properties for many years. He eventually received sufficient income from his apartment units to free him to engage virtually full time in what he loved to do most . . . golf.

He explained his addiction to golf. Every other aspect of his existence played a far less important role to him than the time he spent on the course. He engaged in his irresistible pastime five days each week, mostly at the Chuck Corica, City of Alameda Municipal Golf Course. After an early round of indulging his habit, he whiled away the rest of the day at 19th hole—the golf course cocktail lounge—enjoying the camaraderie of his playing partners and others discussing every nuance of the morning's game.

Nick's interest in overseeing his income properties continued to diminish. The neighborhood in which his Oakland units were located had turned bad during his many years of ownership. They became particularly troublesome and time-consuming to manage. When visiting those properties he carried a firearm and, even worse, they interfered with golf.

Christina met Nick when she came to his Hayward complex looking to rent an apartment for her and Mercedes and Troy. He did rent to them, and in the course of their conversation he told her about his difficulties in Oakland. He accepted her offer to manage those vexing units for him. Nick gladly handed that nasty job to Christina.

Nick accepted Christina's property management skills only because she relieved him of the necessity of dealing with the Oakland properties personally. She presented him with an abundance of reimbursement requests for repairs to the units she represented she had ordered and paid for. He suspected she might be padding the charges, or in some cases, collecting for non-existent fixes. In order to avoid any interruption to his world of golf he so loved, Nick figured to put up with Christina until his properties sold. After all, he reasoned she had taken on a horrible job and if she skimmed a little, so be it.

Selling his properties gave Nick the freedom to invest in potentially profitable, yet less time consuming enterprises. As soon as his escrows closed, he asked if he could make a substantial loan to me and receive regular monthly interest payments. I agreed to accommodate him.

Christina came up with an idea how Nick might invest some of his available cash that involved one of my listings. A couple of years previously, I had arranged a loan from one of my wealthy investors, Kal Harvey to Jason Hunt, a small residential building contractor who occasionally worked on my projects. Kal secured his loan with a first deed of trust which encumbered Jason's property at the corner of Williams Street and Doolittle Drive in San Leandro. The property consisted of a third of an acre lot improved with a former service station building which served as Jason's business office. In time, Jason's business faltered. He became unable to make his loan payments. Kal acquired ownership of the property by way of foreclosure.

Kal's son, Steve, converted Jason's former office into a delicatessen from which he served lunch, predominantly to employees of the numerous industrial facilities in the neighborhood. When Steve's deli reached its optimum income potential, he decided to sell his business and gave me the listing. I placed the business opportunity listing on the Multiple Listing Service where it attracted Christina's attention.

It surprised me when Christina called. We hadn't spoken with each other since the Tribune classified ad incident. She apologized and begged me to forgive her. She explained Troy's cocaine habit at that time had gotten much worse. She said that the only way to avoid beatings from him required her to do anything necessary to provide him with money to support his drug habit, which related to the reason she had scammed me.

She told me that she had convinced Nick to buy Steve's delicatessen and let Troy run it for him. She reasoned that operating the business could elevate Troy's self-esteem which she believed he needed in order to turn his life around. She envisioned the enterprise promised to provide a good income for both Nick and Troy and would not interfere with Nick's favorite activity. I didn't like the idea, but Nick hadn't asked for my advice, and he knew Christina and Troy as well as I knew them.

Christina prepared an offer which Steve accepted. Nick gave Christina a check for $2700 which covered his good faith deposit. She needed to deposit the check into her broker's trustee account and transfer the funds into a Wells Fargo escrow account when she opened the escrow. The purchase contract provided for Nick to put up a down payment and finance the balance of the purchase price with a loan from Wells Fargo Bank. According to the terms of the agreement, Nick had seventy-five days to complete the purchase.

Sixty days passed and I hadn't heard a word from Christina. I called her to inquire as to the progress of the escrow. She told me Nick had decided he didn't want to buy the delicatessen after all. She said he knew he had to forfeit his $2700 good faith deposit to Steve. That afternoon she submitted documents to the escrow company, signed by Nick, canceling the escrow and authorizing payment of the good faith deposit to Steve. She delivered Steve's check to me which I gave to him the same day. It worked out well for Steve; he pocketed the $2700 and we immediately negotiated a sale of his business to a backup buyer.

A month or so passed, I received a call from Nick. He told me he hadn't been able to make contact with Christina. He wanted to know the status of the delicatessen deal. Confused, I explained he had signed escrow documents canceling the transaction and authorizing forfeiture of his good faith deposit.

Stunned, he told me Christina said she had the sale ready to close and collected the down payment check from him, made payable to her broker's trustee account. I called Wells Fargo escrow and the escrow officer informed me they had never received a down payment check. When I explained to Nick that apparently he'd been swindled and Christina could face criminal charges, he asked not to take any action. He promised to contact me later that week.

He called a few days later and let me know he didn't wish to press charges. He felt humiliated because he'd been such a fool, but he believed his unreasonable golf addiction made him partially responsible. He also let me know he had lent Christina a car a couple of months before, when she put hers in the shop for repairs. He knew he'd never see Christina or his car again. After that, Nick visited me often, and now and then I'd run into him at the golf course. We became good friends.

Surprisingly, Christina called me about a year later. She said she wanted to let me know Mercedes had died. She explained she knew I had liked her sister and Mercedes had liked me. Mercedes' body reposed in the same mortuary in San Lorenzo that had processed their mother's body. A complication had arisen which I figured had to be the real reason Christina called me. The mortuary needed $200 more than Christina had to bury her sister. I told Christina I would drop the $200 off at the mortuary that afternoon, and I did.

During one of Nick's visits to my office, he asked me to go with him next door to the donut shop for a cup of coffee. He wanted to speak with me in private, out of hearing of my staff. He told me he learned he had incurable rectal cancer. Nick explained he didn't have much time left. He asked me to assign the beneficial interest in the deed of trust which secured the loan he had made to his daughter, Stacy, who lived in Los Angeles. He asked me to continue making the monthly payments to him until he died and then pay the loan off to Stacy, which I agreed to do.

He lasted another year and, yes, he played golf during that year. I paid off the loan to Stacy, and enjoyed meeting her when she came up to settle her dad's affairs. Nick had spoken of his daughter often, and when I met her I discovered her to be beautiful through and through. I understood his pride in her. I gladly accepted her invitation to the memorial service for her dad, attended by his many golfing pals at his favorite golf course.

I didn't expect to ever hear from Christina again, but I did. She asked me to find a rental for her and Troy. They had no references, and the house they lived in had been sold and they had been given notice to move. After my history with them, I don't know why I bothered but I asked my friend, Karl, whom I had recently handled the sale of a duplex to, if he might be willing to rent them his vacant unit. I didn't paint a very pretty picture of Christina and her son, and still Karl wanted to meet them.

Both Christina and Troy collected welfare in an amount easily sufficient to cover the rent. Karl decided to take a chance. He figured them as potentially good payers because of the difficulty of finding another rental in their circumstances. All went well for a few months, and then as always, it went bad.

Just before Christina and Troy moved into Karl's duplex unit, Karl had a new cement driveway installed. Christina and Troy parked their car—the car they had never returned to Nick—on the new driveway in front of their apartment. The car developed an oil leak and Karl asked them to leave the car parked at the street until they got the oil leaked fixed. I knew they wouldn't risk leaving the car at the curb because they couldn't register it. If the police discovered the car had no current license stickers, Christina and Troy would have lost their transportation.

Karl complained to me, and I called Christina who put me on the phone with Troy. He told me that they couldn't afford to have the oil leak repaired and what did it matter about oil on Karl's driveway. A week after our conversation, they moved. I heard that they had moved in with an elderly widower in Alameda who needed someone to care for him. I wondered how that would work out. In any event, I haven't heard from Christina and her son in years.

CHAPTER ONE HUNDRED FOUR

Yes, my business and my life were good. I had been blessed beyond my expectations and perhaps beyond what I deserved. I often contemplated why I'd been so fortunate. Perhaps, I had the advantage of experiencing some heartbreaking events which guided me around obstacles that might derail the progress of others. Because of a childhood dominated by an alcoholic, sometimes brutal and yet sometimes loving father, I grew to like, but not to trust, most people entirely. Because of what I learned as a kid, in most situations I stayed pretty much in control of my relationships, which kept me out of trouble.

I've never forgotten for a moment when I lived in a world of penury. Although I buy whatever I like, live where I want, and drive cars that hint of my success, and I am generous with those I care for, I practice some fairly unusual economies. I cannot understand why so many financially deprived people are so misguided in how they think about money. For instance, I will see people walk by a penny lying on the floor or ground and never stop to pick it up. A penny is money and a multiple of a million dollars. It doesn't matter that it's only a penny, what matters is how you think about money. I never leave a penny lying on the ground and I suspect few other millionaires do either.

Whenever I entered a dwelling in which a tenant or foreclosed owner had been evicted, invariably, I found the premises strewn with loose change. I'm told that the same is true in repossessed automobiles. I've never found abandoned change in a home or apartment vacated by affluent people. Would you like to learn a good method of determining who in a neighborhood is most likely to be in financial straits? A sure way of knowing is to determine which houses have the porch lights left on during daylight hours.

I know you will think this is ridiculous but no matter, it's true. When a bar of soap has been used to the point it has nearly melted away, it is usually discarded. Not my soap—when it's too small to use, I squeeze what remains onto a fresh bar. In my shower, no matter how small, no fraction of a bar of soap is ever wasted. I suppose to think like that a person would have had to have gone through some fairly rough times, and I have.

Wherever I went, I always stayed on the alert as to how I might spot a business opportunity. Every year, Bud used to have a super bowl party to which he always invited me. Usually Julie and I attended those parties together. We bet on the game, met a lot of interesting people and stuffed ourselves with chili and pie; Bud cooked great chili and I brought the pies, freshly baked at Emil Villas.

At one such get-together, Julie and I visited with Ray Hansen's secretary. Ray Hansen enjoyed a very successful career as an East Bay apartment complex builder. Ray's secretary mentioned her boss needed a short-term loan to cover an unexpected expense. She said he had plenty of equity to use as collateral in any of his apartment complexes, but his problem centered on the fact he wanted the money in just a matter of days. I told her maybe I could help and if her boss seemed interested to have him give me a call.

Early Monday morning, Ray called me. He told me he could use a half million, quick. He agreed to pay my standard interest rate, plus a loan fee of seven thousand dollars. Ray had an idea that might facilitate a fast loan. He asked me to meet him within the hour at the Bank of America on Castro Valley Boulevard in Castro Valley, just fifteen minutes from my office.

When I got there, Ray showed me a huge lump of pure silver in a large safe deposit box. At the current price of forty nine dollars an ounce, I estimated the value of Ray's silver to be around $600,000. He said, "You buy my silver for $500,000 and I will transfer the safe deposit box into your name." We agreed he would buy the silver back for $500,000 in addition to a sum equal to six months interest on that amount, plus seven thousand dollars.

He promised to buy back his silver within six months from the day I bought it from him. I became nervous when in the next few weeks the price of silver on the open market dropped to thirty nine dollars an ounce. I needn't have worried, within the next three months Ray purchased his silver back from me exactly as we originally planned.

CHAPTER ONE HUNDRED FIVE

In our divorce settlement, Sheila acquired ownership of our home in Mulford Gardens. Initially, she took custody of our four children. The kids liked that very comfortable home and community. Both Sheila and I agreed our divorce might prove less traumatic to our children if they continued living there. Soon after our divorce, it surprised and disappointed me when Sheila decided to sell the home.

She purchased a much larger and very beautiful home on Cherry Drive in Hayward, closer to the kitchen remodeling business where she worked and would soon buy. After our breakup, maybe she just needed a change of scenery.

Those days, we pretended we had put aside our differences. Still building and remodeling, I regularly availed myself of the services of her newly acquired company. Additionally, Sheila's step-father had retired from his Air Force job and often worked for me on home remodeling projects, and he and my ex-mother-in-law had invested in my loan business.

During our marriage Sheila and I continually hosted holiday dinners, outdoor barbecues and card parties. Sheila and her new husband maintained that pattern. Sometimes my sister, her family, and even my dates' families accepted Sheila's invitations to attend such gatherings. I thought such congeniality between the kids' mother and I served our children well.

I believed that accepting Sheila's invitations to be okay until Sheila's maternal grandmother directed a pointed question at me. Angelina Netti sat across the table from me at Sheila's Thanksgiving dinner. You may recall that she lent Sheila and me one-half of the down payment toward the purchase of our first property. She looked me straight in the eye and asked, "Why are you here?"

A rhetorical question, of course, but her words clearly told me I shouldn't be there. I had great respect for Mrs. Netti. She emigrated from Italy to the United States at age sixteen to marry, by proxy, a man she had never met. She probably didn't even have a sixth grade education. No matter, she happened to be one of the wisest people I'd ever met and instantly I accepted her admonition.

One day shortly before my marriage ended, Grandma Angelina, in her broken English, made a very prophetic statement, "Val, you are working hard, but I wonder if you know who you're working for." I remained friendly with Sheila for some time but respectfully figured out diplomatic ploys to decline her future invitations.

Before our divorce, while we still lived in Mulford Gardens, Sheila insisted that we build a swimming pool on our property. I adamantly refused. My refusal triggered strong resentment and perhaps triggered the beginning of the end of our marriage. After all, she reasoned if our money belonged to both of us, then why didn't she have the right to have a swimming pool? We just didn't have enough warm days in Mulford Gardens to justify a swimming pool. I knew about the daunting maintenance problems swimming pools presented from my experience managing such properties for others.

I understood the depth of her feelings on the subject and proposed a compromise. I said, "Sheila, please consider this; any weekend our family wants to go swimming, we'll book a room at the Airport Hilton. There's more than one pool there. After an afternoon swim, we can enjoy a nice dinner in one of their excellent restaurants. After dinner, you and I can even go dancing. If we want, we can stay the whole weekend anytime you like. I promise you we'll have more fun, and in the long run, staying at the Hilton whenever we choose will be a lot cheaper than putting in and maintaining our own pool."

She didn't buy my suggestion for even one second—we remained at an impasse. After our divorce, when Sheila moved over to her new Hayward home, she immediately had a beautiful expensive swimming pool installed. Incidentally, it didn't take Sheila another eighteen years to figure out that she and her second husband weren't compatible, I think the marriage lasted only a couple of years. Shortly thereafter, she married someone our kids liked and respected, and a person who seemed to truly adore her.

Eventually, Sheila bought a home with a large, highly-productive orange grove adjacent to the Feather River near Chico, California. She and her husband moved there and she continued to successfully run her business in Hayward from her ranch. She asked me to put her house in Hayward on the market. I turned the listing over to Dawn Chandler, one of my steadily producing agents with whom I thought Sheila felt comfortable.

The residential real estate market dragged extremely slowly at that time. Sheila's Hayward home attracted very little interest. Her financial circumstances dictated that she needed to sell soon. Dawn found an attractive, flashy, unmarried, Mexican-American couple, Frank and Dianna, willing to make an offer. Frank operated an exotic used car business. Dianna, a platinum blond sex pot, arranged weddings, including selling wedding gowns out of her store in the Fruitvale District in East Oakland. The area is so Mexican-oriented, that while there one gets the same feeling they would have in Mazatlan or Puerto Vallarta.

The offer required Sheila to carry back a large portion of the purchase price. Neither Frank nor Dianna had been in their current occupations very long. Consequently, primary lenders agreed to lend only a very small portion of the purchase price. Additionally, the couple had very little cash for a down payment. Frank owned a vacant lot with a view on 166th Avenue, not far outside the San Leandro City limits. I bought Frank's lot for $40,000, which he and Dianna used as their down payment toward the purchase of Sheila's property. We lined up a first loan and Sheila carried back the balance owing in the amount of $51,000 to complete the financing of the purchase price.

Sheila didn't mind carrying the financing. She looked forward to receiving the monthly interest payments from Frank and Dianna. I felt a little nervous about the deal but Dianna assured me, I had nothing to worry about. She asked me, "Val, do you have any idea what Mexican parents pay for their daughters' weddings? You needn't be worried about Frank and me making our house payments."

If not for the sluggish market, I wouldn't have considered advising a seller to accept that sort of a deal. But Sheila had over-improved her property and her only chance of getting enough to recoup her money necessitated that we do what we did. Well, as I halfway expected, the Cherry Drive deal went sour. The payments to the first lender and to Sheila stopped. I advised Sheila to bring the first loan payments up to date, in order to keep the bank from foreclosing and wiping out her second position. She knew that routine well and did exactly as I advised. She paid the first loan payments and started foreclosure under the terms of her note and second deed of trust.

When she began the foreclosure process, in order to remain in possession of the home as long as possible without making payments, Frank and Dianne filed bankruptcy which had the effect of delaying the trustee's foreclosure sale. Damn . . . dealing with savvy deadbeats is truly nasty business. Sheila didn't seem concerned; she knew I wouldn't let her lose on a deal that I got her into. She finally acquired title to Cherry Drive and took possession of the property. I bought it from her at a cash price that made her entirely whole.

Hoping the market might recover in the not too distant future, I decided to rent Cherry Drive out. Not long after my tenants took possession, I got a call from them letting me know the swimming pool needed work. I would have filled it in, except that I'd rented the property with a pool, which obligated me to provide one. It cost me a little over seven thousand dollars to refurbish the damn thing and in a year or so I had to evict my tenants for non-payment of rent. Additionally, they wrecked the house, which took a small fortune to correct.

I fixed the place up, staged it and put it on the market. It took a long time but the property eventually sold. When I figured everything out, the Cherry Drive transaction resulted in a loss to me of $135,000. There is a degree of irony in this story. Remember, prior to the divorce I refused to install a swimming pool at our San Leandro home because of all the terrible maintenance problems and expense associated with owning a pool?

Well, sometimes fate refuses to be denied. Instead of taking my swimming pool beating at 2332 West Avenue 134th in San Leandro, it just happened at 632 Cherry Drive in Hayward instead. Oh, I almost forgot, the vacant lot I bought on 166th Avenue from Frank for $40,000 brought $20,000 three years later. Sheila said that my sole motivation for buying Cherry Drive resulted from my desire to make a profit. Of course, she knows the truth but I'm not about to hear her say, "Thank you, Val."

CHAPTER ONE HUNDRED SIX

You may recall that I introduced Stuart Alexander into my story in Chapter Fifty-Two. Before actually meeting Stuart, I heard a lot about him. He bought up a lot of residential property in Mulford Gardens. One afternoon, Stuart's father, Tweedy Alexander, stopped by my office with a mutual friend, Pete Peterson. Pete introduced us. That marked our first meeting but we certainly knew of each other.

Tweedy's uncle, Joe Natario, was married to my Uncle Gene Frazier's sister, Jessie. The Natarios and the Fraziers both lived within a block of my mother and step-father's home. My Aunt Pauline and Uncle Gene Frazier knew Tweedy well and they had often mentioned me to him, and they had talked about Tweedy to me frequently. Tweedy and I had some things in common: We were close to the same age, we both married young and subsequently divorced. We remained single and each of us owned successful businesses in San Leandro. I suppose the most significant experience we shared happened to be that both of us lost our oldest sons in tragic accidents.

Tweedy operated the Santos Linguisa Factory on Washington Avenue in San Leandro, which he inherited from his aunt who founded the business in 1921. The property where he produced the popular Portuguese sausage included, in addition to the factory, a neighborhood-type saloon and a well maintained older rental house. Tweedy owned several other single family residential rentals, within the immediate vicinity of the real estate his aunt left him. We enjoyed our first meeting, and I suspected we might become friends.

Tweedy mentioned he wanted to meet me because he knew I'd acquired a lot of properties, just as his son, Stuart, aspired to do. He thought I might be able to pass along some helpful advice. He told me Stuart owned eight or nine properties and he continually dealt with remodeling contractors and didn't get on with them very well. I let Tweedy know, "I sure know what that is like especially when you're starting out. But in time, a person learns to select the right guys and how to get the best out of them." Tweedy asked me if I might talk to his son. I told him, "I'd be happy to talk with Stuart. Just have him call me."

I saw Tweedy two more times; first at my Uncle Gene's funeral. I saw him last when I attended his Uncle Joe Natario's funeral in which Tweedy served as a pall bearer. On that somber occasion, I greeted him with a friendly smile. I couldn't help but notice his lukewarm response, which surprised me in view of our congenial meeting in my office. Sadly, from my Aunt Pauline, I learned later the reason for Tweedy's tepid response. He had been diagnosed with incurable lung cancer.

He died and his estate went to his sons, Stuart and his younger brother. The brothers inherited all of their dad's property and took over the operation of the venerable linguisa business. Stuart worked very hard. The terrible fire that destroyed more than twenty-eight hundred homes in the prestigious Montclair and

Hiller Highland districts of Oakland in the early 1990s presented a terrific business opportunity for Stuart.

The City of Oakland required that the foundations of the fire-destroyed houses had to be removed at the expense of the owners by a certain date. I suppose it might be more accurate to say the foundations had to be removed at the expense of the property owners' insurance carriers. Stuart set up a very profitable operation that complied with the city's dictate regarding disposal of the foundations. His services related to those removals spanned several years. Additionally, that experience along with his regular job as a garbage collector led to an active trash-hauling business in San Leandro and adjacent communities.

Aptly demonstrating his ability as a remarkable entrepreneur and carrying on the tradition of his great aunt and father as a successful business person, Stuart's various enterprises provided a considerable stream of income. The time came when his family's reputation played a monumental role in the events that affected Stuart's life and the lives of others. I mentioned earlier that Stuart and his younger brother basically shared their father's estate. The shared ownership of their inheritance ended when Paul lost his life as a result of being run over by a train in the wee hours of the morning within a few blocks of the linquisa factory. I believe it remains a mystery as to the reason for Paul's presence on the tracks.

Even though the money poured in, Stuart's income couldn't keep pace with his propensity for continuing to buy and pay too much for residential properties, mostly in San Leandro. Additionally, he refurbished several of his houses well beyond the limits of sound financial practices. In my opinion, he committed the classical error of trying to make many of his real estate holdings monuments to his elevated ego rather than staying within the boundaries of economic prudence. In order to sate his appetite to become a real estate mogul, Stuart chose to borrow what he needed to keep it all going.

Utilizing the prestige of his successful and highly respected predecessors, long established in San Leandro, Stuart borrowed from family friends and acquaintances. Still, he needed more money so he expanded his borrowing sources to hard money lenders. The Oakland foundation-removal income became just about exhausted. I'm told the trash hauling business diminished as a result of partnership complications and credit issues began to restrict Stuart's ability to borrow.

One afternoon, I received a call from a loan broker who had been trying unsuccessfully to arrange a loan for Stuart. He told me the property on which Stuart wanted to secure the requested loan had a value of approximately two hundred thousand dollars. The commercially zoned corner lot improved with a spacious attractive older house was located just two doors from the linquisa factory. The unfinished remodeling status of the house to make it suitable for business use had hampered Stuart's ability to obtain a loan on his property.

Most lenders will not make a loan against a property being worked on because of potential mechanic liens that might take priority over the lender's security position. Stuart's loan broker knew of my unorthodox lending reputation and wondered if I could help. He told me if making the loan interested me he wanted no fee and asked if he might put Stuart in touch with me. I informed him I'd check out the property and get back to him right away. I liked what I saw and put the mechanics lien reservation at rest, because only Stuart and his regular hourly employees had worked on the building.

The initial meeting at my office with Stuart went well. I agreed to make him a loan in the amount of $96,000 from which I would be paid a commission. We closed the escrow in a week, utilizing Fidelity Title Insurance Company, an escrow company of Stuart's choice and one I rarely used, which resulted in a troubling situation. When I turned my escrow instructions and check for $96,000 into Fidelity, I expected to receive my promissory note and commission check upon completion of the transaction.

Things didn't work out that way. The day the escrow closed Fidelity delivered my documents to the office by messenger service. When I opened the envelope, it didn't contain my $6000 commission check. When I called Fidelity, an embarrassed escrow officer told me she simply forgot to collect my commission from Stuart's proceeds. I thought to myself that would never have happened had I insisted on using my regular escrow company. But I let Stuart choose because I wanted a good start with him. I foresaw doing a lot of business with him and besides, he paid for the escrow service and title insurance.

Such situations can get very sticky. Of course, if Stuart refused to cough up the commission, Fidelity's error made them liable, but I knew collecting would be complicated and time consuming. I thought, *why don't people just do what they are supposed to do?* My consternation proved unnecessary. The errant escrow officer called Stuart and within half an hour he came to my office with a check. What a great beginning. I sold the $96,000 loan to my friend and attorney, Michael Jacobowitz. The commission represented my profit and by selling my position, I had another $96,000 available to invest. Michael trusted me and I found him a pleasure to deal with. Besides, I enjoyed playing golf with him.

Stuart impressed me. His dedicated work ethic and wholesome ambition made me think he had a very promising future. Besides his business-related good qualities, he seemed like a genuine good guy. I stopped by the linquisa factory one day to drop off loan payment books and he loaded me up with a few pounds of Santos Linquisa on the house.

Every Monday evening I took Mom to dinner at Emil Villas. On one such occasion, Stuart sat at the counter when Mom and I passed by him as we headed toward our booth. When we finished our meal, I asked our waitress for the check. She told me, "Stuart already paid your bill." Who couldn't like Stuart?

Within a month I made another loan to Stuart in the amount of $30,000. He secured the loan with a first deed trust on a well located Mulford Gardens property on West Avenue 133rd. Stuart had an insatiable desire to own Mulford Gardens property. He owned a sort of Cape Cod architectural style house at 2417 Marina Boulevard situated on two-thirds of an acre. I used to own that property myself and knew it had promising development potential. The party who sold it to Stuart carried back the financing and secured his loan with a first deed of trust which encumbered the property. I mention the seller carry-back financing because it would become significant relative to my experience with Stuart.

Stuart also owned 2403 Marina Boulevard, a third-acre parcel improved with two houses and adjacent to the eastern boundary of 2417 Marina Boulevard, giving Stuart title to a full acre on Marina Boulevard, the main arterial servicing the San Leandro Marina and golf course complex. By putting together parcels—a process known as "plottage"—in such a strategic location, Stuart created tremendous advantageous investment possibilities.

He explained to me that when the property adjacent to the west side of 2417 Marina Boulevard had been for sale, he had made two attempts to buy it. For some reason, the owners just didn't seem to want to sell to him.

Whenever Stuart bought property he used the services of a real estate agent by the name of Dorothy Saxe. He told me in her capacity as a Realtor, Dorothy had long represented both him and his father. Her relationship with the Alexanders extended beyond her role as their real estate agent. Stuart explained he considered her a valued family friend. He said she had written and presented both purchase contracts relative to Stuart's efforts to acquire ownership of the property at 2417 Marina Boulevard. In each instance the sellers rejected and refused to counter Stuart's offer. Stuart said Dorothy had no idea why she couldn't make any headway with the sellers.

When Stuart let me know how much he had offered, it surprised me the sellers rejected his proposal without at least submitting a counter offer. Although I didn't know the sellers personally, I knew their neighbors. Through that source, I discovered the owners truly wanted to sell, even though the listing had expired. Something didn't seem right. I looked at the situation as an intriguing challenge. I told Stuart if Dorothy agreed to permit me to write and present an offer, and in that one isolated instance act as his Realtor, I might be able to help him.

Stuart assured me he spoke with Dorothy and she didn't mind at all if he worked with me on that one transaction. He insisted on paying too much. I only wrote the contract after I had him sign a statement wherein he had been advised his offer exceeded my estimate of the market value of the property. I prepared the offer and made an appointment to present it to the sellers.

That evening, I arrived at the property and the sellers greeted me cordially. As I recall their first names were Fred and Nancy. We settled around their kitchen table and they offered me a cup of coffee. As usual, I accepted my hosts' offer of refreshments. For maybe ten minutes we made small talk. When I thought that they felt sufficiently comfortable with me, I began the presentation of Stuart's purchase contract.

Fred couldn't conceal that the offer pleased him. Nancy reacted differently. She angrily stalked from the kitchen into the dining room. He followed her and I heard her say to him, "I told you, we're not selling to him."

After a few minutes they rejoined me at the kitchen table. I said, "I couldn't help overhearing what you said in the next room.

Would you consider letting me know why you refuse to sell to Stuart? Believe me, whatever you say will be kept in confidence."

Fred answered for her. He told me decades past, Tweedy Alexander and Nancy both attended San Leandro High School. For some reason, Tweedy, sort of a power on campus, and some of the fellows with whom he hung around, took a dislike for her. They teased her continually through her high school years. Their alleged bullying ruined what should have been a happy time in her life. She had never forgotten and damn well refused to do anything to help Tweedy Alexander's son.

Upon learning her reason for being so adamantly determined not to deal with Stuart, I quickly formulated a strategy. I told her Stuart wanted to pay so much more for the property than its market value, that I wouldn't even prepare the purchase contract until he signed a statement indicating I had advised him of that fact. I told her humorously, "If you really want revenge, what would be better than accepting Stuart's overpriced offer?"

Well, my approach, which I call "kidding on the square," worked. The sellers and Stuart thought I did a good job. I guess deals like that rated high among the reasons I loved what I did for a living.

I suppose you might say Stuart made me think of a "one-eyed Jack." Until then, I'd only seen one side of his face. It started with a call from Mike Jacobowitz. Stuart had fallen behind on his payments on the $96,000 loan I had sold to Mike. Stuart also failed to make his last two payments on the $30,000 loan I made to him. Rumors in San Leandro had spread about Stuart regarding secured and unsecured loans he had accepted from locals on which the payments were delinquent. Some loans had been made from elderly folks who trusted him but began to see another side of Stuart.

My friend, seventy-five year old Cliff Berg and his wife lived on West Avenue 133rd. The Bergs took great pride in maintaining their property. Their home happened to be one of the finest in Mulford Gardens. The back property line of Berg's lot was adjacent to the rear boundary of Stuart's property located at 2403 Marina Boulevard.

Stuart's activity on his property upset Cliff and his neighbors. The rear portion of Stuart's lot had taken on the appearance of a junkyard. Stuart filled it with old cars, crates and items he had accumulated in his hauling business. What happened there had the potential of diminishing the value of real estate in the neighborhood.

The abhorrent undertaking on the rear portion of Stuart's property couldn't be seen from Marina Boulevard. The two houses at the front obscured the view from the street. Cliff, in an effort to gather evidence of the loathsome circumstances adjacent to his property decided to video-tape the offensive threat to the well-being of the neighborhood. As Stuart operated a loader, stacking and arranging items to make more storage space, he spotted Cliff filming him from Cliff's side of the property line.

Stuart jumped down from the loader and headed straight for Cliff who retreated into his home. I believe Stuart followed Cliff right into the house where he severely beat Cliff and left him bleeding on the floor. Cliff called the police and Stuart soon wound up in jail. A couple of days later, Cliff dropped by my office as he often did. He explained what had happened. He told me his wife, not in the best of health, had been traumatized over the situation. She didn't want Cliff to press charges. She abhorred the thought of her husband testifying in court.

Someone had contacted Cliff on Stuart's behalf. I listened to Cliff and felt sorry for him. He seemed extremely concerned about what might happen with his wife if he didn't do as she wished. At the same time, he just couldn't let Stuart get away with what he had done. I wondered if dropping the charges—sure to please Mrs. Berg—in return for cash payment from Stuart might satisfy Cliff's sense of justice. I believe that is exactly how the matter got resolved.

A retired building contractor, Joe DeSilva, who constructed some residential apartments for Bud and me years previously, contacted me. Joe was from San Leandro and of Portuguese ancestry. Being familiar with the excellent reputation of Stuart's dad and great aunt, he made a loan to Stuart. The loan had been secured with a note and deed of trust which encumbered Stuart's property at the northeast corner of Williams and Washington in San Leandro; the same property that secured the $96,000 loan I sold to Michael Jacobowitz. Joe's loan was in second position to Mike's loan. In order to protect his investment, Joe had to cure Michael's loan if Michael initiated foreclosure proceedings.

When Joe called Stuart about the delinquent payments, he said Stuart became belligerent and hung up on him. Discouraged, Joe thought he had lost his money. He and his wife came to the office and I explained that equity existed in the securing property exceeding Michael Jacobowitz's loan and Joe's loan. If Joe initiated a foreclosure under the terms of his securing deed of trust, likely he would either end up owning the property or be paid off by a successful bidder at the foreclosure sale. Well, Joe did initiate a foreclosure and his loan got paid off in full by the party who acquired ownership of the property via the foreclosure process. The new owner of the securing property paid off Michael as well.

Stuart called me and we agreed to meet at my office. In deep financial trouble, he hoped I could help him. He no longer had the ability to service his financial indebtedness. He had lost that prime real estate located at 2417 Marina Boulevard discussed earlier herein. Stuart informed me the person who sold him the property and carried back the financing, took back the property by way of a foreclosure sale. According to Stuart, the foreclosure resulted from his failure to service the note payments. The new owner had listed the property for sale, and Stuart tore down the "for sale" signs on the property twice. He irrationally contended that the lender had no right to foreclose.

Stuart didn't understand that violation of the terms of a secured promissory note left the lender little choice other than initiating foreclosure. I calmly tried to make Stuart comprehend that if lenders couldn't take legal action to enforce the terms of their notes and deeds of trust, no loans would ever be granted. He refused to understand and told me that if he saw anyone placing another for sale sign on 2417 Marina Boulevard, things might get ugly. I took what Stewart said seriously. I didn't consider his words to be idle rancor. After Stuart left my office, I called the Realtor who had the Marina Boulevard property listed. I told him about my conversation with Stuart and suggested that he refrain from placing a sign on the property for awhile. He thanked me and heeded the suggestion.

I called Stuart a couple of days later and suggested he speak with his attorney, Jeffery Rooney, about taking some action to hold off his creditors, giving him time to raise money to make his creditors whole. I told him if I knew who he owed and how much he owed, maybe I could determine whether he had enough equity in his remaining properties to obtain a loan to consolidate his indebtedness. He utilized the services of Dorothy Saxe and his attorney to acquire the information I needed. I let Stuart and his attorney know that even though I'd try, I might not be able to help, and I advised him to continue to pursue other sources of relief.

Stuart's creditors' received a statement signed by him, asking them to provide whatever information I might request regarding his indebtedness. As I studied Stuart's complicated maze of secured and unsecured loans, I discovered even though deeply in debt, he may have had sufficient assets to justify a bail-out loan.

I contacted several of his unsecured creditors. Even though they had or could obtain judgements if Stuart filed Chapter Seven bankruptcy, his financial obligation to them would likely be wiped out. Some agreed to take substantial settlement discounts. I think I'd given them a degree of hope because they seemed to have long given up on ever getting paid. The process dragged slowly because Stuart owed a lot of people. Still, very encouraged, every week I wrote a letter to Stuart explaining my progress and sent copies to his lawyer and Dorothy Saxe. I hoped Stuart appreciated all the work being done on his behalf.

Finally, after weeks of struggling, I felt close to working it all out. I figured I could arrange a loan to Stuart with a single blanket deed of trust encumbering all of his real estate holdings. Although I didn't mention it to Stuart, if I didn't find another lender, I could make the loan myself. The monthly payments should have been well within his ability to handle.

He had provided through Dorothy Saxe detailed information on all his properties with the exception of the linguisa factory property. Dorothy thought that he had about $125,000 equity in that property. If she estimated correctly, I believed I could arrange or make Stuart a loan to put him in good financial shape. Furthermore, I considered if I could help Stuart, I would have performed a valuable service that few could or would do.

In view of Stuart's overwhelming monetary problems, it surprised me when I saw him on television debating with two other candidates as to which of the three of them was best qualified to serve as the City of San Leandro's next mayor. Indeed Stuart did campaign and ran for the office of mayor. Although he didn't win, he made a good showing.

I called and wrote Stuart for the specific information I needed regarding the linquisa factory property. I got no answer. Even Dorothy couldn't seem to get the information I needed. Finally, I let Stuart know I couldn't help him if he didn't cooperate—I got no response. While resting in a hotel in Sacramento, recovering from running a marathon, I got a call from Carman, my office manager.

She told me Stuart was in my office. He demanded the file containing all the information pertaining to his properties he had provided to me. I told Carman to give him the file. He informed her he had located another lender, and he no longer needed my services. When he saw my personal handwritten strategy notes in the file, he demanded those as well. She knew he had no right to my notes and told him she couldn't give them to him. He became very angry. Stuart's aggressive attitude scared her. Another person in the office observed the tenseness of the situation. Carman believed had she been alone he might have injured her to gain possession of the notes.

Stuart left the office with everything Carman had given him. He sat brooding in his car in the parking lot. Carman locked and left the office to avoid any possibility of having to deal with him by herself. I believed no lender other than me would rescue Stuart. I felt sure I could help him. I know it sounds egotistical but I was his only hope. The money meant absolutely nothing to me compared to the knowledge that I had the ability to perform a truly valuable service unavailable from anyone else.

I pondered the foolishness of Stuart's behavior. He cooperated with me until I asked him for information regarding the linguisa factory property. Although it made no logical sense, I figured when he discovered I needed to encumber that particular property with a blanket deed of trust, he just wouldn't take a chance on losing it. He may have been able to tolerate the loss of everything other than the Santos Linguisa Factory. I believe he would have considered such a failure as the ultimate disgrace. The termination of the concern that had given his family status and financial security since 1921 would be intolerable to Stuart. Sadly, in my opinion, he couldn't comprehend that in order to save Santos Linguisa he probably needed to follow my lead.

It's trite I know, but I suppose the old saying of "when it rains it pours" held true in Stuart's life. For some time he had been experiencing an adversarial relationship with government meat inspectors. According to Stuart, the heart of the problem related to the method of smoking the linguisa sausage. The same equipment —which had been in use for more than seventy years—didn't maintain consistent temperatures in compliance with current regulations throughout each batch of meat being smoked. Stuart had mentioned to me that the cost to solve the problem would run about a hundred thousand dollars. He stated, "That's not going to happen."

An antagonistic relationship had developed between Stuart and the inspectors. With the personality traits I'd observed Stuart demonstrating since the buildup of his financial troubles, I easily understood how personality clashes might develop. The inspectors threatened to shut down Santos Linguisa Factory, which angered Stuart. Such an action would not only stop a badly needed source of income, but just as painful, an honored family tradition would have been scuttled on his watch. He wouldn't accept the inspectors' demands and started producing and selling the popular sausage illegally.

On the morning of June 21, 2000 as I drove to an appointment, I received a call from Ed Marvin. He asked, "Val, have you heard about Stuart Alexander?"

"No," I replied.

Ed informed me that Stuart had been arrested for the murder of three meat inspectors and the attempted murder of a fourth inspector at the linguisa factory. A story so bizarre, momentarily I just couldn't believe Ed's words but, of course, he had told me the truth.

Stuart's eventual first degree murder conviction resulted in his death sentence. While on death row at San Quentin Prison he died of a pulmonary embolism. His death marked the end of the only remaining son of his parents.

When I first met Stuart his future seemed bright. A series of ill-thought out moves led to his catastrophic demise. The meat inspectors couldn't have been aware of the depth of Stuart's emotional distress. I suspect at least one of them allowed the difficulty with Stuart to become personal, which was understandable, yet fatal.

CHAPTER ONE HUNDRED SEVEN

Michael Jepson attended high school with Danny, Steven and Valerie. While in his mid-twenties, Michael worked as a real estate salesman in Castro Valley. He operated out of an office by the name of the Property Professionals. The sales staff of that office didn't content themselves just grinding out a living earning commissions. Like me, each and every one of them aspired to do their job in a manner that promised to lead to their financial independence. Mike had allied himself with a group of winners, and I hoped their influence served him well.

From time to time, Mike called me to chat about his progress in the business. One day he let me know he had a chance to buy a house in Floresta Gardens at a bargain price. Floresta Gardens had a reputation as a desirable, middle-class, San Leandro neighborhood. Many San Leandro police officers lived in Floresta Gardens which might have accounted for the fact that people thought of it as one of safest areas in the city. Mike planned to pay cash down and assume an existing loan against the property. He had a problem. He didn't have enough cash to pay the difference between the purchase price and the loan balance that encumbered the property.

He had to close his deal fast or lose it. He didn't have much time to look for a loan to make up the amount of his shortage. I specialized in making fast loans, and I preferred to lend money to someone like Mike. I provided the needed financing and secured my loan in the usual manner. In about two weeks, Mike explained he had another problem. The house needed work and he didn't have enough cash to pay for what he figured needed to be accomplished.

When I thought about it, I realized he really did make a good buy. I asked him if he wanted to take a quick profit and sell his property to me. He jumped at the chance to close the deal fast and move on to his next project. I didn't expect a big gain, but I wanted to try out a new marketing technique and that property seemed particularly well suited for what I had in mind. If my idea worked, it would become a permanent part of my residential property merchandising activity.

Unlike new model homes, I had never seen a used home staged to enhance its selling potential. I mentioned to Carman I wanted to stage the house in Floresta Gardens, which I planned to soon place on the market. I didn't know how to proceed. Buying staging furniture at first seemed unwise because I didn't know if my plan would work. Carman told me she recently received a flyer from a fellow trying to get started in the business of house staging.

I called the number on the flyer and set up an appointment with Bart Norton. Bart agreed to meet me at the office after he got off work at his regular job. He worked as a nurse in an assisted living care home but hoped to develop a career in house staging. Bart and I had one thing in common. We both saw great potential in staging used houses.

After talking with Bart, I determined that he had been making preparations for some time but hadn't yet been able to sell his staging services. He explained the scope and cost of his service. Satisfied with his price, I withheld my judgement of the quality of his presentation until I'd seen it in place. He did his magic and truly impressed me. He furnished every room tastefully and created a warm and cheerful ambience. He periodically changed or rearranged various decorative features throughout the home. The property sold quickly and at full price, which I did not expect.

From then on, I had every one of my marketed properties staged. The investment in staging produced great returns, considering the speed at which the property sold, and the price it brought. After I'd sold six or seven properties utilizing Bart's remarkable talent, I determined staging resulted in twelve to fifteen percent higher selling prices than comparable unstaged houses.

Unfortunately, Bart just didn't have enough furniture and accessories to decorate more than two houses at a time. He simply couldn't produce sufficient income to compensate him for the time he had to invest to do the job right. He had to give up staging. Determined to continue staging without him, I thought of another person who could take his place, who I'll discuss later.

Mike and I continued doing business together, and I figured him to be a progressing success story. Julie and I weren't married, even though we lived together. We often hosted parties to which we invited business associates and friends. Actually, our business associates were our friends; that's just the way it worked in our occupation.

One evening, Mike showed up at one of our parties accompanied by a gorgeous brunette. He introduced her as his favorite escrow officer and his brand new wife. It made me happy to learn Mike had found someone to share his life's adventure. It seemed he'd put everything in place to achieve the degree of success to which he aspired. Even so, as promising as Mike's prospects seemed to be, I knew everything didn't always turn out as expected.

We were acquainted with a lot of the same people and occasionally I heard it mentioned that Mike used recreational drugs. I really didn't attach much credence to such rumors because I figured if he had a problem with drugs it would show up in his business performance. My contact with Mike simply stopped for several months. One morning I got a call from him. He'd found a property listed in Alameda he thought might be of interest to me. We made an appointment for him to show me the property the next afternoon.

Why Mike thought I'd be interested in the property puzzled me. Nothing about it appealed to me. I hadn't seen him for several months and his appearance startled me. Instead of looking trim and fit and dressed like a male model, I saw a sloppily fat, unshaven fellow with sores on his face. We had a close enough relationship that I felt comfortable asking what had happened to him. He seemed relieved to be able to openly discuss what had been happening in his life.

He explained in the beginning of his career in real estate he delighted at being thought of as a rising entrepreneurial star. He told me he had enjoyed showing off his dancing skills almost every Friday evening at popular night spots. He looked forward to snorting a little cocaine to add to his enjoyment of each of those wonderful Friday evenings. Gradually, his use of the illegal drug spanned whole weekends. In time, he just couldn't function absent the addictive stimulant. He realized he no longer qualified as a so called recreational drug user. Rather, he became an addict and his life began to fall apart. And, of course, his gorgeous wife moved on.

Mike's father and mother had been divorced for years. Until his recent death, his dad lived in a desirable hilltop condominium in

Castro Valley with a view of the San Francisco Bay. I received a call from Mike informing me his dad had passed away. He and his younger brother, Ray, inherited their father's condominium. He wanted me to take a look at it. I met Mike and Ray at the unit. I discerned after a little cosmetic work it should be very marketable. Both brothers wanted to sell the property.

Ray owned a pool cleaning service in which he had tied up all his capital. He came across in a very likable positive fashion, as did Mike before his descent into the world of illegal pharmaceuticals. Ray's wife taught school and the couple had a seven-year-old daughter. At that time, Mike and Ray lived totally different lifestyles. I noticed Mike, being the older brother, seemed to intimidate Ray. The prospect of him having to engage with Mike to accomplish the sale of their newly acquired condominium presented problems.

Mike called me because neither brother had any money. He knew I could help. Making a loan didn't interest me because I believed the two of them couldn't work effectively together. I liked Ray a lot and mentally formed a plan. Buying both brothers interest in the property didn't appeal to me. If I did buy the condo, and made a substantial profit, it could appear as if I took advantage of someone not thinking clearly as the result of their father's death. If one member of the family shared in the potential profit it looked better. I offered to buy only Mike's interest. He accepted the cash offer without hesitation and Ray and I became partners.

I wrote out a work format as I did before starting any refurbishing project. My list assigned specific tasks to both Ray and me. I agreed to provide all improvement funds and collect when the property sold. Ray had confidence in my ability and cheerfully let me take the lead. He turned out to be a good partner. The property sold soon after going on the market, and we divided a nice profit. My business association continued with Ray after we sold the condominium. He needed more capital to increase his growing pool service business. I made a loan to Ray and his wife against their home on Covington Avenue in the highly desirable Sheffield Village district in Oakland.

Mike didn't work in the real estate business any longer. He cared for his incapacitated mother in his well located home on Paru Avenue in Alameda. In addition to the house in which Mike and his mom lived, he owned a rental cottage situated at the rear of the parcel. Mike asked me to make him a loan on Paru. I questioned his ability to make payments to me if I granted his request.

In addition to the loan he requested me to make, he had a first loan which encumbered the property. He assured me that if he became unable to service his loan payments, he would sell the property. He did have sufficient equity in his property to pay off his loans and have money left over if he decided to sell. Mike told me he received some income from his mother for the care he provided to her.

For a time he made his payments as agreed. When his mother died, his finances spiraled downward. I received notification that the monthly payments on the first loan had fallen behind. I expected foreclosure proceedings on the first loan to begin soon. I moved to protect my second position loan. In order for my loan not to be wiped out I had to bring the past due payments on the first loan current. I cured the first and gave Mike some time to reimburse me for what I'd paid on the first loan. Not only did he not make up what I'd advanced to cure the first loan, he continued not making his regular monthly payments on the first, and he stopped making payments on my second loan.

I initiated foreclosure and heard nothing from Mike until a few days before the foreclosure sale date. He came to my office and it saddened me to see the state of his physical deterioration. He had even angrier looking sores on his face and had gotten much fatter since the last time I saw him. His formerly beautiful, but currently beat-up, Cadillac sat in our parking lot with someone sitting in the driver's side. I wondered if Mike had lost his driver's license. The Mike Jepson I observed on that day appeared to be a far different man than I knew a few years previously.

I said, "Mike, I don't want your property sold in foreclosure unless you leave me no choice." When I told him, "I'm willing to buy your property." I saw a sense of relief on his hard-to-look at face.

We quickly negotiated a better price than he expected. But he couldn't hide his disappointment when he heard the condition that the major portion of his proceeds would not be given to him until I had complete possession of the property. I didn't want to deal with evicting him, which I knew I'd have to do if I didn't hold on to the money until he vacated the premises.

Mike moved—I disbursed his money, had the house cleaned and I rented it out. Fortunately, through all that, the cottage at the rear had been rented to a couple of female college students. A few months later, Mike called and wanted to make an appointment with me. Someone drove him to the office in an old beater car; the sort of car dopers drive. I watched as he walked across the parking lot and noticed him limping badly. Everything about him seemed even worse than the last time I saw him.

I listened to his sad story. The limp resulted from a broken leg he sustained when he fell out of a tree. The fractured leg failed to knit properly, and the doctors at the county hospital connected the break with a stainless steel bolt. Unfortunately, because of the state of Mike's continuing physical deterioration, his body rejected the bolt. He told me of the unbearable pain he experienced, and I believed him.

Finally, he arrived at the point of his visit. He had broken his glasses and could barely see without them. He wanted to attend a job fair being held in Oakland. Determined to rebuild his life he thought the job fair could be a good beginning. He asked to borrow two hundred dollars to pay for a new pair of glasses.

I refused to lend him two hundred dollars. However, I offered to give him two hundred dollars in return for his promise never to call me again. He promised and I gave him a check. What happened to Mike happens too often. I knew nobody could help him and it hurt to see him like that. A few months later, I got a call from Ray telling me someone had discovered his brother's body under a 580 freeway overpass in Oakland early that morning.

CHAPTER ONE HUNDRED EIGHT

Since entering the real estate business in 1960, it seemed that about every ten to twelve years a steep decline in the prices of and the demand for residential housing occurred. It never failed that the bursting bubble at the peak of the market came as a complete surprise to many real estate entrepreneurs who just didn't believe the rising tide of prosperity could ever abate. Nonetheless, it always happened and the results rarely varied from one financial catastrophe to the next.

With the advent of the turn of the decade into the 1990s real estate recession, I had ample cash. As usual, my activities involved multiple categories of residential business enterprises. Right then though I concentrated on the lending segment of my various modes of operation. The vast majority of borrowers with whom I dealt proved to be financially sound and met the conditions set forth in our loan documents faithfully.

My expanding lending reputation and the severity of the real estate recession brought me into association with a somewhat different variety of borrower. I'd been considering developing a plan of how I might enter into semi-retirement. The "new to me" type of borrower with whom I'd soon come into contact served to delay my withdrawal from a full time work schedule for the next few years. Yes, a trap awaited me.

I heard from several very experienced residential real estate developers. They'd been caught severely financially overextended as a result of the sudden unexpected real estate recession. Riding the crest of a prosperous, seemingly endless real estate boom, they were totally unprepared to weather the bust that threatened to wipe them out. They found their way to me from conventional lenders that had served them in the past, and some instances still had loans with them. The qualifying criteria of those lending institutions prohibited them from going further with those borrowers.

I found them different from those I had dealt with in the past. They owned several properties, and had enjoyed spectacular success throughout their careers … until they needed to contact me. Every cent they had accumulated, through many profitable ventures, had been invested in their current projects. They'd borrowed as much as they could and exhausted their liquid reserves. I placed that unique group into a category I silently and respectfully classified as the "Golden Boys." I admired their accomplishments, and I felt flattered that I might be of service to them.

George Oakes called me. He explained he had been referred to me by a bank he had done business with for years but at that time couldn't help him. I set an appointment to meet George at my office the following morning. In my opinion, everyone in the Bay Area had heard of George. I met him in his early seventies. His family had been in the newspaper business for generations.

George basked in his role as a lawyer and a principal developer of large residential subdivisions, apartment buildings and a multi-story retirement facility. His activity encompassed a career spanning decades centered primarily, but certainly not limited to, the Hayward area. George served as mayor of Hayward in 1963 and 1964 and carried out the duties of a Hayward City Councilman for twenty-two years.

However, despite the broad expanse of his many accomplishments, there hung a seemingly permanent dark cloud over George. Sometime in 1983, he found himself convicted of felony drunken driving resulting from an incident in which he ran over and killed two pedestrians. As part of his punishment, the court ordered George to serve one hundred and twenty nights in jail. Although confined nocturnally, during daylight hours he could manage his sprawling business affairs.

George, accompanied by his wife, arrived right on time for our first appointment in my office. I must say George impressed me. He as well as his wife, Christine, came across as the epitome of genuine charm and grace. As I recall, I think George needed to borrow around $300,000. After talking and getting acquainted, we set an appointment for me to look at their home that afternoon which would serve as collateral, if I decided to make a loan to the Oakes.

Their home sat at the top of Oakes Boulevard in the Hayward hills. Of course, Oakes Boulevard had been named after George. I'd heard he built many, or maybe all, the upscale homes fronting that street. I believe when he finished the last house up the hill near the end of the street, he proceeded to construct his own home on a three-acre parcel which provided a spectacular view of the southern portion of the San Francisco Bay.

The Oakes home consisted of a sprawling, 6000 square foot, one story Spanish Mission style structure. A dramatic walkway shaded by an overhead grape arbor encircled three quarters of the once gorgeous structure. I say "once" gorgeous structure because obviously the years had been as unkind to the home as they had been to the Oakes themselves. I got the feeling that following the tragic circumstances in which George's careless behavior resulted in the death of two people, the glory days of George and Christine had diminished. In any event, in my cursory view, I estimated an investment of around a $100,000 or more might be needed to restore Villa Oakes (my appellation) to its original eminence.

George provided me with a financial statement that listed the numerous properties to which he and his wife held title. I told him I hadn't the time to look at his other assets. I agreed to lend what they requested and encumbered several of their properties under a blanket deed of trust along with Villa Oakes which I believed failed to provide sufficient security. I knew that type of "shooting from the hip" lending represented something no other lender would dream of doing.

That didn't matter though; inundated with other borrowers like George, as a result of the devastating recession, I simply didn't have the time to investigate every securing property. I felt relatively financially secure and those types of borrowers cheerfully did whatever I asked to get the money they needed. Each and every one of them expressed their sincere gratitude for my help. I got the impression they had exhausted all other sources of borrowing money. They didn't mind encumbering nearly every piece of property they owned.

I made the Oakes the loan they requested and for awhile the monthly payments arrived right on time. They delivered the payments to me personally. As they pulled into our parking lot in their Lincoln Continental, I noticed that Christine always drove. I guess the reason for that is easy to figure out. In any event, I always enjoyed my time with George and Christine.

My blanket deed of trust on the Oakes' home being in third position, meant the first and second place lenders had priority over my loan. If the Oakes failed to live up to the terms of either of those loans and the lenders initiated foreclosure proceedings, I would have to bring their payments current in order for my investment not to be wiped out. Sure enough, I received notification from Wells Fargo, the holder of the first loan, that the bank had initiated foreclosure. I talked with George about the situation. He explained he just couldn't make the payments. I felt bad for him; he seemed ashamed. I thought it may have been the first time in his long life he'd found himself in that position.

Normally, I would have brought Wells Fargo's payments current and initiated my own foreclosure. George told me, "Val, you don't have to go through the foreclosure process; Christine and I will just deed the property to you now and move out."

I appreciated his offer, but it wouldn't work. If I foreclosed I not only had to pay Wells Fargo, the lender in first position, but I had to pay other creditors whose debts encumbered the property and had priority over my loan. No, I planned to proceed somewhat differently.

I decided to simply show up at the Wells Fargo's trustee's foreclosure auction on the Alameda County Courthouse steps in Oakland and engage in the bidding process in an effort to acquire ownership of Villa Oakes. The purpose of that strategy follows: Wells Fargo's loan balance and foreclosure costs totaled around $300,000. That figure would equal the minimum opening bid required by the foreclosing trustee. If I got lucky and the other creditors behind Wells Fargo—but ahead of me—hadn't filed foreclosure in order to protect their interest, and if there were no competing bidders at the auction, I might be able to buy the property in the vicinity of $300,000.

I had loaned the Oakes around $300,000. If I acquired ownership of the property for $300,000 and sold it for $600,000, I would have recovered all the money I'd paid for the property, plus what I had loaned to the Oakes. Before being permitted to participate in the verbal bidding process, I had to show the trustee's auctioneer a cashier's check for the maximum amount I could offer. No one except the trustee and the party showing the check are supposed to know the amount of that limit. Of course, a bidder can increase the maximum amount of the bid by producing another cashier's check.

Being very experienced at that game, I showed a check indicating a much larger amount than I intended to pay for the property. In that case, I planned on a maximum of a little more than $300,000, but I submitted a cashier's check for $600,000. I did that just in case a dishonest trustee might be in cahoots with one of the bidders. I didn't want any potential competing bidder to have any inkling of what I might be willing to pay.

Another party approached the auctioneer to show his cashier's check which disappointed me. I'd hoped to be the only bidder. Other than myself, I didn't expect to see another $300,000 cash buyer in that recessionary market. Maybe, I'd get lucky and he'd drop out early in the game. I didn't get lucky. One of spectators who loved to hang around the foreclosure sales just to watch the action, informed me the other bidder happened to be a wealthy doctor. Worse yet, the good doctor wanted to make Villa Oakes his home. My strategy had run into trouble.

The bidding began: I got caught up in the pure excitement of the auction and lost all sense of reality. In $25,000 increments the doctor and I quickly reached $500,000. I knew if I raised the bid another $25,000 he would do the same. I increased my bid by $100,000 and reached my limit of $600,000.

I looked at my competition and for a moment had no idea as to his next move. He looked back at me and shook his head in a manner that told me I'd won. Won! *What the hell did I win?* I'd just paid twice the amount I intended to pay. I felt a little queasy. The doctor walked over to me. He asked for my telephone number. He said he wanted to call me in a few days to see if we might negotiate a sale of Villa Oakes to him. Man ... how I hoped I'd get that call but it never came.

To just break even, I had to net $600,000 from the sale of Villa Oakes. That didn't seem likely to happen for two reasons: A severe real estate recession existed and the property suffered from significant deferred maintenance.

I had the once elegant, faded-blue fabric window awnings spray painted to restore their original beauty. Jim Stagg, a painting contractor, and one of my best friends painted the interior of the home. Other repairs and improvements included retiling some floors and re-carpeting others, plus totally landscaping the expansive grounds. John Manuel, a meticulous contractor, rebuilt the massive rotted deck overlooking the stunning San Francisco skyline. Villa Oakes looked new again.

Julie accomplished the staging. She had her dazzling baby grand piano moved from her Alameda waterfront condo to the Villa Oakes living room. She staged every house I placed on the market, and nobody did it better. But what she accomplished at the top of Oakes Boulevard turned out to be a work of art. Bill Carrish, a friend and connoisseur of vintage collectable automobiles told me, "What you need to add more panache to this place is a classic car in the garage."

Bill figured right. Jerry Chastain had sheetrocked and textured the interior of the three car garage. How could I better show off his fine work than by parking Bill Carrish's splendid Zimmer Roadster inside? No way would I drive that gaudy car to the property. My secretary, Lee Wirt, seemed delighted to take care of that for me.

In addition to staging Villa Oakes, Julie had consulted with me and guided me through every phase of the extensive renovation program. She fell in love with the property from the moment she first saw it, and frankly, she saw more there than I did. Her enthusiasm led me to make an unprecedented (for me) decision. I decided to list the property with her firm Summers Real Estate Company. That didn't go well with the agents in my office, of course. No matter, I had gotten into that deal pretty deep and only an agent with Julie's positive enthusiasm had a chance of generating a sale that could make me whole.

Right after I signed the listing agreement, Julie contacted her friend and customer, Skip Everett. Skip and his wife, Doctor Nancy Everett owned the Sierra Academy of Aeronautics at the Oakland International Airport. Although not necessarily pertinent to this story, Doctor Everett delivered one of Julie's two granddaughters, Mallory Bickley, into this world.

Skip arranged for one of his pilots to take color aerial photographs of her new listing. The dramatic pictures highlighted an eye-catching, glossy informative brochure that accompanied the listing distributed by the MLS. That beautiful brochure truly made one think of the former Oakes estate as a magnificent Spanish or Italian villa.

I placed the property on the market at $900,000, which would net me a fair profit. I didn't feel confident I could get anywhere near that amount. I found nothing for sale in the area that could compete with what we had to offer. We resolved to just do a good job of promoting and hope for the best. Plenty of lookers came by and some made low ball offers, but so far it didn't look very promising.

Occasionally, George Oakes showed up when Julie held the house open. He told potential buyers interesting tidbits about the property. I agreed to pay a commission of ten percent of the selling price, instead of the usual six percent. The generous commission agreement brought a larger than normal number of real estate agents out to inspect the property.

You will recall the lot consisted of around three acres. The house had been constructed at the northwest corner of the parcel, leaving plenty of room to build two more houses. If the site could be divided into three view lots, the value of the property would increase substantially. I put out some feelers to the homeowner's association to try to determine if there would be any opposition to creating three lots. An adjacent neighbor got word back to me that if I made an application to subdivide, I should expect his opposition to my proposal.

Disheartened, but not quite ready to give up on my idea, I visited the Office of the City of Hayward Planning Commission to see what their attitude on the subject might be. If the planning staff discouraged me, I'd forget about filing an application. When I talked with the head of the staff, Mr. Hal Davis, he said, "You know, there's something about this that rings a bell, let me check back in the old files."

Some time passed before Mr. Davis reappeared. When he came back, he had some startling news. He held a sheet of paper in his hand which he extended to me. Apparently, at some point years ago, George Oakes filed an application to divide his three acre parcel into three lots. His application had been approved and the paper Mr. Davis handed me confirmed the approval. That, indeed, counted as one of those instances I refer to as "magic time."

Judy Rose, an agent with Allied Brokers brought in a purchase contract at the listed price. Her buyer wanted to trade an acre located in Hiller Highlands in Oakland toward the purchase price. The buyer lost his house on the acre parcel as the result of the catastrophic fire that destroyed 2800 homes in 1992. According to Judy, he had no desire to move back to Hiller Highlands and had found Villa Oakes to be just what he wanted. His offer provided that I take his lot in trade at a value of $200,000.

Julie and I immediately drove up to Hiller Highlands to look at the lot. We really liked the location. We had been told the Golden

470

Gate and the Oakland Bay Bridges could be clearly seen from the subject parcel. If that statement held true, I wouldn't have disputed the value given the lot at $200,000. Unfortunately, from any place on the site, nearby houses blocked an unobstructed view of the bridges. We could see only the southern portion of the bay, thereby placing the market value of the property more in the range of one $100,000.

I called Judy and informed her of the results of our inspection. The next morning, she presented me with a purchase agreement complying with my request as to the value of the buyer's property. We quickly closed the escrow. The new owner bought some of the staging furniture including Julie's baby grand piano. I started thinking about my acquisition in the Oakland hills. I noticed the lots in the neighborhood happened to be far smaller than mine. I thought it might be a reasonable proposition to try to divide my acre into three building lots. If I succeeded, perhaps the three separate parcels could be sold at a significantly higher price than what I had paid for the site.

I hired a surveyor to prepare a topographical plot map showing how he believed the parcel should be divided. I presented the map to the City of Oakland planning staff along with my application to divide the parcel. The planning staff informed me a hearing would be scheduled in which the public would be invited to voice their opinion regarding my application. Prior to the hearing, I met with several of the closest neighbors at one of their homes. I'd been in this situation many times in my real estate career. I knew exactly what to expect. I figured to hear a lot of negative comments, and I did.

As charmingly as I could, I explained that each of my three proposed lots would be larger than any one of theirs. After an hour and a half into the meeting, most of the opposition had been diminished. The remaining objection came from an adjacent owner to one of the proposed lots, who expressed concern that a new house might negatively impact his view.

Diplomatically mentioning it seemed likely my application would be approved, notwithstanding his objection, I suggested perhaps his concerns could be put to rest if he bought the lot that had him worried. That way he could control the development of the parcel. He asked me to meet with him and his wife the following afternoon to discuss numbers. The couple bought the lot for $71,000 the same amount each of the other two sold for.

I still had other loans with George Oakes; on some of which he made his monthly payments faithfully. Other of the Oakes loans were complicated to settle, but in time, did get resolved. By that time I had made loans to several members of the Golden Boys group. None of them could meet the obligations set forth in the securing loan documents they had signed.

Nonetheless, I didn't consider them deadbeats; they were honest and ethical, and every one of them tried to work with me to the best of their ability to live up to their responsibility. There is no point in telling about my experiences with each and every one of those borrowers. To do justice to that endeavor would require writing another book. Eventually, although it took years and scores of serpentine negotiations and dealings, I think in the end I recovered all the money I lent to those fellows.

One more story about one of the Golden Boys. I think someone from World Savings and Loan directed Donald Mendez my way. Donald worked as a contractor, primarily engaged in remodeling commercial buildings in San Francisco. He had expanded activities into building three homes in Hayward which were about ninety-five percent finished, and they were gorgeous. He also owned several rental houses in good areas in the East Bay area. He worked out of two industrial condominiums on Clawiter Road in Hayward that he owned, along with three other adjacent identical units.

Donald found himself severely overextended and several of his property loans were close to going into foreclosure. He impressed me; he came across as a very intelligent person. I felt if any of "The Faded Golden Boys" might succeed in spite of that damn recession, I thought it could be Donald. I made him the loan he requested and secured it with a deed of trust blanketing every property he owned, except his home.

He made his payments as long as he could. He ran out of funds and the payments on my loan, as well as the loans senior to mine against his other securing properties, stopped. There were seemingly endless negotiations and renegotiations and meetings with Donald and his wife in their attorney's office that got us nowhere. Eventually I had no choice. I filed for foreclosure. No over-bidders came to the trustee's foreclosure sale. It appeared as if the loan balances on the Mendez real estate exceeded the properties' value. Consequently, I acquired title to twenty-something over-encumbered properties in one day.

It seemed little or no equity remained in the properties. It looked as if I might end up losing the funds I had lent to the Mendezes. Actually, I sold one of the houses in Hayward that Donald had recently finished remodeling and picked up a few thousand dollars. Every Mendez property which I acquired ownership of via foreclosure was encumbered with a loan. I contacted each of beneficiaries of those loans and tried to negotiate a cash discount with them in an effort to create some equity. They responded negatively to my appeal—most of them had started foreclosure which threatened to wipe out my loan security.

I mentioned earlier my blanket deed of trust to the Mendez's encumbered five industrial condominiums. I knew nothing about that type of property. The savings and loan association that held the loan senior to mine on the five units, had failed. Its assets were taken over by a federal government agency known as the

Resolution Trust Corporation (RTC). It encouraged me that the RTC hadn't initiated foreclosure. They didn't even call or write demanding payments and I didn't make any monthly payments on those loans.

I called the RTC in an attempt to accomplish a cash discount. No one I spoke with seemed to know which department would be interested in talking with me. Each time I called, I found myself directed to someone in another department, who in turn directed me to yet another department. Concurrently with calling, I also wrote letters.

Donald Mendez still operated out of two of the units for which he paid me some rent. I leased two of the units to Duane Phelps, who bought, refurbished and sold Harley Davidson motorcycles. I leased the remaining condo to Richard Freitas, a remodeling contractor and a friend of Phelps. For once I didn't complain about governmental inefficiency.

Duane wanted to buy the two units he leased, plus the two presently occupied by Donald Mendez. Richard Freitas also preferred to be an owner rather than a lessee. After a few months, I finally got in contact with someone in the RTC who could talk with me about reducing their loan balance for a cash settlement. He told me their decision would be subject to the opinion of an appraiser, chosen by the RTC, as to the appraiser's estimate of the market value of the property.

I met with the Roger Perkins, the appraiser selected by the RTC. Roger seemed friendly and very appreciative that I'd prepared a substantial file of market data to help him prepare his appraisal. It turned out Roger worked with many of the fellows who made a career of bidding at foreclosure sales on the steps of the Alameda County Courthouse. I knew most of those guys as well. We engaged in a little idol gossip about some of our mutual acquaintances. I thought about inviting Roger to lunch, but on second thought, figured that might be pushing it.

In about two weeks, a call came, followed by a letter from the RTC informing me my offer relative to discounting the balance owing on RTC's loan in the amount of $171,000 had been accepted. I paid off the RTC immediately before someone changed their mind. I sold the condos to Duane Phillips and Richard Freitas. I carried most of the financing, collecting monthly interest payments for a year, at which time they paid me off in full. I invested a lot of time and work, but I got back every cent I loaned to the Mendezes.

CHAPTER ONE HUNDRED NINE

Early in my career, I wanted to determine the reason why some people who had risen to a level tantamount to financial independence would lose all they had worked to acquire. There are many causes of such failure. Some of those include ill-heath, drug and alcohol addictions, womanizing, carelessness in protecting good credit and a tendency to take unjustified chances, instead of adhering to prudent investment principals. None of the preceding would ever pose a threat capable of overwhelming my own quest to achieve my life's goals.

Nevertheless, there is one menace that poses a threat to all entrepreneurs, especially those involved in the real estate business. I'm talking about ruinous litigation. There are myriad situations by which wealth is redistributed through exposure to the legal system. In an effort to avoid involvement in the courts resulting from my lack of knowledge, in 1963 I enrolled in a college course regarding preparation of legal contracts. That extremely fortuitous decision served me well over the following decades.

I took pleasure in drawing legal contracts related to my own accounts and did so frequently, year in and year out. With the exception of the following case described herein, I've rarely been in court over my forty-some years in business. So confident of my ability to avoid legal entanglements until the advent of the following situation, I mistakenly never purchased "Errors and Omission" insurance.

Sometime in 1994, Carman Holder, my most active salesperson and office manager, and I were served court papers naming us as two of four defendants in a lawsuit. The action stemmed out of a circumstance in which a property in Hayward that had been listed by Carman and sold through another office had drainage problems. The plaintiffs who purchased the property alleged the sub-area of the house continuously flooded. The buyers contended the defendants could have, or should have, informed them of the condition before they bought the property. They asked the defendants to settle the matter for around $100,000.

In my estimation and based on extensive experience, the cost to repair the damage and correct the cause of the problem should have been more in the vicinity of $20,000 to $25,000. The first news Carman and I received regarding a problem came in the form of the lawsuit. We called the former owners. They admitted they had known of the drainage problem and were agreeable to settle the matter for $20,000.

I knew greed motivated the case, and I found it disgusting. The lawsuit had nothing to do with just getting the damages and corrective work accomplished. The desire to make a nice fat windfall profit drove the plaintiffs and their attorney. Otherwise, a couple of telephone calls from the plaintiffs' attorney to the other defendants and us would have led to a quick solution.

Normally, if you're sued, you hire a defense lawyer. As the case drags on, the attorney fees keep adding up. It's an old ploy; you get weary of the mounting legal expense and eventually settle even if you are convinced you're innocent and would likely prevail in court. With due respect to my lawyer friends, I've often considered that a person involved in litigation has three adversaries; the plaintiffs, their attorney and your own attorney. I'm not entirely sure which of those three are the most dangerous.

Carman and I were knowledgeable of our responsibility relative to the circumstances of the case. We'd taken the time to obtain legal advice and felt reasonably certain if we decided to litigate the matter, our chances of prevailing in court were favorable. But we contemplated how much it might cost to win and what if luck went against us. We didn't want to go to court. I called the plaintiffs' lawyer and told him we would pay $5,000 to be dropped from the case. He rudely informed me that my offer didn't deserve consideration.

At that point, I made a fateful decision that may not have been among my smartest moves. I decided Carman and I had to fight the lawsuit and act as our own attorneys. My decision had nothing to do with money. I needed to fight a patently unfair system. A worn cliché, "a man acting as his own lawyer has a fool for a client," hopefully wouldn't apply to Carman and me. We filed an answer and our case took on a life of its own. Over a period of three years, Carman and I defended ourselves using tactics totally unexpected and disappointing to the plaintiffs' openly hostile attorney.

The multiple depositions exhausted us. One of the other defendants, the broker for the selling office, died during the course of the case. We effectively, albeit awkwardly, utilized the full array of legal maneuvers available to us. The plaintiffs called in an expert witness; we responded with, in my opinion, the presentation of a far more capable expert witness. We filed a complex Motion for Summary Judgment. The plaintiff's furious attorney accused us of purposefully trying to increase his client's legal fees.

Finally, just prior to having the matter litigated in court, a party selected by the court to attempt to negotiate a pre-trial settlement, suggested the other side might accept a settlement offer from us in the amount of $7,500. I pretended disinterest, but Carman pleaded with me to make the offer. Acting as I if agreed in order to please Carman, we made the offer, which the opposition immediately accepted. I'm forever grateful to Carman for letting me save face.

I learned the plaintiffs' attorney lowered his fee to his clients from $25,000 to $5,000. I believe the sellers of the property settled for the amount that they agreed to pay from the beginning. All concerned had endured three years of unnecessary grief, expense and heart-wrenching turmoil. I repeat, for my part, that battle had nothing to do with money. Would I do it again? Of course, I would.

CHAPTER ONE HUNDRED TEN

I suppose had I not got mixed up with the Golden Boys in the early 1990s, thoughts of planning for retirement or redirection would have been the dominating force in my life. But for the next few years, cleaning up the complications of recovering what I'd invested with those fellows definitely kept me in the real estate business. Financially, the goals I'd set for myself had been reached. Making good money, of course, still motivated me. But the profit I earned from my varied business activities, in my mind just counted as a way of keeping score. How I ran up the score, relative to the game I played, represented what excited me.

National statistics indicate that the average full time real estate agent doesn't really do well financially. That is especially true if the prodigious time they must invest to earn their living is taken into account. It is easy to see why most of them fare so poorly. The activities to which they devote their business pursuits are far too narrowly circumscribed. Their failure to recognize the wide spectrum of economic opportunity available within the real estate profession severely limits income potential. Yes, if done correctly, indeed it is a profession.

By 1999, all but a couple of the Golden Boys hangovers had pretty much been reasonably resolved. Shirley McGuire from the San Leandro office of Coldwell Banker called me. Shirley, like several local agents contacted me when they listed a difficult to market property, yet to the right buyer presented extraordinary profit possibilities. Even though I operated my own real estate company, they knew I would act as their customer and expect no part of the sales commission. The tactic kept them calling. Of course, the potential of substantial gain came with ample risk.

Shirley explained that she had just listed a home in Bayo Vista, considered probably the most prestigious subdivision in San Leandro. The houses situated on the west side of the streets that ran north to south offered magnificent unobstructed views of the San Francisco Bay and the City of San Francisco's dramatic skyline. I met Shirley at noon at the property on the day she called me.

The circa mid-1960s, former showplace Rancher presented a stunning, even better view than I expected from almost every room in the house. Oh boy … but what a problem. The long, numerous gaping cracks in the interior and exterior walls and the severe undulating floors throughout the structure reminded me I lived in earthquake country. The devastation seemed to emanate from a drainage problem which had undermined the stability of the substructure.

Shirley took the listing in the high two hundred thousands. She showed me a geologist's report and bid to correct the basic problem in the range of the mid-sixty thousands. Of course, his estimate had nothing to do with effecting sorely needed cosmetic improvements. I considered the stigma that often remains, even after correction has been accomplished, when a hillside house undergoes such impairment. In pristine condition, I thought that the property might sell for around $375,000 to $400,000.

I told Shirley I would pay $150,000. Of course, unless the out-of-state seller agreed to carry some financing, any purchase required cash. Shirley explained the seller would not carry any financing. I knew no lender would make a loan on the property in that condition. Shirley wrote the contract, but the seller rejected it, and accepted one in the range of $250,000. Shirley let me know she had presented several other offers; all at least $100,000 more than mine. I thought, *oh well, you can't win them all.*

About two months passed, and I took a call from Shirley. She asked me if I might be still interested. The other contracts fell through, primarily for two reasons: either because inevitably no lender could be found to finance the purchase, or pending buyers backed out because they developed the fear they wouldn't be able to stop the basic cause of the damage. The second reason concerned me as well.

Shirley and I met at her office and I signed a purchase offer for $152,000. I agreed to pay $2,000 more than my original contract because I felt I needed to demonstrate to the seller my willingness to fairly negotiate. The seller accepted and I knew I faced a challenge. The question in my mind lingered, *can I make this work or am I going to lose my fanny?*

I called Dan Marzilli, the owner of Gen Tech Termite Company. Dan, as honest and reliable as any person I'd ever met in the structural pest control-related business, also operated a heavy duty earth stabilizing concern. Dan took the geologist's report I got from Shirley. After a week passed, he let me know he could accomplish the work outlined in the report for $45,000. The cost for Dan's company to do the job came in around $25,000 less than the bid from the geologist who prepared the report.

A massive amount of work had to be accomplished. It required digging twelve-foot-deep, three-foot-wide holes in and around the house, which had to be filled with steel and concrete. The job proceeded slowly. Periods of several days sometimes lapsed between the times Dan's crew showed up. Although he never complained, I began to think Dan bid the project too low, and in order to stay financially viable, scheduled the work on my job in between other projects. As usual, inundated with my other house fix-up projects and remodeling activity, within reason of course, it didn't matter how long Dan took to finish Hillside.

The longing to move toward a different way to live started to influence my decisions more and more. I began the slow, arduous task to eventually extricate myself from the residential real estate business. I didn't hate what I did; I just needed a change. Although I never asked anyone to move, whenever a tenant vacated one of my properties, it almost always got totally remodeled and sold. Anytime I purchased a property, upon completion of renovation, I sold it.

I knew many people who had been acquiring property seemingly forever would never truly be able to redirect their lives because they refused to sell anything—they didn't want to be taxed on their profit. Generally, after they departed this mortal coil, their kids had little compunction about disposing of their newly inherited assets. I refused to fall into that trap.

The real estate recession had passed. Property prices increased rapidly. I owned three shoreline properties on Neptune and thought about selling at least two of them soon. An unsightly old Craftsman-type rental house located near the intersection of Neptune Drive and Williams Street seemed to adversely affect the surrounding properties.

A group of beer guzzling, disheveled appearing guys could usually be observed day and night lounging around on the front porch and steps of that neighborhood detraction. The location of the untidy mess bothered me. Situated within a hundred yards of my home and not much further from my other Neptune Drive real estate, that eyesore posed a potential problem. Williams Street provided a convenient access to Neptune Drive. When I placed my bayside holdings on the market, potential buyers would likely drive by the Williams Street rental before they reached Neptune Drive. The situation threatened to interfere with the optimum marketability of my properties.

Heading to my office on a cold, rainy, February morning in 1998, I drove by that Williams Street irritation and observed a pleasant surprise. As I'd done so many times, I wondered at the timely inexplicable vicissitudes that so often occurred in my life. A Century 21 "for sale" sign graced the front lawn of the property. I immediately called Peggy Deadder, the listing agent whose name had been attached to the sign. I gave Peggy my usual spiel. I asked that she consider me her customer, and I didn't want any part of the commission.

As with most agents, my proposition pleased Peggy. What she told me next, I'd already surmised. The property needed lots of work. Due to the tenant situation, it wouldn't be easy to see the interior of the house or gain access for lenders and various inspectors. I liked what I heard because it diminished the threat of competing buyers. I said, "Peggy, let's do this the easy way. Please prepare a purchase agreement wherein I will buy the property and pay all cash. I won't have to inspect the inside and I'll buy the property in its 'as is' condition and release the seller from any liability in connection with needed repairs."

I offered a little less than the listed price, but not much less. The contract provided the house be vacant at close of escrow. But if the seller resisted that provision it wouldn't be a deal killer. A grateful Peggy got the deal accepted and I had my work cut out for me.

I engaged the services of my two friends and terrific remodeling contractors, Jerry Chastain and Steve Keffer. I let those two do their thing, which they do so very well, and in a short time the property transformed from an ugly duckling into a gorgeous swan, so to speak. Carman negotiated the sale of the property to a young couple who accomplished even more improvements. I made a fair profit, but more importantly, I improved the marketability of every property in the area.

I got ready to sell my home, thinking Julie and I would move into Hillside when Dan finished his work there. I sort of hated to sell my Neptune Drive home. It had been the finest home I'd ever lived in. I considered it a showplace, and I knew I'd miss living next to the bay and waking up to the sound of the pounding surf.

I planted a "for-sale" sign on the property and immediately got a call from Dianne Anderson, a single, twenty-six year old Federal Bureau of Investigation agent. Dianne impressed me as the sort of young lady that every parent would want their daughter to become, or their son to marry. She owned a condominium in the popular Seagate complex just blocks from Neptune.

She looked at my home and didn't try to hide the fact that she loved the place. She asked if I would consider buying her condominium and almost new Ford Explorer in order to facilitate her ability to purchase Neptune. I accommodated her wishes, and she became the new owner of my Neptune Drive home. I quickly sold the Seagate condominium and the Ford Explorer became my main source of transportation for the next few months.

Dan Marzilli did an excellent job on Hillside. No visible clue existed as to the stability problems that once beset the site. A certified geologist approved the work, as did the San Leandro Building Department, and Julie and I moved in. We marveled at the spectacular bay view from the west side of the house. In order to further enhance the desirability of the feature most likely to sell Hillside, I decided to build a large deck covering most of the backyard. I reduced the structure I envisioned to paper, setting forth the elevation and dimensions. I showed the drawings to one of my regular contractors. He bid the job too high.

For several weeks, I'd been utilizing the landscape maintenance services of Kevin Chung and his small crew, all Vietnamese immigrants. I found Kevin to be reasonable and reliable. He continually asked if he might increase the scope of work he performed for me. I inquired if he knew how to build a deck. He laughed at my question. He took my drawing, priced the materials, and in a few days gave me a bid. The amount of his bid astounded me. Kevin bid half of what my regular contractor wanted. I asked, "Kevin, are you sure you can build my deck for this price and come out okay?"

Smiling, he answered in his really hard-to-understand version of the English language, "Don't worry boss, I know what I'm doing."

Well, Kevin built the deck. It turned out absolutely gorgeous, and I knew selling Hillside promised to be about as easy as anything I'd ever done. From then on, almost every fix-up I did got a new deck and Kevin built most of them. I had one problem with Kevin. I had the hardest time understanding him— sometimes the effort gave me a headache. I didn't think I'd ever learn Vietnamese so hoped he'd learn to speak better English.

I put the property on the market. An offer came in from another office. A former very popular and well known San Leandro vice mayor made the offer. The amount of his bid almost reached my asking price. The agent told me his buyer really wanted the property. He assured me his client would pay the full listed price if he had to. I still appeared frequently before the San Leandro City Council, applying for zoning changes. That potential buyer, although no longer in office, remained politically well-connected locally. I reasoned, if he owed me a favor, he might use his considerable influence with the City Council to get them to look favorably at my rezoning submissions. I told the agent I would consider the offer and get back to him in two days.

The next morning my doorbell rang, and I opened my door to an elderly, distinguished looking gentleman. His pleasant voice revealed a man of education. Mark Hudson introduced himself, saying he saw the for-sale sign and wondered if he might have a look inside. The proper procedure would be to call the phone number on the sign outside and arrange for an appointment, but I took an instant liking to the fellow and invited him in. As he toured the premises, I sensed his strong attraction to the property. He asked if he could bring his daughter who lived two blocks away back in ten minutes. Sandra and her father looked the place over together and she said, "Dad, this is perfect, you'll be happy here."

Mark wanted to make a deal . . . quickly. I let him know it pleased me that he liked my place so much, and explained about the other party who also wanted to buy my property. I told him I'd let him know my decision before the end of the week. I regretted disappointing him, but I knew better than to negotiate with two potential buyers at the same time—those situations never ended well—at least for me.

I arrived at my office at eight the next morning and found Mark waiting at the door for me. He apologized for being pushy and asked if I could spare a few minutes. Naturally, I gave him the courtesy of speaking with him. Mark described his situation. He told me his wife of forty-some years had died recently. He lived in the Golf Links district in Oakland in a home he and his wife shared for over thirty-five years. They raised their children there. Tears welled in his eyes as he told me his memories just wouldn't let him live there any longer.

Because of the location of my house on Hillside, only minutes away from his daughter and grandchildren, he believed that God led him there. Mark didn't need to sell his home in Oakland in order to buy Hillside. He could close immediately. He explained if it would sway my decision to favor him, he'd be happy to list the Oakland property with my office.

The next thing he said sealed the deal. Before driving to my office that morning he had attended early mass at Assumption Catholic Church to ask God to influence my decision. Within the next two weeks, Mark became the happy owner of Hillside Drive. For some strange reason, I decided not to take the listing on Mark's Oakland property. I suggested he list with a broker based in Oakland, which he did, and his property sold immediately. I had walked away from an easy commission. Sometimes intuition is hard to understand. Julie and I lived at Hillside for less than a year. During that period, we restored the property to a level that exceeded its former glory.

CHAPTER ONE HUNDRED ELEVEN

In 1999, Julie and I moved from Hillside into a house on Morgan Drive in San Ramon that I bought from Ed Schmucker. We lived in the house on Morgan Drive until February, 2001. While in Morgan, we had the house painted, had new carpet installed and replaced the kitchen counter top in addition to replacing the garage doors. The lot, around a third-acre, needed substantial landscaping, which we accomplished at a cost of several thousand dollars. The two-story house seemed a little large for just the two of us.

While living on Morgan, I repeated a profitable maneuver that worked well for me over a period of twenty-five years. When prices were rising in residential real estate, as they were then, I found it to be a smart move to buy a house in a new subdivision that hadn't yet been built. All that's required to lock in the current price is to put up a small good faith deposit. It usually takes months before the house is finished and not until then is the buyer is required to complete the purchase. Generally, by the time I'd have to actually pay for the property, it would be worth considerably more than the price I contracted for when I put up the deposit.

I liked the new Thomas Ranch subdivision in San Ramon and visited the sales office and looked over the drawings of the elevations of the homes that would be constructed in the tract over the following months. We picked the location to be developed last. The longer it would take for our selection to be finished, the better. We chose a less expensive, smaller model at around $500,000. I'd found that values of the initially less-costly properties in a new subdivision rose the fastest. I paid an extra $5000 for a lot with an unobstructed view of the scenic nearby hills. Paying extra for a lot with a view is always a smart move. Hoping to mesh the timing just right, I listed Morgan with Carman. I wanted to sell Morgan and close escrow just about the time we could move into the Thomas Ranch house.

Effective in March of 2000, Carman took over the ownership of Val Barry Realty. She paid me a monthly fee for the use of my broker's license. I still had a desk in her office, which I utilized a few days out of the week, but the business belonged to her.

We planned for the arrangement to last until she got her broker's license, which she seemed in no hurry to do. She hadn't time to study for the test. She did too much business. Carman's approach to operating a real estate office differed from mine. She liked the glitz of a classy office environment, where my concentration stayed glued to the bottom line. In any event, I saw her as a savvy, energetic, highly-ethical business person destined for success.

Morgan sold and in September of 2000, we moved into 900 Regalo Way in Thomas Ranch. We enjoyed the home immensely. It had a little over 2300 square feet of living space within one of best laid out floor plans we'd ever lived in. It had really been a smart decision to pay extra for a lot with a view. Although we lived close to shopping, movies and all the other conveniences we liked, that part of San Ramon seemed a little like living in the country.

Julie and I had always lived very busy lives and, even though neither of us reported to an office anymore, we remained very active. Notwithstanding the fact that we filled our days with a plethora of projects, somehow the environment in which we operated seemed more relaxed. Concurrent with carrying out my intent to dispose of my real estate holdings and wind down my loan business, Julie and I truly had a good time.

At the age of 59, Julie received her Bachelor of Arts degree from Thomas Edison State College. She conducted her studies on-line. We flew to Trenton, New Jersey for her graduation. Then she immediately began working toward earning a Master's Degree through Cal State University. She made me proud and a little intimidated.

I loved long-distance running which I did four or five days each week. Often Julie ran with me. In 1983, she had suffered a near-fatal heart attack and underwent a four-way by-pass operation. Even so, she had restored her health to the point she regularly ran and occasionally competed in five-kilometer fun runs.

Our lives were full. We relished escaping to the movies and every chance we got we hung out with our grandchildren. The biological source of the grandkids didn't matter, because in our hearts they were just our grandchildren. Julie and I fit well together; we adored each other and I couldn't picture my life without her.

CHAPTER ONE HUNDRED TWELVE

Even though I intended to dispose of all my real estate as expeditiously as possible, I still took advantage of the many good buys that came my way. My reputation for relieving other Realtors of their trashed listings—in which I took no portion of the commission—had grown significantly. Buying opportunities from that source continued on a regular basis. That might seem to be at odds with my wish to redirect my activities away from real estate but just the opposite held true. By acquiring additional property now and then, my very capable work force didn't leave me between jobs, because no in-between-jobs time existed.

How I handled it insured that the guys would be available anytime I needed them. They truly enjoyed working on my projects. I paid the price they asked and because I had complete confidence in them, they pretty much were given free rein. And of course, they knew I owned a lot of houses I wanted remodeled as they came available, so years of work lie ahead if they stuck with me. Steve Keffer and Jerry Chastain were not only my primary contractors but we regularly played golf together also.

John Litvinchuk, a highly respected, long time San Leandro Realtor called me when he listed a property that just didn't work for the average buyer. I made an offer on one such listing in Washington Manor, an area in which John specialized. The house and grounds reflected the conditions that often resulted from the occupancy of heavy drug users. We did our typical job of restoration and upgrading. The former blight-on-the-neighborhood sold as soon as it hit the market. Sure I made money, but I knew we had served the community as well.

About a year after the property sold, I received a visit at Carman's office from Lloyd, one of the fellows who had worked on the property. Lloyd, about twenty-eight, seemed as devoted a fundamentalist Christian as I'd ever known. Every day he wore a different tee-shirt bearing a religious logo. Well, the shirts meant very little to me, but what Lloyd said to me that day underscored the veracity of his faith. He asked if he could talk with me in private outside. I thought, *Uh oh, he wants to borrow money.* I had been dead wrong. He hadn't come there to receive money. He wanted to *give* me money.

He explained when he and Jerry prepared the dopers' Washington Manor bathroom for remodeling, they removed the old medicine cabinet. In the resulting void they discovered a loaded .38 caliber revolver and a bundle of cash. Jerry and Lloyd divided the cash. Jerry bought Lloyd's one-half interest in the pistol. Lloyd's conscience bothered him ever since. He came to square accounts with me. He believed because I owned the house, the hidden treasure should have been mine. I sincerely thanked him for the valid demonstration of the extent of his deeply held beliefs. Tongue in cheek, I said, "Lloyd, you live on a boat—maybe you know something about the 'Mariners Code of Salvation Rights.' Under that concept, I'd like you to consider what you found while working in that house to be yours."

With few exceptions, every house I placed on the market looked as good or better than it appeared when new. We accomplished so many remodels, we had the process down to a science. I utilized a Vietnamese contractor—who imported his materials from China—to install gorgeous new natural wood kitchen and bathroom cabinets on which granite composite countertops were installed. If you called contractors that advertised in the Yellow Pages, you'd get a price for a kitchen like ours for a minimum of $25,000. I never paid more than $5000.

Occasionally, when we had several fix-ups in progress at one time, I had Carman list a property to be sold in its "as is" condition. For instance, I bought a Neptune Drive shoreline property for $295,000 and rented it out for a year. Actually, the house needed a lot of work. Nonetheless, it seemed that the market got hotter by the week and due to the scarcity of waterfront residential real estate it quickly sold for $500,000.

Sometimes I'd have Carman or one of her agents ask certain tenants if they might be interested in buying the home in which they resided. It happened some of them did want to buy. In such cases, I didn't have the house fixed up. If the property needed repairs, I gave the buyers a credit, and they could have the needed work accomplished at their convenience.

The drastically reduced qualifying requirements by lenders and extraordinarily low interest rates created a frenetic buying environment at that time. In some cases, buyers could borrow more than a hundred percent of their purchase price. I'd been in the business long enough to know at some point exorbitant prices coupled with foolhardy lending practices had to go real bad.

In the many years I'd spent in real estate I became accustomed to the inevitable recurring peaks and valleys of prices, but I'd never seen anything like I witnessed at that time. Thousand-square-foot, 1950s-circa homes in blue-collar neighborhoods that just a few years previously sold for around $100,000, brought $500,000—sometimes more. Although the phenomenon started around 1995, the madness reached its peak between 2003 and 2005.

That unbelievable market couldn't last forever. I had so many remodeling projects in progress I had to work alongside my contractors to keep things moving at an accelerated pace. When I say I worked alongside my contractors, what I mean to say is I acted as a "gofer", inasmuch as my job required me to "go for" material to keep them progressing. Yes, I guess you might describe me as a flunky, but I became a very rich flunky. Carman managed my rental properties and began serving some of my tenants notices to move so I could get the properties ready to market. I wanted to sell every piece of real estate I owned before the madness ended, which I knew would happen.

Sometimes human nature can be confusing. One of my favorite contractors, who I will call Bob because I don't want to embarrass him by using his real name, worked for me for years. I bought properties and Bob, an expert at fixing up houses, did his thing, and I sold each property for a very good profit. Bob and I repeated that process over and over, year in and year out. Bob, unlike most contractors I knew, had enough money to do for himself what he did for me. When I asked Bob about that, he indicated that for some reason he lacked confidence or he blamed his wife.

One day, while I worked with Bob on one of my houses, he posited an interesting situation. Beth, a lady living across the street from him, explained that her father, due to severe health problems, had to be admitted into a convalescence facility. The father owned a home in a desirable neighborhood in San Leandro in which he and his now deceased wife had raised Beth and her sister.

In order to come up with funds to meet the unexpected expenses caused by the life-altering circumstances resulting from the abrupt deterioration of the father's health, Beth needed to sell her dad's house. She told Bob and his wife she had the Power of Attorney that gave her the right to sell the property, which she wanted to do fast.

I asked Bob, "Why don't you do yourself and your neighbor a favor and buy the house? We're in a great market and the property is well-located. If you offer a clean, fast cash deal, you probably can get a good buy."

Bob . . . whiney Bob, told me his wife would never let him take the risk. I decided on a strategy intended to demonstrate to Bob what existed out there for him if he would adjust his thinking a little.

I said, "Bob, ask Beth if she and her family members would be interested in a cash, 'as is' offer for $430,000 that would close in one week. If they decide to accept my proposition, I will hire you to do what is needed for me to get the highest price for the property. When it's sold, if there is any profit, I will split it with you fifty-fifty." Bob liked the idea, yet I told him, "You can do this by yourself, and keep all the profit if there is any."

Beth and her sister reacted with relief when Bob told them about my verbal offer. He set up an appointment for me to meet with Beth at her home to formalize the transaction. I drew up a contract containing a clause stating the seller knew the value of the property exceeded my purchase price.

The agreement pleased Beth and her family. Beth abhorred the idea of going through the usual marketing steps. I felt good when she expressed her gratitude that there were people like me available in such situations. About a month and a half later, Bob and I split a net profit of around sixty-thousand dollars. He continued to work on my houses. As yet, he hasn't ventured into the world of an entrepreneur.

CHAPTER ONE HUNDRED THIRTEEN

For the past few years, I'd tried not to face a troubling and, in its inception, a slowly developing situation that I kept hoping might just go away, but it didn't. Ever since my step-father died, Mom—who had always been self-sufficient and independent—gradually moved into a world clouded by varying degrees of dementia. At first it didn't seem so bad. I called her every day and took her to dinner every Monday evening to wherever she wanted to dine.

Although my mother always argued with me, I'd never forgotten how she worked so hard for so many years for my sister and me. Long ago I made a silent promise to myself to try to pay my mother back for the sacrifices she endured for her kids. I thank God for blessing me with the desire, the will, the opportunity and the ability to keep that promise.

I'd gladly given Mom and our step-father all-expense paid vacations, including new clothes, to the East Coast and Hawaii. Practically every piece of furniture, including the television in their home, and an almost new automobile in their driveway, passed from me to my parents. Mom had the ability to buy whatever she might have wanted. She never asked me for any of the things I gave her.

That didn't matter because what I did for Mom, I really did for myself. Things just worked that way between us. Strangely, she showed no physical affection toward my sister and me, nor did we to her; yet there existed an inviolable, unspoken bond between us. Clearly, we would always, without hesitation, do whatever seemed necessary to protect each other.

Either I or Julie, and occasionally my kids, Valerie or Paulie, took Mom for her regular medical appointments. My sister's husband, Morgan, had died of cancer a few years earlier. Sherie lived in Oregon with her new husband. Even though she generously helped with our mother when she visited California, the major portion of caring for Mom fell to me.

While still in good shape, Mom loved to cook for her family. If anyone of her family dropped in unexpectedly and happened to be hungry, she could whip up something delicious on a moment's notice. I think every grandkid had a favorite Grandma Vada dish, which delighted Mom to prepare for them. My mother adored all her grandchildren. Her affection, her door and her pocketbook remained always open to them. Each of them believed him- or herself to be her absolute favorite. It pleased me immensely that my mother expressed such tender loving warmth toward those kids.

Things went downhill for Mom. Hygienically, my mother's mode of living continually declined. She had an old, vicious cat she, and she alone, dearly loved. We'd learned if you didn't want to get bitten and scratched, you had better not try to pet it. The fact that Mom permitted and even encouraged that angry little varmint to lounge around on her kitchen table, didn't whet the appetite. My mother developed an incontinence problem and her home reeked of urine. When I tried to discuss the situation, she denied that it existed.

Mom's ability to function independently continued to deteriorate. She could no longer operate her washer and dryer. She put orange peels in the freezer compartment of her refrigerator, rather than in the garbage. I appreciated Julie's involvement with Mom—she looked in on Mom several times each week. Often Julie took her to lunch, the bank, medical appointments or wherever my mother needed to go.

On July 18, 2002, Julie's mother, who lived in Klamath Falls, Oregon, died suddenly of a blood clot. Julie loved her mother deeply. For years, she assisted her mother in many ways, including financially. Sadly, relations between the two had been strained at the time of her mother's death. Julie's well-meaning advice didn't go over well with her mother. Even though a strong bond had existed between them, it troubled Julie that death intervened before they reached a resolution of their differences. I learned that Julie's disappointment served to enhance her efforts to pursue the best interests of my mother. My mother and I and my whole family benefitted immensely from Julie's presence in Mom's life.

One day, Mrs. Ray, Mom's friend and neighbor who lived just across the street, stopped Julie and let her know she occasionally walked with Mom to the bank. She explained Mom often withdrew several hundred dollars in cash and placed it into a paper bag. Mrs. Ray had no idea why Mom did that, and neither did I. Mrs. Ray explained Mom relied on the bank tellers to fill out her deposit and withdrawal slips because she had lost the ability to do it herself.

To protect my mother, and ultimately my sister and myself, from a looming catastrophe, I made a bold move solely designed to protect my mother. I convinced Mom to sell me and Sherie her three properties, including the home in which she resided. Sherie knew we needed to protect our mother, but buying a half-interest in Mom's property at that time wouldn't work for her.

I had Sherie sign a waiver in which she opted not to participate with me in the purchase of our mother's properties. I bought Mom's real estate holdings and she carried all of the financing, secured with a promissory interest-bearing note. Effectively, I'd taken control of my mother's money, which would be used to pay her living expenses. I knew I had the experience and the mindset to guarantee my mother's needs would be accommodated for the rest of her life. In the event her financial requirements eventually exceeded the amount I owed her, then I personally would provide for her support throughout her remaining days.

I arranged to have Meals on Wheels deliver food to Mom's home every day. When I visited her, I discovered she hadn't eaten even half of them. One of her neighbors called my office and left an angry message for me that Mom came by her house begging for food. I set up an account at Ploughman's, one of Mom's favorite restaurants, so she could have her meals there daily. She liked walking to Ploughman's and walking served her well.

Valerie's trusted friend, Fred, had a gay, unemployed brother named Sammy around fifty years of age. Sammy had extensive experience caring for the elderly and happened to be between jobs. Based on Fred's recommendation, after a lengthy interview with Sammy, who I found to be affable, and with my sister's approval, I hired him to care for our mother on a full-time basis. Sammy lived in the studio apartment attached to Mom's home. I placed his name on the Ploughman's account which delighted him.

I had the house thoroughly cleaned to eliminate the odor of urine and hired Genelle, an experienced, compassionate, black female caregiver to bathe Mom several days each week. I hoped Mom would be able to enjoy her twilight years in her own home. I wanted to get things off to an auspicious beginning. As soon as I thought Sammy and Mom had become comfortably acquainted, I sent them off on a week's vacation to Hawaii. Sammy had never been there and his gratitude seemed genuine.

At first things seemed to go well. In time though, I suspected Sammy's gay lifestyle interfered with his responsibility to care for Mom properly. I began getting reports that young men stopped by the house late at night. My sister drove down from Oregon occasionally and stayed at our mother's home for a few days. On one such visit, my sister found a stranger washing his car in

Mom's driveway where Sherie wanted to park her $60,000 Lexus off the street.

When she asked the fellow to move his vehicle, he told her Sammy gave him permission to wash his car in our mother's driveway. He told Sherie he'd move when he finished. My sister demanded Sammy have his friend clear the driveway immediately. Sammy reluctantly confronted his pal, but he did and my sister got her way. Another time someone knocked on Mom's door after eleven at night. Sherie opened the door to a young guy looking for Sammy. She told him to go around to the back and knock on Sammy's door. We began to wonder about Sammy.

One day, Julie brought Mom back home after lunching out. Sammy, who was always trying to impress Julie, wanted to play a video about housecleaning shortcuts for her. He inserted the cartridge into the DVD. Instead of housecleaning tips, while standing there in front of the television, Julie, Sammy and my ninety-one-year-old mother watched three butt-naked men cavorting in heavy gay sex. Mom screamed and she resisted Julie's efforts to turn her away from the action while Sammy frantically fumbled in an effort to turn the thing off. Exasperated, he exclaimed, "Damn ... Blockbuster must have given me the wrong tape again."

I stored staging furniture in the garage I had built behind Mom's house. One night around ten, as I unloaded furniture from my truck into the garage, I saw through the kitchen window Sammy and Mom at the dinette table drinking wine. I'd never known my Mom to drink ... ever. The next day, I called my friend Fred, Sammy's brother. I told Fred about my misgivings about Sammy. Fred asked if he could drop by the office to discuss the matter. I told him, "Now's a good time for me, Fred."

Fred immediately apologized for ever recommending Sammy. He told me he'd discovered his brother's interest in carrying on with young men exceeded his interest in providing quality attention to my mother. He suspected Sammy regularly plied her with wine. He thought his brother served wine to Mom to put her into a deep alcohol-induced sleep state. In such a condition she didn't interfere with his nocturnal activities.

Mom didn't wake up until after ten each morning, giving Sammy plenty of time to get his overnight visitors out of the house. It became clear Sammy's level of assistance toward the well-being of my mother fell far short of my expectations when I engaged his services. That week, on Wednesday, Fred accompanied me while I informed Sammy my mother no longer needed him. I told him if he cleared out of the apartment the next day and signed a total release of all liability form, he would receive $2500. Sammy complied, with the full knowledge he'd blown a good deal. I thanked Fred for being a straight up guy and took Mom to my house.

Julie and I brought Mom to live with us for the next two weeks. Still involved in our pressing real estate business affairs, we managed to give my mother all the attention she craved. Julie seemed like an angel; she treated my mother with deep love and respect. Mom became like a small child. The level of her insecurity broke my heart. Our roles had reversed; she became the child and I became the parent. I gave her what I could because she did the same for me many decades in the past. She couldn't bear for me to be out of her sight.

She constantly asked when she could go back to her home. I lied and said she could go back as soon as she got well. Of course, I would have been delighted for her to be in a mental state in which she could go back to her home, but I knew it wouldn't happen and it tore me apart to lie to her, but I did anyway. One morning, I resolved to sit next to her for as long as she needed me. With the exception of a couple of restroom breaks, I conversed, consoled and comforted her for twelve hours.

My sister came down from Oregon and stayed with us to help find a suitable assisted-care home for Mom. Sherie provided great help. She contacted an Alameda County senior advocate group for placement referrals. She and I looked at a large facility in Hayward. While there I saw one of my former MGIA dedicated adversaries in a wheel chair with spittle drooling down his chin. I said hello to him, but he had no idea who had spoken with him. The thought of our mother living in that awful place brought tears to my sister's eyes.

The next day, we inspected a six-patient care home set up in an attractive residence in Pleasanton, just minutes from my home. We called it the Solomon House because Mr. and Mrs. Solomon, a middle aged Indian couple, owned the business. The pleasant couple operated several comparable facilities in the community. Mrs. Solomon, a registered nurse, frequently visited the premises to check on the residents, which gave reassurance to my sister, Julie and me.

The availability of the cheerful master bedroom with a full bathroom and sliding glass door accessing a lovely tree-shaded, inviting deck pleased us. Sherie and I believed our mother could be happy there. Bernadette, the charming Filipina cook and maid told us she prepared and served meals to the residents in the combination dining and family room three times each day.

She explained sometimes the residents watched television in the family room, even though each of them had a television set in their room. Except for two days every week, Bernadette lived on the premises. If Mom became a resident there, it would be Bernadette and her two-day-each-week replacement's daily routine to bathe and dress her.

Sherie and I decided to move our mother into the Solomon House and made the necessary arrangements with Mr. and Mrs. Solomon. Afterward we passed the evening with Mom and told her what we'd decided. While Sherie and I sat with Mom, Julie discreetly moved Mom's wardrobe, television, bedroom furniture and personal items into what would be her new living quarters. My mother, verging on panic, said, "Val, you know I want to go back to my home."

Again, I lied to her and explained, "Mom, when you get well, we'll move you back to your home."

That placated her temporarily, but on our way to the Solomon House the next morning, I had to repeat the lie to calm her down. I felt like a heel. We introduced her to Bernadette who did her best to make Mom feel at home. Mom liked Bernadette, and Bernadette quickly made Mom feel comfortable. Sherie and I visited with Mom in her beautiful room until Bernadette served lunch. We left our mother having lunch with four other residents.

Sherie headed back to Oregon. Julie and I—actually Julie more than I—visited Mom frequently. In the beginning, when we went to the home, we generally found her in the family room engaged in conversation with another resident, an elderly black lady. The other residents, all younger than Mom, spent most of their time in their rooms watching television, or reading, or involved with their computers. Bernadette told us other than bathroom breaks, Mom remained in the family room from early morning until bedtime. She would not stay in her room by herself, which I found disconcerting because her room cost much more than the other residents' accommodations.

In a few months, the elderly black lady, Mom's steady companion, left the home. Other than when Bernadette found time from her chores to spend time with her, Mom watched television by herself. Mom had always been a "people person"— she wouldn't last long in those conditions. To help alleviate the situation, we followed Solomon's recommendation that we enroll Mom in a county-sponsored senior daycare program which cost fifty dollars each month. A van picked up Mom four days each week and delivered her to a former elementary school facility that provided a variety of senior-appropriate activities. After four hours at the center, the van returned her to Solomon House. I wanted more for my mother.

Julie started contacting other assisted-care homes that might be better suited to meeting Mom's needs. Julie investigated Tiffany Gardens in Livermore. The home had around thirty patients who seemed mentally on par with Mom. The well-staffed facility provided daily activities designed to keep the residents challenged and entertained. Delicious, health-oriented meals were prepared by trained chefs and served in a dining room reminiscent of a first class hotel. Tiffany Gardens cost about equal to Solomon House. We quickly relocated Mom. The first day, as we helped her settle in, unnerved by the change, she begged me to take her back to her home in San Leandro, or home with me and Julie, or back to Solomon House.

Again, I lied when I told her if she stayed for two weeks and wanted to leave, I'd accommodate her wishes. The lie seemed to satisfy her. I prayed she would forget my promise. The circumstances reminded me how I felt when I left my six-year-old son Danny at Bearskin Meadows diabetic summer camp decades past. Don't ever believe dealing with the complications of aging parents is easy, because it isn't.

We found Tiffany Gardens to be cheerful and beautiful. Not once did I detect the odor of urine, so prevalent in assisted care homes we'd investigated. The wonderful meals and continuous fun activities gave the place the ambiance of cruise ship living. Tiffany Gardens had a wonderful caring staff. Within a short time after my mother moved there, her attitude changed dramatically. One afternoon, while visiting with her in the fragrant, flower-filled garden, she expressed how much she enjoyed living there and wondered why Julie and I didn't move in. Julie took the time to locate that haven for the aged, and I'm not sure she'll ever truly know how grateful I am to her.

Even though the wild real estate market still dominated my time, I managed to drop in on Mom each week. Sherie still lived in Oregon and visited Mom as often as she could. Julie kept very busy doing my extensive bookkeeping and staging the houses I continually marketed. For a while, Mom still attended the senior center we enrolled her in when she resided at the Solomon House. Unfortunately, she experienced an incontinent-related incident on the bus while en route to the center which resulted in her dismissal from the program.

Julie visited Mom more often than I, and she made the effort necessary to get acquainted with the Tiffany Gardens' staff. She bought pastries at Costco for the other patients and told them they came from my mother. She made sure all the staff who worked with Mom received gifts on holidays. As a result of Julie's efforts, Mom became a favorite in the home.

As a young girl on the farm, Mom loved her horse, Topsy. Julie regularly drove Mom out to Bollinger Canyon Road. While enjoying a tasty treat, they parked and watched the horses in the fields and stables, clearly visible from the car. Whenever I visited Mom without Julie, my mother expressed her disappointment.

Mom still communicated with us, but not effectively; we observed her gradually shutting down. Although the Tiffany Gardens staff remained lovingly attentive to her basic needs, caring for other residents prohibited them from giving her prolonged personal visitation attention. In an effort to slow Mom's regression deeper into the fog of dementia, Julie engaged the services of Karen and Adele. Both ladies—retired academics—conversed with and read to elderly individuals on a one-on-one basis in an effort to stimulate mental clarity. At a total cost of around four hundred dollars per month, both ladies alternated with each other spending about five hours each week with Mom.

Karen and Adele formed a warm relationship with Mom that did indeed provide a degree of mental stimulation. While in

Tiffany Gardens, surprisingly, my mother began exhibiting an attitude of loving affection toward my sister and me. That struck us as wonderful, new, and totally unexpected. Julie mentioned the change in Mom to Karen. Karen told Julie that she believed the tender affection our mother had begun to display represented her true nature which she couldn't show before. Karen might have been correct; Mom experienced some very cruel circumstances in her life that likely influenced how she dealt with her children. In any event, her cheerful smile and motherly hugs sure made me feel good. When it became apparent that Mom had gotten all she could from Adele and Karen, we bid them an appreciative farewell.

PART SIX

JULIE

"fulfilled dreams, the good life and Arizona"

CHAPTER ONE HUNDRED FOURTEEN

Though I had made an ironclad pledge to myself decades ago never to marry again, I hadn't anticipated a casual remark would make me rethink that pledge. Julie's youngest granddaughter, Mallory—and in my heart, *our* granddaughter—had taken a part-time job with Carman. I know everybody brags about their grandchildren, but in our case, we just told the truth. Carman said if she thought she could have had a daughter like Mallory, she would have had children. Carman told me something else. She said Mallory confided in her that because Julie and I hadn't married, she didn't know how to describe her relationship with me. What Mallory said to Carman made me ashamed of myself.

I realized that Julie and I should be married. I wanted her to be my wife. Not because of what Mallory told Carman and not because of all she had done for my mother and the rest of my family, but because I loved her and never wanted to be away from her. Julie and I took care of each other; we truly wanted the best for one another. I'd waited a long time to ask her to be my wife. I prayed I hadn't waited too long. She accepted my proposal. We flew to Reno and entered into a union that made my life about as perfect as it could ever be. Now, Mallory could call me Grandpa or Papa Val or whatever else she could think of.

By 2005 Julie and I had lived in and enjoyed the Thomas Ranch home since 2000. Residential real estate prices still shot skyward, but I knew that dynamic had to change. I listed Regalo Way with Carman at nearly twice what I had paid for it just five years before. It sold quickly for just short of a million dollars.

We moved to Copper Ridge, a beautiful, large apartment complex in the hills of San Ramon. Our unit overlooked the seventeenth fairway of the Canyon Lakes golf course. The development, in the process of being converted to individual condominiums, made us think about buying our unit. We liked living there and had been informed when the condo conversion reached completion, renters who decided to buy would be offered a purchase price discount. The proposition tempted us, but our plans at the moment were indefinite.

Julie's long-time best friend, Joana Oster, had moved from California to Phoenix, Arizona. Joana and Julie shared a friendship as true and beautiful as any I'd ever seen and they missed each other. Julie gave me an expensive and totally unexpected gift; a three-day golf instruction session with an ex-touring professional golfer, Jim Samsing, at the Wig Wam golf complex in Goodyear, Arizona. Let me tell you, I truly needed help with my golf game and that trip offered a great chance for Julie and Joana to get caught up.

Each daily session of the three-day golf school had been scheduled to last eight hours. I guess I judged the quality of my game as maybe just short of being in the toilet. The thought of spending hours alone with an instructor of Jim Samsing's stature intimidated me. But happily, when I met Jim, I realized I had nothing to be concerned about. He seemed as friendly and as easy to be with as any one of my regular California foursome. At about the fourth hour into the first day of instruction, we got rained out.

It looked as if the inclement weather might last for the next week. Jim told me not to worry, he'd fly to California to complete my instructions in a couple of weeks at no extra cost. Well, we planned to be in Arizona for three days, so now that we had some spare time we decided to explore a little.

The ambitious highway construction and the huge number of proposed regional shopping centers in the planning and development stages impressed me. Everything I saw emphasized the expectation of large population increases for that part of Arizona. What I saw there promised substantial elevations of property values. We checked out prices and discovered residential properties selling for less than half what they would have brought in the Bay Area. Yet, the wages between the San Francisco Bay area and the Phoenix area didn't appear to relate to the disparity of residential real estate prices between the two states. I thought maybe we could make some money in Arizona.

Early on the Sunday morning of the day we had to fly back to California, we drove our rented car through Del Webb's Sun City Grand subdivision (SCG) in the City of Surprise. *What a beautiful community.* We stopped at the SCG tract sales office to inquire about purchasing a new home. They didn't open that early, but Julie took a marketing flyer from a box outside the office.

Immediately after we got back to California, Julie called the sales office and spoke with Shirley Nensel, a sales agent with the company. Julie learned from Shirley very few unsold properties remained in the tract. We decided we wanted to buy a home next to a golf course. Shirley told Julie all the golf course lots except four had been sold. That evening when I arrived back at our apartment, Julie and I discussed what Shirley had said to her.

We decided to put a deposit down on a golf course lot on which a home wouldn't be built for quite some time. Perhaps by the time we needed to complete the deal, some months down the road, we could sell our property for quite a bit more than we paid for it. The builder had several models from which we could select to be constructed on the lot. Julie took responsibility for making that decision. The next morning, Shirley let Julie know only three golf course lots remained. It looked as if we'd have to move fast. Julie decided which of the models she liked. By putting up a five thousand dollar good faith deposit over the phone, using our Visa card, we tied up our lot selection.

508

The developer offered the following deal: by paying the full purchase price in cash at the time of signing the purchase agreement, the builder agreed to pay us six percent interest on that amount of money on a per annum basis until completion of the purchase. In an effort to extract the most profit out of the transaction, indeed we did pay the full purchase price up front. We looked forward to owning 20929 Grand Staircase Drive, in the city of Surprise—our first Arizona property.

From then on, Julie agreed to take control of the SCG transaction. She flew back to Surprise from California five times to monitor the construction process. She turned those trips into fun-filled excursions. Twice she brought our daughter-in-law, Virginia Barry and our granddaughter, Katrina Barry, and on two other trips Julianna Fleming, another granddaughter, accompanied her. I got the impression they liked Arizona.

Upon completion of construction, a couple of days before signing our final closing papers, we did a final walk-through inspection. I hadn't seen the house before and what I saw surprised me. I viewed a top quality, 2800 square-foot beauty, on a golf course, selling for the same price that I sold fifty-five-year-old, 1000 square foot, cheaply built houses back in California.

Finally, while waiting to meet with the escrow officer to complete our purchase, Julie brought up the subject which I'd guessed had been on her mind for some time. She said, "Maybe we should try living in Arizona. We have nothing to lose. We've sold most of your properties in California. You've paid off every one of your lending investors. The only person you owe is your mother. If for some reason we aren't happy here, we can always sell Grand Staircase and move back to California."

I responded, "You're right Hon. We're sort of retired, and I suppose the change could do us good."

We moved from Copper Ridge and rented a one-bedroom apartment on Stanley Boulevard in Pleasanton, California close to Tiffany Gardens. We planned to fly or drive to Stanley Boulevard from Arizona each month to maintain close contact with Mom. With my sister driving down from Oregon to visit Mom fairly often and the grandkids dropping by to see her occasionally, Mom wouldn't be lonely for family.

We moved down to Grand Staircase in Arizona and enjoyed living there immensely. Julie bought me a one-year golf pass for thirteen hundred dollars. The pass gave me discounted green fees on any of the four SCG courses. Golfing on those lush courses seemed like playing on a deep pile green carpet. To break even on the cost of the discount pass, I figured I'd have to engage in a minimum of forty-four rounds within the one year period. I loved the game, but my monthly trips back to California made it difficult to make the pass pay off. My life seemed better than I ever thought it could be. In addition to me running a few miles every other day, Julie and I worked out regularly at one of the community's two recreational facilities.

At Cimarron Center and Sonoran Plaza, the two physical fitness and learning centers in SCG, there are around eighty different subjects available for study to residents of the community. Julie and I enrolled in Jim Matui's creative writing class. Over the years, in the course of my business, I had to learn to write contracts covering the scope of my operations. With so much practice, I suppose I'd effectively developed the ability to transfer my thoughts to the written page. In Jim's class we wrote a very short story each week and read it to the class, who critiqued what we'd authored. I derived a lot of enjoyment from the time I spent in Jim's class.

In 2009, I submitted my running composition *The Grey Runner* to the prestigious Arizona Authors Annual Writing Contest. The contest judges selected my submission as one of the winning entries. While still a little lightheaded over that unexpected success, I made the decision to write the story you are reading now.

Life in Arizona turned out great, but I missed our friends and family in California. The flight from Oakland International or Sacramento airports takes less than two hours. Kids and grandkids started spending holidays and vacation times with us. We played golf, visited the Grand Canyon and had wonderful times. My regular golfing foursome flew down for a couple of good-time days. We played three rounds of golf, which delighted me, especially because I could still just barely beat them.

We treated every visitor we picked up at Sky Harbor Airport to lunch at Durant's, the iconic restaurant located in downtown Phoenix. Joana's sister, Carol, and her ex-husband, Jack McElroy, own Durant's. Joana is the day manager and anytime we showed up she comped us to special hors d'ourves and desserts. The place is gorgeous and the cuisine is as good as it gets.

It's not an inexpensive eatery but when your meal is over you know you've had your money's worth. Movie-makers, drawn to the captivating charm of Durant's, have shot numerous cinematic scenes there. It's commonplace to observe local and national celebrities enjoying the delightful ambiance in the place. I've been told that it used to be frequented by Bugsy Siegel and Del Webb. Whenever I'm in Durant's, I get the feeling that's where it's happening.

CHAPTER ONE HUNDRED FIFTEEN

This chapter is a reprint of a letter from me to my daughter, Valerie, describing my 2008 Christmas day activities, relative to one of my trips from Arizona to California to visit Mom.

December 2008

Dear Valerie:

I hope you had a wonderful Christmas. Dean called me, which I guess you know. I enjoyed talking with him. It sounds like his life is together. Neal called me also. Learning that he is moving to Sacramento into a far more comfortable home with the prospects of beginning an apprenticeship makes me hopeful that some very positive things are happening for him.

I'd like you to know how deeply your gift touched me. Thinking of the hours you spent embroidering Rudyard Kipling's poem "If" for me reminds me of what a wonderful daughter you are. Julie is listening to her music for the second time.

Before I talked with you about my back problem, I had decided to forget about seeing any more doctors and attempt to correct the condition through self-applied physical therapy administered at home. However, your encouragement has convinced me to continue seeking professional medical assistance.

Valerie, I'm so pleased that you arranged to get the family together to celebrate Christmas. You really "stepped up to the plate" and I'm proud of you. It's always been my wish that my children be close. Clearly, you are the one most likely to bring that about.

This time I came alone to be with Mom for Christmas. Julie has always done so much for her, but wasn't up to coming with me this time. The past few days have been different. When Julie and I fly to California together, we rent a car at the airport so we will each have a car while we're there. I keep my BMW in Pleasanton. While in California, we go our separate ways—I play golf and Julie visits Joan and Mallory. We even visit Mom separately.

This time (December 21st) I took the BART shuttle from the Oakland Airport to Coliseum BART station. I rode BART to Pleasanton and caught the number ten bus which stops near our Pleasanton apartment. I enjoy riding the BART train. Looking down from my elevated rail car at the areas in which you and your brothers grew up, and observing the panorama of the communities in which I spent so many years chasing my dreams, is somewhat therapeutic. The fact that the car in which I rode smelled of urine wasn't too distracting.

Riding the bus is fascinating to me. The regular fare is a dollar eighty-five, but people over sixty-five pay only eighty-five cents which makes no sense to me. It seems that young people with children have the greater need for a discount. Of course, when I say that, I'm thinking of my family about five decades ago. I haven't traveled by bus since I was a teenager. What an interesting experience. I didn't hear anyone speaking English. Mostly, I heard Spanish, in addition to variations of Asian and one or two languages I couldn't identify. I sort of felt like I was a foreigner in my own country, but I didn't mind.

About three-thirty that afternoon, I drove over to Tiffany Gardens to attend their Christmas party. I expected to see Steven, Virginia and Katrina there, but was surprised and really pleased that Paulie and Rachel also showed up. The party, more crowded and chaotic than last year, brought a lot of joy to Mom and her pals. I think Mom didn't exactly know who we were, but she still had a good time. When I read her the Christmas card I brought for her, signed "Val", she looked at me closely and asked, "Are you Val?" She has her good days and foggy days. When the staff gives her cough medicine, she has difficulty staying awake and remembering.

I wanted to be with Mom on Christmas morning to give her a gift Julie had selected, a very pretty watch. I had reservations to fly back to Arizona at four, Christmas afternoon. I had spent the 22nd and 23rd and Christmas Eve day playing golf and spending time with friends. I missed Julie. We must have called each other at least twenty times.

At nine-thirty on Christmas morning, I delivered Mom's present. She loved the watch. As her world grows smaller, it takes very little to make her happy. At 95-years-old, Mom's world is indeed very small, but I'm convinced she is as happy as she can be, which pleases me immensely.

I drive back to the apartment and pack my one "carry on" bag with the wrapped presents given to me at Mom's party by Steven and Paulie and their families. I wanted to open them Christmas night with Julie. At ten-thirty a.m. I head out toward the closest number ten bus stop. It's raining and cold walking the half mile to catch the bus to the Pleasanton BART station.

After waiting for a half hour at the bus stop in the bitter cold, it dawns on me that maybe the bus schedule changes on holidays. After all, this is Christmas. I call Julie on my cell and voice my concern. She tells me she will check the bus schedule on the Internet and call me right back. After a few minutes, Julie calls and tells me that on holidays the bus doesn't service my stop. I can catch it at Santa Rita Road and Valley Avenue in twenty-six minutes. I can get there in time if I hurry.

I don't mind jogging to reach my stop in time because moving fast is warming. I reach Valley Avenue and Santa Rita Road with six minutes to spare. There's a problem—I see no sign of a bus stop. What am I supposed to do? I cross Santa Rita Road and walk into a service station convenience market. The clerk behind the counter is serving the only customer in the store. When he's finished, I approach him and say, "I know this is a strange question, but do you think there's anyone around here that would give me a ride to BART for twenty dollars?"

That last customer half way out the door overhears and says, "I'll give you a ride, but I'm not going to charge you—not on Christmas morning." I thank him and walk with him to his pretty much of a junker car. I wait while he clears the clutter off the front passenger seat to make room for me. The inside of the car is as ratty as the exterior. Numerous empty cigarette packs and small cans which once contained—now consumed—some sort of energy drink litter the car's interior.

My benefactor introduces himself as Jim. He asks me if there's enough time for him to stop at a Seven-Eleven store before he delivers me to BART. I tell Jim because of his generosity, I now have ample time. I wonder what he needs at Seven-Eleven that he couldn't have bought at the service station market where I had observed him buying cigarettes. He comes out of the store with several cans of the same energy drink once held in the empty cans strewn about in his car.

On our way, Jim calls his girlfriend. He explains he will be slightly delayed arriving at her place because he is taking me to the BART station. Jim tells me he is divorced and has three grown children who all live out of the Bay Area. He seems sad, and I feel sorry for him. I tell him I don't live near my kids either.

When we reach our destination, I try to hand him a twenty dollar bill which he adamantly refuses. I tell him, "Jim, you're a great guy, and I appreciate that you are against accepting payment for doing a good deed on Christmas, but at least use this to buy something for your girlfriend." I leave the bill on my seat as I exit Jim's car.

I ride the train to the Coliseum station. When I insert my BART ticket into the slot which I expect will cause the egress door to open and allow me to exit the station, it doesn't happen. An electronic readout display instructs me to see the station agent. The agent inserts my ticket into some sort of testing apparatus to determine the cause of my problem. I'm told the same ticket used to enter the station must be used to exit. She asks me if I have another ticket on my person which I discover I do. Utilizing the correct ticket, I'm able to leave the station.

I catch the airport shuttle. Because I'm over sixty-five the cost to ride the shuttle is a dollar instead of three. I still think the wrong age is getting the break, but I pay a dollar anyway. I arrive at the airport near one p.m. My flight is scheduled to leave at four-ten. Instead of a direct flight to Phoenix that takes around an hour and forty-five minutes, my plane will make a stop in Los Angeles extending my travel time approximately an hour and fifteen minutes.

There are other flights to Phoenix. The airport doesn't appear very crowded. Maybe not many people travel on Christmas Day. I decide to try to get an earlier flight. The lady at the ticket counter tells me that for an additional sixty-five dollars she's able to book me on a direct non-stop three o'clock flight. I'm tickled. Maybe now I can be home in time to enjoy Christmas dinner with Julie, Julianna and Julianna's boyfriend whom I haven't met yet. Julianna is visiting for a couple of days and after Christmas dinner in our home, she plans to go out with her fellow. Sometime in January she will be starting a new job at Phoenix Children's Hospital.

As I proceed through airport security, the X-ray-type machine reveals that a couple of the wrapped presents from Steven and

Paulie contain liquid. Unless I'm willing to dump the packages, they must be checked through "baggage." I'm escorted out of the security area and directed to the baggage counter.

Now, it's necessary to go through the security line again. I proceed to Gate 24 to await my three o'clock flight. I sit there reading the "brain candy" detective fiction novel written by Betty Webb who gave a talk at a recent Arizona Authors Association, a group to which Julie and I belong. Arizona Authors' members include published authors and writers who aspire to be published such as Julie and myself. I bought Ms. Webb's book when I heard her give a talk. I wanted to compare her speaking presentation with her writing style.

It's getting very close to flight time and there's no plane parked out by Gate 24. A middle-aged woman sits down beside me. She appears congenial and I off-handedly comment, "It's sure turning out to be a long day." She responds in a friendly manner and a pleasant conversation develops. I tell her about my kids and my grandchildren and she does the same.

A mother of four children and a grandmother, her first husband and the children's father left her a widow a few years ago. She explains that the loss of her husband devastated her. She has remarried, and I get the feeling she's happy. Since she works in some sort of an academic capacity at a college in Stockton, California, I feel encouraged to tell her about Julie acquiring a Masters' Degree in her sixties.

When I mention that Paulie has published two books and that both Julie and I enjoy writing, she explains that she has published a book. Apparently, her first husband enjoyed success as a radio sports announcer. Over the years, during his life and following his demise, she expressed her admiration of his accomplishments in numerous brief written passages.

In time, after he died she gathered her writings and photographs that related to her deceased husband and wrote the book that she has published. The book is entitled, *Firefly Moments of Transition*. My airport friend's name is Norma Peterson, but the author of her book is listed as Lee O'Kelly which is Norma's maiden name. She thinks the name O'Kelly might be commercially superior to Peterson. I tell Norma I'd like to buy a copy of her book. She lets me know I can order a copy on line from *Author House*.

My plane departs over an hour late. I catch the Sun City airport shuttle Julie reserved for me. On the drive home, I have an interesting conversation with the shuttle driver. He works seven days a week, including holidays. He says in order to support his family he can't afford days off. Before he reported for work today, he enjoyed a Christmas dinner featuring menudo (stomach tissue of cattle) and tamales prepared by his wife. He says he has lived in Arizona all his life. I guess he's in his sixties. His son is twenty-seven. At first, I think he's Hispanic but the more we speak I realize he is Indian. He posits an interesting theory. We're driving through densely developed residential subdivisions and passing numerous shopping centers. He claims the increasing volume of annual rainfall results from the abundant non-native plants related to the aggressive landscaping activity. He predicts that in a few years our weather patterns will continue to change. I hope that he's correct. Maybe our summers will eventually be cooler.

I arrive home around eight thirty. After paying the shuttle driver fifty-two dollars, including a ten dollar tip, I enter a spic-and-span home and enjoy a wonderful holiday dinner. By the appearance of the house, Julie hasn't gotten much rest during my absence. I'm disappointed that Julianna and her boyfriend have left but it feels real good to be home. Indeed it's been a long and tiring day, but I wouldn't trade this Christmas Day for any other. I think of it as a microcosm of my whole life. Love, Dad

CHAPTER ONE HUNDRED SIXTEEN

Near the start of this story I indicated the importance of running in my life after the end of my first marriage. I mentioned that I had authored an essay-length article that pretty much recounts my running activities. That prize-winning article was published in the 2009 *Arizona Literary Magazine* and reappears and comprises chapter one hundred sixteen herein.

THE GREY RUNNER

It's April 18, 2005, the day I exercise my earned right to participate in the 109th Boston Marathon and every long distance runner's dream. It's been a nine-year uphill battle, sometimes literally to qualify for this venerable event. I'm seventy and am not going to pretend that isn't old. The twilight years have arrived, and I'm just not ready for them. Running the Boston and spending five days with loved ones just might be what I've needed to buoy my flagging self-esteem.

My wife, Julie, and I flew nine relatives from California several days earlier to enjoy the wonderful ambiance of Boston. Shortly after checking into our hotel, Julie and I visited the marathon exposition. To help memorialize the experience we purchased a plethora of marathon- related souvenirs.

We discovered that Boston is a tourist's sightseeing paradise. It is, after all, the birthplace of our nation. I especially enjoyed exploring the centuries-old graveyards with their markers and tombstones with pithy engravings. Thousands of long dead folks whose lives were every bit as precious and complex to them as ours are to us gives me pause. After all, don't all of us before we depart this mortal coil, desire exactly the same things? Maybe I'd like, "He ran the Boston at 70" engraved on my headstone.

There's a feeling of community and camaraderie in Boston this week. We've seen crowds of people wearing blue jackets commemorating the 109th Boston Marathon. Thousands of strangers connect in the spirit of the event. I'm thrilled to be part of this. The lobster dinners are expensive, but I don't care—they're worth every penny.

People often ask why I keep running and I reply with an old Mutt and Jeff joke, wherein Mutt asks Jeff, "Why do you keep hitting yourself in the head with that hammer?" Mutt replies, "Because it feels so good when I stop."

Running works for me. It's been a surefire way for me to keep physically and mentally fit. In thirty years, I've run thousands of miles, all leading me here. Last night, a few of our group enjoyed the marathon runners' dinner consisting of spaghetti, salad and garlic bread. I loaded up on carbohydrates, hopefully sufficient to stay with me through today.

At around 6:30 this morning, we were bused from Boston to the town of Hopkinton, the starting location of the race. Corralled in a holding area on the grounds of a high school, I'll have to wait until the marathon commences. The course goes through several typical small New England picturesque towns on an undulating road finishing in Boston at Copley Square, alongside the Boston Public Library. This is my tenth marathon and the pinnacle of my running experiences. Whenever I meet someone who has completed, I automatically consider that person a proficient athlete. If I'm able to finish, I will earn that status.

Approximately 21,500 runners will participate today. Many who start won't finish. God, I hope I won't be one of those. Only around a hundred of the participants are in my age group. I look forward to visiting with a few of these old-timers while waiting for the start of the race. What brought them here today? Perhaps like me, a strong desire to resist surrendering to the infirmities of advancing age. Everyone I meet today seems to have a story.

A taciturn older man, Paul, tells me that in his hotel room last night, something unusual for him occurred. Emotionally overwhelmed, he broke down in tears at the realization that he would actually be running in the Boston today. He informs me that his wife commented that during their forty years of marriage she had never seen him in tears. I feel what this means to him. What he's planning to do today is awesome for anyone, but especially for someone who's been around for seven decades. It's unlikely he will ever do it again. I think he could only tell a stranger whom he'll never see again about his crying jag. Another fellow, Jack, belongs to a seniors running club in Alabama. He says that after a long hot run, the members stand in leg high barrels of ice water for around twenty minutes. That's a new one on me, but I sure would like to try it. This surely is a special group and I'm proud to be one of them.

Due to the large number of marathoners, it takes about twenty minutes from the time the race begins for me to reach the starting line. While moving ahead, I'm surprised to spot Phil Martin. Phil is two years younger than I. We have competed against each other in half marathon events in the San Ramon and Danville areas back in California. We've become fierce competitors. In five races, he's beaten me three times. He doesn't see me and I don't approach him. I won't engage in a grueling contest against Phil today. I've decided to purposefully run slower than my normal pace. It's especially important to avoid any injuries. Getting hurt could prevent me from finishing the race and I'm not willing to repeat what I did after getting hurt in my first Boston qualifier. Even so, I'd sure like to even the score between Phil and me. There's little chance of that happening this time.

I'm thinking of what it took for me to get to this moment. Thousands of lonely miles on tracts and trails, the runners' highs and lows, shin splints, foot injuries, silent and sometimes faltering determination delivered me here today. I take a deep breath and look at the sea of athletes ahead of me. Damn, this is exciting. I try to relax in spite of my racing *pulse and pounding heart. Can I really do this? The sound of the starting pistol resonates in my ears. I smile inside and start back to Boston.*

Thousands of enthusiastic spectators cheer us along every mile. I've experienced powerful support in other races but not equal to this. When we wish to speak to anyone around us, we have to shout in order for our voices to carry. In addition to the ample official water and Gatorade stations, exuberant supporters cool us with spray from garden hoses, and offer restoring snacks. The crowd goes wild as a group of five fully uniformed U.S. Marine marathoners pass by. I, along with others, shout my congratulations and gratitude to them. My youngest son, Paulie, served as a marine in Desert Storm and I understand what we owe these men. I guess I've been this happy before, but right now, I can't remember when.

The course seems no more difficult than the other marathons I've run, until I reach the twenty-mile mark and see the last of the four Newton Hills approaching. It's called Heartbreak Hill. This far into the race, on a warm afternoon, Heartbreak Hill deserves the name, but I vow not to let it stop me. Then something happens, a thing called, "hitting the wall." I'm close to complete exhaustion. My legs weaken and my pace drops. I feel as if I can't take another step. But I just can't stop now! I remind myself of the times I've been here before and yet prevailed. This is my decisive moment. I've started too many things in my life that I've failed to complete, like the boat I spent weeks constructing and before finishing, lost interest and gave it away. I've enrolled in at least four Spanish classes and still can't understand much beyond como se llama. Redemption for these and most of my other shortcomings wait for me at the finish line. Ignoring the feeling I've been run over by a truck, from somewhere deep within I summon the energy to continue. Recalling the powerful message from Rudyard Kipling's poem, "If", seems to help.

> *"If you can force your heart and nerve and sinew,*
>
> *To serve your turn long after they are gone,*
>
> *And so hold on when there is nothing in you*

Except the Will which says to them,

Hold on!"

Until the end of an eighteen-year marriage that began in my teens, I lived a somewhat sedentary life. During that period I worked through a succession of different jobs until at twenty-five, I began a promising real estate career. Ironically, just about the time I achieved a level of financial security I'd labored for years to reach, circumstances that truly qualified as "irreconcilable differences" brought my marriage to an end. Disoriented, confused and unsure of what the future held for me, at thirty-six I sensed that my physical conditioning and mental well-being would bear heavily on the quality of life I hoped to experience post marriage. I decided to try jogging, which had become a popular fad.

I began my jogging routine, lumbering along a bayside trail at the San Leandro Marina. I soon discovered it would take a lot of work to get into shape. After repeating the process a few times, I began to feel more confident and fit. I looked and felt better than I had in years. The length and quality of my workouts increased gradually. Jogging became running and if I had to miss a session, I felt deprived. Excess fat disappeared and awareness of the rewards commensurate with my dedication to the project grew.

Although I ran three or four times each week for years, which kept me in good shape, I didn't begin running competitively until I reached my late fifties. It was then that I began participating in ten kilometer (six and two tenths miles) races, mostly in the San Francisco Bay Area.

My addiction to running reached new heights on October 15, 1995. Starting near the Pacific Ocean on a chilly, foggy morning, I won the first place award in age division sixty to sixty-nine, at the eighteenth Annual Half Moon Bay ten kilometer race. When I won, I beat seventy-five percent of all the other racers, regardless of age.

Over the years that followed Half Moon Bay, I won dozens of first place racing awards, mostly throughout the nine Bay Area counties. I loved the sport and continuously extolled its benefits to friends and family and anyone who would listen. Everything—and I mean everything—I did, I did better because I ran.

Eventually, I began entering half marathon competitions and occasionally moved up to a full marathon. The time came when the lore of the Boston captured my imagination. I promised myself to invest whatever effort it might take to participate in that world class event. At the time I didn't realize that qualifying would be a nine-year long journey. To be eligible to run in the Boston one must complete a USA Track & Field (USATF) certified marathon (twenty-six miles three hundred eight-five yards) within a time corresponding to the runners' age group. My first attempt at qualifying occurred in 1996.

The evening before the Fifteenth Annual California International Marathon (CIM), I checked into the Holiday Inn in Folsom, less than a mile from the start of the race. A two-hour early morning drive from the San Francisco Bay Area would have saved the hotel expense, but I thought I'd perform better if I were well rested. The CIM course runs slightly downhill and ranks among the five highest rated marathons to produce Boston Marathon qualifiers. The race commences on the Folsom Dam and progresses along the historic California Forty-niner Gold Rush Trail, finishing in Sacramento in front of the state capital. I had logged at least 500 miles in preparation. Around eight thousand runners gathered in the dark before starting the race at seven a.m., in cold damp weather that threatened rain. To protect against chill and moisture, I wore a plastic garbage bag with holes cut out to accommodate my head and arms. After a few warming miles, I discarded the bag.

At each mile marker, the runners heard an announcement as to how long it would take to complete the race at our current rate of speed. To qualify for the Boston, I needed to average nine minutes and sixteen seconds per mile. By the tenth mile, I easily maintained an eight and a half minute per mile pace. This seemed a lot easier than I had anticipated. Then I began to feel a pinch in my right heel as it hit the pavement. By the sixteenth mile, the pain became unbearable, rendering me incapable of continuing. It hurt even more to know I wouldn't qualify that day. A pickup bus, there to convey incapacitated runners drove past. Disheartened, I waved it over. I looked in and saw no passengers. In spite of my injured foot and the cold, hard, wind-driven rain, I decided that I just couldn't ride that bus alone. I resolved to keep going on my own power.

Forgetting the distance remaining in the race, I chose a visual focal point, usually a set of stoplights half a mile ahead. I promised not to give up before reaching that point. Moving in a gait that I describe as sort of a stumbling jog, I continued repeating the process. Near the twenty-third mile, I saw an exhausted runner some yards ahead staggering from one side of the road to the other. He looked as if he was near collapse and I wondered why the course officials hadn't already assisted the fellow. The gap between us closed. He turned to me and sputtered, "Hang in there buddy, you can do this!" Dear God, he thinks I'm worse off than he is! I looked away to hide my tears.

Four hours and forty-five minutes after the start of the race, I staggered across the finish line and received my completion medal. A few days later, a sports doctor diagnosed my foot injury as severe plantar fasciitis. It seems I managed to detach the fascia connective tissue on the bottom of my right foot from my heel. The injury prevented me from running another marathon for three years. Strangely, I considered the Fifteenth Annual CIM among my best races. I didn't qualify, but I felt like a winner. I had discovered a degree of strength within me that I never knew existed before that day.

I tried the CIM again in December 1999 and encountered a ferocious storm with up to fifty miles per hour gusts of wind, driving cold rain into my face. I finished, but not within the Boston qualifying time limit. I wondered if I would ever succeed and if I should even keep trying. Maybe I just didn't have what it took. Though I continued competing in ten kilometer races and an occasional half marathon, I put thoughts of Boston into my mind's recycle bin.

I registered for the Eighteenth Annual Lake Chabot Trail Challenge Half Marathon in Castro Valley and awoke early, excited and anxious to compete on June 3, 2001. Trail Runner magazine designated the Chabot Trail Challenge as one of the country's most scenic courses. I've heard it said that the course is as difficult as it beautiful, and I agreed having run it three times previously.

For two months before the race, I ran the most difficult portions of the trail repeatedly during the week and traversed the entire course on Saturday mornings. I hoped to finish in two hours and twenty minutes, which would likely place me among the first three runners in my age division and entitles me to a trophy. I had finished this event first in my division three times, but each race seemed more taxing.

I arrived at Lake Chabot early to do a few warm-up sprints and stretch my muscles. Meandering through the crowd of nearly four hundred, I spotted my friend, Victor Moreno. Victor, seventy-one, had received a diagnosis of cancer three years previously and after the removal of a section of intestine, he became an avid runner. He believed the cancer wouldn't return if he kept running. Inspired by Victor, I chatted with him for a few minutes and wished him the best of luck.

I stopped for a moment to visit with my pal, Jerry Chastain, a very competitive runner. Although the words were unspoken, we both knew he intended to best me that day. Being fifteen years his senior, I thought he had a good chance. Nonetheless, I accepted his silent challenge.

The few contestants in my age group had a small gold circle pasted on their on their racing number bibs. Having raced against most of the gold circle competitors, I had a good idea of my competition. That is until I saw a silver haired stranger, wearing bright red running trunks and a gold circle on his bib. He stood among the elite runners at the starting line. He looked like a serious runner.

At eight sharp, in response to the retort of the starting pistol, the race began. Our jovial noisy pack headed west on the winding trail through a mild hilly terrain adjacent to the northeast shore of gorgeous Lake

Chabot. The narrow trail permitted only the front-runners to move out fast. The rest of us only jogged until the pack spread out enough to establish our desired pace. Damn ... that silver-haired guy in red trunks had moved out of sight before I'd run a half mile.

After 1.6 miles of gentle rolling hills past the north shore of the lake, we came to Cameron Loop, which left and circled back to the main trail, covering a distance of a mile. The first half of Cameron Loop inclines steeply adjacent to a delightful gurgling brook, which cascaded down toward Lake Chabot. Even as I strained to climb the demanding slope, I still appreciated the beauty surrounding me. I passed Jerry struggling up the hill. I saw pain in his face. It looked as if he might have developed a leg cramp. I expected there would be more leg cramps as the Chabot Challenged progressed.

Reaching the top of Cameron loop I headed down hill at full speed, a technique I had worked out during training. A rocky trail this rough and uneven causes runners to slow their pace considerably to avoid falling. Very carefully, I had practiced aggressively accelerating down the hills. I believed the technique would serve me well.

Four miles into the race, Live Oak appeared; a daunting mile and a half, steep, scrub oak bordered, narrow, rocky and dusty grade, often referred to as Hell Hill. Probably the most punishing segment of the course, about half the pack walked the hill. I continued running, albeit slowly. The sound of heavy breathing replaced jovial chatter and joking. Reaching the crest, I raised my arms skyward, a poor imitation of Rocky Balboa.

Two miles further, we veered left onto Loggers' Loop, which for a half mile declined precipitously under a shadowy dense forest canopy, then ascended another mile back to the main trail. I never run Loggers Loop alone. It's creepily dark and forbidding. Mountain lions live in those hills.

Soon we progressed within earshot of the Redwood Road Rifle and Pistol Range, where we heard gunfire over the next mile. In every Chabot

Challenge in which I've participated, one or more of the racers pretend they've taken bullet. Although always funny, there is no chance of an accidental shooting, as a large hill separates the firing range from the course. As they fire at their targets the shooters are positioned with their backs to the runners.

Arriving at a point where the trail dropped around five hundred feet over a distance of two miles, I employed my fast downhill strategy. Within this stretch, I passed everyone in front of me. I had little doubt that I would run the course within my goal of two hours and twenty minutes.

At around eight and a half miles, I crossed Stone Bridge, a picturesque structure made of large rocks, built in the 1930s under the auspices of the Federal Works Administration. I looked down and saw the trout filled sparkling creek flowing toward the lake. Just beyond the creek crossing, we reached Jackson Grade. Though half the length of Live Oak, yet nearly as steep, that far into the race, Jackson Grade wouldn't be easy. The difficult course began to wear me down, but my dedicated training gave me confidence.

Just after the tenth mile, the inviting clear blue water of Lake Chabot came into view again. As I reached the eleven-mile mark from an elevated portion of the trail, I spied a runner with silver hair wearing bright red trunks about a quarter mile ahead. His pace now seemed slower than mine. I figured he normally ran faster than me, but being unfamiliar with the taxing course, I suspected going out too fast had zapped his endurance. I caught up with him and as I passed him, he looked my way. We both knew that only I stood between him and a first place trophy.

If I could make him believe he had absolutely no chance of beating me, he might give up. I gambled and sprinted ahead at twice his speed, hoping he wouldn't guess I couldn't run that fast for more than fifty yards. Experience told me not to look back to see if the ploy worked. If I glanced back too soon he might have guessed my plan and decided to challenge. A short distance farther, the trail circled back toward where the race began. As I crossed Lake Chabot Dam, my peripheral vision revealed *a silver haired man in bright red trunks fading out of sight. In long distance racing, sometimes strategy beats speed.*

Another mile and three-quarters along the western shore of the lake, I reached the finish line. The digital racing clock informed me that I'd completed the race in two hours and nine minutes. Feeling tired, yet invigorated, I retrieved a soda from an ice-filled barrel. I found a shady spot with a view of the finish line and reclined on the soft cool grass.

After a few minutes, the silver haired man in bright red trunks approached, shook my hand and congratulated me. I thanked him for helping me do my best. Silently, palpable mutual respect between two old guys recapturing their youth filled the moment.

Together, we relaxed and enjoyed watching others complete the race. Soon, the officials presented awards to the winners in each of twelve categories. Though confident that I had placed first in my age group, I didn't expect and hardly believed what came next. I learned that I'd set a new course record in my division in addition to winning a Road Runners Club of America, State of California championship. My success at Lake Chabot made me start thinking about Boston again.

I decided to run another Boston qualifier on October 3, 2004, in Sacramento. I missed qualifying by a scant seventeen seconds. In less than a month, I tried again at the Silicon Valley Marathon in Los Gatos. Nearing the end of the race, I leaned forward, forcing tired legs to move just fast enough to keep me from falling on my face. About to fail to qualify again, I quickly calculated which qualifier to sign up for next, when, to my surprise, my son, Steven, an avid marathoner, stepped out of the crowd of sideline observers. He yelled, "Dad, only 200 yards to the finish—you can do it!" His encouragement brought a surge of renewed motivation. I qualified for the Boston with fifteen seconds to spare. I will never forget the wonderful sense of elation I felt that day.

***

Shakily, I get past Heartbreak Hill. Just a few miles left, but I'm hurting. As I enter Boston, I see Phil Martin standing off to the left side of the course, bending over vigorously rubbing his lower legs. It looks like he's experiencing leg cramps, shin splints, sheer exhaustion or maybe all three. As I pass Phil, he looks at me, surprised. Clearly, he's finished running today. The chances of evening the score between Phil and me just got better.

With a mile remaining in the race, the course makes an abrupt left turn and the elaborately decorated finish line comes into view. My heart fills with joy because I know nothing can stop me now. I'm no longer concerned with developing an injury. The cheering throngs and inspiring music from several bands on the sidewalks renew my energy. I sprint to the finish line faster than I've run at any previous point in the race.

As I cross the delicious line, exhausted with every muscle in my body aching, I can't help but think that the twilight years will work out alright. After all, I just completed the Boston Marathon.

Julie and I, along with the rest of the family, rendezvous in our designated post race meeting area where I receive warm congratulations on this day's milestone. While I ran today, most of the family watched the Red Sox beat the Toronto Blue Jays at Fenway Park Things just couldn't be much better.

After a few minutes, for the first time ever, I get a severe case of leg cramps. I think of Phil Martin. Julie and I take a cab back to the hotel where I stay the remainder of the evening, resting and enjoying the events surrounding the occasion. The Julie will bring my dinner from the restaurant.

Alone, lying on my bed, I hear my cell phone ring. It's Jim Stagg, an old high school pal who I haven't seen in a couple of years. Jim just wants to chat. He has no idea where I am. When I tell him what I did today, he says, "Damn, Val, are you crazy, don't you know you're seventy years old?"

I smile ... "I sure do Jim."

CHAPTER ONE HUNDRED SEVENTEEN

With the arrival of 2009, I figured I had to be about the luckiest guy alive. When we moved down to Arizona, I invested a few million dollars through Edward Jones Brokerage into what I considered to be safe positions I didn't have to worry about. The modest returns produced a few hundred thousand dollars annually. Other income came from the free and clear rental properties I still owned in California, managed by Carman. But the most exciting money-making activity in which I participated, almost daily, had to be the "put" and "call" options segment of the stock market. The percentage of return stayed consistently high and, in my opinion, the way I worked it, the odds of winning favored me. You know, those who say, "if it sounds too good to be true, it's not" aren't always right.

Julie and I worked out regularly at the fitness centers in SCG. I played enough golf to satisfy the urge, ran every other day, and took on-line college courses and Spanish language classes at one of our community centers. Just for the fun of it, Julie taught a course entitled "The World's Major Religious Perspectives" based upon her studies in pursuit of her Master's Degree. She enjoyed teaching and as always, she went all out, bringing in fascinating guest speakers and drafting large colorful charts which truly engaged her students. The school genuinely wanted her back which flattered her, but after two semesters new projects attracted her attention.

As I mentioned earlier, we lived in a beautiful house adjacent to the sixteenth tee of the Cimarron Golf Course. Although I enjoyed residing next to the golf course, the view didn't excite me. You will recall, when we bought our home all but three golf course lots had been sold. The lots with the best views had been taken.

One morning, as Julie and I walked to Sonoran Plaza to attend one of our classes, we noticed a Realtor setting up to hold a house open on a golf course property. He asked us if we'd like to look inside. We had no interest in buying but out of curiosity we accepted his invitation. The property overlooked a small lagoon and afforded us a view of the two hundred yard, three par, seventeenth hole of the Cimarron Golf Course. What we saw from inside the house and the beautifully finished patio impressed us.

From decades of experience, I had learned to quickly spot signs that indicated when owners had lost interest in their home. I saw those signs all over the property. The house, larger than the one we lived in, had more square footage than we needed. But the view captivated us so I asked the Realtor if he might consider presenting an offer to his seller in an amount considerably less than the listed price. I let him know I could pay cash immediately and close escrow in just a few days.

He smiled but didn't offer to draw a contract. Although congenial, his body language told me he thought reducing my proposal to writing would be a waste of his time. He let me know he considered the value of the property to be considerably more than the price I wanted to pay. He said he'd mention our conversation to the owners and took my cell number. An hour and a half later as we left our class at Sonoran Plaza, my cell phone rang. The Realtor had talked with the owners in California where they searched for a house to rent. They wanted to see my verbal commitment in the form of a written contract.

Long story short: we bought the property, did some fix-up work and moved in. We listed Grand Staircase for sale. We left most of our furniture in place. Grand Staircase showed beautifully. Julie had it looking like a model home. We didn't know to what extent the housing bubble in 2010 had burst, especially in Arizona.

I think I've advised other sellers a thousand times, "The first offer will often be the best." Trouble is, I don't always follow the advice I give to others, which is what happened on Grand Staircase. Within a week after listing the property, our Realtor presented us with a clean cash offer of $620,000.

It happened so soon after listing our property I arrogantly figured we could get more. We learned as soon as we turned down their proposition, our potential buyers purchased another home a few blocks away.

For some weeks, Julie hadn't been feeling well. She experienced continual pain throughout her body. At night, sometimes her intense discomfort led her to leave our bed and try to fall asleep on the carpeted floor. It took a lot for her to complain so when she did, I worried. In 1983, she had suffered a near fatal heart attack and underwent a four-way heart by-pass operation. She diligently followed a heart-healthy regimen which included, among other things, regular aerobic exercise and a variety of medical surveying procedures, including stress and electrocardiogram tests.

Because she monitored the condition of her heart and arterial system so carefully, we didn't suspect a heart problem. However, as an experiment when Julie took a Nitrostat tablet which is designed to relieve angina (heart related pain), indeed, the discomfort she felt temporarily subsided. We decided to check into the emergency clinic at Banner Estrella Hospital. Banner Estrella is a hospital where most serious heart conditions in our area are treated. It also happened to be next to Julie's cardiologist's office.

I parked in the hospital parking lot—Julie felt worse with each step we took toward the emergency entrance. About two hundred feet from our destination, she stopped and sat on a landscape planter wall, too weak to walk further. For the first time, we both recognized the severity of the situation. I ran to emergency and quickly explained the situation. I grabbed a wheelchair and sprinted back to Julie.

The emergency medical staff conducted a number of tests. They informed us she needed to remain in the hospital overnight. At that point we had no idea of the source of her problem. Around ten p.m. I told her I'd head home and return early the following morning. She seemed comfortable and looked forward to a good night's rest.

I called her from home the next morning. She said her doctor explained they needed to take additional tests. She sounded calm, which made me feel the same. As I drove to I-10 from Grand Avenue toward Banner Estrella, my cell phone rang. The call came from Doctor Kline, Julie's cardiologist. He asked when I expected to be at the hospital. I answered, "In about twenty minutes." He said he'd bring me up to date regarding my wife's condition as soon as I arrived. The urgency in his voice scared me.

I reported to the nurses' station on the floor where Julie had been taken. Doctor Kline and his associate, Dr. Amenio, immediately took me into a small room with a battery of computer-type screens. They showed me a hastily prepared pencil drawing of a diagram of the arteries that supplied blood to Julie's heart. The doctors explained the tests indicated blockage of her arteries which caused her discomfort and threatened a heart attack.

The situation called for the doctors to perform an angiogram, wherein a devise incorporating a tiny camera is fed into an artery at thigh level, and maneuvered up to the heart for the purpose of examining the extent of the blockage. Doctor Kline, pointing to the diagram, told me the artery in which they inserted the widening apparatus had split very near Julie's heart creating a life threatening situation.

Doctor Arthur Murphy, a renowned young heart surgeon, hopefully possessed the elevated level of surgical skill needed to save Julie. Just as he drove his new Porsche Carrera out of the hospital parking lot, Dr. Kline contacted him on his cell phone.

As Doctor Kline and his associates carefully explained the situation, they told me that at that very moment Doctor Murphy had begun to perform open heart surgery on my wife. I asked Doctor Kline to forget about the penciled diagram and to please level with me regarding Julie's chances. He quietly explained that Dr. Murphy would do his best—not exactly what I had hoped to hear.

I retreated to the waiting room where the impact began to sink in. In the early morning of the day after I left Julie at the hospital, she called various family members to let them know about the tests being run on her. Now, as I sat in the waiting room, Julie's daughter, Joan called me to learn about her mother's status. I explained what I knew and asked her to pass on the information to the others. I tried to act calm, but I sensed that she suspected my terror.

The calls started coming in. My daughter Valerie, a registered surgical nurse, called me from Oroville, California. Very familiar with Julie's procedure, she wanted to fly down right then. I thanked her and asked her to please not come yet. I wanted to stay as close to Julie as possible. I didn't relish the thought of having to pick anyone up at the airport.

Next, I heard from Julianna, the granddaughter who worked at Phoenix Children's Hospital. She insisted on leaving work to sit with me in the Banner Estrella waiting room. I explained she could do nothing there and I needed to be alone. I just couldn't stand the thought of loved ones observing my distressed state.

Julie and I enjoyed more than a wonderful relationship—we enjoyed a nearly perfect relationship. We'd both endured some pretty difficult times but figured those periods in our lives meant nothing because we had each other. The stark reality of the possibility I might lose what truly gave my life meaning slammed me as if I'd been run over by a truck. I sat in the waiting room with my eyes closed, trying to communicate with God. I felt a warm tender hand cover mine. Julianna . . . she came to be near us, even though I asked her not to. *Thank you, God.*

Around eleven a.m., I got a call from Joan. I didn't want to worry her but she demanded I be candid. When she learned the gravity of the situation, she insisted on catching the next Southwest flight to Phoenix. Julianna agreed to pick her up at the airport. Time dragged as slow as molasses in January. Julianna and I sat quietly side by side, hardly speaking. Although we didn't speak, we silently shared our feelings. I wanted desperately to know Julie's condition, yet at the same time, I didn't want to know. At least as long as I didn't hear otherwise, I could assume she still lived. My emotions seemed to take a roller coaster ride. She didn't deserve to die, and I couldn't imagine living without her.

I sat for hours in that waiting room. Thoughts about my near perfect life with Julie and how Joan, Valerie and Julianna had responded to the utter terror of the situation flooded my mind. It occurred to me with just a couple of exceptions, women had always been good to me. I only hoped I'd been half as good to them.

At about five in the afternoon, a nurse asked me to come out into the hall. To say I feared what she might tell me couldn't begin to express how I truly felt. It surprised me to see Doctor Kline and another doctor waiting there for me. Doctor Kline introduced me to Doctor Arthur Murphy who told me he had just completed performing a successful three-way heart by-pass procedure on my wife. I felt as if a mountain had been lifted off my weary shoulders.

Doctor Murphy, with his long hair and youthful-appearance, sort of reminded me of a rock star. I imagined he'd faced many people in similar circumstances and had actually become accustomed to receiving adulation on a level with an actual rock star. I expressed my complete respect and admiration, and let him know I considered him a bona fide hero. I couldn't begin to imagine the feelings a person living in his world experienced.

Julianna picked up Joan at Sky Harbor Airport in Phoenix and brought her to the hospital. Julie woke up in recovery with her only child at her bedside. She groggily asked Joan for the time. Joan told her, "It's a few minutes after two."

Julie said, "Let's get out of here. They want to operate on me."

Joan answered, "Mom, it's two in the morning—and they've already operated."

Julie's cardiologist believed Julie's heart complications had left her with double pneumonia. He insisted she remain in the hospital for a full two weeks. Joan slept on a comfortable couch in her mother's room every night of her mother's stay at Banner Estrella. She even took most of her meals with her mother. Except for bathroom breaks and an occasional visit to the excellent cafeteria, she never left her mother's side. For a hospital room, the accommodations seemed quite pleasant. The delicious food and the third floor view of the Phoenix Mountains reminded me of a luxury hotel. I asked Julie if she thought we might book a getaway weekend there sometime.

I brought Julie home. Our insurance included coverage for a registered nurse to make house calls during Julie's recovery. Not being Julie's first such experience, she needed only one nurse visit. For a while, she slept on a hospital bed which had been delivered and set up for her the morning she arrived home. Now, we figured with a couple weeks rest, she'd be back to normal—hardly!

She had been home about five days when she showed me a small red rash on her left side. We thought it might be a heat rash. In just a few days, the mild break-out developed into painful angry sores. Julie had shingles which results from the same virus that causes chickenpox.

In Julie's case, no medication relieved her agony. For at least the first month, her misery increased with each passing day. The suffering brought on by her shingles affliction far outweighed the wretchedness she endured which led to her latest by-pass operation. We knew as awful as shingles are, they aren't life threatening. Eventually the inflammation cleared up, but an aching discomfort known as post-herpetic neuralgia remained.

Grand Staircase hadn't sold yet and summer had arrived—not a good time to sell property in Arizona. Julie made a great decision. She wanted to take the property off the market until fall. She had the house dazzling and beautifully furnished. Actually the wonderful amenities available in SCG make it a veritable resort community. About half the residents there leave for cooler locations in the summer. Even though it's hot, the diminished seasonal population makes the area quite pleasant.

We decided to invite family members, one after the other, to stay at Grand Staircase over the summer. We also included Carman and her fiancé in the invitation. After all, she is like family. They all had the use of our almost new Toyota truck to drive wherever they wished. There are a lot of things to see in Arizona. It all worked perfectly.

The ladies received massages at Cimarron Center. Some of them took advantage of the exclusive community swimming facilities and fitness centers. We took them out for dinner, played golf, and went to movies and dinner shows and left them free to do things on their own. Carman and her fiancé drove up to Sedona and on the way home stopped at one of the many Indian gambling casinos and won twelve hundred dollars.

Seven different groups stayed at Grand Staircase over the summer of 2011. We wanted to show them one of the best vacations of their lives, and I think we did just that. September arrived and we listed Grand Staircase with Lilly Mitsui of Longs Realty. Lilly is the wife of Jim Mitsui, my former creative writing instructor. She is just the sort of agent we needed. She's resourceful and inspires confidence and her high volume of sales attests to the fact she works very hard and very smart. Lilly delighted us by successfully negotiating the sale of Grand Staircase to a Canadian couple.

CHAPTER ONE HUNDRED EIGHTEEN

Within the parameters of my ability, desires and ambitions, I suppose my goals to date have met with success. That being said, however, there is a conundrum most everyone achieving aspirations similar to mine will likely experience. No matter how self-effacing and modest I've tried to behave regarding my accomplishments, I've encountered a certain amount of vitriolic envy, often from unexpected sources.

You will recall back when I still worked for Ed Marvin I had three lots listed for sale on Fairway Drive. I bought one of the lots and moved a house onto it which resulted in a profitable project. When I approached the owner about buying his other two lots, I received an adamant refusal.

He explained, "I know you paid what I asked, but I can't stand the idea you made a profit off the deal. It's okay if you handle the sale of the other two lots, but I won't sell them to you." I negotiated the sale of his remaining lots to a party who built condominiums on them.

Early in my real estate career, I developed a wonderful relationship with Golden West Savings and Loan Association. They seemed to think I could do no wrong. I dealt with Chad Scott, the manager of Golden West's Castro Valley branch. Golden West charged me interest rates and gave me service comparable to their competitors. For years, because Chad and I got along so well I directed my business to Golden West.

When World Savings and Loan bought Golden West, most of officials I had dealt with either retired or went with other lenders. World put Chad in charge of their Hayward branch. I planned on doing business with World through Chad. Boy ... did I miscalculate. Whenever I called him for a loan, he acted cold and rude. He seemed nothing like he had over the past years. I asked for a loan commitment on one of my properties just before placing it on the market. That afternoon, Chad met me at the property to make an appraisal.

As usual he was unfriendly. I figured I had nothing to lose so I asked him about his behavior toward me. To my surprise he answered my question candidly. He said, "I've been doing you favors for years while you've been getting rich and you've never done a damn thing for me."

I wanted to tell him, "That's bullshit" but I didn't. Over those years he facilitated my acquisition of loans from Golden West who I gave all my business. It had been a two-way street.

Nonetheless, I remained calm and friendly—I didn't want to give up without making some effort to restore our past congeniality. I lied and told him I understood his position and asked him what I could do for him. He said, "I've been looking to buy a home and this property is exactly what I want. I'd like you to sell it to me for $41,500." The property would sell for more, but I decided to accommodate Chad. We agreed to meet in my office later that day around six, and I would draw the contract.

As we parted, he seemed like his old self—just as friendly as I'd ever seen him. About three, I got a call from him. He instructed me to forget about the deal. When I asked him what was wrong, just before he hung up on me he answered, "If I bought your property, you would claim you did me a big favor and say I promised you preferential borrowing treatment." Chad disappointed me, and I never spoke with him again.

Of course, I experienced other instances in which my perceived triumphs inspired resentment, but in that regard, I think Sheila disappointed me the most. As I stated earlier, in spite of our divorce we seemed to develop a friendly relationship which endured for years. I thought the fact we enjoyed an amicable association enhanced the security of the children. Years passed and suddenly, to my utter confusion, she ended the cordiality that had existed between us. It serves no good purpose here to discuss the things she said about me or her mysterious anger toward me. She never gave me an explanation, but I can only assume it's a plain case of jealousy. No matter, although circumstances dictated that Sheila and I go our separate ways, not for a moment did I ever stop wishing the very best for her. Notwithstanding the irritation, paradoxically, perhaps being the object of envy is tantamount to receiving a compliment.

CHAPTER ONE HUNDRED NINETEEN

Traveling from Arizona to California each month to visit Mom created stress. We found it difficult to establish a comfortable living routine when we had to be away from our home a few days every month. Although we could easily afford it, keeping the Pleasanton apartment and paying for parking storage of my BMW so I'd have a car at my disposal in California, and related expenses cost plenty. While in California, in addition to seeing Mom, we visited friends and relatives and took care of my lingering real estate business. To fit everything in while there, Julie and I went our separate ways and this necessitated renting a car for her.

Even though Tiffany Gardens and the staff there had become Mom's loving home and family, Julie and I considered if we found a similar facility for Mom in Arizona we could visit her far more often. Julie said if my mother lived close by she would love to see her every day. I knew Julie meant every word. Since her own mother died, it became obvious to me that her relationship with Mom filled a void in Julie's life. We visited several assisted care establishments near our home.

Each of the homes we investigated had things in common. Most of them were housed within modern architecturally pleasing structures. The members that made up the staff of every residential complex we looked into were mostly white women. They dressed like and communicated as you might expect of nurses in a hospital setting. The environment seemed cool— nothing like the warm and loving setting Mom enjoyed at Tiffany Gardens. I didn't think Mom would last a year in Arizona, so we decided not to make any shifts in her living habitat, and I couldn't bring myself to take her so far from her beloved grandchildren.

I'd mentioned previously herein, although my mother would give her life to protect her children, and I happily tried my best to make things easy for her, we hadn't always gotten along well. I rankled in response to her eternal criticism and often found myself at odds with her. That unpleasant dynamic had changed— we had become affectionate with each other. I often found myself massaging her arms and shoulders as we sat and talked.

I told her she enjoyed the lifestyle to which she had become accustomed because of her wise investment strategies. She loved to hear me talk like that and her accomplishments made me proud. She had been employed as a food waitress most of her working life, and she lived better than most professional people her age. I didn't mention it to her, but had I not taken control of her finances, things might have turned out differently. Not really though—I would have always been there for Mom, regardless of her financial situation.

Ingrown toenails became a problem for Mom. The staff at Tiffany Gardens, by law, couldn't trim the toenails of the residents. Sometimes the condition resulted in an infection. When that occurred, a physician had to be called in who always removed the toenail. I didn't want my mother over time to lose all her toenails. It became my job each time I flew up from Arizona to clip my mother's toenails. That was definitely something I didn't enjoy; and a service I think I would only perform for a disabled member of my immediate family. I'm not sure, but I think Mom enjoyed the process.

Mom had resided in Tiffany Gardens for the past seven years. Every day the staff provided entertainment, but her favorite activity was playing bingo. She won often and enjoyed her participation so much that if she had become engaged in a game during a visit, I just sat back and watched. The prizes she and the other winners received might be a small tube of toothpaste or maybe a couple of cookies, but nothing very exciting. When Julie became aware of how much the game meant to Mom, she began donating better prizes she bought at Costco, which made the activity even more fun. The staff and residents always cheerfully welcomed a visit by Julie. She never went there empty-handed.

My mother never lost her unusual sense of humor. One day, while she and I visited in the Tiffany Gardens dining room between meals, a little, rather addled old lady with two cookies in her hand, shuffled up to us and just stood there and stared at us. Something behind her momentarily distracted her. She placed the cookies on the table next to Mom and turned to see what was going on. In a flash Mom plopped the cookies into her mouth. When the little lady turned back and tried to figure out where her cookies went, Mom sat there quietly with a mischievous smile on her face.

Each winter Mom developed a cough that seemed to get worse with every succeeding year. In 2010 the severity of her condition required a trip by ambulance to the Valleycare Health System Hospital. When she recovered sufficiently to leave Valley Care, an ambulance transported her to Silver Oakes Nursing Home instead of Tiffany Gardens. Silver Oakes is immediately adjacent to Tiffany Gardens and both facilities are owned by the same person. Weak and disorientated, Mom had lost the ability to feed herself. Until she could regain strength and the ability to take her meals unassisted, she wouldn't be returning to Tiffany Gardens.

Distance and busy schedules worked to make it difficult to see my kids as often as I would have liked. Julie and I planned to host a reunion with them and available grandchildren in Hawaii. A couple of days before the family flew to Oahu, Mom's health took a turn for the worse. The trip had been planned for some time. The hotel reservations had been made and difficult work vacation schedules were in place. Although Julie and I felt apprehensive, we didn't mention anything about Mom's faltering condition and proceeded to our family rendezvous in Honolulu. They all had a wonderful time, and Julie and I believed we had accomplished something important.

When we returned, I spoke with Mom's doctor and he told me what I'd guessed. He reminded me that my mother had been around for 98 years. The next one of those respiratory relapses would likely be her last. Julie, Sherie and I and those in the family who lived in California visited Mom frequently, even though I think much of the time she no longer recognized us. After any visit with Mom at Tiffany Gardens, I left feeling good. Whenever I left Silver Oakes, I wondered if I'd see her again. On February 8,

2011, I got a call from my sister informing me that our mother had died. I'm grateful that my niece Demi had been with her at the end.

We held a service for Mom, arranged and paid for years ago at Santos-Robinson Mortuary in San Leandro, just blocks from where she resided for over forty years. The event that initiated the pre-arranged funeral service for Mom occurred in 2005 when I received a call from Lone Tree Cemetery where my step-father had been interred. The official wanted to know the life status of my mother. He asked if she still planned to eventually be buried next to my step-father, because she had reserved the site for herself at the time of his death.

With approval from me and my sister—who resided in Oregon —in order to avoid last minute confusion and take advantage of prices available at that time, Julie and Mom planned and set up our mother's future funeral arrangements. Julie formulated an effective pragmatic non-emotional strategy. Julie's own mother had very recently passed on. She asked Mom to help her with planning her mother's last rites which Mom happily agreed to do.

Unbeknown to my mother, instead of making plans regarding another person, she actually set up her own arrangements. Julie instructed her as she proceeded to make various selections not to consider the expense. Mom selected a beautiful Thomas Kincaid theme. She picked out a handsome coffin and even a lovely dressing gown in her favorite shade of blue. I am grateful to Julie for handling that difficult process for us.

Mom outlived all of her friends and I expected a very small turnout at her service. What a gratifying feeling to see the Farewell Chapel packed with those who came to pay their last respects. I hadn't seen some of those people in years. My three children and Sherie's oldest son, Eric, and his daughter, Beth, each stood and addressed those in attendance.

I hoped Mom heard four of her grandchildren and a great-granddaughter eloquently describe loving and sometimes humorous memories of their grandma. Each of them expressed the belief that he or she was their grandmother's absolute favorite. The stories they told brought smiles as well as tears. They were truly grateful to have loved and been loved by such a person. Listening to and watching my three children made me appreciate the self-confidence I had always wished for them being demonstrated on that memorable Saturday morning. As I heard their beautiful words, it came to me that my mother had to be about the most generous person I'd ever known.

Mom left her estate to my sister and me. Her assets at the time of her death consisted of the $600,000 I owed her. As trustee of my mother's revocable trust, I disbursed $300,000 to Sherie and accordingly was relieved of my debt by way of inheritance of the remaining three hundred thousand dollars. After waiting for a few months for any unknown claims to surface against Mom's estate, in 2011 I disbursed $60,000 to each of my three kids and Julie, thereby dividing my inheritance of $300,000 by five. I felt good because I knew I had pleased Mom.

CHAPTER ONE HUNDRED TWENTY

I've pretty much related herein some (certainly not all by a long shot) of the incidents in my life that brought me to this place on my journey. Although we're near the end of this part of my story, I'm sure not at the end of the best part of life. I truly believe my best days are still out ahead, and I genuinely hope yours are too. I'm rich and I'm happy. Maybe you would like to be rich and happy as well but not sure you can achieve that status. By the way, being financially rich doesn't necessarily equal happiness, although it helps considerably.

Perhaps, if you consider some of the hurdles I encountered along this odyssey and somehow dealt with successfully, you might be encouraged. My mother divorced my father, a loving, yet sometimes brutal alcoholic around my eleventh birthday. The insecurities a child feels as a result of living in the sort of family war zone in which I found myself left me with inhibitions I struggle with to this day.

I suffered from debilitating migraine headaches from childhood. I dropped out of high school to take on the responsibilities of a married man. By the time I reached my 22nd birthday, I struggled to support a wife and three children. At age 18, my marketable skills beyond a rudimentary labor classification equaled zero. Some of the awful jobs I had to take to allow me to barely provide for my family emphasized the extreme cost of my bad decisions. We found ourselves in such bad financial shape, that I think some folks idea of poverty might have been a step up the economic ladder for us.

I got sick and tired of being broke. As I stated herein previously, "I was broke, but never poor." Paradoxically, some financially wealthy people are *poor* in mind and heart. I read multiple self-help books, determined to escape from the wretched existence of economic deprivation. They all helped tremendously, but the most valuable asset I owned and still do own is an overwhelming *desire* to live a victorious life. Everything successful follows desire.

Of course, every one of us desires success. No . . . I'm not talking about the average wishful thinking level of desire. I'm talking about the depth of desire that dominates every waking minute of the day or night. I call it "Deep Desire." Deep Desire never sleeps and is so inculcated within one's heart, mind and soul that it is impossible to resist or deny. Deep Desire is so powerful that it can even bring you together with a mate that truly makes life a continuous, delicious adventure, as it did for me.

If Deep Desire is possessed by an individual, every decision he or she makes is consciously and subconsciously directed toward the inevitable achievement of one's cherished goals. Deep Desire is rare, which I imagine is the reason why around ninety-five percent of the retirees in this country live far less affluently than they did when they were employed. You might ask, "How can I develop Deep Desire?"

I suggest you give serious contemplation as to what you really want in your life. No . . . I don't mean a compromised existence that just gets you by, but within the parameters of your true potential, what would you truly aspire to achieve if you held the power to make your dreams come true? Imagine your life as you would like it to be. Set goals and determine what you need to do to reach those goals. Libraries are full of books about people who have climbed the ladder of success. Read those books for inspiration. Okay, you have figured out what you want; picture yourself living as you truly want to live. Keep up that mindset, develop faith that it's all there for you, and soon Deep Desire will take over and it will happen for you.

Please know the decisions you make today can shape the quality of your life for the rest of your days. To help me reach decisions that will deliver success to my world, I often employ the following procedure: whenever I find myself wrestling with the pros and cons of a particular course of action, I accelerate my mind five years into the future. From that distant vantage it is easy to determine what decision I should be making currently.

Understand that my Deep Desire isn't limited to monetary accomplishment. Oh no … the cliché that money won't buy happiness is about as true as anything you will ever hear. I've tried to live a lifestyle that delivers the highest level of mental and physical health available to me. We all endure handicaps, some more severe than others, still I'm convinced that if one acquires Deep Desire, those handicaps only serve to sweeten one's ultimate success. Before I say goodbye, please know I wish you the very best. It is well to remember, not everyone is going to be thrilled with your inevitable success. What matters is that you will be happy with your success.

THE END